DEVELOPING EFFECTIVE STUDENT PEER MENTORING PROGRAMS

A Practitioner's Guide to Program Design, Delivery, Evaluation, and Training

Learning
Resources
Centre

MAVERING
COLLEGE

Peter J. Collier

Foreword by
Nora Domínguez

Sty/us

STERLING, VIRGINIA

Published by Stylus Publishing, LLC
22883 Quicksilver Drive
Sterling, Virginia 20166-2102

Library of Congress Cataloging-in-Publication Data
Collier, Peter J. (Peter John), 1947-
Developing effective student peer mentoring programs:
a practitioner's guide to program design, delivery, evaluation and
training / Peter J. Collier.
    pages cm
Includes bibliographical references and index.
ISBN 978-1-62036-075-0 (cloth : alk. paper)
ISBN 978-1-62036-076-7 (pbk. : alk. paper)
ISBN 978-1-62036-077-4 (library networkable e-edition)
ISBN 978-1-62036-078-1 (consumer e-edition)
1. Mentoring in education–United States. 2. College students–
Services for–United States. I. Title.
LB1731.4.C65 2015
371.102--dc23
                                                    2014044190

13-digit ISBN: 978-1-62036-075-0 (cloth)
13-digit ISBN: 978-1-62036-076-7 (paperback)
13-digit ISBN: 978-1-62036-077-4 (library networkable e-edition)
13-digit ISBN: 978-1-62036-078-1 (consumer e-edition)

Printed in the United States of America

All first editions printed on acid-free paper
that meets the American National Standards Institute
Z39-48 Standard.

Bulk Purchases

Quantity discounts are available for use in workshops and for
staff development.
Call 1-800-232-0223

First Edition, 2015

10   9   8   7   6   5   4   3   2   1

To all program directors and mentors who are the frontline troops in promoting college student success; to my mentors: David Morgan, Amy Driscoll, Michael Toth, and Grant Farr; and most of all to my wife, Christina, without whose support I never would have realized my own educational dreams.

CONTENTS

FOREWORD

The United States suffers from less-than-satisfactory graduation and retention rates nationally, averaging 59% (National Center for Educational Statistics, 2014). Students frequently report feeling a lack of connectivity and social support from their educational institution. This lack of integration into college life often hinders students' achievement and increases the likelihood of failure in completing their intended degree. This trend is indicative of institutional failure to properly implement programs and provide support systems that students need to develop a sense of purpose in higher education. To combat this issue, peer mentoring can be an excellent way to strive toward students' college success, and Peter J. Collier's book *Developing Effective Student Peer Mentoring Programs* provides a strong argument for continued application of peer mentoring programs for undergraduate student success.

During a time when the economic and social landscape is fraught with conflict and social tension, mentoring is recognized as a useful tool to engage students and increase the likelihood of student success and degree completion (Beatrice & Shivley, 2007; Black & Voelker, 2008; Colvin & Ashman, 2010). Although valuable for all, peer mentoring is particularly vital for nontraditional students; throughout the book, Collier and his vignette contributors place additional focus on effectively reaching underserved minority students, first-generation college students, veteran students, transfer strudents, and international students. Peer mentoring is a cost-efficient option for universities to provide support for students, and can be adapted and used in many different contexts. As institutions of higher education suffer through persistent budget cuts and lack of resources, operating on sometimes nonexistent budgets, both educators and administrators need to implement programs that are effective and cogent. Peer mentoring is not only beneficial for retention and graduation rates but also rewarding for the peer mentors and their mentees. In comparison to hierarchical mentoring programs, the implementation of a peer-mentoring program is economical (Minor, 2007; Cerna, Platania, & Fong, 2012) and compensation for mentor services can be offered in a variety of ways that benefit tight university budgets and reward students for their contributions.

Scholars have been immersed in the study of developmental relationships since the 1970s, and empirical research in the field supports its continued attention across all fields, particularly in higher education. Scholars such as David Clutterbuck, Kathy Kram, Lois Zachary, Robert Garvey, and many others have paved the road for the use of mentoring as an integral component of professional and educational pursuits. This book makes ample mention of Kathy Kram's (1983) foundational research and builds on and draws upon the idea that mentoring serves two primary functions: career development and psychosocial support (Kram, 1983). The concept of *mentoring* represents a multitude of meanings depending on the context. In this book, Collier reframes and expands on this ideology to fit a contemporary framework of peer mentoring for undergraduates in higher education.

With the multitude of social and financial pressures placed on students entering higher education, students require encouragement and incentive to embark on their educational journey. A deep understanding of the bureaucratic, political, social, and personal pressures that surround the crisis of low graduation and retention rates must be antecedent to the design and implementation of a peer-mentoring program. This volume does a great job of acknowledging this importance, dedicating the first half of the book to exploring these frames. The question, "Why should we use peer mentors?" garners a great deal of attention in this book. Without a solid understanding of the students' needs and the constantly shifting educational landscape existing and new programs may not be successful. Institutions of higher education are in need an all inclusive evaluation of the benefits and best practices guiding the design, development, and implementation of a peer-mentoring program. Collier provides just that, and more.

While peer-mentoring programs have gained popularity in higher education, uneven application of best practices and unclear program goals allow for a significant variation in the effectiveness of these programs. The quality and effectiveness of a peer-mentoring program is largely contingent on the commitment of the program coordinators and the extent to which the program is specifically designed to meet the unique contextual characteristics of the population to be served. This book provides a comprehensive look into the multiple facets, conceptual frameworks, and paradigms surrounding peer mentoring in higher education. This book covers the who, what, why, when, and how of peer mentoring in a way that is seamless, coherent, and straightforward, so that both the novice and seasoned mentoring professional can draw valuable information from its content.

This book offers not only a wealth of knowledge pertaining to successful peer mentoring in higher education but also the nuts and bolts that are required to establish a mentoring program. It delivers strategies for implementation, suggestions on how to navigate budgets and bureaucracy, and approaches on how to train and educate peer mentors. It also addresses how to evaluate and maintain existing programs. There are so many mentoring programs currently in place at colleges all over the nation, and it can be difficult to ascertain which of these programs are effective, and which models should be duplicated and in what contexts. The nature of scholarly debate over what mentoring is and is not has engendered a contemporary perspective, which emphasizes that there is no one-size-fits-all program in mentoring. Collier's book makes use of palpable vignettes of different types of mentoring programs to reemphasize situations where peer mentoring has worked, and prepares its mentoring coordinators and leaders to overcome potential barriers to success. The use of these case studies also illustrates the diverse populations served by peer-mentoring programs and shows that an individual program design is reliant on many factors, such as funding and university size.

This book is organized in a manner that is straightforward and easy to digest. The first four chapters of the book are dedicated to a critical evaluation and discussion of the overall landscape of peer mentoring in higher education. In Chapter 1, Collier explores the definitions of *peer mentoring* and its functions and how peer-mentoring programs are categorized and differentiated. Subsequently, Chapter 2 discusses how peer mentoring can address the degree completion crisis among college students as well as relevant models for both traditional and non-traditional students. Collier integrates his own model, the two-path model of student performance, which offers a promising archetype for use on nontraditional student populations and stresses the cultural capital component in peer mentoring. In Chapter 3, Collier identifies the adjustment issues and barriers that may arise during students' undergraduate degree. Chapter 4 follows with a more detailed discussion on how peer mentoring can provide relief from these adjustment issues and how students can persevere with confidence and a stronger sense of purpose.

Chapters 5 through 9 are dedicated to the actual implementation and maintenance of the program, and cover important components such as program design and peer mentor recruitment strategies (Chapter 5); different possible modes of delivery and a discussion of each method's strengths and limitations (Chapter 6); necessary content and materials (Chapter 7); how to properly train peer mentors (Chapter 8); and how to properly evaluate your program and its components (Chapter 9). Collier concludes this book with an overall assessment of peer mentoring in higher education. He brings a unique and valuable perspective to the table, and emphasizes the importance of tailoring each program to its audience while committing to highest standards and the best of practices.

As the president of the International Mentoring Association and director of the Mentoring Institute at the University of New Mexico, I have immersed myself in the study of developmental relationships and have seen their positive effects through my work. I consider this mentoring handbook a vital tool for any institution that is looking to establish a peer-mentoring program, and I recommend its use to those who have already implemented programs in their search to improve on their model and thus the program's overall effectiveness. I believe that by explicitly defining and demonstrating all of the multifaceted aspects involved in creating a mentoring program, and by addressing the best strategies to approach this subject, *Developing Effective Student Peer Mentoring Programs* is a must-read for anyone interested in implementing a peer mentoring program on their college campus.

Nora Domínguez
President,
International Mentoring Association;
Director,
Mentoring Institute,
University of New Mexico

ACKNOWLEDGMENTS

I would like to first acknowledge the contributions of the authors of the mentoring vignettes in this volume: Vynessa Ortiz and Mary Virnoche (Humboldt State University); Phil Larsen, Lydia Middleton, and Adam Baker (University of Michigan); Elizabeth Erickson (Sacramento State University); William L. Gannon, Stephanie Sanchez, and Felipe Amaral (University of New Mexico); and Paul Braun and Jill Townley (Portland State University).

I am also grateful to all the program directors, staff, and faculty members who shared information on their mentoring programs: Pat Esplin (Brigham Young University), Pam Person and Greg Metz (University of Cincinnati), Adrienne Mojzik, Ryan Padgett, and Jennifer Keup (University of South Carolina), Nora Domínguez (University of New Mexico), Kate Tisch and Beth Monhollen (Alverno College), Gretchen Palmer (Utah Valley University), Ronnie White (Mississippi State University), Lisa Ruebeck (Lehigh University), Michael Samano (Lane Community College), John Stewart (Lewis and Clark College), Kali Lettemaier-Laack (University of Michigan), Allison McWilliams (Wake Forest University), Brigette Coble (Metropolitan State University of Denver), Phylis Martinelli and Dana Herrera (St. Mary's College), Lacey Hunter (Southern Oregon University), Miguel Santiago (Oregon State University), and Signe Bishop (Oregon Campus Compact).

The Students First Mentoring Program, described in Vignette 2, was my first large-scale, hands-on experience designing and delivering mentoring support for first-generation students. I would like to thank my Fund for the Improvement of Postsecondary Education program officers David Johnson and Krish Mathur; the Students First Mentoring Program staff: Barbara Holland, Collin Fellows, Cathy Gordon; the mentors: Regina Arellano, April Armstrong, Kristen Collins, Nicki Harwood, Robin Johnson, Heather Lindsay-Carpenter, Samantha Lopez, Julie Parker, Hannah Schmalz, Chris Solario, Joel Strong; and all the students who enthusiastically contributed to the success of the program.

My mentoring research and program development efforts have been strongly supported by Portland State University. I have been particularly fortunate to have been able to work closely with Tom Keller, Kay Logan, and my colleagues at the Center for Interdisciplinary Mentoring Research; and the administrators, faculty members, and mentors of Portland State's University Studies program, specifically Sukhwant Jhai, Yves Labissiere, Dana Lundell, Carol Gabrelli, Annie Kneppler, Mirela Blekic, Rowanna Carpenter, and Jacob Sherman. I also want to acknowledge my colleagues at Portland State University who contributed many of the exercises included in this book and willingly shared their mentoring expertise: Mary Ann Barham, Jolina Kwong Caputo, Carlos Crespo, Melanie Dixon, Toeutu Faaleava, Dan Fortmiller, John Freeouf, William Garrick, Sara Lynn Haley, Lisa Hatfield, Joan Jagodnik, Tonya Jones, Kevin Keckses, Kathi Ketcheson, Paul Latiolais, James Looney, Ahn Ly, Linda Mantell, Lisa McMahon, Dalton Miller-Jones, Lianne Kehaulani O'Banion, Jose Padin, Steve Reder, Candyce Renolds, Aimme Shattuck, Amy Spring, Rita Stacy, Olivia Thomas, Lorna Tran, Janelle Voegele, and my students Christa Zinke, Cristina Restad, and James Foutch.

Finally, I would be remiss if I did not acknowledge the support I received from Portland State's JumpStart Program faculty and coparticipants in writing this manuscript. I especially want to thank Dannelle Stevens for all her encouragement and help in transforming my ideas into this book.

Peter J. Collier
Portland, Oregon
January 2015

INTRODUCTION

Peer mentoring programs are a lot like espresso bars. Several of them can be found around every college campus, they seem to spring up overnight, and once college students start making use of their products, students wonder how they would ever get through school without them.

Still, there is a paradox associated with college student peer mentoring programs that must be addressed. On the one hand, colleges and universities have increasingly turned to peer mentoring programs as part of their efforts to facilitate student success and retention. On the other hand, in many instances programs may lack clear, explicit explanations of how peer mentoring is supposed to bring about the range of positive effects its champions claim it can deliver. At a time of reduced resources and increasing demands for accountability, it has become all the more important for programs to adhere to the highest standards of rigor in terms of defining outcomes and evaluating program effectiveness. One of the main points of this book is that program evaluation cannot be separated from design, delivery, content selection, and mentor training choices and issues. This book also emphasizes the importance of considering the comparative strengths and weaknesses of different modalities in relation to program goals, and makes the case that recycling old formats may not deliver the desired results.

This book emphasizes the importance of intentionality and quality in student mentor training. Tools are provided to help you design your program so there are explicit connections between delivered mentee services and training content. Furthermore, it includes extensive discussion of the value of rigorous evaluation of mentor training as a way to establish that positive program effects are because of peer mentoring and not prior conditions or extraneous situational elements.

Program coordinators face some important but underdiscussed measurement issues when trying to establish their programs' effectiveness. First, many times, evaluation is limited to outcomes desired by funders or administrators (e.g., retention) in situations where it is difficult to isolate the effects of a mentoring program on those outcomes. Second, many programs do not collect data that could be used to establish their effectiveness because of a lack of understanding about which student adjustment issues can be realistically addressed by peer mentoring. It is hard to be clear on what evaluation questions should be asked, the types of information that are necessary to address those questions, and how and when to collect that data without specifying how mentoring is supposed to affect the issue program administrators are trying to address. This guide provides the tools, based on theories of student development, college success, and persistence, to help readers design programs with greater intentionality that will demonstrate their programs' effectiveness to all stakeholders.

This book takes a unique approach to supporting peer mentoring. It is designed to be a resource for a wide range of college student peer mentoring programs. In addition to exploring issues associated with designing universal access programs, this book explicitly focuses on helping develop targeted programs for three large groups of underserved students: first-generation, international, and veterans of the armed forces. It is intended to primarily serve as a resource for student affairs professionals and program coordinators who are developing a new college student peer mentoring program or are trying to refine an existing one. However, it could also serve as an invaluable supplementary text in courses designed to train future peer mentors and leaders.

This guidebook is divided into two sections. Part One (Chapters 1 through 4), "What Is Peer Mentoring, and Why Does It Work to Promote Student Success?" provides the conceptual foundation for your mentoring program. Chapter 1 starts by providing some background on peer mentoring and then introduces a rubric for categorizing college student peer mentoring programs. Chapter 2 explores the issue of why college degree noncompletion is so important, reviews models of traditional and nontraditional student persistence, and explains how peer mentoring could have an impact on each of those models. Chapter 3 reviews a range of college student adjustment issues, including those specifically experienced by first-generation, international, and veteran students, and provides several tools for identifying the issues of the students your program serves. Chapter 4 connects what peer mentoring can accomplish to student adjustment issues and provides a tool you can use to determine which of your students' issues peer mentoring can realistically address.

Part Two (Chapters 5 through 10), "What are Nuts and Bolts of Developing a College Student Peer Mentoring Program," shifts the focus to more practical issues. Chapter 5 walks you through materials on program design, such as developing a time line, budgeting, hiring program staff, recruiting mentors and mentees, and developing job descriptions and program policies and forms. Chapter 6 discusses the strengths and limitations of different modes of delivery, including face-to-face, e-mentoring, and hybrid approaches. Chapter 7 focuses on program content, distinguishing among universal, group-specific, and program-specific content areas. This chapter also explains the value of organizing and sequencing content materials to facilitate mentees' information recall and higher–quality decision making. Chapter 8 starts by summarizing some important issues to consider when setting up mentor training, then introduces more than 20 mentor training exercises you can use in your program. Chapter 9 explains why rigorous evaluation is important to demonstrating your program's success. This chapter introduces several different evaluation designs, identifies different types of evaluation data and data collection tools, and shares examples of how to appropriately measure specific program goals. In addition, the sets of resources at the end of Chapters 5, 6, 7, 8, and 9 include examples of key program documents, a mentor training curriculum, and evaluation materials. Developing a peer mentoring program that works also involves maintaining your program once you've gone through all the work of getting it started. Therefore, Chapter 10 explores potential challenges and issues that might arise once your program is in operation and provides some strategies other programs have used to address these issues.

Two features of this book are particularly distinctive. First, this guide explicitly discusses multiple ways program-size decisions will affect the development and implementation of your peer mentoring program. Second, a series of case studies of successful programs of different sizes and that focus on different educational transitions (Vignettes 1–6) has been included to illustrate best practices in the key areas of design, delivery, evaluation, and training. It is my hope that this book will prove to be a valuable resource as you move forward in developing a new mentoring program or revising an existing one.

PART ONE

WHAT IS PEER MENTORING, AND WHY DOES IT WORK TO PROMOTE STUDENT SUCCESS?

I

WHAT IS PEER MENTORING, AND HOW IS IT USED IN HIGHER EDUCATION?

> College students benefit from participating in a variety of different peer mentoring programs; programs can be categorized in terms of level of inclusiveness, duration, and approach in addressing students' needs.

Chapter 1

- defines *mentoring* and introduces the dual-function model of mentoring;
- explains the differences between hierarchical and peer mentoring;
- reviews what is already known about how peer mentoring positively affects college students;
- explores peer mentoring's relative advantages in regard to facilitating college student success; and
- introduces a rubric of peer mentoring programs based on inclusiveness, duration, and approach in addressing students' needs.

A mentor empowers a person to see a possible future, and believe it can be obtained.

(Hitchcock, 2015)

Within higher education, mentoring is increasingly associated with efforts to promote student success, which includes helping students stay in school and complete their degrees in a timely manner. The large number of national-, state-, and local-level formalized programs, as well as a wide range of other student success promotion efforts that include a mentoring component, attest to this approach's popularity among college presidents and administrators (Crisp & Cruz, 2009; Girves, Zepeda, & Gwathmey, 2005; Quinn, Muldoon, & Hollingworth, 2002). Peer mentoring programs are particularly popular. Sixty-five percent of the public four-year colleges and universities included in American College Testing's (2010) "What Works in Student Retention" survey reported having peer mentoring programs with goals of promoting student success and retention.

What Is Mentoring? What Is Peer Mentoring?

Mentoring seems to mean one thing to businesspeople, another to developmental psychologists, and something else to academics. Although in higher education there is no universal agreement on a single definition of *mentoring*, this book uses a definition from the National Academy of Sciences: "Mentoring occurs when a senior person or mentor provides information, advice, and emotional support to a junior person or student over a period of time" (as cited in Lev, Kolassa, & Bakken, 2010, p. 169).

Kram's (1983) work on mentoring relationships in a business context serves as the basis for most discussions of mentoring functions. She proposes that mentoring relationships serve two primary functions: career development and psychosocial support.

> Through career functions, including sponsorship, coaching, protection, exposure-and-visibility, and challenging work assignments, a young manager is assisted in learning the ropes of organizational life and in preparing for advancement opportunities. Through psychosocial functions including role modeling, acceptance-and-confirmation, counseling, and friendship, a young manager is supported in developing a sense of competence, confidence, and effectiveness in the managerial role. (pp. 617–618)

This dual-function model of mentoring is supported in the higher education literature (Crisp & Cruz, 2009, p. 528; Terrion & Leonard 2007, pp. 149–50). There is agreement that college students' mentoring experiences include broad forms of support including professional/career development and psychological support that includes role modeling (Brown, Davis, & McClendon, 1999; Campbell & Campbell, 1997; Davidson & Foster-Johnson, 2001; Kram, 1985; Rendon, 1994). For college students, career development can be thought of as academic support and includes mentors promoting academic success and facilitating mentees' efforts to complete their degrees.

Differences Between Informal and Formal College Student Mentoring Relationships

Formal student mentoring in higher education refers to structured and intentional relationships where mentors and student mentees are matched by a third party, such as mentoring program staff (Eby, Rhodes, & Allen, 2007). Similarly, informal student mentoring refers to naturally occurring supportive relationships students have with older and more experienced individuals such as advisers, professors, or other students (Rhodes, Grossman, & Resch, 2000). Many times informal mentors actually provide the impetus and encouragement that lead college students to get involved in formal mentoring programs. This book focuses on formalized peer mentoring relationships.

Differences Between Hierarchical and Peer Mentoring for College Students

Hierarchical mentoring for college students involves individuals from two different social positions, such as faculty–student, adviser–student, or counselor–student. This is similar to a mentoring relationship in a business context where a senior manager mentors a junior staff member. Although Kram's (1983) original work in mentoring research focused on hierarchical mentoring, her later research identified how mentoring functions are slightly modified in peer relationships (Kram & Isabella, 1985).

Peer mentoring describes a relationship where a more experienced student helps a less experienced student improve overall academic performance and provides advice, support, and knowledge to the mentee (Colvin & Ashman, 2010). Unlike hierarchical mentoring, peer mentoring matches mentors and mentees who are roughly equal in age and power for task and psychosocial support (Angelique, Kyle, & Taylor, 2002; Terrion & Leonard, 2007). Although a peer mentor may or may not be older than the mentee, there is a considerable difference in each one's level of college experience.

What Do We Know About the Impacts of Peer Mentoring on College Students?

Researchers have established that participating in college student peer mentoring programs provides mentees and mentors with a range of positive outcomes. Participating in peer mentoring programs leads to positive outcomes for mentees in regard to each of the aspects of Kram's dual function mentoring model (Terrion & Leonard, 2007, pp. 149–150).

Peer Mentoring and the Career Function in Higher Education: Academic Success and Staying in School

For college students, the career development function in Kram's (1983) model takes the form of mentors providing help to students who are trying to complete their college degrees. In order to better understand how peer mentoring serves a career development function for college students, it helps to look at key indicators of college student career achievement such as academic success and staying in school. It may be worth clarifying terms that are sometimes used interchangeably, although they do not mean the same thing. *Persistence* is an individual-level variable that refers to whether a student continues his or her education, regardless of institution, and *retention* is an institutional variable describing the rate at which students remain at the institution where they initially enrolled (Collier, Fellows, & Holland, 2008).

Although it may seem obvious, researchers have established a relationship between academic performance and college persistence, particularly first-year persistence. It also turns out that the number of credits successfully completed during the freshman year is a particularly important variable in predicting degree completion. Research shows that the lower the number of credits completed during a college student's freshman year, the less likely that student is to complete any type of certificate or degree program (Chen & Carroll, 2005; Miller & Spence, 2007).

Peer mentoring increases mentees' intentions to stay in school and graduate. College students who participate in peer mentoring programs report stronger intentions to stay in college and complete their degrees (Sanchez, Bauer, & Paronto, 2006; Thile & Matt, 1995). The theory of reasoned action from psychology argues that individuals' stated intentions are the best predictors of their subsequent actions (Ajzen & Fishbein, 1970). Therefore peer mentoring programs, by positively affecting mentees' intentions to stay in school and graduate, actually contribute to increasing these students' chances of graduating.

Peer mentoring promotes mentees' academic success at college. Participating in peer mentoring programs is associated with improved student retention rates in numerous studies (Beatrice & Shively, 2007; Black & Voelker, 2008; Colvin & Ashman, 2010; Hall, 2006; Harper & Allegretti, 2009; Terrion, Philion, & Leonard, 2007; Thomas, 2000; Torres Campos et al., 2009). Peer mentoring also has an impact on the likelihood of students' academic success by improving grade point average (GPA; Collier et al., 2008; Pagan & Edwards-Wilson, 2002; Roberts, Clifton, & Etcheverry, 2001; Rodger & Tremblay, 2003; Thile & Matt, 1995; Thomas, 2000) and the number of credits successfully completed (Campbell & Campbell, 1997; Collier et al., 2008; Rodger & Tremblay, 2003). For example, in their study of students on academic probation, Pagan and Edwards-Wilson found that students' retention rates and GPAs improved during the time they participated in a peer mentoring program (p. 214). Other studies found that mentees reported feeling that they acquired social capital, in the form of connections to other students and faculty, from their interactions with peer mentors and that these increased connections had a positive impact on GPA and retention rates (Roberts et al., 2001; Smith-Jentsch, Scielzo, Yarbrough, & Rosopa, 2008).[1]

Peer Mentoring and the Psychosocial Support Function in Higher Education

Researchers agree that college student mentees highly value the support provided by peer mentoring relationships (Awayaa et al., 2003; Harper & Allegretti, 2009; Johnson-Bailey & Cervero, 2004; McDougall & Beattie, 1997; McLean, 2004; Mee-Lee & Bush, 2003; Ruthkosky & Castano, 2007; Sands, Parson, & Duane, 1991; Terrion & Leonard, 2007). For example, Ehrich, Hansford, and Tennent examined 159 research-based higher educa-tion articles and found that in 42.1% of studies, mentees reported that the support they received from the mentor was the most positive outcome from the relationship (as cited in Terrion & Leonard, 2007). Interestingly, per-ceived support from peer mentors can result in a range of different positive outcomes for mentees.

Peer mentoring helps transitioning students adjust to the university. New students who participated in peer mentoring programs credited mentors with facilitating their university transitions (Beatrice & Shively, 2007; Hall, 2006; Ruthkosky & Castano, 2007). For example, Hoffman and Wallach (2005, p. 72) found that four-year college mentors were able to dispel many myths about the university held by community college mentees and eased these students' fears of transitioning. Mentees also reported an increased sense of campus connection and increased satisfaction with their universities (Colvin & Ashman, 2010, p. 128; Sanchez, Bauer, & Paronto, 2006).

Peer mentoring affirms mentees' beliefs they can succeed as college students. Students making the transition from high school, community college, or another educational system to a university must learn a new role or a new version of the role of college student.[2] Several studies found that students who participated in peer mentoring programs demonstrated increased levels of confidence in this new role (Smith-Jentsch et al., 2008, p. 194; Allen & Poteet, 1999). Peer mentors model the college student role, observe their mentees' efforts, and then provide mentees with feedback that gives them legitimacy as "real" college students.

Mentees increase their knowledge and use of available campus resources such as the library, computer labs, and health services by working with peer mentors (Beatrice & Shively, 2007; Hall, 2006; Ruthkosky & Castano,

2007). This is important for student persistence because a main part of successfully acting the college student role is knowing how to appropriately use campus resources.

In addition, participating in a peer mentoring program improves mentees' levels of motivation and perceived self-efficacy (Hoffman & Wallach, 2005; Smith-Jentsch et al., 2008, Thile & Matt, 1995). Smith-Jentsch and colleagues note that when a mentor shares "his/her personal history including successes, failures, and lessons learned, these vicarious experiences should have a positive impact on mentees' self-efficacy as well" (p. 197).

Peer mentoring provides mentees with safe allies for sharing personal and college concerns. New students making the transition to college face an unfamiliar and complex environment. They must deal with a range of new issues and struggle to find other people in whom they can confide. Several studies found that mentees viewed peer mentors as allies with whom it was safe to disclose personal issues and information (Beebe, Beebe, Redmond, & Geerinck, 2004, p. 305; Garvey & Alfred, 2000). Mentees also reported that they viewed peer mentors as approachable sources of expert knowledge about college because of their academic achievements (McLean, 2004; Mee-Lee & Bush, 2003; Ragins & Cotton, 1999; Schmidt, Marks, & Derrico, 2004). Mentors had already succeeded in the very same college context that mentees aspired to succeed in themselves. Because of their acknowledged college expertise, mentors were able to initiate discussions with mentees on academic coping skills and other concerns including time management and getting help with class work (Steinberg, 2004).

Peer mentoring is particularly effective at promoting college success for students of color and other underrepresented student groups. Many colleges and universities use peer mentoring to facilitate unrepresented student groups' college transitions (Collier et al., 2008; Good, Haplin, & Haplin, 2002; Jackson, Smith, & Hill, 2003; Santovec, 1992). Peer mentors serve as role models and provide encouragement and support for these students who must deal with the range of college adjustment issues all new students face while struggling to adjust to a context where their home culture is no longer dominant (Shotton, Oosahwe, & Cintrón, 2007; Thile & Matt, 1995). For example, Jackson and colleagues (2003, p. 97) described how peer mentors provided new-to-college Native American students with models for addressing some of the conflicts that arise as students struggle to develop bicultural identities.

Participating in peer mentoring programs has been shown to be associated with improved retention and academic performance for several groups of students of color including Latino/Latina (Thile & Matt, 1995), African American (Good, Haplin, & Haplin, 2000; Thile & Matt, 1995), Native American (Gloria & Robinson-Kurpius, 2001; Jackson, Smith, & Hill, 2003; Shotton, Oosahwe, & Cintron, 2007), and Asian American students (Kim,

Goto, Bai, Kim, & Wong, 2001). For example, Kim and colleagues found that Asian American students participated in a peer mentoring program because they believed doing so would facilitate their transitions to higher education. Although Asian American students are not typically thought of as a group that needs additional academic support in moving to the university, these students valued their mentors' help with maintaining their ethnic identities and dealing with the model minority stereotype that places additional pressure on students to succeed academically (pp. 2419–2420). Peer-mentored first-generation students, those for whom neither parent completed a four-year U.S. college degree, also have been shown to demonstrate higher average GPAs, credits earned, and retention rates than nonmentored students (Collier et al., 2008, p. 8; Pagan & Edwards-Wilson, 2002, p. 214).

Peer mentors benefit from supporting mentees. Although the major stated goal of all college student peer mentoring programs is to benefit mentees, peer mentors also benefited from their participation in these programs. Mentors reported improved academic performance (e.g., Good, Haplin, & Haplin, 2002, p. 377), personal growth (e.g., Falchikov & Blythman, 2001), improved communication skills (e.g., Terrion, Philion, & Leonard, 2007), and increased understandings of themselves as students (e.g., Bunting, Dye, Pinnegar, & Robinson, 2007). For example, Good and colleagues (2002), describing mentors' experiences in a minority peer mentoring engineering program, noted that

> mentors realized that they were acting as role models for the freshman students . . . (and were motivated) to incorporate learning strategies learned and emphasized through the program into their own work and study sessions . . . because they wanted to ensure that they were role modeling the most effective techniques for their mentees in and out of the workshop and lab settings. (p. 380)

Mentors also acknowledged that in the process of helping mentees learn about available campus services and resources, their own levels of social capital increased through the formation of relationships with faculty and university professionals who provided student support services (Terrion et al., 2007, p. 51).

What Are the Advantages of Peer Mentoring?

One underexplored issue in discussions of the impact of mentoring on undergraduate college student success concerns the relative effectiveness of hierarchical and peer mentoring approaches. Both approaches have been shown to facilitate new students' adjustment to campus (hierarchical: Pascarella & Terenzini, 2005; peer: Ruthkosky & Castano, 2007); increase students' satisfaction with their university (hierarchical: Cosgrove, 1986, p. 119; Tenenbaum, Crosby, & Gliner, 2001, p. 326; peer: Ferrari, 2004, p. 303); and have a positive impact on average GPA, credits earned, and retention (hierarchical: Campbell & Campbell, 2007, pp. 137, 143; peer: Rodger & Tremblay, 2003; Colvin & Ashman, 2010, p. 128). However, in regard to issues associated with setting up mentoring programs, there are times when using a peer mentoring approach seems to provide advantages.

Cost

Peer mentoring programs that support college students are viewed as relatively less expensive than hierarchical mentoring programs that use faculty or staff mentors for the same purpose (Campbell & Campbell, 2007; Cerna, Platania, & Fong, 2012; Minor, 2007). Minor says that "in times of stagnant or diminishing financial resources and increased benefit costs for full-time employees, peer mentors represent a cost-effective way to meet educational goals and address retention issues" (p. 65). A report from MDRC on the effectiveness of a peer mentoring program at two Achieving the Dream colleges in the Boston area noted that administrators at both colleges viewed the peer mentoring program as "a more cost-effective alternative to hiring full-time faculty to provide similar services" (Cerna, Platania, & Kong, 2012, p. ES4).[3] Colleges and universities find additional cost savings by compensating mentors with resources at no great cost to the schools but that peer mentors highly value, such as stipends (e.g., $500 per semester at the East Carolina University College of Business, www.ecu.edu/cs-bus/success/peermentor.cfm), academic credit (e.g., University of Washington First-year Interest Group, http://fyp.washington.edu/become-a-student-leader/fig-leaders; St. Mary's College of Maryland's peer mentor program, www.smcm.edu/corecurriculum/FYS/PeerMentor.html), and textbook scholarships (e.g., University of Memphis's First Scholars program, www.smcm.edu/corecurriculum/FYS/PeerMentor.html). Since mentor compensation is a major cost for peer mentoring programs, Minor suggests ways to develop cost-effective peer mentoring compensation strategies that include consulting with potential mentors about what they value as well as working with academic affairs to creatively use existing resources like course credits (p. 65).

Availability of Potential Mentors

Another relative advantage of employing a peer mentoring approach for supporting college students has to do with the availability of potential mentors. On any college or university campus, many more experienced students are available to serve as peer mentors than faculty and staff. Although faculty and staff are highly committed to helping students succeed at college, their multiple job demands can limit their availability to participate in formal peer mentoring programs. However just because large numbers of experienced students/potential mentors are present on college campuses does not guarantee these students will choose to participate in peer mentoring programs. Motivation is an important consideration. Many peer mentors report they initially got involved in peer mentoring programs out of a desire to give back to other students and return the support they received when they were trying to make the adjustment to college.[4] Issues of motivation underlie another potential advantage of employing a peer mentoring approach to supporting college students.

Why Might Peer Mentoring Be Particularly Effective for Promoting Undergraduate Student Success?

Although no research directly compares hierarchical and peer mentoring with the same populations of students, the question still remains: Which approach is more effective? A possible explanation might lie in exploring one positive effect of peer mentoring that is not shared with hierarchical mentoring: Students who are mentored by peers report increased confidence in performing the college student role (Allen & Poteet, 1999; Smith-Jentsch et al., 2008, p. 194). In the course of supporting mentees, peer mentors model the successful college student role. However when faculty and staff support student mentees, they are not modeling the successful college student role because they are not students. This difference, whether role modeling does or does not occur, may have an impact on mentees' interpretation of mentors' actions. How mentees interpret mentors' motivation for their action has an effect on perceived mentor credibility. Although both forms of mentoring result in positive outcomes for students, peer mentoring may be relatively more effective in promoting undergraduate college student success because of issues associated with credibility.

The social-psychological concept of credibility is a useful frame for understanding why peer mentoring is relatively more effective for supporting college students. The person who sends a message is called the *message source*. Mentors are message sources. A message source's credibility is a critical element in the process of persuasion (Pornpitakan, 2004). Credibility is made up of two components, expertise and trustworthiness. *Expertise* refers to the source's degree of knowledge of factual information associated with the issue in question; *trustworthiness* refers to the degree to which the source is perceived as being likely to accurately share this related factual information (Hovland, Janis, & Kelley, 1953). The source's perceived self-interest influences the relative importance of trustworthiness and expertise (McGinnies & Ward, 1980).

Imagine you are receiving information from someone who is trying to convince you of the superiority of one type of computer versus another. On one hand, when the source is a computer salesperson who has a great deal to gain if you are persuaded, then even though the salesperson has expertise, it is much more important for you to find someone you consider trustworthy. If, on the other hand, the source is a friend who has nothing to gain from your compliance, then your friend's relative level of computer expertise takes on a greater importance. Your friend might be trustworthy, but if your friend doesn't know much about computers you are unlikely to be persuaded by his or her recommendation.

Credibility and Hierarchical Mentoring

Those in higher education agree that in a hierarchical mentoring relationship the faculty member or adviser mentor has greater college expertise than the student mentee (Campbell & Campbell, 2007; Lev, Kolassa, & Bakken, 2010; Packard, 2004; Pascarella & Terenzini, 2005). In regard to credibility, a less examined question is: To what degree do student mentees perceive their faculty or staff mentors as trustworthy? One factor that affects perceived trustworthiness is past history. Have the mentor and mentee successfully interacted before? The mentee's perceptions of the mentor's motivation in offering help are another major component of perceived mentor trustworthiness. Some mentees might discount a mentor's expertise-based advice if they see the mentor as self-serving and someone who is just doing a job.

Credibility and Peer Mentoring

It is interesting that while the peer mentoring literature identifies mentor expertise and trustworthiness as necessary conditions for promoting student mentee success, the two concepts are rarely combined in discussing credibility. In regard to the importance of expertise, several researchers have noted that in order to be effective, a peer mentor must be academically successful and have the expertise in the field (Johnson, 2002; McLean, 2004; Mee-Lee & Bush, 2003; Ragins & Cotton, 1999; Schmidt et al., 2004; Terrion & Leonard, 2007). For example, McLean (2004) noted that student mentees sought advice from seniors who were mentors because seniors were perceived as able to offer more useful advice in regard to working through specific issues and finding campus resources. It is also agreed in the literature that trustworthiness is crucial for establishing successful peer mentoring relationships (Bouquillon, Sosik, & Lee, 2005; Garvey & Alfred, 2000; Johnson-Bailey & Cervero, 2004; Pitney & Ehlers, 2004). Beebe (2004) pointed out that stable peer mentoring relationships are based on the degree to which mentees and mentors feel comfortable in sharing personal experiences and information.

Credibility, Role Understanding, and Mentoring Undergraduate Students

One way roles are learned is through role modeling, watching other more experienced students enact the college student role. The other way roles are learned is through interactions with others in complementary roles; for students this means interacting with faculty members or advisers. In these interactions, the student gets information from faculty members or advisers about how they think the student role should be played and then tries to live up to those expectations.

Hierarchical Mentoring of Undergraduate Students

Hierarchical mentoring of undergraduate students does not involve role modeling. A faculty mentor is not modeling the college student role when sharing ideas with an undergraduate student mentee on how the student should study for an exam to earn a good grade. Instead, what is happening is that the mentor is sharing knowledge of faculty members' expectations of undergraduate students. The faculty mentor is not a student, yet the mentor is sharing an understanding of the standard that faculty use to judge the quality of their interactions with undergraduate students. Clearly this is very useful information and serves as evidence of the mentor's relatively higher level of expertise. Mentees who can turn this information about expectations concerning their behavior into effective interactions with other faculty members have a better chance of college success (Collier & Morgan, 2008). However, an issue associated with credibility may arise in hierarchical mentoring relationships. When a mentee is not sure of the mentor's motivation for sharing this information, that student might discount some of the potential benefits of the mentor's shared expertise.

In a hierarchical mentoring relationship, the undergraduate student mentee is being asked to accept the mentor's advice because of the mentor's acknowledged higher level of expertise. The mentor is viewed as knowing what's best for the student, like a manager knows what's best for a new employee, or a parent knows what's best for a child. However, since the mentor is obviously not a student it may be unclear to the mentee whether the mentor's expertise-based advice is based on the mentor's past experiences as a student or based on how the world appears to work from the perspective of the mentor's current role as a faculty member or student affairs professional. The mentor clearly has expertise, but when credibility is considered, the key question becomes, Is the mentor trustworthy? For a new-to-campus college student, it may not be clear why the mentor is taking the time to help; maybe helping is just part of the faculty or staff person's job. The student may not be completely clear on what to expect from someone in a faculty member or staff mentor role, much less how a person who is accurately enacting the faculty or staff mentor role should act because of a lack of familiarity with that role.

Peer Mentoring Undergraduate Students

With peer mentoring, the situation is different. Although both hierarchical and peer mentoring seek to promote student mentee success at the university, there is a difference in role relationships. Compared to the complementary faculty member and undergraduate student roles of a hierarchical mentoring relationship, with peer mentoring only one role is involved. The mentor and mentee both share the undergraduate student role.

In regard to trustworthiness and credibility, the mentee's struggle to understand the mentor's motivation is no longer an issue. The peer mentor is seen as trustworthy because the peer mentor is a college student, the same as the mentee. The mentor's motivation for helping is assumed to be the same as the mentee imagines it would be when he or she helped another student; one student helps another because they are all in the same boat. Even if the mentee knows the mentor is being compensated for participating in the mentoring relationship, the *near peer* nature of the mentor-mentee relationship causes the mentor to be seen as more similar to the mentee than faculty members or staff.[5] In a peer mentoring relationship, the goal is not moving from one role into another or understanding faculty expectations for undergraduates. Instead, the goal of peer mentoring is facilitating the development of college student role mastery by assisting the mentee in becoming more expert in a role the mentor already occupies.

The peer mentor models the role of a successful college student to promote the mentee's development of role mastery. The peer mentor shares not only his or her knowledge of faculty members' expectations for students but also time-tested personal strategies the mentor has used in successfully meeting those expectations. The peer mentor has a high level of expertise, based on previous success in enacting the mentee's current role, because he or she is already an upper-division college student (Terrion & Leonard, 2007, pp. 153–154). The mentor's expertise and relatively greater level of trustworthiness provide an unambiguous message to the mentee that following the strategies suggested by the mentor will most likely lead to mentee success because these strategies clearly worked for this mentor as an undergraduate student.

Therefore, because role modeling is present in peer mentoring relationships but not in hierarchical ones, and because of the importance of similarity on trustworthiness and credibility, peer mentoring may be relatively more effective in mentoring undergraduate students because of student mentees' perceptions of peer mentors as being more credible. However, because there is no research that directly compares perceptions of credibility for hierarchical and peer mentors with the same populations of students, the argument that peer mentors may be viewed as more credible by mentees remains a hypothesis.

In review, employing a peer mentoring approach to supporting college students' transition and adjustment to the university has two clear advantages: cost and availability of potential mentors. In addition it has been suggested that peer mentoring may be particularly effective for mentoring undergraduate students because of issues associated with credibility.

How Can Peer Mentoring Programs Be Categorized?

Now that the strengths of peer mentoring and the positive college student outcomes associated with this approach are clarified, the Peer Mentoring Program Rubric (Table 1.1) is a good starting point for thinking about developing your own college student peer mentoring program. Although subsequent chapters of this book categorize peer mentoring programs in different ways (e.g., how peer mentoring is delivered, what is evaluated, how evaluation is conducted, and the nature and extensiveness of mentor training), it is helpful at this initial stage to situate your program-to-be in terms of three meta-level dimensions: inclusiveness, duration, and approach to addressing students' needs.

TABLE 1.1
Peer Mentoring Program Rubric

Inclusiveness	*Duration*	*Approach to Addressing Students' Needs*
Universal: *Open to all students*	Short term: *One semester or less*	Targeted: *Addresses student needs at one point in time*
Tailored: *Designed for a specific audience*	Long Term: *More than one semester*	Developmental: *Responds to student needs as they evolve over time*

Inclusiveness: Which students are being served? Inclusiveness refers to the distinction between universal and tailored programs. A universal program is provided to all students, regardless of their year in school, GPA, family status, race or ethnicity, age, gender, or sexual orientation. First-year experience programs that include a peer mentoring element are universal programs. For example, Portland State University (PSU) requires all freshmen, except those on a separate honors track, to complete a year-long sequence of general education courses in the University Studies' Freshman Inquiry program (see www.pdx .edu/unst/freshman-inquiry). PSU senior undergraduate student mentors assist faculty members in course delivery and also run separate weekly discussion sessions in which freshmen mentees explore course readings and assignments in small-group settings. Mentors encourage freshman mentees to use these sessions to discuss some of the college adjustment issues they are experiencing and collaboratively work out possible approaches to resolve these issues.

A tailored program is offered to only a subgroup of students; it is tailored to fit the needs of those students. Examples of tailored interventions include returning women students' programs (for women who have taken a break from school and are now returning, www.pdx.edu/wrc/empower-ment-project), Student Support Services-TRIO programs (for underrepresented students with academic issues, www.pdx.edu/dmss/TRIO-SSS), veterans' programs (for current and postservice military personnel, www .veterans.msstate.edu/programs), and conditional admission programs (for students who may have academic preparation issues, www.gcsu.edu/success/bsoverview.htm). For a tailored intervention to be successful, the intervention must focus on addressing crucial college student adjustment issues particular to the group you are trying to serve.

A theoretical-conceptual foundation for the intervention is necessary to suggest which of several possible issues should be emphasized to best produce success for the group of students your program intends to serve. For example, if historical trend data suggest students from a particular group tend to be underprepared academically, an intervention that solely focuses on building social networks will not necessarily result in higher academic success and persistence.

Duration: How long will your program provide mentoring services for students? A *short-term peer mentoring program* is defined here as one that lasts one semester or less, while a long-term program lasts more than a single semester. Short-term peer mentoring programs are only intended to provide mentee support for a relatively short period of time, such as the University of South Carolina's 101 programs for freshmen (www.sc.edu/univ101). *Long-term peer mentoring programs* cover a greater period of time, ranging from year-long programs (e.g., California State University, Fullerton's Louis Stokes Alliance for Minority Participation program, http://lsamp.fullerton.edu) to comprehensive programs that provide continuous support from initial enrollment though graduation (e.g., PSU's Diversity Scholarship program, www.pdx.edu/dmss/diversity-scholars).[6]

Again, a theoretical foundation to support your choice regarding the duration of your intervention is necessary. One perspective on college student support interventions suggests that the key to promoting student success is providing continuous support from initial enrollment through graduation (e.g., the Federal Student Success Services Program, www2.ed.gov/programs/triostudsupp/index.html; Ford Family Foundation Scholarship program, www.tfff.org/?tabid=65). Another perspective is that interventions can be successful by focusing on key transitions or narrower periods of time during students' academic careers (e.g., first-year experience programs such as University of South Carolina's Freshmen 101 and the federal Ronald E. McNair Post Baccalaureate Achievement Program, www2.ed.gov/programs/triomcnair/index.html). The issue is not that one perspective is right and the other wrong. The important point is that in order to develop an effective college student peer mentoring program, you must be clear about why your program is designed to run as long as it does and how your choice of duration interacts with your choices of level of inclusiveness and approach to meeting student needs.

Approach to addressing students' needs: What are the differences between a targeted and a developmental approach to dealing with students' college adjustment issues? A targeted, or single point in time, college student peer mentoring program that emphasizes helping students at a particular stage of development, deals with one or more specific issues that are of immediate concern. For example, a targeted program might serve students who are on academic probation with a program goal of helping mentees get off probation and return to regular student status.

A developmental mentoring program is based on the premise that students' needs change over time, even when dealing with the same issue. The concerns students have in their early efforts at addressing a particular college adjustment issue might not be the same when dealing with that same issue later in the same academic year. In a developmental mentoring program, the goal of the program is to improve students' abilities to deal with a particular issue over time. Peer mentors begin mentoring relationships by working with student mentees where they are in terms of a specific college adjustment issue. Mentors subsequently provide more sophisticated approaches and strategies for mentees to use as they develop more nuanced understandings of that same adjustment issue.

Although student progress through higher education is based on a model of developmental learning, whether or not your peer mentoring program needs to incorporate a developmental perspective depends on your program goals. If you are designing a targeted peer mentoring program that is focused on time-bounded issues such as helping international students acclimate to a U.S. university environment or assisting aspiring graduate students to prepare to take the Graduate Records Examination, then a developmental approach may not be important for your program.

However, this is not the case for many college student peer mentoring programs. Material that students may not completely understand or find valuable during the early stages of their educational careers may take on increased importance at later stages when it becomes clearer why this material is relevant. This issue of matching your program goals with what peer mentoring can realistically accomplish is discussed in greater depth in Chapter 4.

This peer mentoring program rubric is used in several different ways throughout the rest of this book. First, it is used to situate the different case studies presented in Part Two. Second, this rubric is reexamined in greater depth in Chapter 5 in regard to developing your own college student peer mentoring program. By determining where your proposed program fits within this rubric, you will facilitate your subsequent decisions about design, delivery, content, evaluation, training, and evaluation of training.

Subsequent chapters of this book explore the issue of identifying and understanding college student adjustment issues in greater depth. Chapters 2 and 3 detail several models of student persistence and development. Chapter 3 also explores some important college adjustment issues all students face, as well as issues specific to three groups of students targeted in this book: first-generation, international, and veterans. Chapter 4 reexamines the rubric in greater detail and provides some useful tools for identifying the important college adjustment issues your targeted students are likely to be dealing with.

Chapter 1 provides the first layer of the foundation you'll need to develop your own peer mentoring program by presenting the dual-function model of mentoring, reviewing what is already known about how peer mentoring positively affects college students, and introducing the peer mentoring program rubric. The next chapter is a discussion of why the issue of promoting college student persistence is so important for students, colleges, and larger communities. It reviews models of college student persistence and explores how peer mentoring might promote student persistence in each model.

Notes

1. "Social capital . . . exists in the relations among people" (Coleman, 1988, p. S100). Coleman argues that individuals can access one another's human capital (i.e., the embodiment of skill sets and knowledge bases) and other valuable resources (e.g., prestige, status, and money) through participation in social networks. "Social capital is defined by its function. It is not a single entity, but a variety of different entities having two characteristics in common: they all consist of some aspect of social structure, and they facilitate certain actions of individuals who are within the structure" (p. S98).

2. Roles are understood as positions in the structure of society and the sets of expected behaviors associated with those positions (Becker, 1963; Mead, 1934). Roles are not as much tangible objects as much as they are shared generalized ideas that individuals use to direct goal-related actions such as succeeding in a particular college class (Callero, 1994).

3. MDRC, a nonprofit, nonpartisan education and social policy research organization created in 1974 by the Ford Foundation and a group of federal agencies, is dedicated to learning what works to improve programs and policies that affect the poor. MDRC is best known for mounting large-scale demonstrations and evaluations of real-world policies and programs targeted to low-income people. For more information, see www.mdrc.org/about/about-mdrc-overview-0.

4. See John Jay College, "In Peer Mentors' Own Words," http://jjay.bfmdev9.com/sasp-peer-mentors; George Washington University School of Engineering & Applied Sciences, "Meet the Mentors," www.seas.gwu.edu/meet-mentors; University of Louisiana at Lafayette, "Peer Mentors," http://firstyear.louisiana.edu/content/get-involved/peer-mentor

5. In a college context, a *near peer* refers to a student who differs from the mentee in terms of characteristics such as educational level or specific academic experiences but is very similar in terms of others such as age, major, knowledge of popular culture, or recreational interests (Edgcomb et al., 2010, p. 18).

6. The goal of the Louis Stokes Alliance for Minority Participation program is to increase the number of targeted students who graduate with degrees in the sciences, technology, engineering, or math (STEM). The targeted students have faced or face social, educational, or economic barriers to careers in STEM. PSU's Diversity Scholarship Program supports outstanding students from diverse backgrounds, including racial and ethnic backgrounds that are traditionally underrepresented in higher education. The Diversity Enrichment Scholarship gives preferences to those who are Oregon residents, demonstrate financial need (federally defined), are first-generation college students, or are students completing their first bachelor's degree. The scholarship is renewable.

HOW CAN PEER MENTORING HELP ADDRESS THE CRISIS OF COLLEGE STUDENTS NOT COMPLETING THEIR DEGREES?

College students who leave college before finishing their degrees are a major cost to the nation, their colleges, and themselves. Peer mentoring can have a positive impact on the issue of college student persistence.

Chapter 2

- explains the importance of the issue of college students' degree noncompletion;
- presents the costs of degree noncompletion to the nation, colleges, and students;
- explores models of traditional and nontraditional student persistence;
- examines how race and class differences have an impact on college student persistence; and
- discusses how peer mentoring might affect each model of college student persistence.

The direction in which education starts a man will determine his future in life.

(Plato, 2000)

The U.S. higher education system is facing a crisis. Too many students are dropping out of college before completing their degrees (Symonds, Schwartz, & Ferguson, 2011, p. 2; Waldron, 2012).

What Is the Issue of Degree Noncompletion?

Even though the U.S. higher education system is ranked as the best in the world (see www.universitas21.com), America ranks only 16th out of 26 developed countries in regard to the percentage of 25- to 34-year-olds with college degrees ("Bachelor's Degree Attainment," 2012). According to the National Center for Educational Statistics, about 58% of full-time, first-time students who begin at a four-year college complete a bachelor's degree in six years, and about 26% of full-time, first-time students who begin at a two-year college complete either a bachelor's or associate's degree in a three-year period (National Center for Education Statistics [NCES], 2012b; Symonds et al., 2011, pp. 4, 11).[1] There is also a relationship between type of institution and students' graduation rates. Among bachelor's degree seekers, students at private nonprofits demonstrated the highest graduation rate (65%), followed by students at public institutions (56%) and those at private for-profit schools (28%; NCES, 2012a).

What Are the Costs of College Students Not Completing Their Degrees?

When students leave college without completing their degrees, the negative effects ripple outward and affect students, their former colleges, and the communities. Figure 2.1 shows the widening circle of costs associated with degree noncompletion.

National- and State-Level Costs of College Students Not Completing Their Degrees

Students who do not complete their degrees dramatically affect government tax-based revenues over their time in the workforce. Adults 25 to 34 years old with college degrees, working year-round, earn about two thirds more than high-school graduates and about 40% more than someone who attended college but did not complete a degree. This means that a college graduate's lifetime earnings can be as much as half a million dollars more than those of a high school graduate

Figure 2.1   The Widening Circle of Costs From Degree Noncompletion

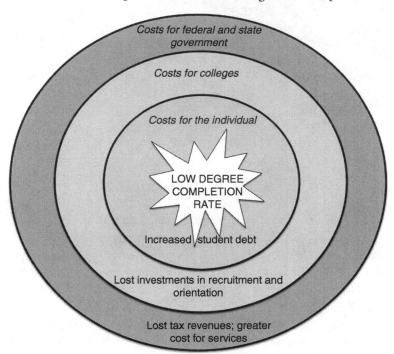

(Schneider & Lu, 2011). Since the federal government and 41 state governments rely on income taxes to fund government services, students who do not
complete their degrees represent a major loss of tax revenue (Moreno, 2014).

*Students who do not complete their degrees are more likely to require
government-funded public support services.* They are also more likely to incur
costs for federal, state, and local governments. Health care is one area where
lower educational levels correlate with increased societal costs. Individuals with
only a high school degree are more than two and one-half times more likely
to report not having health insurance than those who complete a bachelor's
degree and slightly less than two-thirds times more likely than those with an
associate degree ("Health Insurance Coverage," 2009). A similar pattern can
be found when looking at individuals who reported having only government
health insurance. High school graduates were 77% more likely than those
with a bachelor's degree and 53% more likely than associate degree holders to
only have government health insurance ("Health Insurance Coverage," 2009).

Educational level also has an impact on a related health issue—births to
unwed mothers. High school degree holders' nonmarital birth rates were more
than three and one-half times greater than the rate for those who completed

bachelor's degrees and twice the rate of those with associate degrees ("Non-marital Births," 2005).

Students who do not complete their degrees are less likely to be civically engaged in their communities. Political and social scientists from Jefferson (1894) and de Tocqueville (1840) to Putnam (2000) and Krueger and Lindahl (2001) in the present day agree that an educated citizenry is essential for a country's economic and civic success. There is a direct relationship between educational level and voting. Individuals with associate degrees are more likely to vote than high school graduates and those with less than a high school education, and those with bachelor's degrees vote at higher rates than those in all other categories ("Voting for Presidential Candidates," 2012).

Volunteerism is a major benefit for society. Volunteers provide free services to others in a range of situations where local, state, and federal governments would have to provide the same services if volunteers were not present and active. Bachelor's degree holders are more than twice as likely as high school graduates and 50% more likely than a combination of those with "some college" and an associate degree to report volunteering in their community ("Volunteer Rates by Educational Attainment," 2009).

Considering the range of national- and state-level costs associated with the issue of degree noncompletion, it is not surprising that in the United States initiatives aimed at increasing college degree attainment rates are being promoted at the federal and state levels.[2]

College-Level Costs of College Students Not Completing Their Degrees

Students who do not complete their degrees cost colleges by reducing tuition-based funding streams. With the recent trends in state- and federal-level defunding of higher education, colleges and universities have had to incresingly rely on tuition dollars for an increasing portion of operating budgets ("How to Limit Opportunity," 2011; "State Disinvestment in Higher Education," 2013).[3] For example, in the 1960s state funding made up 80% of the University of Michigan's general fund budget; in 2013–14 the state appropriation dropped to less than 17% of the same budget ("Understanding Tuition," 2013). Therefore, students who leave college before completing their degrees represent a significant loss of tuition revenue for colleges and universities.

Although the loss of any student because of degree noncompletion is fiscally important for colleges and universities, even greater financial concerns are associated with students from some specific subgroups who drop out. International students, who represent an increasing percentage of U.S. college student enrollments, make up one such subgroup. Because these students pay almost three times as much in tuition as native students, international students who do not complete degrees represent a major loss of revenue for colleges and universities (Lewing, 2012). Student veterans are another fiscally important subgroup. They also make up an increasing percentage of the U.S. college student population and bring with them federal educational benefits under the Post-9/11 GI Bill (Cook & Kim, 2009; Fusch, 2011a). Colleges and universities have a vested financial interest in promoting veterans' college success as Congress is paying increased attention to student veterans' degree completion rates (Shane, 2013). Any cutbacks in veterans' educational benefits would translate into decreased tuition revenue for colleges and universities.

Students who do not complete their degrees cost colleges money by keeping them from recouping all their initial investments in orientation and support services. A sizable amount of colleges' student processing and support costs are actually accrued during the first year. However, all the cost is not recovered until later in a student's undergraduate career. According to 2009 *University Business* calculations, it costs a college or university an average of about $6,000 to recruit, enroll, and process each new student (Raisman, 2009). So when a student drops out, that student takes at least $12,000 out the door with her or him. The student not only costs the college or university the initial $6,000 average financial investment that school made to recruit and enroll the student, but also must be replaced with another student, which means the school must incur another $6,000 in costs (Raisman, 2009).

Student-Level Costs of College Students Not Completing Their Degrees

Students who do not complete their degrees are more likely to default on student loans. The rising amount of college student loan debt has become a pressing issue in higher education, with no easy solutions in sight. In 2011, two thirds of graduating seniors had student loan debt with an average of $26,600 per student ("Student Debt," 2012). Student borrowing has increased to the point that a majority of freshmen at all institutions now borrow to pay for their education (Nguyen, 2012). In a 2012 analysis of borrowing patterns of college graduates and dropouts in the period 2001–2009, the percentage of students who borrowed to finance college increased from 47% to 53% (Nguyen, 2012). Not surprisingly, borrowers who dropped out were more than four times more likely to default on their loans (Nguyen, 2012).

Students who do not complete their degrees are more likely to be unemployed. Unfortunately the relationship between education level and likelihood of being unemployed mirrors the one between education and income. Individuals with baccalaureates were almost 92% *less* likely to be unemployed than those with only a high school degree ("Education and Training Pay," 2013). Students leaving college in 2009 entered the labor market during a 19-month recession that officially ended in June of that year. Although the economic downturn made it harder for new college graduates to find jobs, borrowers who dropped out before completing a degree faced even greater challenges. Student borrowers who dropped out experienced higher unemployment rates and made less money than those who graduated (Nguyen, 2012).

What Are Some Relevant Models of College Student Persistence?

It is clear that when college students leave school without completing their degrees, there are far-reaching negative impacts on multiple levels of society. Therefore it is important to understand what happens to students after they enroll in college that affects their decision to complete their degrees or to drop out.

Models of Traditional College Student Persistence

Traditional college students are between the ages of 18 and 22 and enter college immediately after graduating from high school (Hurtado, Kurot-suchi, & Sharp, 1996). Two useful models for understanding traditional college student persistence are Astin's (1977, 1984) student involvement model and Tinto's (1975, 1987, 1993) student integration and persistence model.

Student Involvement Model
Astin (1984) proposes that the extent to which a student is engaged and involved in the actual process of his or her education is an excellent predictor of academic success and degree completion. For Astin, *involvement* refers to "the amount of physical and psychological energy the student puts into his or her academic experiences" (p. 297). Academic experiences can be very general, such as involvement in campus activities, or very specific, such as studying for a specific examination.

Astin (1984) also establishes that peer groups can have an impact on the level of student involvement in the learning process; students whose friends are engaged in campus activities are more likely to become involved themselves. Not surprisingly, the amount of available time a student has also affects the ways students get involved in the campus community as well as how deeply involved they are during any single experience (Astin, 1977).[4] Faculty members can promote students' levels of college involvement by designing assignments that improve the likelihood of students' engaging with their own learning. Peer mentoring programs can help students get involved in their education by connecting them to opportunities to take part in campus activities.

Student Integration and Persistence Model

Tinto (1975, 1987,1993) proposes a multivariate model to predict whether students depart from college prior to graduation. Tinto bases his model, to a great extent, on the degree of fit between the student and the institutional environment.

In this model an individual arrives at college with a package of assets including individual attributes, such as intelligence or creativity; precollege schooling experiences, such as the availability of advanced placement courses in high school; and family background characteristics, such as parents' educational or income levels. These assets have an impact on two kinds of commitment that in turn have an impact on the students' desire to complete a degree, which Tinto (1975) refers to as "academic integration" (p. 96). These variables also affect the students' desire to get a degree at a particular institution, or what Tinto calls "social integration" (p. 96).

For Tinto (1975, 1987, 1993) academic and social integration are important predictors of whether students decide to persist or drop out of college. With all other factors held constant, the more a student feels academically integrated at school, the more that student will be committed to completing a college degree. Similarly, the more socially integrated students feel, the more they will commit to completing degrees at their colleges (Tinto, 1975, 1987, 1993).

Tinto's (1975, 1987, 1993) and Astin's (1977, 1984, 1993) models provide insights into the persistence-related experiences of traditional college students, and both models have been used to inform student support efforts. However, traditional students are actually in the minority in college campuses as the number and percentage of nontraditional students are rapidly increasing (Carey, 2010).

Models of Nontraditional College Student Persistence

Although the details of the definition of *nontraditional students* may vary, according to the NCES (2013), age (i.e., older than 24), enrollment status (i.e., part-time), and background characteristics, particularly race and class, differentiate nontraditional from traditional college students (see also Carey, 2010; Jones & Watson, 1990).

The nontraditional/traditional student distinction is important in regard to understanding persistence-related experiences because of racial and social class differences in degree completion rates. According to the NCES (2012b), Asian/Pacific Islander students had the highest six-year graduation rate at 69%, followed by White students at 62%, Hispanic students at 50%, and Black and American Indian/Alaska Native students at 39% each. Unfortunately, racial gaps widen as students move up the degree ladder. White students starting at two-year institutions have about the same likelihood as Black, Hispanic, or Native American students of earning an associate's degree but are more than half more likely to earn a bachelor's degree than either Black or Native American students (NCES, 2012b). The six-year graduation rate for White students starting at four-year institutions is 61.65%, compared to 39.5% for Black students, 50.1% for Hispanic students, and 39.4% for Native students (NCES, 2012b).

There are two ways of describing students' social class, family income, and parents' level of education. Regardless of which criteria are used, higher social class translates into higher college degree completion rates. High school graduation rates across income groups are comparable because of the U.S. policy of mandatory education until youths are at least 16 years old ("Unequal Family Income," 2013).[5] However, students from families in the top income category are more than 96% more likely to complete a bachelor's degree by age 24 than students from families in the next quartile, and almost three times more likely to do so than students from families in the lowest quartile ("Unequal Family Income," 2013). Although bachelor's degree completion rates among all students (dependent at age 24) increased by 73% from 1970 to 2011, the majority of this change occurred for students from families in the top two income quartiles ("Unequal Family Income," 2013).

Class based on parents' educational levels has a similar effect. First-generation students, without a parent who completed a four-year degree at a U.S. college, are more than 60% less likely to complete a bachelor's degree than students whose parents earned a bachelor's degree or more (Carey, 2010; Chen & Carroll, 2005; NCES, 2012b; Nunez & Cuccaro-Alamin, Nuñez, & Carroll, 1998). Nationally, first-generation students make up 47% of all entering college students but 53% of all entering students at two-year schools (Collier et al., 2008).

Although Astin's (1977, 1984, 1993) student involvement model and Tinto's (1975, 1987, 1993) initial version of the student integration and persistence model are widely cited in the student persistence literature, neither really describes the college experiences of nontraditional college students or students of color. Several theorists have built on the foundation of Tinto's work to try and address this issue. Guiffrida's (2006) student connection model and Collier and Morgan's (2008) two-path model are useful for gaining a better understanding of how race and class affect nontraditional college student persistence.

Student Connection Model
Guiffrida (2006) adapts Tinto's model to make it more culturally sensitive and applicable to students of color and other underrepresented students.

Guiffrida (2006) adds cultural norms and values from the students' home culture to the preenrollment packages of individual attributes, previous schooling, and family support that entering students bring with them to college. When nondominant group members retain their home culture norms and values, they feel better connected to friends and family, and this connection enables them to continue at college.

Guiffrida (2006) also emphasizes the importance of academic and social connection rather than integration to express the degree to which students experience membership in different campus communities. Students' relative levels of academic connection depend upon their classroom experiences. Students get feedback from faculty members in the forms of grades and other evidence of intellectual development.

Students' relative levels of social connection depend upon interactions and relationships in two social systems, the campus and their home. In the campus social system, students' relationships with other students and with faculty members outside the classroom context affect their degree of social connection. However, maintaining relationships in students' home communities is also important to groups of underrepresented and nontraditional students. Research shows that Latino, Chicano, Navajo, and African American students all perceived the support from families and members of their home communities as providing cultural connections and "nourishment" that helped them deal with the adversities of college (Guiffrida, 2006, p. 458).

Guiffrida's (2006) modified model of persistence draws attention to how difficulties in social connections can affect persistence among underrepresented students and students of color. However, less attention has been paid to how race and class differences affect students' experiences in the academic system and subsequent academic connections.

The Two-Path Model of Student Performance

Collier and Morgan's (2008) two-path model of student performance focuses on how differences in students' family-based social class have an impact on their understanding of the college student role and their experiences in colleges' academic systems. As noted in Chapter 1, a role is a set of expected behaviors for someone who occupies a specific social position, such as a parent, bus driver, or college student. People from the same culture or subgroup tend to share similar understandings for a role such as college student. The primary way roles are learned is through observing others' role modeling; individuals figure out what to do by watching what others do in the same role. They also learn the benefits and obligations of claiming a particular role by observing what happens to others when they take on that role. The two-path model proposes that role mastery, knowledge of the explicit and implicit aspects of the student college role, is a resource students draw upon in their efforts to succeed in their course-based interactions with professors (Collier & Morgan, 2008).

The development of role mastery typically begins with role playing, where a person performs a conventional version of the role in question. Over time, students progress to role making as they develop their own version of the role based on previous role performances (Collier & Morgan, 2008). The shift from role playing to role making reflects an increase in expertise.

Differentiated role mastery refers to an individual's relative level of ability to successfully learn how to recognize and respond to different standards for a role (Collier 2000, 2001; Collier & Morgan, 2008). Individuals become more expert college students as they add additional versions of a role to their problem-solving tool kit. This gives them more options about how to perform the college student role.

This conceptualization of role mastery or increasing expertise as a resource is closely related to Bourdieu's (1973, 1984) concept of *cultural capital. Cultural capital* can be defined as "proficiency in and familiarity with dominant cultural codes and practices" (Aschaffenburg & Maas, 1997, p. 573). The educational system is the primary vehicle by which the culture of the dominant class is transmitted and rewarded according to Bourdieu (1973, 1984). Dumais (2002) notes that although schools require students to have the ability to recognize, receive, and internalize the values of the dominant culture, they do not necessarily provide students with opportunities to do so. Instead, "the acquisition of cultural capital and subsequent access to academic rewards depend upon the cultural capital passed down by the family, which in turn, is largely dependent on social class" (p. 44).

Student success in regard to the two paths of this model depends upon knowledge of the explicit and implicit aspects of the college student role. Explicit knowledge of the college student role is acquired in classrooms and other formal learning settings, and implicit knowledge of the role is typically acquired through interpersonal relationships, such as with families, that occur outside the classroom (Collier & Morgan, 2008; see Figure 2.2).

The lower path of this model represents a traditional achievement model of education and focuses on how a student learns course content. On the lower path, a student's academic abilities determine how well he or she understands course material, which then determines how well the student performs academically. Most of the activities along this path consist of formal learning, involving knowledge that is typically explicit and codified (Eraut, 2000). The upper path in the model expands on the traditional achievement model by including students' understandings of faculty expectations as an additional influence that mediates the relationship between students' academic skills and their academic performances (Collier & Morgan, 2008).

Figure 2.2   Two-Path Model of College Student Performance

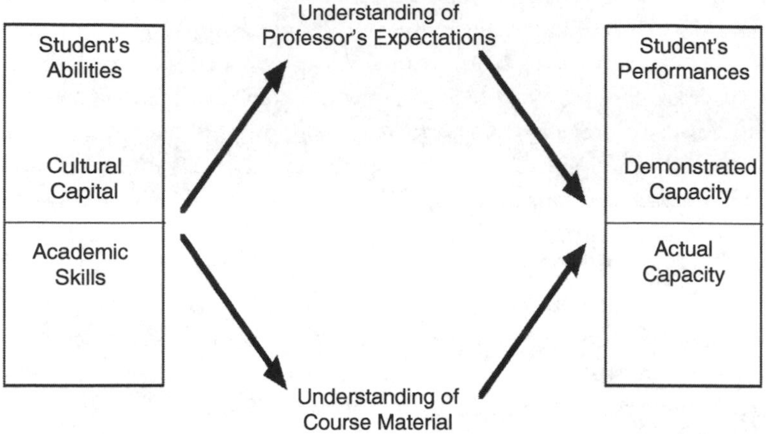

In the two-path model, the ability to understand course material and display basic college level skills, such as writing a paper or reading college-level texts, captured in the lower path, is a necessary but not sufficient predictor of how well a student will perform in class. Cultural capital, in the form of knowing how to be a successful college student in regard to understanding professors' expectations, is also necessary for the student to ultimately demonstrate knowledge of course materials. Knowing how to be a successful college student refers to important information and strategies, such as how to get questions answered, determine what to study for an exam, or find help with academic writing assignments. These upper-path activities can be characterized as informal learning, emphasizing knowledge that is typically personal and implicit (Eraut, 2000). Comparing two students with an equal understanding of the course material, the student with a better understanding of a faculty member's expectations will perform better in that professor's class (Collier & Morgan, 2008).

Consistent with its dual-path approach, the model distinguishes between two parts of student performance, *actual capacity* and *demonstrated capacity*. Actual capacity refers to the full set of what the student knows and understands in regard to course materials. Demonstrated capacity refers to the student's ability to express what he or she knows and understands. Demonstrated capacity is what a faculty member uses when assigning grades (Collier & Morgan, 2008). When a student complains, "I knew so much more than I got to show on that exam," the student is really saying, "My actual capacity is greater than I demonstrated on the exam."

Sometimes this lack of fit between actual and demonstrated capacity is the result of students not understanding the professor's expectations regarding what or how much content needs to be mastered to succeed in the class. At other times, a student's inability to demonstrate all that he or she actually knows is the result of ignoring the professor's time management expectations.

Regardless of the reason, a student who does not understand the professor's expectations ends up with a demonstrated performance that does not accurately represent all that student actually knows. Students who begin college with more family-based cultural capital in the form of understanding how to be a successful college student are more likely to make sure they understand what their professors expect from them and act accordingly. First-generation and other nontraditional students may unintentionally demonstrate less than they actually know in a class assignment simply because they were not clear on the professor's expectations for that assignment. The two-path model draws attention to how social background differences affect an individuals' ability to perform the college student role.

How and Where Peer Mentoring Might Affect College Student Persistence Models

Chapter 1 established that peer mentoring is positively associated with improved college success, including persistence, for traditional and non-traditional college student mentees. This section examines how and where peer mentoring positively affects each of the student persistence models introduced in this chapter.

Peer Mentoring and Astin's Student Involvement Model: Increasing Mentees' Engagement and Involvement in Their Own Learning

As noted earlier in this chapter, Astin (1984) proposes that the extent to which a student is engaged and involved in the actual process of education is an excellent predictor of academic success and degree completion. Mentors' modeling of the college student role is a particularly effective tool for helping mentees understand the benefits of being an engaged learner. In a review of the literature on peer mentoring and college student success, Jacobi (1991) notes:

> From (the Student Involvement Model's) perspective, mentoring can be viewed as a vehicle for promoting involvement in learning. The mentor would encourage and motivate the student protégé to deepen his or her involvement in learning and would provide opportunities for particular kinds of involvement. (p. 523)

It is not so much the specific activities modeled by peer mentors that are important as that these modeled activities encourage student mentees to more actively participate in their own educations. Peer mentoring promotes mentee involvement in learning through mentors demonstrating the positive effects of involvement.

Incorporating service-learning components into peer mentoring programs is an effective way to promote engagement, citizenship, and community involvement. When mentors model a version of the college student role that includes service to others beyond the boundaries of the college, mentees act accordingly. By observing their mentors' interactions with community members in service-learning experiences, mentees learn how to act in interactions with community members, when to act, and the benefits and costs associated with civic engagement. Interestingly, when mentees participate in service-learning experiences, it can serve to increase their engagement in their own learning, subsequent academic performance, and persistence (Cress, Burack, Giles, Elkins, & Stevens, 2010, p. 1). This approach can be particularly effective for programs serving nontraditional students. In the Midwest Campus Compact Citizen-Scholar (M3C) Fellowship Program, college student mentees, supported by peer mentors, provided direct service in multiple community projects. The student mentees, many of whom were first-generation or low-income students themselves, demonstrated higher grade point averages and retention rates than a comparison group of similar students (Cress et al., 2010).

Peer Mentoring and Tinto's Student Integration Model: Validating Mentees and Increasing Their Feelings of Belonging

In Tinto's (1975, 1987, 1992) model of student integration, experiences in a university's academic system have an impact on a student's level of academic integration and, subsequently, that student's level of commitment to earning a college degree in general. Similarly, experiences in the school's social system affect the student's level of social integration and subsequent level of commitment to completing a degree at that institution.

In regard to how peer mentoring might affect student success in Tinto's model, Jacobi (1991) states,

> Emotional support would show the strongest links to integration. . . .
> For example, student mentors could promote a feeling of belonging or
> integration among students by offering them acceptance, validation, and
> friendship. . . . Role modeling, from this perspective, would also be a means
> of socialization. (p. 524)

This suggests that the greatest impact of peer mentoring on student success, in regard to Tinto's (1975, 1987, 1992) model, happens in the university's social system. Peer mentors can make mentees aware of different opportunities to participate in campus activities, and through role modeling, help mentees better understand the institutional culture by participating in these activities themselves. In this way mentors increase mentees' awareness of opportunities for becoming connected to campus and more actively engaged in their own education.

Peer Mentoring and Guiffrida's Student Connection Model: Helping Mentees Retain Home Cultural Values and Connections While Still Succeeding in College

Guiffrida's (2006) student connection model emphasizes that persistence among students of color and other nondominant student groups involves remaining connected to their families and home social systems as well as successfully negotiating the university's academic and social systems. Peer mentoring programs can help mentees feel more socially connected on campus by linking them to networks of similar students from their same cultural backgrounds, such as Las Mujeres, a student group for Chicana/Latina women at PSU (www.facebook.com/MujeresPSU). Peer mentors, particularly those from the mentee's same racial/cultural group, can also validate mentees as legitimate college students by modeling a version of the college student role that emphasizes the importance of maintaining home community connections while staying actively engaged at college.

Peer Mentoring and Collier and Morgan's Two-Path Model: Importing Cultural Capital and Strategies for Student Success

Collier and Morgan's (2008) two-path model of student performance emphasizes how family-based cultural capital in the form of knowledge of how college works has an impact on student success in colleges' and universities' academic systems. Peer mentors can help mentees understand what professors expect and achieve positive college outcomes by sharing their college student expertise. Role modeling is the key. When mentors model the successful college student role, they share practical problem solving knowledge as well as providing mentees with backstage information on how the culture of higher education works. In addition, mentors are providing mentees with cultural capital that mentees were not able to acquire from other sources by helping them recognize which version of the college student role might work best in specific classes.

Peer mentoring can lead to positive student outcomes by affecting two different parts of the upper path of the model. The first place is at the point where students' cultural capital levels affect their success at figuring out professors' course-related expectations. Consider a situation where a mentee approaches his peer mentor for help with understanding a professor's expectations for an assignment that asks the mentee to document the stages in the development of writing a high-quality paper for a class. When the mentor recommends that the mentee try a strategy that worked for the mentor in the past, the mentor is sharing his or her understanding of the professor's expectations and a specific solution with an excellent chance of successfully addressing the issue in question. Because the mentor's recommended strategy is time tested, it is likely to have a better chance of strategically addressing the issue than any strategy the mentee could have developed on his or her own.

The second place is at the point of the upper path where students turn their understandings of professors' expectations into actions that demonstrate their mastery of the content as well as their understandings of the professors' expectations. When the mentor shares his or her strategy for addressing the issue of how to proceed with the writing assignment, the mentor provides the mentee with a step-by-step script for turning the professor's expectations into mentee work that demonstrates content mastery and understanding of the professor's expectations.

What Are Some Important Higher Education Transitions That Affect College Student Persistence?

All the college student persistence models presented in this chapter are overarching, general models in that they try to explain students' persistence-related experiences regardless of where students enter higher education. However, higher education transitions are key points in the larger process of college student persistence. Examining the different ways students make the transition into higher education can provide additional insights that are relevant to our interest in developing peer-mentoring-based student support programs. The following are five important transitions in higher education.

From High School to College

In 2012 the number of new freshmen entering college was 2,121,000, with 57.9% of them beginning at four-year schools and 42.1% at two-year schools ("College Continuation Rates," 2013). New freshmen enter a college environment that can be exciting and intimidating, stimulating and overwhelming. Decision making becomes more complicated for students moving from the more structured high school context to college because of the exponential increase in possible alternatives and level of personal choice. The highly stimulating college environment can make it hard for new students to know what to pay attention to first, which choices affect important outcomes, and how differences in choices affect those outcomes.

From a Two-Year Community College to a Four-Year College

In 2011 just under 7.5 million students were enrolled in community colleges (NCES, 2012b). Many more students begin at community colleges with the intention of completing a four-year degree than actually transfer to four-year schools or complete four-year degrees. Different surveys report that between 50% and 80% of community college students intend to complete a four-year degree.[6] Nationally, it's difficult to show exactly what the transfer rate is from community college to a four-year institution because of a lack of comprehensive annual tracking of student movement (Barker, 2013). However, several more locally focused studies can provide some insights into two-year to four-year transition trends. For example, in 2006 slightly less than 3,000 students out of a new student cohort of 4,400 at St. Louis Community College said they planned to transfer to a four-year college or university; by 2009 only 30% had actually transferred (Barker, 2013). In another study of a 2006 community college cohort, 13% of Portland Community College students graduated with an associate's degree (which could enable them to transfer to a four-year college or university) while 26% transferred before completing their degrees ("2010–11 Institutional Effectiveness," 2011).

Community college transfer students face several issues that students who begin at four-year schools do not face. One surprise for many community college students who seek to transfer is that destination four-year schools do not accept all their credits. Some community colleges have signed articulation agreements with four-year schools to address this issue, but there is no uniform policy among four-year schools. This means that credits from a specific community college that are accepted at one school might not be accepted by another (Barker, 2013). This problem can be particularly acute for first-generation or low-income students who may not understand how the community college to four-year college transfer process works.

Returning Students' Transition From the Community to Higher Education

The number of individuals seeking retraining or credentials necessary for career changes has been steadily increasing since the 1990s. This trend has led to even greater numbers of returning students during the last recession and period of slow economic recovery. In addition there has been a surge in the number of veterans returning to college after completing their service (Cook & Kim, 2009; Fusch, 2011a). After the 10-year period from 2001 to 2011 when high levels of active duty personnel were maintained because of two major overseas conflicts, there was a major scaling down in the armed forces. Returning to college is an attractive alternative for veterans because of the Post-9/11 GI Bill education benefits available to them along with the lack of available civilian jobs.

From Undergraduate to Graduate School

According to the Council of Graduate Schools, 441,000 students began graduate studies in 2011 (Allum, Bell, & Sowell, 2012). Institutions that participated in the annual survey reported receiving nearly 1.88 million applications across all fields of study leading to master's or doctoral degrees and graduate certificates (Allum et al., 2012). The transition from undergraduate to graduate school is as great as moving from high school to college for many students because of unavoidable life challenges. This transition involves shifts in expectations for learning, new relationships with faculty members and other students, and changes in the version of the college student role necessary for graduate school success.

From One Educational System to Another

Educational systems are socially embedded institutions strongly influenced by the society as a whole, taking whatever form was best adapted to the realities of existence at the time and particular place in which they were established.[7] This means that secondary and postsecondary education can and will differ between societies during the same historical period, such as present-day U.S., Japanese, and Afghan educational systems (Kerr, 1991, Chapter 1).

International students who transfer to U.S. colleges experience educational system differences on a much more practical level. International students must deal with all the issues new freshmen encounter, including a new hyperstimulating context, trying to connect to other students, difficulties in navigating the explicit and implicit guidelines of the university, and making sense of faculty expectations for students.

However, international students face a much more complicated path when moving from their home systems to U.S. colleges and universities. They must learn the U.S. educational system's basic set of expectations for college students and then they must use this knowledge to appropriately interact with faculty, staff, and other students in their U.S. colleges.

How Can Educational Transitions Be Integrated Into the Peer Mentoring Rubric?

The Peer Mentoring Program Rubric (Table 1.1), introduced in Chapter 1, is a useful way for thinking about developing your own college student peer mentoring program in terms of three meta-level dimensions: inclusiveness, duration, and approach to addressing students' needs. In light of how important differences in transitions into and within higher education are in understanding college student persistence, it now seems important to add "type of higher education transition" to the list of dimensions making up the rubric (see Table 2.1).

TABLE 2.1
Revised Peer Mentoring Program Rubric

Inclusiveness	Duration	Approach to Addressing Students' Needs	College Transition
Universal: *Open to all students*	Short term: *One semester or less*	Targeted: *Addresses student needs at one point in time*	High school to college
			Two-year to four-year college
			Returning student reentering college
Tailored: *Designed for a specific audience*	Long term: *More than one semester*	Developmental: *Responds to student needs as they evolve over time*	Undergraduate to graduate school
			One educational system to another

As noted in Chapter 1, the Peer Mentoring Program Rubric is used in several different ways throughout the rest of this book, particularly to situate the different case studies presented in Part Two.

Chapter 2 establishes the importance of promoting college student persistence and degree completion and explores how peer mentoring might promote student persistence within the frameworks of four theoretical models. In addition, this chapter makes the case for expanding the Peer Mentoring Program Rubric to reflect the importance of understanding how differences in transitions into higher education impact college student persistence. The next chapter focuses on identifying and understanding the specific adjustment issues students must address to succeed and persist in college. Particular attention is paid to the adjustment issues faced by three targeted groups of students: veterans, international, and first-generation students.

Notes

1. An additional 9% of students who begin college at two-year schools complete some form of certificate program (NCES, 2012a).
2. In October 2012, 494 public colleges and universities, members of the Association of Public and Land-grant Universities and the American Association of State Colleges and Universities, committed to accessible, affordable, and quality public higher education for all students through Project Degree Completion. This initiative aims to increase the U.S. degree completion rate to 60% by 2025, which would require increasing the number of students earning baccalaureate degrees by 3.8 million over the next 12 years. There are initiatives to improve state-level degree completion rates in every state. For example, in 2011 the state of Oregon introduced a 40-40-20 educational attainment goal. By 2025 the target goal is for 40% of adult Oregonians to hold a bachelor's or advanced degree, 40% to have an associate's degree or postsecondary certificate, and all adult Oregonians to hold a high school diploma or equivalent ("From Goal to Reality," 2012).
3. State fiscal support efforts for higher education have fallen back to where they were in the mid-1960s.
4. Peer groups can have an impact on the level of student involvement in the learning process (Astin, 1984).
5. In 2011, the gaps in high school graduation rates among the top three quartiles were each less than 10%, and the gap between the rates for the top and bottom quartiles was only 27% ("Unequal Family Income," 2013).
6. At least two studies document the transfer intentions of community college students (Horn, 2009; Provasnik & Planty, 2008; see also "Act on Fact," 2006). This report indicates that 50% of students surveyed indicated that "transfer to a four-year college or university" was a "primary goal," while 21% listed transfer as a "secondary goal" (p. 5).
7. *Educational system* refers to all the elements in a given society that are recognized as legitimate components of that society's deliberate efforts to transfer knowledge, values, and attitudes to either prepare young people for adult roles or prepare older adults for new roles (Dewey, 1916).

3

WHAT ARE THE IMPORTANT ADJUSTMENT ISSUES COLLEGE STUDENTS MUST ADDRESS TO PERSIST AT COLLEGE AND COMPLETE THEIR DEGREES?

The first step in developing an effective college student peer mentoring program is to identify the key adjustment issues your targeted group of students face.

Chapter 3

- introduces meta-level student development issues including increasing autonomy, refining social skills, and developing self-authorship;
- reviews shared adjustment issues all new college students face;
- explores adjustment issues associated with the different higher education transitions discussed in Chapter 2;
- elaborates on specific adjustment issues that are critically important for international students, first-generation students, and student veterans; and
- shares some tools for identifying the important college adjustment issues faced by the students your program serves.

Before anything else, preparation is the key to success.

(Bell, 2015)

The work you do before actually implementing your college student peer mentoring program will go a long way in determining just how successful your program will be. The underlying purpose of most college student peer mentoring programs is to help students make smoother transitions to college and promote their subsequent success and degree completion. However, the adjustment issues these students face exist on several different levels: meta-level developmental issues, issues associated with different higher education transitions, and issues specific to certain targeted groups of students.

How Can We Understand College Student Development Issues?

College student development issues transcend classroom experiences and strongly affect a student's persistence at college (Mattanah, Hancock, & Brand, 2004, p. 213). Developmental theorists have defined the *transition to college*, which typically occurs in late adolescence, as a period when individuals must deal with issues of autonomy and the development of identities that transcend their families of origin (Arnstein, 1980; Baxter Magolda, 2001, 2004; Chickering, 1969). Students who successfully addressed these issues reported better social, academic, and emotional adjustment to college (Larose & Boivin, 1998; Schultheiss, & Blustein, 1994); greater social connectedness and less loneliness (Brack, Gay, & Matheny, 1993); and lower levels of depression and anxiety (Armsden & Greenberg, 1987; Vivona, 2000). Those who did not were more likely to suffer emotional distress and less likely to persist (Astin, 1999; Mattanah et al., 2004). College development issues seem to be a double-edged sword. While failure to adequately address these issues is associated with negative outcomes, they also provide students with opportunities for growth.

Student Development Theory

Chickering's (1967; Chickering & Reisser, 1993) student development theory explains how attending college provides students with several important opportunities for personal growth. First, the college experience provides students with an opportunity to develop intellectual competence. When students attend college, they acquire discipline-based intellectual content and the specific skills associated with content. English majors learn what differentiates Victorian from Renaissance literature; civil engineering majors learn how to calculate the load-bearing capacity of a bridge or highway; and students in general education classes, regardless of their majors, learn to write in different academic styles, think critically, and make logical arguments. Differences in intellectual competence development are reflected in students' grades, so it is imperative for students with intellectual competence issues to receive assistance if they are to remain in school. Peer mentors can help these students deal with this issue in several different ways. Mentors can make mentees aware of relevant campus support resources such as tutoring programs and learning centers. In addition, mentors can share their personal stories of overcoming learning deficits as well as modeling appropriate behavior for seeking help.

A second college student developmental issue or opportunity has to do with how well students refine their social skills. Students try out an increasingly sophisticated set of social skills while attending college. Chickering and Reisser (1993) describe this as developing interpersonal competence. Attending college provides students with opportunities to acquire valuable social capital in the form of social networks that provide benefits in multiple other areas. New college students must interact with a much wider range of people at college than they did in the past, which can pose problems for some students. Peer mentors can help mentees refine their social skills by making mentees aware of opportunities to interact with students from other social groups and by modeling appropriate social behavior.

Another developmental issue has to do with how students handle the increased autonomy that attending college brings. Many students experience higher levels of independence when they begin college than at any earlier time in their lives. They are required to be more self-sufficient and to take more responsibility for realizing important life goals. College can serve as a transition point between a relatively dependent role in a student's parents' household to total independence and living on one's own. Peer mentors can assist students dealing with autonomy issues by explicitly discussing what colleges expect from students, sharing their own stories, and modeling responsible behavior.

Student development theory proposes that as students develop in competence, autonomy, and social relations, they face another issue or opportunity—how to deal with potential changes in self-concept. From this perspective, the issue of student self-concept or core self-development involves finding roles and styles in the college context that are genuine expressions of self and that further sharpen self-definition (Chickering & Reisser, 1993, p. 46).[1]

Self-Authorship Theory

Baxter Magolda's (2001, 2004, 2009) self-authorship theory also explores college student development issues related to autonomy and self-concept development in conjunction with a larger epistemological question: What is the basis for knowledge? *Self-authorship* refers to a person's internal capacity to articulate his or her identity, beliefs, and social relationships (Baxter Magolda, 2001). This perspective emphasizes that student development is an ongoing, multidimensional process that occurs in three separate dimensions (cognitive, intrapersonal, and interpersonal) as well as in the interconnections among these dimensions (King & Baxter Magolda, 2005, p. 574). In the period between leaving high school and making one's place in the world, young people keep searching for, and in many cases revising, their personal answers to three questions: How do I know what I know? Who am I? and What do I want in relationships? (Baxter Magolda, 2009, pp. 9–10).

Cognitive development involves deciding what to believe and value, as well as assumptions about how knowledge is acquired (Baxter Magolda, 2009, pp. 9–10). This process involves shifting ideas about the quality and accuracy of information, as well as what constitutes legitimate ways for how knowledge is learned.

Intrapersonal development involves figuring out who we are and how we view ourselves. Several different types of identities make up the self-concept.

> Role identities are based on the different social structural *positions* individuals hold, such as spouse, worker, and parent, social identities are based on individuals' memberships in certain groups as in persons being Democrat, Latino, or Catholic. Person identities are based on a view of the person as a unique entity, distinct from other individuals. Here, the focus is on the qualities or characteristics individuals internalize as their own, such as being more (or less) controlling or more (or less) ethical. (Burke & Stets, 2009, p. 112)

In the early stages of a person's life these identities or views of self typically come from family, elementary and secondary schools, and other social groups the person belongs to. College involves a shift in how students see themselves in regard to possible careers, spirituality, gender, sexual orientation, and political affiliation. Students try on new identities and then reflect upon how well each identity works in regard to accomplishing important life goals.

Interpersonal development involves interacting with others and recognizing how we want to interact with them (Baxter Magolda, 2009, p. 10). College students must adjust from familiar parent-child and high school student-teacher relationships to more nuanced college relationships with professors, other students, and additional members of the college community. A major aspect of these new relationships involves students trying to understand the expectations that others have of them as well as what they can expect from others in different college relationships.

To make the most of their time at college, students must progress along a continuum of self-authorship. Baxter Magolda (2001, 2009) discusses how a student moves from relying on external formulas, in the form of others' visions for how that student should proceed in college and life, to a crossroads or transition stage, where the student is torn between following others' visions and listening to his or her own internal voice. In the final stage, self-authorship, the student is now clear about her or his own values and comfortable making decisions based on his or her own internal voice (Baxter Magolda, 2009, p. 10). A self-authored student would be more likely to choose a major that interested him or her and think critically about the courses he or she signs up for (Pizzolato, 2008). Unfortunately many traditional-age college students enter college without these skills (Baxter Magolda & King, 2008, p. 8).

When students enter college they rely heavily on external authorities such as parents or professors for what they believe, how to learn, how to define themselves, and how to build relationships with others. This is logical considering the complexity of the college context these students are entering. However, as students encounter new experiences, expectations, and responsibilities, they may find that the way they have been living their lives is conflicting with their new sense of self. The career path that seemed perfectly laid out from the perspective of a new high school graduate may become increasingly problematic because of reappraisals of skills, such as one's ability to pass college statistics, or new understandings of possibilities for employment with certain degrees. Family-based time lines about settling down into more permanent relations and forming families may no longer fit with new understandings of career paths, sexual orientation, or relationship options.

The issue of developing self-authorship can be thought of as a quest for authenticity. Peer mentors can help guide students through the transformation from external definition to self-authorship through a combination of support, modeling, encouraging reflection, and developmental stage-appropriate communication. It is not realistic to expect new freshmen to have already developed their internal voices to the degree necessary to successfully make all the decisions required for college success. Peer mentors can assist new students in moving along the developmental continuum by providing initial external formulas for college success that work based on peer mentors' own experiences. These are more likely to help mentees succeed in their early college efforts while allowing them time to begin to develop their own internal voices. Mentors need to model how to make sense of newly acquired college knowledge; what constitutes appropriate college student behavior; and how to appropriately approach key interpersonal interactions with other students, professors, and staff. But having mentors model appropriate behavior is not enough. Mentors must also explain to their mentees why the mentor chose to act, think, and interact in these ways. Reflection can be used to help mentees recognize situations where they had been aware of personal values and their internal voice, and the degree to which they acted in accordance with the authentic or self-authored self.

Also, since self-authorship is a developmental process, nontraditional, older, or returning students may begin college further along the self-authorship continuum than traditional-age students. Peer mentors need to adapt how they support and challenge mentees to authentically correspond with mentees' stages of self-authored self-development.

Student development and self-authorship theories draw attention to the importance of helping students address meta-level issues of autonomy, social skill maturation, self-concept development, and authenticity if they are going to persist and succeed at college. The next section focuses on more specific adjustment issues all college students must address.

What Are Some Important Issues Faced by All College Students?

All students must address some basic adjustment issues to succeed at college.

Sense of Belonging

A student's sense of belonging and connection to the campus community are major factors in determining whether she or he will persist in college or even stay at a particular school (American Council on Student Financial Assistance, 2005; Terenzini & Pascarella, 1994; Tinto, 1993). New students' abilities to develop satisfying peer relationships strongly affect their feelings of belonging (Terenzini & Reason, 2005). Many students struggle to make friends in their new college environment. Some have difficulty finding others who share their values and interests even when they are offered a chance to interact with a new group of peers, such as in a residence hall setting.

Preparation

A student's level of preparation not only affects whether he or she gets into college, but also is a prime predictor of whether the student will persist at college long enough to complete a degree (Adelman, 2006; Bedsworth, Colby, & Doctor, 2006). Two good indicators of level of preparation are students' grades in college-level mathematics courses and whether students need to complete one or more remedial classes (Bedsworth et al., 2006). Students' freshman year performance is strongly dependent on level of preparation (Pascarella &

Terenzini, 1991), and poor freshman year academic performance is associated with a lower likelihood of degree completion (Allenswoth & Easton, 2007).

Negotiating Bureaucracy

Colleges and universities are bureaucracies, and students must learn to negotiate these bureaucracies to persist and complete their degrees. New students must address a range of bureaucratic issues including having transcripts evaluated, completing preenrollment mathematics and writing placement, setting up information technology (IT) accounts for mail and computer access, paying tuition bills, and following the proper chain of command for addressing issues with faculty members or other students.

Time Management

Time management is another issue all students must address to succeed at college. One expectation that faculty members and advisers universally have is that students should spend two to three hours reading, studying, and working on course materials outside class for every hour of class time. In reality, students expect to complete the required work in the amount of time they have available after meeting other priorities, including work demands, family obligations, recreation, and hanging out with friends (Collier & Morgan, 2008).

Finding Campus Resources

Colleges and universities are spatially huge. Classrooms, departments, faculty and administrative offices, and student support services are scattered across large geographical areas, which can make it challenging for students to figure out where they have to go. Many students turn to online campus services to help locate needed resources. However, typical college websites are organized to reflect the school's administrative hierarchy, such as which faculty members are in a specific department or which program staff report to which administrator. This format makes it difficult for students to search for and find the services they seek.

To further complicate the issue, there typically is too much information on most campus services Web pages. Even when students locate a possible source of assistance, they must sift through large amounts of information to find out if this source can provide the needed services and how to go about accessing the help the source provides. Many students end up feeling overwhelmed by the process of trying to locate needed campus resources and give up without getting the help they need.

Financial Issues and Managing Money

Developing financial literacy is an important issue that has an impact on college student persistence and degree completion. Applying for financial aid and keeping track of all the details can be an overwhelming process. Students need to know what different types of financial aid are available, how to fill out and submit the Free Application for Federal Student Aid form, and how to proceed after they receive an award. They also need to know where to go online and in person to get financial aid questions answered.

College students also struggle with managing their money. Creating a budget is one of the most important things college students can do to manage their finances and make sure they pay their bills on time. Paying bills on time helps students establish and maintain good credit. Unfortunately, some students do not realize that the decisions they make about finances as they attend college could have a lasting impact later in life.

Personal Well-Being and Physical and Mental Health

Students must appropriately deal with physical and mental health concerns to succeed at college. While college transitions can be very exciting, they are also major sources of stress for students, especially new freshmen (Fisher & Hood, 1987; Towbes & Cohen, 1996). Social support, particularly parental support, can serve as a buffer to the stress associated with making the transition to college. The irony in this situation is that the college transition time is typically characterized by students' increased expectations of independence. This expectation can lead new students to reject offers of parental support that might have proved useful in reducing stress levels. Students have to take greater responsibility for their own health-related decisions, including making the time for regular exercise and sleep.

Understanding the Culture of Higher Education

All students in transition have to develop or refine their understanding of the culture of higher education, regardless of the specific type of transition they make. Understanding the culture of higher education is an umbrella category that includes a wide range of specific issues, such as the appropriate use of office hours; figuring out how to address a professor; the relationship between major choice and career paths; and understanding what constitutes plagiarism, an appropriate source, or how to prepare for examinations.

This type of knowledge is an example of what Robert Sternberg (1985) calls "practical intelligence" (p. 258), which is a person's knowledge about how the world works, and is used to set realistic goals to get things done. While all students must deal with understanding-the-culture-of-college issues, students from middle- and upper-class families tend to start college with more of this valuable practical intelligence because of their family's greater familiarity with higher education and social networks that include other children of more educated parents. Many times, college-related practical intelligence takes the form of tacit knowledge, which is knowledge a person has available but may not initially be aware that she or he possesses (Polanyi, 1966, pp. 3, 7). What is interesting is that many times, individuals operating on tacit knowledge are not always able to articulate the decision rules they are using to navigate the situation in question. Even students from families with college-educated parents may still be anxious about dealing with the new college culture.

What Are Important Student Adjustment Issues Associated With Specific Higher Education Transitions?

Students experiencing each of the transitions discussed in Chapter 2 must address specific sets of adjustment issues that are relevant to your interest in developing peer-mentoring-based student support programs. Part of the challenge of each transition has to do with students trying to figure out appropriate and effective strategies for addressing issues and for taking advantage of different opportunities associated with each transition.

From High School to College

Missed Opportunities and Not Recognizing Potential Problems
Freshmen's lack of familiarity with the new college context may make it hard for them to recognize potential adjustment issues until they become problems. On the flip side, inexperienced students many times do not take advantage of potential opportunities that could benefit them personally, academically, and careerwise. This can happen for two different reasons. First, students may not recognize potential opportunities as such. Second, sometimes students who are new to higher education lack enough college student expertise to take advantage of opportunities, even when an opportunity is recognized.

Change in Basic Student-Teacher Relationship
New freshmen quickly learn that the basic student-teacher relationship at college is different from what they experienced in high school in large part because of college faculty members' multifaceted job expectations. However, recognizing that the relationship is different and understanding the implications of those differences for students' college success are not the same thing.

At college only one part of professors' responsibilities has to do with student instruction. This affects the nature of interactions they have with students, including their availability and how much time they spend meeting with students outside the classroom. This means that students must take more responsibility for making sure they understand course materials and assignments than they may have had to do in the past.

Changes in Explicit Norms and Consequences

Many freshmen find that in college, explicit norms, such as standards for what constitutes plagiarism, may be very different from those experienced in high school. In addition, there are further expectations. New freshmen may completely miss implicit expectations that more experienced students recognize, yet they still face the same consequences. For example, a junior or senior, aware of the deadline and option to drop classes, may choose to drop a difficult non-major class to protect his or her GPA. Meanwhile, in a similar situation, a new freshman, oblivious to the option of dropping classes, may persist in a class he or she is having problems with and end up with a low or failing grade.

From a Two-Year Community College to a Four-Year College

Transfer students have already developed understandings of the college student role, what they believe to be the college instructor role, and how to approach fundamental student adjustment issues. However, their perceptions of apparent similarities regarding the contexts, norms, and expectations for students between the community college and university may result in unanticipated adjustment issues.

Need to Revisit Issues Already Thought to Have Been Mastered

Community college transfer students discover that making a successful transition to the university involves a much more nuanced understanding of issues they thought they had already mastered based on their experiences at the community college. For example, while community colleges and four-year universities have multiple buildings located at different physical locations on the college campus, the increase in geographical size of a university can mean that even taken-for-granted aspects of student life can all of a sudden become problematic, such as getting from one class to another when they are not in the same building.

Greater Variety in Professors' Expectations

Transfer students must deal with much more variation in university faculty members' expectations for students than the students typically experienced at a community college. One size does not fit all when it comes to trying to respond appropriately to four-year-college faculty members' expectations. To be effective in upper-division courses, transfer students need to have multiple strategies for identifying and responding to professors' expectations as well as the ability to recognize when one approach rather than another will be more effective.

Efficiency and Effectiveness

Because community college transfer students are more likely to succeed academically and persist during their first year at a four-year college or university than new freshmen, efficiency and effectiveness issues tend to be much more important. Efficiency involves completing a degree in a timely manner. An example of efficiency would be when a student makes sure he or she begins a required three-course sequence in the fall term to avoid waiting a second year until the course is offered again. Effectiveness means maximizing the benefits of attending a four-year college or university. An example of effectiveness in getting a strong letter of reference for graduate school would be a transfer student who makes an effort to build a personal relationship with a professor in his or her first one or two semesters at the university, compared to a student who began as a freshman at the same school who might wait until his or her third year on campus to even consider starting the relationship-building process. To be an efficient and effective transfer student, the student must understand the culture of four-year colleges and universities as well how to make the most of opportunities and resources available at the institution the student is attending.

From Undergraduate to Graduate School

The transition from undergraduate to graduate school provides students with opportunities for professional preparation and socialization, but it also brings adjustment issues different from those students may have faced as undergraduates.

Balancing Commitments

While many undergraduates have had to deal with the issue of balancing school, work, and family commitments, the demands of graduate school make maintaining home, work, and school balance even more difficult. Many new graduate students must juggle competing teaching assistant or research assistant responsibilities and increased academic workloads along with learning the new version of the student role while continuing to fulfill outside obligations to family members, friends, and employers.

Differences in Expectations

New graduate students find there is a qualitative difference between expectations for undergraduate and graduate students. Graduate work involves more demanding coursework and a different approach to learning. The new graduate student can no longer wait for the professor to provide the right answer. It is likely there is no single right answer, and the student is expected to be an engaged learner who plays an active role in his or her own education.

Changes in Academic Relationships

Transitioning students find that academic relationships change when they begin graduate school. Graduate students are expected to have more nuanced relationships with faculty members, including taking more initiative in seeking out faculty advisers as well as becoming comfortable in more equal intellectual exchanges. Relationships with other students change during this transition period. Students now must judge their performances against those of a new comparison group, the members of their graduate cohort.

Changes in What It Means to Be a Successful College Student

Many transitioning students are surprised to learn that the understanding of what constitutes being a successful college student that they shared with other undergraduates changes in graduate school. Typically, new graduate students take on the version of the college student role that worked for them as undergraduates only to discover that professors have much different expectations for them in their new role.

Returning Students' Transition From the Community to Higher Education

Several of the developmental issues discussed earlier are not quite as important for returning students. For example, most returning students do not find college to really be an opportunity for establishing autonomy as they have typically lived independently on their own for some time before returning to college. Still, many of the issues associated with new freshmen and transfer students' adjustment to college are also important for returning students, such as understanding a new context, navigating the campus, and connecting with peers. Returning students also experience some issues not faced by other groups of students.

Skill Erosion

Although returning students, as the name implies, attended college in the past, the college they experience today is much different from the one they remember. Many returning students have concerns about skill erosion in terms of basic educational competencies such as writing academic papers, working with statistics, or conducting library research.

Changes in the Level of Role Mastery

Returning students are in an unusual position in regard to how they feel about their relative level of college student role mastery. For students making the transition from high school or community colleges, learning how to be a successful four-year college student is a logical extension and advancement from their previous student roles. These students see becoming a successful four-year college student as desirable and as an improvement from previous roles because mastering the four-year college student role is associated with positive outcomes such as greater earning power and access to a career.

However, many returning students have already experienced a level of mastery in regard to some different role in either business or the community that came with its own associated social respect and prestige. Taking on a *becoming* role such as college student may be difficult for someone who has already been recognized as a legitimate expert in another well-respected role. This particularly can be an issue for veterans who in the course of their service performed roles that required extensive training and involved high levels of responsibility yet did not directly transfer into jobs in different sectors of the civilian economy.

From One Educational System to Another

International students need to take advantage of the same developmental opportunities as new native students, specifically developing greater intellectual competence, increased autonomy, and improved social relations. International students also have an additional opportunity: They have the chance to learn more about another culture from an insider's perspective, which can be particularly valuable in today's global economy. The specific adjustment issues these students face are discussed in the next section, which examines adjustment issues for the three groups of students featured in this book: international students, first-generation students, and veterans.

What Are Some Important College Adjustment Issues for International Students, First-Generation Students, and Student Veterans?

Although many colleges offer peer mentoring programs that serve all students, such as first-year experience programs, many other programs target subgroups of students identified as needing specific support services.

International Students

U.S. universities and colleges currently enroll more international students than those of any other country in the world (Institute of International

Education, 2012). Many times, international students are not prepared by their home countries' secondary school systems for their American college experiences (Zhao, Kuh, & Carini, 2005). Although international students on U.S. college campuses face many of the same problems U.S. students face, they also must deal with several unique challenges.

Differences in Professors' Expectations

In U.S. higher education, learning is seen as a collaborative process, and most U.S. college professors expect students to be actively engaged in their own learning. International students struggle with differing cultural expectations about faculty-student roles (Fusch, 2012; Hopkins, 2012). Many of these students come from educational systems in which faculty members are not approachable. U.S. professors' almost universal expectations of critical thinking and student participation in class discussions can be difficult for international students from educational systems that stress rote memorization (Bartlett & Fischer, 2011; Fischer, 2011). American concepts of intellectual property don't always clearly transfer to students from collectivist cultures that discourage individualism. For example, some East Indian students turn in papers copied word for word from source material. What these students see as being respectful, college faculty members see as cheating (Fischer, 2011; Fusch, 2012).

Adjusting to New Assignments and Different Grading Criteria

International students at U.S. colleges and universities have to adjust to different types of assignments and different computations of academic success from what they were used to in their previous schools. International students from systems where course grades were based on a single end-of-year exam sometimes need to be reminded that term papers and quizzes also count toward their final class grade (Fischer, 2011). Some international students have little experience writing term papers and struggle doing independent research and citing sources appropriately (Bartlett & Fischer, 2011; Fischer, 2011; Hopkins, 2012). In addition, when U.S. professors include class participation as part of the course grade, many international students are unintentionally penalized because of their reluctance to speak up in their classes. These inside-the-classroom adjustment issues involve students having to learn a new version of the college student role to succeed at U.S. colleges.

Culture Shock

Most international students report some degree of culture shock when they begin their studies in the United States (Furnham, 1988; Olaniran, 1996, 1999; Selvadurai, 1992; Thomas & Althen, 1989; Zhai, 2002; Zhao et al., 2005). In addition to having to deal with new classroom expectations, student sojourners must also adjust to U.S. values and customs as part of dealing with aspects of everyday life that native students take for granted. International students often lack local knowledge of available resources and how to solve daily life problems in a new country such as getting a bus pass or finding a Laundromat (Olaniran, 1996).

Language Proficiency

Language proficiency can be a major source of stress for international students since language skills have an impact on many other college adjustment issues. Typically, international students' English language skills preparation prior to their arrival at U.S. colleges focuses on academic English; however, students also need to be familiar with American idioms and college slang to be successful in social interactions (Chen, 1999; Lacina, 2002; Poyrazli, Senel, & Kavanaugh, 2006). Some international students avoid interactions with native students because their lack of confidence in their social language skills leads them to think they will not fit in (Olivas & Li, 2006). Unfortunately, this becomes a self-fulfilling prophecy. Their lack of confidence in social English skills leads to avoidance of interactions with native students. The international student then sees the lack of successful interactions with native students as evidence of not fitting in. This leads to the student's even greater negative feelings about ever being able to fit in the U.S. college environment and even greater avoidance of interactions with native students.

Building and Maintaining Support Networks

International students struggle to develop support networks or maintain social support from family and friends. Many times international students turn to online, Skype, or instant-messaging relationships with family or friends in their host and their home countries (Fischer, 2011; Ye, 2006). Staying connected to friendship networks has a positive impact on how international students deal with their sojourns to U.S. colleges (Furnham & Alibhai, 1985; Ye, 2006).

International students are sensitive to changes in their relative social status in their host country. They go from being a member of the dominant group, with many taken-for-granted privileges and advantages, to being a part of a clear numerical and ethnic minority. Many times the social standing they enjoyed in their home countries is not recognized as important in the United States (Al-Sharideh & Goe, 1998). International students are also more sensitive to what they perceive as prejudice and discrimination in the United States, compared to permanent residents or visiting scholars from the same country (Sodowsky & Plake, 1992).

Even the concept of friendship is understood differently in different cultures (Lacina, 2002). Because the United States is a highly individualistic culture, friendship is viewed as less permanent in more collectivist countries (Bulthuis, 1986). International students can feel confused watching other students interact on U.S. campuses as it appears that American students are friendly to everyone they meet.

Homesickness

Although loneliness is an issue for all new college students, international students report much higher levels of homesickness than native students (Lacina, 2002; Olaniran, 1996; Rajapaksa & Dundes, 2002/2003; Yi, Giseala Lin, & Kishimoto, 2003). Attending college in the United States may be their first time away from home for younger international students. Homesickness also seems to be associated with other international student issues. Students with lower levels of English language proficiency report higher levels of homesickness (Duru & Poyrazli, 2007; Poyrazli & Lopez, 2007). Similarly, international students' relative level of homesickness is associated with students' perceived levels of discrimination (Poyrazli & Lopez, 2007). However, international students with higher levels of social support report lower levels of homesickness (Duru & Poyrazli, 2007; Yeh & Inose, 2003).

First-Generation Students

First-generation students, whose parents did not complete a four-year degree at a U.S. college or university, are a large group of undersupported students. Compared to students from more educated families, these students have lower rates of enrolling in, persisting in, and graduating from college (Engle, Bermeo, & O'Brien, 2006; Engle & Tinto, 2008).

First-generation students also experience the transition to college differently than traditional students (Terenzini, Springer, Yaeger, Pascarella, & Nora, 1996; Thayer, 2000; York-Anderson & Bowman, 1991). While first-generation students share the same issues regarding financial literacy, prior preparation, campus connection, and navigating campus that other new students face, understanding college culture, differences in family background resources, and role mastery are particularly important issues for them.

Financial Issues

First-generation students struggle with financial literacy issues because, compared to students from more educated families, they are more likely to come from lower-income families (Bui, 2002; Choy, 2001; Oldfield, 2007). It is critically important for them to obtain accurate information on managing the financial aid system and understanding alternative funding sources (Chen & Carroll, 2005, Engle, 2007).

Financial issues affect many other areas of first-generation students' college experiences. They are more likely to work off campus and take classes part-time while working full-time, characteristics that are associated with lower retention rates (Choy, 2001; Richardson & Skinner, 1992; Terenzini et al., 1996).

Prior Preparation

First-generation students are more likely to have preparation issues and require tutoring services than students from more educated families. Unfortunately, first-generation students are also less likely to be enrolled in rigorous high school curricula than students from more educated families (Saenz, Hurtado, Barrera, Wolf, & Yeung, 2007). Because of this difference, first-generation students are more likely to need remedial course work once they've enrolled in college (Choy, 2001).

College Campus Connection

First-generation students are less likely to live on campus and therefore less likely to develop relationships with professors or become involved in student clubs and organizations (Billson & Terry, 1982; Richardson & Skinner, 1992; Terenzini & Pascarella, 1994; Terenzini et al., 1996). For students to become connected to college, the campus must be seen as welcoming to all students. Underrepresented student groups in particular seem to benefit from being able to maintain ties to their cultural and home communities (Guiffrida, 2006; Hurtado & Carter, 1997; Smith, 2007).

Navigating the Campus

First-generation students have a particularly difficult time finding campus resources to help them address specific adjustment issues. Because of their lack of familiarity with higher education, these students do not know what kinds of issues to expect once they are in college and are less likely to receive informal family support in coping with problems (Adelman, 2006; Thayer, 2000; Vargas, 2004).

Understanding the College Culture

First-generation students struggle to understand the college culture, particularly professors' expectations for students. These students who are new to higher education are not sure how to proceed initially or what they must do to be seen as legitimate college students. First-generation students are at a disadvantage for two related reasons: differences in levels of family background resources and relatively lower levels of role mastery.

Differences in levels of family background resources. First-generation students, compared to students from more educated families, enter college with relatively lower levels of family background resources, which has an impact on their levels of academic and social integration at college. While most first-generation students start learning about how college works near the end of high school or after they enroll at college, many traditional students' parents have been preparing their children for college since the day they began kindergarten (Collier & Morgan, 2008).

Relatively lower levels of role mastery. First-generation students come to the university with less understanding of the student role and less capacity to build their existing knowledge into genuine expertise. Regardless of whether students are aware of multiple versions of the student role, they typically are only comfortable using a single version of the role. First-generation students have less experience in pattern recognition either in understanding the university's expectations for students or recognizing effective role-based problem-solving strategies. While traditional students are employing previously acquired role knowledge to differentiate expectations of professors in each class, first-generation students are usually struggling to understand the university's expectations in general (Collier et al., 2008; Collier & Morgan, 2008).

Student Veterans

Many student veterans are reenrolling in college after time away from school because of deployment or required training. In essence, fulfilling their military obligations has forced them to "stop out" of their education. Unfortunately, stopping out has been associated with lower degree completion rates and a longer time to degree completion (Livingston, 2009; Pascarella & Terenzini, 2005). Student veterans must deal with financial and academic issues similar to those of all new students. Like other returning students, student veterans face the issue of having to juggle pursuing their academic goals with family and work responsibilities. However, student veterans often face additional challenges that even other nontraditional college students do not face, particularly administrative, social, and personal issues.

Financial Issues

Student veterans face financial issues that are similar to and different from those faced by other college students. The first, and biggest, similarity is that veterans identify financial issues as their greatest college concern. The second similarity is that veterans, like other college students, struggle to get accurate information about available financial resources. However, there are several important differences. Student veterans report confusion about their GI Bill benefits, and a lack of strong guidance in figuring out which benefits are available to them or how to access those benefits (Cook & Kim, 2009; Fusch, 2011). Financial issues can overlap with administrative issues on many campuses because student veterans often have to navigate multiple departments or offices to access the range of benefits and resources supposedly available to them.

Academic Issues

Student veterans face many of the same issues other transitioning students do, particularly figuring out professors' expectations. Veterans report that their military service both positively and negatively affected their efforts to make the transition to higher education. Many veterans credited the discipline and do-it-yourself attitude fostered by military service as the source of their increased academic focus and seriousness of purpose once they returned to college (Livingston, 2009; Sachs, 2008). However, some veterans acknowledged they had forgotten key academic concepts related to their major or the general education curriculum during their deployment (Livingston, 2009). Other classroom-related issues included difficult in concentrating and test-taking anxiety (Student Affairs Leadership Council, 2009).

Administrative Issues

Administrative issues refer to university policies that directly affect student veterans. While these issues may vary between campuses, specific veterans' concerns include some schools' lack of flexibility in regard to military students' somewhat unpredictable deployment schedules, and whether colleges will recognize and award credit for civilian courses completed while in the military and give credit for specific skills learned as part of formal military training (Cook & Kim, 2009; Fusch, 2011).

Campus Navigation

Like many other groups of students making the transition to college, student veterans have to learn to find the appropriate campus resources to deal with their specific issues. However, a somewhat unique problem among these students is that veteran-specific information is not available from a single source (Student Veterans of America, 2008). An unanticipated consequence of a lingering do-it-yourself military pride is that student veterans are sometimes less inclined to seek out and take advantage of formal academic support resources like tutoring (Livingston, 2009). Many times student veterans will try to get their questions answered at a campus veterans' center when they do not feel comfortable contacting campus offices that could refer them to services (Fusch, 2011).

Culture Shock

Student veterans often experience culture shock as they try to make the transition and assimilate into the civilian college environment (Cook & Kim, 2009; Livingston, 2009). The differences between military and college life are particularly striking as they try to adjust from the service's rigid, regimented, and structured work environment with high levels of accountability to the varied, flexible, and laissez-faire college culture (Cook & Kim, 2009; Livingston, 2009; Summerlot, Green, & Parker, 2009).

Lack of Connection
Another social issue for veterans has to do with a general lack of involvement with their campuses. Veterans often find dormitory life unattractive because they tend to be older in age, more mature, and have different life experiences. Many student veterans report little interest in joining typical college clubs or organizations because of differences in priorities and difficulties in relating to nonmilitary peers (Livingston, 2009; Student Affairs Leadership Council, 2009). Some student veterans tend not to disclose their military affiliation or veteran status to avoid dealing with other students' stereotypes of veterans as politically conservative males (Livingston, 2009; Student Affairs Leadership Council, 2009).

Personal Issues
One striking difference between veterans and other groups of returning students is that veterans are dealing with high levels of physical and psychological injuries (Ford, Northrup, & Wiley, 2009; Sachs, 2008). One of the greatest needs for many student veterans is help in dealing with psychological problems such as post-traumatic stress disorder (PTSD) and depression (Cook & Kim, 2009; Ford et al., 2009; Lokken, Pfeffer, McAuley, & Strong, 2009; Tanielian & Jaycox, 2008). It is unclear how many student veterans are dealing with mental health problems, but according to Department of Veterans Affairs' (VA) data, 27% of Afghanistan and Iraq campaign veterans using VA services have been diagnosed with PTSD (Bagalman, 2011; Brancu, Straits-Tröster, & Kudler, 2011; Tanielian & Jaycox, 2008). College disability services have reported an increase in student veterans with multiple injuries or a combination of PTSD and unresolved anger applying for services (Sachs, 2008). These kinds of psychological issues can make it difficult for veterans to build relationships with other students.

How Can You Identify the Adjustment Issues the Students in Your Program Face?

One of the first things you need to do when setting up a peer mentoring program is identify the needs of your target population of students.

What Are the College Adjustment Issues These Students Are Facing?

This is an important question for several reasons. First, all adjustment issues are not of equal importance. Because no single program can address all the issues a targeted group of students face in adjusting to college, a key step in establishing program priorities is ordering issues in terms of their relative importance to student success.

Second, it is important to remember that students' adjustment to college is a developmental process. This means that when specific issues must be addressed is also an important consideration for peer mentoring programs. Over time, all students develop more sophisticated understandings of how college works. As they continue to become more informed consumers of higher education, issues that were very important in the early portions of their transitions become less critical, and new issues that were initially off the radar become more salient. Students' brains are full of new information as they make transitions in higher education. Therefore peer mentoring programs that can categorize the issues they provide support for according to relative importance and the student's developmental stage will also contribute to reducing students' levels of information overload.

Finally, peer mentoring may not be the most appropriate way to address some student adjustment issues. (Chapter 4 explores what peer mentoring can realistically accomplish in addressing college adjustment issues.) You can build a solid foundation for your peer mentoring program by establishing program priorities that are relevant to student adjustment needs and appropriate for mentoring.

Identifying Student Adjustment Issues

Several points should be considered when you are trying to identify the important adjustment issues your targeted group of students must address to succeed at college. The first point has to do with perspective: Who is best equipped to identify these students' college adjustment issues? It is critically important that the issue identifier has requisite college student expertise. This then suggests that either more experienced students or advisers, support staff, or faculty members who regularly work with the targeted students would be most appropriate. The second point has to do with process: How should you go about identifying these important student adjustment issues?

Tools for Identifying Student Issues

The following are two tools to help you identify your targeted group of students' adjustment issues.

Charrette

A *charrette* is a term used in architecture that describes a collaborative process of design improvement (Juarez & Thompson-Grove, 2003). More recently,

Exercise 3.1. How to Use a Charrette to Identify Student Adjustment Issues

Once you have identified the target group of students your peer mentoring program will serve, such as new freshmen, transfer students, or international students, determine who among your campus community are experts on the adjustment issues facing those students. If your peer mentoring program is targeting new freshmen, then campus experts would include more expert students (e.g., juniors, seniors, and graduate students), faculty members who teach first-year courses, and student affairs professionals such as advisers, health center counselors, financial aid advisers, resident hall supervisors, and orientation leaders. Invite your campus experts to a meeting scheduled at a time that is convenient for the greatest number of these people.

In preparation for the meeting, tape several large sheets of butcher paper on the walls of the meeting room. Make sure you have an adequate number of colored markers available. Because student adjustment is a developmental process, label the sheets with each of the academic terms or semesters your school uses to divide up the year. If you are going to have a large number of participants, you may want to have two sheets for each semester or term. You will need a group facilitator and a note taker.

When the participants arrive, review the purpose of the charrette with them. In this example, we are trying to identify all the college adjustment issues new freshmen face during their first year on campus. Emphasize that all ideas are important. Make sure everyone knows that you are interested in distinguishing between issues that are important in one or more terms of the year and those that are term specific, and point out the different sheets of paper corresponding to the different academic terms or semesters. To start the idea generation stage of the process, provide participants with colored markers and ask them to start writing down their ideas about adjustment issues on the different sheets of butcher paper hanging on the walls of the meeting room. If a participant agrees with an idea that is already on the sheet of paper, ask her or him to put a checkmark next to the idea to signify agreement. By having people write their ideas on the sheets of paper on the wall rather than using a paper on a table, all the other participants can see which issues have already been identified, prompting new ideas from others. Allow 15 to 20 minutes for participants to contribute all the ideas they can think of, extending or shortening the amount of time you spend on this task based on the amount of participation.

After all the participants are finished generating ideas and adding them to the sheet of paper on the wall, the facilitator begins the clarification stage of the process by reviewing the responses for each term or semester with the group. The facilitator totals the numbers of responses for the same issue and asks individuals in the group who identified this issue as important to briefly explain why and why it needed to be addressed in this term or semester. The facilitator tries to consolidate similar ideas into a single term or phrase while regularly checking with the participants who generated the initial ideas to make sure the consolidated term still captures the intended meaning of the original points. The facilitator also asks the group to reconsider the chronology of the listed adjustment issues, for example, checking to see whether an issue introduced in the fall semester also might be relevant in the spring semester. The note taker records all the comments from the group discussion. After the clarification or discussion, the facilitator thanks the group for participating, and everyone leaves the meeting.

The final stage in the process, the review, takes place sometime after the group meeting. Once the note taker has organized the meeting notes, the peer mentoring program team reviews the lists of term-specific adjustment issues. A final document of all the issues, organized by terms or semesters, is then circulated to all the charrette participants to review and comment on. The peer mentoring program team incorporates any additional thoughts and comments from the review stage into a final list of student adjustment issues. The greatest strength of the charrette as a tool for identifying student adjustment issues is the synergy that can arise when campus experts interact face-to-face. On the flip side, the greatest potential problem with using this tool is finding a time when all or the majority of your campus experts can meet to consider the potential adjustment issues your targeted group of students face.

the charrette process has transcended disciplinary boundaries and been employed in a range of situations, including developing curricula, creating a climate action registry, smoothing the process of Leadership in Energy and Environmental Design certification in green building projects, and refining software design (California Climate Action Registry, 2001; Del Monte, 2006; Perez, 2010). The charrette process is based on the idea that individuals working together tend to produce better work than individuals working alone. The charrette is a useful tool for identifying the adjustment issues the students you hope to serve with your peer mentoring program will face.

Delphi Method

The Delphi method is another tool that can be used to identify students' adjustment needs. It is a way of combining opinions of experts whose knowledge is relatively incomplete on how to address an issue (Cuhls, 2003). This tool has been used successfully in multiple contexts, including science, business, and education. Originally developed by the RAND Corporation, the Delphi approach typically consists of two rounds of anonymous surveys. Prior to completing the second round of surveys, participants are provided with the group results from the first round so that their second round responses are informed by others' input.

One advantage of using the Delphi method is that it is generally easier to get all or most of your campus experts to participate because they do not have to rearrange their schedules to try to meet all at the same time. However, unlike the charrette, there are two costs associated with using the Delphi method. First, the Delphi method takes longer to complete because of the two waves of surveys and analyses. Second, the mentoring program staff expends more time and effort to conduct the two rounds of analysis compared to only one round for the charrette. Which tool will work best for you depends on your resources and circumstances.

Exercise 3.2.   How to Use the Delphi Method to Identify Student Adjustment Issues

There are four steps, several of which are repeated, in the Delphi method: preparation, surveying participants, analysis, and implementation. The preparation step is similar to preparing to identify student issues adjustment using the charrette. First, identify the target group of students your peer mentoring program will serve. Second, identify campus experts (e.g., more experienced students, faculty members, student affairs professionals, and other staff), who are familiar with the adjustment issues facing your targeted group of students. The third part of the preparation step involves asking your campus experts to identify important adjustment issues your targeted students are likely to face. The mentoring program team then combines all the initial expert responses into a single list of potential student adjustment issues.

Surveying participants is the next step in the process. The initial list of issues is distributed to the group of participating experts, and they are asked for their feedback about how important each issue is for students' college success. The experts are also asked to share preferred strategies for addressing each issue. Analysis of Step 1 data does not have to be overly involved. Many times, simple frequencies or percentages are the easiest way of presenting results (Cuhls, 2003). The results of the first round are distributed to the group so that each expert has an idea about how the rest of the group responded. Experts are now surveyed a second time using the same list of adjustment issues that have been reordered so that the issues identified by the greatest number of participants in the first survey are now at the top of the list. Once again the experts are asked for their feedback about how important each issue is for students' college success and the preferred strategies for addressing each issue, taking into account the group's response to the first survey. After the survey, the second round of responses are analyzed, and the results are shared with the entire group. The final step is implementation: How can you apply the accumulated information?

Chapter 3 explores college student adjustment issues on several levels: developmental issues, issues faced by all students, issues students must address at different higher education transitions, and issues associated with the three groups of students targeted in this book—international, first generation, and veterans. This chapter also introduces two tools for identifying student needs, the charrette and the Delphi method. Both tap into the expert knowledge of more senior students, faculty members, and staff on your campus who either have experienced the transition your targeted students are making or have previously helped similar students successfully make that transition. One big question remains: How will your peer mentoring program use the needs information collected through the charrette or Delphi method? Before you can answer that question, you need to understand what peer mentoring can actually accomplish in promoting student success. Chapter 4 will help you understand what is possible to accomplish with peer mentoring. After you combine the needs of the target group of students with what is possible to accomplish using a peer mentoring approach, you should have a realistic idea about what you want to try and to accomplish with your specific program.

Note

1. *Self-concept* (2003) is a general multidimensional construct that refers to the whole set of attitudes, opinions, and cognitions that a person has. Lewis (1990) identifies two fundamental aspects of the self-concept: the existential self, the sense of being distinct from others while exhibiting constancy, and the categorical self, awareness of membership in specific categories including those based on values, personality, and social roles.

4

HOW CAN PEER MENTORING HELP COLLEGE STUDENTS ADDRESS SPECIFIC ADJUSTMENT ISSUES AND HAVE A POSITIVE IMPACT ON PERSISTENCE AND DEGREE COMPLETION?

The second step in developing an effective college student peer mentoring program is matching the identified adjustment issues of your targeted group of students with what peer mentoring can realistically accomplish in promoting student success.

Chapter 4

- reflects on what peer mentoring can realistically accomplish in promoting college student success and retention;
- reviews how individuals make decisions;
- discusses how expertise development leads to better decision making;
- describes how better decision making leads to college success;
- explains how mentoring can promote high-quality outcomes for less expert students;

- introduces the adjustment issue and the peer mentoring matching tool;
- connects what peer mentoring can accomplish to international, first-generation, and veteran student issues; and
- provides an exercise to help you determine the appropriate uses of peer mentoring in your program.

Promise me you'll always remember: You're braver than you believe, and stronger than you seem, and smarter than you think.

(Guers, 1997)

In the 1997 movie *Pooh's Grand Adventure: The Search for Christopher Robin* (Guers, 1997), A. A. Milne's beloved character Christopher Robin reminds Winnie the Pooh that he is much more capable than Pooh believes himself to be. In that moment, Christopher Robin is mentoring Winnie the Pooh, although some people might find it difficult to imagine that a stuffed animal needs this level of support. Mentors can help college students recognize abilities and capacities in themselves when students are unsure if they will be able to make it at college.

What Can Peer Mentoring Accomplish?

While peer mentoring is a very effective tool for promoting college student success and retention, it is not a magic bullet for solving any and all problems students face as they make transitions in higher education. To be clear, there is *no* direct causal relationship between students' participating in a peer mentoring program and mastering specific content material or completing a particular degree program. Instead, there are positive associations between participating in peer mentoring programs and students' college success and persistence. What peer mentoring can do is directly affect key intervening variables that have been associated with a greater likelihood of college student success and persistence. Previous research, introduced in Chapter 1, establishes that peer mentoring can

- increase mentee engagement and involvement in learning (Jacobi, 1991, p. 523),
- increase mentees' feelings of campus connection (Colvin & Ashman, 2010, p. 128),
- provide emotional support including validating mentees as legitimate college students (Rendon, 1994; Smith-Jentsch et al., 2008, p. 194),
- help mentees navigate college (Terrion & Leonard, 2007, p. 151),
- help mentees identify and use campus resources to address adjustment issues (Beatrice & Shively, 2007; Ruthkosky & Castano, 2007; Torres Campo, 2009, p. 168), and

- improve mentee decision making (Collier et al, 2008, pp. 131–133; Collier & Fellows, 2010).

Although Chapter 2 presents explanations of how peer mentoring could promote engaged learning and campus connection as part of exploring how peer mentoring might affect Astin's (1977, 1984, 1993) student involvement model and Tinto's (1975, 1987, 1993) student integration model, this section explores how peer mentoring might bring about the additional positive effects on student success and persistence identified in the literature.

Providing Emotional Support and Validating Mentees as Legitimate College Students

Chapter 1 notes that mentees consistently report how important their mentors' emotional support is to them (Harper & Allegretti, 2009; Ruthkosky & Castano, 2007). First-generation and underrepresented students who may question whether they really belong in college particularly value this kind of support (Ishiyama, 2007, p. 457). Mentor support increases mentee success by validating them as legitimate college students.

Chapter 1 also introduces the idea that as students make transitions in higher education, they figure out how well they are enacting the college student role through social feedback. In addition, the discussion of differentiated role mastery in Chapter 2 draws attention to the fact that not all self-referent feedback is equal when it comes to validating a student's role enactment efforts (Collier, 2000, 2001; Collier & Morgan, 2008). The most effective feedback comes from others who understand and are using the same version of the role the student is using. The fact that peer mentors are successful students at the same school the mentees are attending lends weight to the mentors' feedback. So when the mentor validates a mentee's effort by acknowledging that the mentee is a legitimate college student, the mentee is more likely to believe that feedback.

Helping Mentees Navigate Your College

Peer mentoring can have an impact on two different aspects of navigating college that directly affect transitioning students, the first of which is geographical. The sheer geographical size of a university can make even taken-for-granted aspects of student life, such as getting from one class to another when they are not in the same building, unexpected sources of stress. A peer mentoring program can help new students deal with geographical navigation issues by providing them with campus maps and walking them around the campus either in groups or in mentor-mentee pairs to identify important campus resources. Even if mentees have already participated in a campuswide orientation, revisiting important campus resources like the library, financial aid office, computer labs, or advising center reinforces the earlier information and allows further mentor-mentee contact. Mentors should encourage students to use campus landmarks to help them figure out where specific classrooms are located, find campus parking lots, or return to their dormitories.

A second important aspect of navigating college has to do with helping new students figure out how to proceed in key interactions with university personnel, which is necessary for college success. Through role modeling, peer mentors provide mentees with a set of scripts that improve the students' chances of enacting key components of the university student role successfully in interactions with others (Collier et al., 2008, p. 71). Examples of student success scripts include how to communicate with professors, how to act on the first day of class, how to make the most out of a meeting with an adviser, or how to get financial aid questions answered. Many peer mentoring programs make these scripts available as program resources in the form of handouts, Web pages, e-mails, or links on Facebook (Collier et al., 2008). These success scripts help students navigate the upper path of the two-path model discussed in Chapter 2 (pp. 32–35) by making explicit specific elements of college student role behavior that would normally remain implicit. The underlying idea is that when students follow these proven scripts for taking on the college student role, they will have a better than average chance of success at the university because these scripts have been shown to work in the past.

Using Campus Resources to Address Adjustment Issues

While providing new students with a geographical orientation to campus and scripts for dealing with faculty members and university staff is useful, these introductions do not guarantee that students will find the resources they will need to succeed at college. Peer mentors need to do more than just provide their mentees with information about campus resources. They should explain to mentees how specific campus resources are associated with specific student issues. In addition, mentors should share personal strategies for how to effectively use different resources in ways that improve the likelihood of college success.

For example, while new students may remember from orientation where the library is located and that the library provides physical and electronic access to books and journals, they may not realize the library is also a source of help for writing a research paper. As part of a regular mentor-mentee meeting, the mentor can show the mentee how to navigate the library website and access tutorials on identifying appropriate sources, formatting citations, and working through the steps in preparing a research paper. The mentor presents information to the mentee in the form of a script that facilitates storage and recall from memory by connecting a student adjustment issue, such as writing a research paper, with a specific campus resource, such as the library, and a strategy for using that resource to address the issue, such as instructing the mentee to use the website to access tutorials on putting together a research paper.

Improving Mentee Decision Making

One important way that peer mentoring can help transitioning students succeed at college is by helping them make better decisions. Through role modeling, peer mentoring leads to higher quality decision making and ultimately college student success.

How Do Individuals Make Decisions?

Decision making refers to how an individual combines goals and knowledge to determine a course of action (Tversky & Kahneman, 1974). Good decisions are effective alternatives that are possible in the current context and that allow for realization of the person's goals (Hastie, 2001, p. 656). Good decisions require an understanding of the context. Peer mentors' greater familiarity with the context of higher education provides the foundation to help student mentees make good decisions. A decision consists of several basic elements: an uncertain decision situation, alternatives, outcomes, and consequences (see Figure 4.1).

Figure 4.1   Decision Diagram

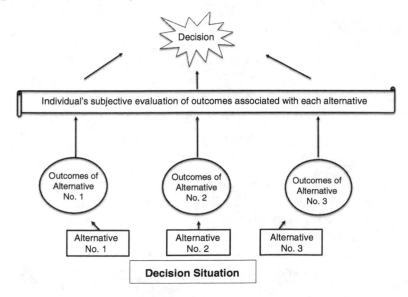

An individual facing a decision situation must consider how alternative choices might lead to achieving a particular goal. Even after he or she chooses one alternative, uncertainty remains because multiple outcomes are possible. Outcomes are publicly describable situations at the end of each decision path, while consequences are an individual's subjective evaluation of each outcome (Hastie, 2001; Tversky & Kahneman, 1974). Subjective expected utility theory proposes that each alternative course of action is evaluated by weighting its total expected satisfaction with the odds that the associated consequences will occur (Von Neumann & Morgenstern, 1944).

Newell and Simon (1972) describe decision making as a four-step process.

1. Identifying: The individual must identify the issue or desired goal.
2. Developing solutions: The individual must call up from memory strategies that might potentially address this issue.
3. Selecting an optimal solution: The individual must evaluate each strategy and choose one that provides the greatest chance of a successful resolution of the issue in this context.
4. Putting the cognitive solution into action: The individual must act by doing the tasks that represent the solution in its action form. It is not enough to have a strategy; the person also must know how to put that strategy into action.

Two issues are associated with the decision-making process that are relevant to our understanding of how peer mentoring can promote higher quality decision making for undergraduate students.

- How does the student decision maker come to understand the decision situation? Which strategies does the student consider as possible choices? (Hastie, 2001, p. 658). This issue relates to the decision maker's college student expertise level.
- Where does the decision maker's information about alternatives, consequences, and events come from in the first place? How does the student use this information to construct the computations of values of different consequences and the odds of each occurring? (Hastie, 2001, p. 658). This issue has to do with the student decision maker's depth of familiarity with the culture of higher education.

How Does Expertise Development Lead to Higher Quality Decision Making?
On a fundamental level, all decision making is based on trial and error. Once the individual has identified the issue, he or she calls up as many possible

solutions as the individual is aware of and selects the one most likely to produce the desired outcome in addressing the issue. If that choice is successful, that individual stores that information in memory as a preferred solution to that problem. However, if the initial solution proves to be unsuccessful, the individual returns to the set of possible solutions and selects the solution with the next best chance of succeeding. This process continues until either the issue is successfully addressed or the individual runs out of possible solutions. The process of coming up with a preferred solution can be thought of as expertise development, which in regard to dealing with college student adjustment issues is the same as role mastery.

How Does Higher Quality Decision Making Lead to College Student Success?
Differences in level of expertise can have an impact on the quality and speed of decision making. Compared to a novice, an expert is

1. Faster in recognizing an opportunity or potential issue. An expert more quickly recognizes an opportunity in terms of what possibly can be achieved in a specific situation, as well as what issues must be dealt with now to avoid larger problems in the future. The expert's advantage here has to do with a deeper understanding of the context of the problem or opportunity.

2. More likely to have multiple strategies or lines of action that are plausible ways of addressing the issue. Here again, the expert's greater familiarity with the context allows him or her to only consider strategies that are possible in the current context.

3. More likely to be realistic in evaluating how successful each line of action might be in addressing an issue. An expert and a novice will evaluate the benefits and consequences of possible strategies differently. The expert will base his or her evaluation on either personal experiences or an awareness of others' experiences using specific strategies in that context. The novice's evaluation is based on *guesstimates* of the transferability of strategies used in other contexts.[1]

4. More likely to choose a high probability of success strategy from the available choices. The expert will choose from a limited set of potential strategies that all have a fairly high likelihood of success because the expert is already familiar with strategies that work and those that don't in this context. The novice may actually have to choose from a larger universe of potential strategies because of a lack of familiarity with the context. Unfortunately, the novice must evaluate all these strategies even though many of them have a relatively low likelihood of success because of a lack of familiarity with what works in this context.

5. More likely to be able to turn a chosen strategy into action that can successfully address the issue. The expert's successful past experiences gives him or her the confidence to use a chosen strategy so that others recognize and understand the actions as the expert intended them to be understood. As a result, the expert student takes less time to make better quality decisions that are more likely to lead to positive outcomes.

An expert student has multiple advantages in the process described in this model. Step 1 is problem recognition. Although a novice and an expert student may recognize that the problem to be solved is how a student can determine what needs to be done to earn a good grade in a particular professor's class, there will be significant differences in how each goes about coming up with a strategy for earning a good grade in that class.

Because of past successful and unsuccessful experiences, the expert student puts the professor into one of several categories, each of which is associated with different expectations for students. For example, "She is X type of professor" may mean the professor values creativity in writing over length or a large number of sources cited in an essay. Because of the expert's greater experience in acting out the college student role, the expert will have had opportunities to validate the accurateness of his or her categorization system based on the outcomes from interactions with different professors.

Note that a student does not need extensive experience playing the college student role in order to develop a categorization system for professors. A new freshman may quickly develop a naive categorization system based on the shaky assumption that the more formally dressed a professor is, the more difficult that professor's class will be. However, using this naive categorization as a basis for deciding which classes to drop or persist in will probably not lead to positive outcomes. So the expert's advantage in the area of problem recognition may not result in a quicker decision but will certainly result in a higher quality one because of greater accuracy and the time-tested nature of the expert student's categorization system.

Steps 2 and 3 relate to the generation and evaluation of possible strategies or solutions. When trying to decide on a strategy to address the professor's first assignment of an essay comparing and contrasting the ideas of two theorists, the expert student initially invokes one or more contingency plans that reduce the number of key situational variables to which he or she must pay attention in order to succeed in this assignment in this type of class to a small manageable number. For example, since this an upper-division sociology theory course, the expert decides it is not necessary to include methodical details when citing articles in the essay for this class. Step 3 is the evaluation of different strategies. The expert student is more likely to realistically evaluate the relative effectiveness of each of the strategies in this smaller subset, based on past experiences of dealing with sociology professors' essay assignments. Compared to a novice, the expert student calls up a relatively smaller number of plausible strategies, although each of those strategies has a relatively high likelihood of success. The expert still must go through a trial-and-error process with each of a limited subset of strategies, but this happens relatively quickly because of the small number of strategies under consideration. Therefore in the area of generation and evaluation of possible strategies or solutions, an expert student's advantage should lead to quicker and better quality decisions than a novice would make in the same situation.

A novice student faces a much more complex process in regard to generating and evaluating possible strategies. The less experience a student has in the college domain, the less certain that student is in knowing what constitutes an appropriate strategy for addressing this problem in this context. For example, a student who also works as a roofing contractor may find that giving a prospective client a bottle of wine when he bids on a job results in a higher percentage of clients giving him what he wants—in this case, getting the roofing job he bid on. However, while this strategy might work in the roofing business, if this same student/roofer gives a professor a bottle of wine in hopes of getting a good grade on the essay assignment, the student will find this to be a strategy with a very low likelihood of success. A novice student, compared to an expert, ends up taking much more time to sift through a much larger pool of possible strategies. It also will take the novice student much longer to evaluate all the possible strategies. Therefore, an expert student's advantage should lead to quicker and better quality decisions than a novice would make in the same situation.

Steps 4 and 5 involve putting the chosen strategy into action. Here again, the expert student's greater familiarity in acting out the college student role provides an advantage. The expert has already observed which strategic actions professors seem to interpret as closely matching their college student expectations, and which actions the same professors view as inappropriate for someone who is a legitimate college student. The expert knows which actions to emphasize to increase the chances of the professor interpreting the student's actions favorably. For example, a professor might conclude that a student is conscientious because the student visited the professor during office hours and asked if there were copies of past essays that the professor would allow him or her to view to clarify assignment expectations.

Novice students' lack of experience may lead them to adopt what they think are student-appropriate behaviors that the professor interprets in a less favorable manner. For example, a novice student who asks another student in the class what he or she thinks the professor's expectations for an essay assignment are rather than speaking directly with the professor may unintentionally give the professor the impression the student is lazy. The expert student's advantage in the area of putting the chosen strategy into action results in better outcomes. The end result is that expert students, compared to novices, take less time to make better quality decisions that are more likely to lead to positive student outcomes.

How Can Mentoring Promote Better Outcomes for Less Expert Students?

Peer mentors can help mentees achieve positive college outcomes by sharing their college student expertise and providing mentees with insights into the university's expectations for successful students. Role modeling is the key. It is not enough that a mentor models the college student role, the mentor must also explain to the mentee why the mentor has chosen the alternative problem solving strategy. The mentor not only shares practical knowledge, but also provides the mentee with backstage information on how the culture of higher education works. Consider a situation in which a mentee approaches a peer mentor for help with understanding a professor's expectations for an assignment that asks the mentee to document the stages in developing a good paper for a class. When the mentor recommends that the mentee try the strategy of outlining the paper, writing a first draft, getting peer review, writing a second draft, taking the second draft to the writing center for review, and incorporating writing center revisions into the final draft of the paper because "the strategy has worked in the past," the mentor is sharing a personal understanding of the professor's expectations and a specific solution with a high probability of success in addressing the issue in question.

For the mentee, accepting the mentor's advice amounts to replacing a process that requires a significant effort and has a low likelihood for success with a simple judgment task that is highly likely to result in a superior outcome. Instead of the mentee using his or her limited experience to try to figure out which alternative strategy will produce the best outcomes based on trial and error, the decision is now based on a much simpler yes or no process: "Should I accept this strategy as the best one to use because the mentor recommends it?" As explained in Chapter 1, it is the peer mentor's credibility that encourages the mentee to follow the advice that is offered.

When the mentor shares his or her expertise in the form of strategies that work, one consequence is higher quality decision making by the mentee. The mentee spends less time setting up the problem and working out a viable solution and more time working on the actual task. For the mentee, spending more time working on the actual assignment leads to better academic outcomes. In the language of the two-path model from Chapter 2 (see pp. 32–35), the mentee's demonstrated capacity now more accurately reflects his or her actual capacity.

Mentees receive additional benefits from successfully adopting the mentor's experience-based strategy that leads to positive academic outcomes. First, the mentee's success in using this strategy increases the likelihood the student will act in similar ways when confronted by similar problems in the future. Second, the mentor's effective problem-solving strategy serves as a scaffold the mentee can build on to develop strategies for dealing with other issues using a problem-solving process similar to the one that just worked in this situation.

How Can You Match What Peer Mentoring Can Provide With Specific Student Issues?

This section contains a useful tool in Table 4.1 for matching what peer mentoring can realistically accomplish with the college adjustment issues the students in your peer mentoring program are facing.

Columns 2 through 7 in Table 4.1 correspond to the six advantages peer mentoring can realistically provide: increasing mentees' engagement and involvement in their own learning, increasing mentees' feelings of campus connection, providing emotional support and validating mentees as legitimate college students, helping mentees navigate college, helping mentees identify and appropriately use campus resources to address adjustment issues, and improving mentee decision making. The horizontal rows correspond to different college student adjustment issues.

The next three sections provide examples of how to connect realistic ideas about what peer mentoring can accomplish with international, first-generation, and veteran student issues discussed in Chapter 3.

What Can Peer Mentoring Realistically Contribute to Promoting International Students' Success?

To illustrate the second step in developing an effective peer-mentoring program, let's examine what peer mentoring might be realistically able to accomplish in a program targeting international students. In Chapter 3, several international student issues were presented. Specific issues included understanding professors' expectations for students, adjusting to new assignments and different grading criteria, dealing with language proficiency concerns, dealing with culture shock, dealing with homesickness, and building and maintaining support networks (see Table 4.2).

Let's start by thinking about how the different ways peer mentoring can facilitate student success might apply to each issue. The peer mentoring function, providing emotional support and validation, affects each international

TABLE 4.1
The Adjustment Issue: Peer Mentoring Matching Tool

	What Peer Mentoring Can Provide					
Targeted Students' Identified College Adjustment Issues	Increased Engagement in Learning	Increased Campus Connection	Increased Feelings of Emotional Support and Validation as Legitimate Students	Improved Campus Navigation Skills	Improved Resource Identification, Appropriate Usage, and Link to Issues	Improved Decision Making
Issue No. 1						
Issue No. 2						
Issue No. 3						
Issue No. 4						
Issue No. 5						
Issue No. 6						
Issue No. 7						
Issue No. 8						

student issue because these students are struggling to adjust to the new U.S. higher education system while also negotiating the cultural and social context of a different country. Peer mentors can facilitate international student success by anticipating students' concerns, answering mentee questions, and reassuring students that they will succeed in their studies at U.S. colleges and universities.

For Issue No. 1, understanding professors' expectations, peer mentoring functions such as increasing engagement in learning, identifying resources,

TABLE 4.2

Using the Adjustment Issue: Peer Mentoring Matching Tool for an International Student Program

Targeted Students' Identified College Adjustment Issues	What Peer Mentoring Can Facilitate					
	Increased Engagement in Learning	Increased Campus Connection	Emotional Support and Validation as Legitimate Students	Improved Campus Navigation Skills	Resource Identification, Appropriate Usage, and Link to Issues	Improved Decision Making
Issue No. 1 Understanding professors' expectations	X		X			X
Issue No. 2 Adjusting to new assignments and different grading criteria	X		X		X	
Issue No. 3 Dealing with language proficiency concerns			X		X	
Issue No. 4 Dealing with culture shock		X	X	X		
Issue No. 5 Dealing with homesickness		X	X	X		
Issue No. 6 Building and maintaining support networks		X	X	X		

and improving elements of decision making might be relevant for addressing this issue. Role modeling is very important here. First, mentors might encourage mentees to become actively engaged in their own learning by demonstrating through their actions the benefits of involvement. For example, a peer mentor might model an appropriate strategy for understanding professors' expectations by going to his or her own professor's office hours during the first week of class to clarify class expectations and encourage the mentee to do likewise. The mentor should also explain to the mentee why this strategy is likely to produce solid academic outcomes by weaving in past personal experiences in which the mentor successfully used this strategy in other classes. The mentor then could put the suggested strategy into a script for action by providing the mentee with a list of topics to include in the discussion of expectations with the professor. Examples of possible mentee-professor conversation topics include how the professor wants to be addressed, grading criteria for the course, whether copies of previous papers or exams are available for a student to review before an assignment is due, the professor's policy on late papers, and the professor's preferred citation format for papers or essay exam questions. Helping the mentee develop the strategy of visiting a professor during office hours to clarify expectations into a step-by-step script is an example of a second function of peer mentoring: improving the quality of mentee decision making.

Issue No. 2, adjusting to new assignments and different grading criteria, is similar to Issue No. 1 in that both involve trying to understand a professor's expectations. Grading criteria are another aspect of professors' expectations. As mentioned in the earlier discussion of using office hours to clarify professors' expectations, understanding grading criteria is one of the topics a mentor should include in the script for the mentee prior to the meeting with the mentee's professors. If the grading criteria in the mentee's course include points for class participation, the mentor might share his or her own past positive experiences with participating in class discussions along with tips on ways the mentee might more easily participate. As noted earlier, some international students do not have previous experience with writing term papers and citing sources. For a mentee who is struggling to understand how to proceed with a term paper assignment, the mentor can help by first linking the term paper issue to key resources, such as the writing center and library website, and showing the mentee how to use each resource appropriately. For example, the mentor could help the mentee explore the library website until the mentee finds the library tutorial on how to use library resources to put together a research paper. Once the mentee has a first draft of the term paper, the mentor then provides a step-by-step script on how to use the writing center to get feedback on grammar, sentence structure, and proper citations.

The mentoring function of identifying resources, linking resources to issues, and showing mentees how to use resources appropriately seems to be one way peer mentoring can have an effect on Issue No. 3, dealing with language proficiency concerns. A mentor who is familiar with the relevant campus resources can connect a mentee with language proficiency concerns to resources like the English as a Second Language program, language labs, and student conversational groups. In addition, the mentor can give the mentee simple strategies for making the most of each resource, such as how to set up an appointment and who to talk with at each resource.

Issue Nos. 4, 5, and 6, dealing with culture shock, dealing with homesickness, and building and maintaining support networks, are best addressed by the peer mentoring functions of increasing campus connection and improving campus navigation skills. As noted earlier, sojourning inter-national students miss their home culture, families, and friends. Mentors can help their mentees address these issues by encouraging the mentees to explore the campus website to find appropriate international student groups on cam-pus. A mentor then can encourage even a shy mentee to attend student group meetings by sharing his own past positive experiences in student groups and offering to attend the first meeting with the mentee to lend support. Inter-national student mentoring programs can organize activities for mentors and mentees that also provide an opportunity for mentees to connect with other students from their home country who are participating in the program.

What Can Peer Mentoring Realistically Contribute to Promoting First-Generation Students' Success?

Based on the discussion in Chapter 3, first-generation students' issues can be grouped into finding needed resources, understanding the college culture, understanding professors' expectations, and building support networks (see Table 4.3).

The peer mentoring function of providing emotional support and validation has an impact on all first-generation student issues because these students do not have the experience base to know whether their cur-rent adjustment issues are idiosyncratic or typical of what all new students encounter. Peer mentors can reassure and validate first-generation student mentees by sharing personal stories of their own experiences in dealing with similar issues during college transitions.

The peer mentoring functions of identifying resources and improv-ing campus navigation skills can directly affect Issue No. 1, finding needed resources. First-generation students do not know what is available in regard to support services, much less how to use available services appropriately,

TABLE 4.3

Using the Adjustment Issue: Peer Mentoring Matching Tool for a First-Generation Student Program

Targeted Students' Identified College Adjustment Issues	What Peer Mentoring Can Provide					
	Increased Engagement in Learning	Increased Campus Connection	Emotional Support and Validation as Legitimate Students	Improved Campus Navigation Skills	Resource Identification, Appropriate Usage, and Link to Issues	Improved Decision Making
Issue No. 1 *Finding needed resources including academic support and help with financial literacy issues*			X	X	X	
Issue No. 2 *Understanding the college culture*		X	X	X	X	
Issue No. 3 *Understanding professors' expectations*	X		X			X
Issue No. 4 *Building support networks*		X	X	X		

because of their lack of familiarity with higher education. Peer mentors should start by assisting their mentees in finding specific resources to deal with immediate adjustment issues. For example, in the beginning of the fall term a mentor could walk a mentee through a tutorial on the financial aid office website that addresses how to manage student's financial aid awards. After helping the mentee address other issues during the students' first term on campus, the mentor could encourage the mentee to reflect on how the pair located relevant resources as part of the peer mentoring function of providing emotional support and validation. Using these initial successful resource-locating experiences as a scaffold, the mentee, with the mentor's guidance, might then develop a general approach for locating needed resources that could be applied to other issues that might come up in subsequent terms.

First-generation student Issue No. 2, difficulties in understanding the college culture, and Issue No. 4, the need to build support networks, arise from the combination of a lack of familiarity with higher education and lower levels of college connection. The peer mentoring functions of increasing campus connection and improving campus navigation skills can help address these issues. Peer mentors can provide mentees with information about different opportunities to participate in campus activities and build support networks by connecting with other students. Because many first-generation students are also members of underrepresented racial and cultural groups, building support networks for these students involves maintaining home community connections and staying actively engaged at college. (See the discussion in Chapter 2, pp. 37, on how peer mentoring affects Guiffrida's [2006] student connection model.) Through the mentoring function of resource identification, mentors can help mentees from underrepresented groups learn about and connect to on-campus clubs and community groups that serve students from the same cultural background as the mentees. Through role modeling, peer mentors can help mentees appreciate the value of increasing campus connections in order to understand college culture by participating in these activities themselves and sharing with mentees the benefits they derive from doing so.

Issue No. 3, difficulties in understanding professors' expectations, is closely related to the earlier issue of difficulties in understanding college culture. Recall the discussion in Chapter 2 (pp. 32–35) of the two-path model that first-generation students are less likely than traditional students to begin college with the requisite knowledge of the college student role that is necessary for them to recognize and respond appropriately to professors' expectations. The peer mentoring functions of increasing engagement in learning and improving decision making can help first-generation students address this issue. Peer mentors can help mentees better understand what professors expect from them by modeling an appropriate version of the student role

and sharing proven college success strategies. It is not enough that a mentor models the college student role, the mentor must also explain to the mentee why the mentor has chosen one alternative over others. In the language of the two-path model, this amounts to the mentor's transferring or exporting cultural capital to the mentee. As noted in the discussion of decision making earlier in this chapter, when the mentee accepts the mentor's problem-solving strategy, the result typically is a faster, higher quality decision that is more likely to lead to positive academic outcomes.

What Can Peer Mentoring Realistically Contribute to Promoting Student Veterans' Success?

Based on the discussion in Chapter 3, student veterans' issues can be grouped into finding needed resources, dealing with administrative issues, dealing with culture shock, understanding professors' expectations, building support networks, and dealing with personal issues.

Similar to the earlier discussions of international and first-generation students' issues, the peer mentoring function of providing emotional support and validation is important in addressing each student veteran issue. Peer mentor credibility, based on similarity because of previous military service, is particularly important for working with student veterans. Peer mentors who are veterans themselves can facilitate mentee success by sharing their own stories of successfully addressing adjustment issues while moving from the military to a college (see Table 4.4).

The peer mentoring functions of identifying resources and improving campus navigation skills can directly affect student veterans' Issue No. 1 and Issue No. 2, finding needed resources and dealing with administrative issues. Dealing with administrative issues has to do with understanding university policies that pertain to veteran students so peer mentors can help by providing mentees with information about which university offices deal with these policies as well as sharing strategies used by other student veterans in trying to resolve these types of issues in the past. Some student veterans need to connect to academic support services such as tutoring because of their concerns about academic skill erosion. Peer mentors can help mentees locate academic support resources and demonstrate through their own actions that normal and appropriate college student behavior is asking for and taking advantage of these services. Also, as noted in Chapter 3, while all students deal with financial literacy concerns, student veterans' financial issues are more specific, relating to accessing and managing GI Bill benefits. Peer mentors can provide student veteran mentees with current benefit information

TABLE 4.4
Using the Adjustment Issue: Peer Mentoring Matching Tool for a Student Veterans Program

Targeted Students' Identified College Adjustment Issues	What Peer Mentoring Can Provide					
	Increased Engagement in Learning	*Increased Campus Connection*	*Emotional Support and Validation as Legitimate Students*	*Improved Campus Navigation Skills*	*Resource Identification, Appropriate Usage, and Link to Issues*	*Improved Decision Making*
Issue No. 1 *Finding needed resources including academic support and help with financial literacy issues*			X	X	X	
Issue No. 2 *Dealing with administrative issues*			X	X	X	
Issue No. 3 *Dealing with culture shock*		X	X	X		
Issue No. 4 *Understanding professors' expectations*	X		X			X
Issue No. 5 *Building support networks*		X	X		X	
Issue No. 6 *Dealing with personal issues*			X		X	

as well as connect them with specific contact people at appropriate campus resources such as the financial aid office.

Student veterans share several issues with international and first-generation students. All three groups of students experience some form of Issue No. 3, dealing with culture shock, and the peer mentoring functions of increasing campus connection and improving campus navigation skills are helpful in helping address this issue. Both of the other groups of students share student veterans' Issue No. 4, understanding professors' expectations, which is directly affected by the peer mentoring functions of increasing engagement in learning and improving decision making. Likewise, the peer mentoring functions of increasing campus connection and improving campus navigation skills can help student veterans address Issue No. 5, building support networks. Because student veterans are less likely to live on campus or have much interest in joining typical college clubs or organizations, peer mentors can help mentees build a sense of college connection by facilitating their linkage with the campus veterans' center or a local chapter of Student Veterans of America.

Finally, the peer mentoring function of resource identification is critical for addressing Issue No. 6, dealing with personal issues. As discussed in Chapter 3, student veterans, compared to other students, are dealing with much higher levels of physical and emotional injuries. Peer mentors need to be able to help mentees connect with campus resources such as the Office of Disability Resources and the counseling center. In addition, it is particularly helpful when mentors can share stories of how they or other student veterans benefited from services provided by these facilities.

What Are Appropriate Uses of Peer Mentoring for Your Program?

This chapter demonstrates through three examples that while mentoring may not be appropriate for addressing every college adjustment issue for every targeted group of students, by matching what mentoring *can* do with specific issues, you can get an idea about what might be possible for your own peer mentoring program to accomplish. Exercise 4.1 walks you through the steps of determining the appropriate uses of peer mentoring in your program.

This chapter reviews multiple ways peer mentoring can help mentees address a range of college adjustment issues. This chapter also introduces the adjustment issue peer mentoring matching tool and walks you through the steps to determine appropriate uses for peer mentoring in your program. Now that you know what is possible, the next step is to actually start designing the program. However, I

Exercise 4.1.   What are appropriate uses of peer mentoring for your program?

Step 1. Start with the list of college adjustment issues your targeted group of students face that your program team developed in Exercise 3.1, the student adjustment issue charrette, or Exercise 3.2, the Delphi method for identifying student adjustment issues. Consolidate similar issues into single ones whenever possible.

Step 2. Insert the identified college adjustment issues for your targeted group of students into the first column of adjustment issues in the peer mentoring matching tool (see Table 4.1).

Step 3. Working with your program team, consider which of the six mentoring functions might be appropriate for addressing each issue, and place a checkmark in the appropriate column. Referring to the three examples in this chapter, many times more than one mentoring function might be appropriate. If none of the mentoring functions seem to be able to address the issue, remove them from the matching tool and put them aside for future consideration.

Step 4. Review your list. Are there issues that now seem similar to each other and might be combined under a single heading, particularly if the same peer mentoring function addresses them all? Once you have combined similar issues, your final list provides you with a blueprint of what is possible to accomplish with peer mentoring in the program you are developing.

must add an important caveat: Just because it is possible to address a range of specific adjustment issues, it does not mean you necessarily will want to or be able to address each issue. The choices you make about which issues your program will address and how you want to address them will affect and be affected by the duration, design, content, mode of delivery, evaluation, mentor training, and evaluation of mentor training associated with your program as well as the resources available to support your program. Part Two of this book explores in greater detail each aspect of putting together a successful peer mentoring program.

Note

1. A *guesstimate* (n.d.) is defined as an estimate made without adequate information.

PART TWO

WHAT ARE THE NUTS AND BOLTS OF DEVELOPING A COLLEGE STUDENT PEER MENTORING PROGRAM?

Vignette 1

HIGH SCHOOL TO COLLEGE TRANSITION-FOCUSED PROGRAM

Retention Through an Academic Mentoring Program

Vynessa Ortiz and Mary Virnoche, Humboldt State University

TABLE V1.1

Inclusiveness	Duration	Approach to Addressing Students' Needs	College Transition
Universal: *All first-time freshmen*	Long term: *First two semesters*	Developmental: *Responds to student needs as they evolve over time*	High school to college

Humboldt State University (HSU) is one of 23 campuses in the California State University (CSU) system. It is a rural campus with 74% of its students originating from areas more than 250 miles away (HSU Institutional Research & Planning [HSUIRP], 2012a). In fall 2012, HSU served 8,116 students through 49 baccalaureate degree majors, 12 graduate programs, and 14 credential programs (HSUIRP, 2012a).

In response to student retention concerns, HSU piloted the Retention through Academic Mentoring Program (RAMP) in fall 2012 as part of a systemwide CSU initiative. The program provided one-on-one peer mentoring for all first-time HSU freshmen. Academic mentors worked with freshmen throughout the academic year, beginning with orientation week and ending with finals week of the second semester.

Institutional Context: HSU Retention and Graduation Rates

RAMP was designed in response to institutional concern about below average retention rates. During the period prior to the program pilot, student groups at highest risk for attrition at HSU included underrepresented minority (URM) students, particularly Native American and African American students, as well as students whose poor first-year academic performance placed them on academic probation. HSU was also concerned with declining retention rates for all male students.

The HSU RAMP pilot was part of a larger graduation initiative to address systemwide retention issues (CSU, 2013). The HSU goal was to increase the graduation rates of URM students by 15% with an overall increase of 12% for all HSU students (HSUIRP, 2012b, p. 2). According to HSUIRP, "our greatest opportunity to increase retention and later graduation rates is by increasing the retention of students in the first two years" (HSUIRP, 2012b, p. 3). Between 2002 and 2012 an average of 27% of first-time undergraduate students left HSU in their first year while an additional 13% left by the end of their second year (HSUIRP, 2012b, p. 4). Between 2005 and 2011 there was a 6% differential between first-year retention of HSU male and female students. While 76% of female students returned for a second year at HSU, only 70% of male students returned (HSUIRP, 2012b, p. 5).

During their first year, URM (73%) and non-URM (75%) students graduated at about the same rate. URM student graduation rates then fell, creating a 5% differential that appeared in the second year and again in the third year (HSUIRP, 2012b, p. 6). Yet greater issues with the retention of some URM students were masked by the high retention of HSU Latino students compared to other URM groups. The disaggregated 2008–2010 data indicate that Latino students actually had the highest average first- to second-year retention rates, 1% higher than White students, and 6% to 14% higher than other URM groups (Meris & Webley, 2012, p. 16). While Latino student second- to third-year retention rates dropped slightly below that of White students (-3%), the 2007–2009 averages indicate that White students were retained in this second period at rates 6%–14% higher than Black, Asian/Pacific Islander, and Native American students (Meris & Webley, 2012, p. 17). First-generation and family income status did not affect retention rates until the third year when data showed a 4% to 5% URM/non-URM differential in retention (HSUIRP, 2012b, p. 8).

Program Description

HSU faculty and staff had been discussing the development of a comprehensive peer mentoring program for several years. Given CSU's systemwide initiative and few changes in retention and graduation rates from other efforts, in the spring of 2012 a retention task force of faculty, staff, and administrators directed Residence Life to plan and launch a program. The group asked Vynessa Ortiz, a Residence Life coordinator and coauthor of this vignette, to take the lead and become the first RAMP coordinator.

During that first year RAMP was located administratively in the Department of Housing and the RAMP coordinator reported to the associate director of Residence Life. Beginning in the second year, the RAMP coordinator reported to the associate vice president for Inclusive Student Success, a newly created office designed to provide oversight and direction for the many offices and initiatives launched to address student success.

In the months preceding the launch of RAMP, a mentor search committee selected undergraduate and graduate students to serve as the first group of mentors. The search committee included the RAMP coordinator and staff from the Academic and Career Advising Center, the Learning Center, Residence Life, First Year Experience, and Leadership & Engagement offices. It was a competitive hiring process that required successful candidates to maintain a current semester and overall GPA of 2.7 or above, have previous student leadership experience, secure faculty recommendations, and have attended the university for at least two semesters by the time their contracts began in fall 2012. The committee gave selection priority to students who had a strong connection with their academic departments, demonstrated an understanding of the needs of first-generation students, and had strong cultural competency skills. The committee also selected several candidates with exceptional qualifications, including previous experience with peer mentoring, to serve as lead mentors.

RAMP mentors completed six two-hour training workshops in spring 2012. Lead mentors participated in two additional workshops. In fall 2012 all mentors returned to campus the week before the start of classes and participated in training and preparation for the incoming mentees. They worked about 40 hours a week during the preterm period and about 20 hours per week during the academic year. RAMP mentors selected in spring 2012 earned $10 per hour and lead mentors earned $12 per hour.

The RAMP coordinator assigned each mentor a caseload of 25 students and asked the mentors to meet regularly with mentees in one-on-one meetings focused on academic progress. Mentors primarily held in-person meetings, but they also used Skype, phone calls, text messages, and sticky notes on residence hall doors to maintain contact with their mentees. The program coordinator asked mentors to work through their caseloads in three-week periods called mentor cycles. This meant that mentors met with about eight students each week. These meetings lasted about 30 to 45 minutes each. In theory, each mentor was supposed to meet with each of his or her mentees five or six times each semester or about 10–12 times in the academic year. This schedule was designed to allow the mentors to get to know each student, regularly monitor each mentee's academics, and be able to follow up on student issues and concerns.

Each mentor cycle had its own curriculum or theme, consistent with RAMP's developmental approach to addressing first-year students' issues. These Three-Week Themes were established based on information from a Student Stress Calendar and information collected in two three-question surveys administered by RAMP several times in a term (Westminster College, 2013). The mentors used the Three-Week Themes to create a timely focus for their mentee meetings. Each curriculum included student-learning outcomes, discussion questions, information to review with students, items for follow-up, and a list of resources. For example, while September is most associated with homesickness, October issues include midterm pressure and stress.

Mentors created an agenda for each mentee meeting based on the Three-Week Theme as well as the individual student's goals and academic plan. These meetings focused on academic success from a holistic perspective, so mentor-mentee pairs covered a range of topics including how to address family concerns, health, friendships, relationships, sexual health, finances, drug and alcohol use, identity, and spirituality. All RAMP mentors worked with their mentees to explore majors, create four-year educational plans, and do early career exploration. Mentors also encouraged their mentees to get involved with campus organizations.

Throughout the year, the RAMP coordinator developed a series of academic and social activities specifically for freshmen. RAMP collaborated with other campus entities to offer academic workshops on topics ranging from communication skills to financial literacy. RAMP also hosted large social events using on-campus facilities such as the swimming pool, recreation center, and the quad. One of the best attended events was Dinner With the Faculty where faculty members joined students for dinner in the dining hall. Mentors served as faculty-student bridges by introducing their mentees to faculty members and encouraging them to dine together.

The RAMP coordinator also organized four study sessions each week that were incentivized through a frequent study points program. For each hour a student attended a study session, he or she earned a point. More points meant more chances to win prizes such as an iPad, Kindle, or gift card to the campus bookstore. These study sessions were widely attended. Freshmen who lived off campus reported that these sessions were especially useful for them.

Evaluation

The HSUIRP office was responsible for the evaluation of the RAMP pilot program. During the 2012–2013 pilot year, HSUIRP collected quantitative and qualitative evaluation data from RAMP mentees at three points in the academic year and from mentors at the close of the first year.

First-time full-time undergraduates in the first RAMP cohort were 5% more likely (78%) to return for a second year compared to the five-year average retention of earlier cohorts (73%) (HSUIRP, 2013, p. 4). The first-year retention gender gap also showed signs of closing. The 2012 cohort had a 4% gender gap in first-year retention compared to the five-year average gap of 5.6% favoring females (HSUIRP, 2014, p. 5).

While non-URM and URM students showed increases in their first-year retention rates compared to the earlier five-year average, non-URM students showed the greatest gains. Eighty-one percent of non-URM RAMP students returned for a second year compared to the 74% non-URM five-year average, while 74% of URM RAMP students returned compared to the 72% five-year average (HSUIRP, 2013, p. 6). URM rate increases were primarily attributable to the increased retention of Hispanic/Latino students (HSUIRP, 2013, p. 14).

Avid mentees who met with their mentors at least three times in the first semester were 11% more likely to return to HSU for a second year than those meeting less frequently with their mentors (81% compared to 70%; HSUIRP, 2013, p. 7). The avid non-URM male mentees showed the highest gains linked to their mentoring engagement; 85% of these students returned compared to 65% of students who had met less frequently with their mentors. Avid non-URM female mentees also showed strong gains in first-year retention; 87% returned compared to only 70% of those who had met less frequently. While avid URM female mentees had a slight (3%) gain in first-year retention (77% compared to 74%), URM male avid mentees were retained at almost the same rate as those meeting less frequently with their mentors (72% compared to 71%; HSUIRP, 2013, p. 7).

It is possible that URM RAMP mentoring differentials have been masked by URM student participation in other programs (HSUIRP, 2013, p. 7). URM students also participate in programs such as Latino Peer Mentoring, Native American Programs, and the Education Opportunity Program. In these programs students are exposed to intensive outreach and mentoring. Therefore, it is possible that some URM students engaged less frequently with their RAMP mentors because they were already being mentored in other programs. To isolate URM RAMP retention outcomes, future analyses will control for URM students' mentoring experiences in other HSU programs.

Training

Mentors received extensive training before and during their mentoring experience. Training began in the spring a few weeks after their selection and before their mentees even arrived on campus. This spring training included six two-hour workshops. During spring training mentors learned about program goals and objectives, student development theory, principles of mentoring, HSU demographic and retention information, cultural competency skills, leadership, and locating campus resources.

Mentors returned to campus two weeks before the first day of the fall academic term. They participated in a 40-hour, weeklong training session. While spring training was more conceptual, the fall training focused on the technical aspects of the job including role-playing and other methods to help mentors develop hard and soft position-related skills. In the fall training the mentors learned about advising on class registration, building an academic plan, making referrals, using campus technology systems, advising styles, supporting students in crisis, administrative processes, leading a mentor meeting, academic policies, and academic success strategies.

Social justice was a key training theme. Several sessions were designed to address social justice topics including safe space training, working with diverse student populations, serving and supporting undocumented students, accessible mentoring and inclusivity of students with disabilities, and understanding power and privilege. Each fall session incorporated opportunities for dialogue and the practice of new skills.

Once the academic year began, mentors participated in a weekly one-hour training session on additional timely and emerging topics. Several campus and community organizations made presentations on themes such as suicide prevention, serving former foster youth, and assisting students with finding off-campus housing and career development. In addition, mentors met bimonthly with their core group, which included one lead mentor and 8–13 academic mentors. Mentors with mentees living in the same residence hall area were generally in the same core group. During core group meetings, mentors learned more about the particular focus for each given Three-Week Theme. The RAMP coordinator developed and aggregated training information and materials in an online courseware site that all mentors could access. The online training site included PowerPoint presentations and handouts from every in-person training session, articles about higher education, and links to key academic policies.

The RAMP coordinator developed student-learning outcomes for fall and spring training programs. Pre- and posttraining surveys were administered to measure mentor-training outcomes. Mentor outcomes included the ability to describe dimensions of serving first-generation college students as well as increased knowledge of academic and administrative policies and referral processes. Outcomes also included the ability to write specific, measurable, achievable, results-focused, time-bound (SMART) goals for academics and health (Doran, 1981). The RAMP coordinator also surveyed mentors after their first semester on the job. This end-of-semester survey measured the mentors' experience and their perceptions of the alignment between the trainings and the work they actually performed.

The training assessment data for RAMP were also used to inform the early stages of planning a common all-university student leadership training program. At the time of this writing, student affairs division staff members were still working on that common training. In 2013 a pilot cohort of major-based peer mentors focused on sophomores and junior retention in four majors participated in parts of the RAMP training. More development is needed on identifying the critical core training all leaders should participate in.

Reflection

While RAMP was still in a pilot phase, those working on related university issues and implementing other organizational changes began integrating RAMP mentors into new structures and processes. For example, in 2012, upon the request of an instructor of a course with a high fail rate, the RAMP coordinator worked with mentors to facilitate mentee meetings with tutors. In 2013, RAMP mentors were designated as first responders for the fall launch of MAP-Works (EBI MAP-Works, 2013) on the HSU campus. MAP Works is a Web-based system for data collection, integration, storage, analysis, and reporting. It integrates institutional data with student self-report data to automatically generate retention risk reports for students as well as alerts to identified staff or faculty members.

In 2013 a planning group of student affairs staff members, faculty members, and administrators developed the structure for the Centers for Academic Excellence to provide more culturally relevant advising and support. In late 2013 a director of the centers was hired to manage professional staff coordinators in each center: African American, Asian and Pacific Islander, Latino, and Native American. The new structure built on some preexisting programs and expanded the capacity for HSU to address the needs of all students of color. At the time of this writing, there was discussion about shifting part of the RAMP mentoring function into these new centers and coordinating more targeted peer mentoring through these centers, including mentoring beyond the first year.

In 2013, the Office of Diversity and Inclusion funded major-based peer mentoring pilot programs in environmental resources engineering, liberal studies, elementary education, politics, and sociology. These mentors focused on sophomores and juniors with greater attention to linking academic advising to career planning. Faculty members leading these programs, including Mary Virnoche, were experimenting with methods to structure the transition between RAMP mentors and major-based mentors.

While the institution found RAMP mentors could provide critical ground-level links to first-year students, the RAMP structure itself required attention and changes to reach its full potential. The mentor hiring process needed changes to facilitate the recruitment of more students of color. The mentor matching process needed systems to allow for more nuanced and mentee-driven matching.

In 2013, HSU began researching mentor matching methods. RAMP staff members were interested in being able to ask incoming students to identify and rank key characteristics for a potential mentor. Staff felt that such a system would in theory align mentees with mentors with whom they most strongly identified. For example, if a student ranked ethnicity and geographic location as most important, the student could be matched with a mentor with the same ethnicity and possibly also from the same area of the state. All of these changes were part of multiple institutional strategies to best identify student needs and support academic success and community in culturally sensitive environments.

5

WHAT DESIGN ISSUES MUST YOU CONSIDER IN SETTING UP A PEER MENTORING PROGRAM?

Program design is the glue that holds all the pieces of your peer mentoring program together. You can increase the likelihood of program success by thoughtfully considering design choices and the implications of those choices.

Chapter 5

- demonstrates how to develop a program time line and identify each step in that time line;
- discusses issues relating to budgets, funding, and institutional commitments;
- describes the process of developing job descriptions for key program staff and mentors;
- reviews the steps in identifying, recruiting, and selecting mentors;
- explains strategies for locating potential mentees and recruiting them for your program;
- identifies key policies, procedures, and program forms needed for any mentoring program; and
- explores how design and program size interact with each of the program dimensions in the peer mentoring program rubric.

> *Organizing is what you do before you do something, so that when you do it, it is not all mixed up.*
>
> (Milne, 2015)

> *What really matters is what you do with what you have.*
>
> (Wells, 2015)

Program design is the key to peer mentoring program success. Design encompasses all the planning and structural aspects of your program, including locating funding, budgeting, staffing, establishing the program location, making decisions about mode of delivery and program content, and putting a system of data collection and storage in place. It also involves determining the number of mentees and mentors; hiring mentors; recruiting and orienting mentees; deciding on program content; and developing job descriptions, program policies, and forms.

Design is like the recipe for your favorite cookie. Initially, only the baker pays any attention to the recipe. The baker's efforts will be judged on the final outcomes. Cookies will be eaten only if they taste good. Program design is very much the same. While the design will influence all the other elements of your program, in the end the design will get the same amount of attention the recipe for a cookie gets. Your program will be judged successful if it works or "tastes good." Only then will someone pay enough attention to the design to ask you for the recipe.

Chapter 3 showed you how to establish the need for a peer mentoring program to support a particular group of students at your college or university by identifying those students' particular college adjustment issues. Chapter 4 then walked you through the steps of developing program goals by connecting the college adjustment issues faced by your group of students with what peer mentoring can realistically accomplish. You are now ready to design your program.

The design and structure of your mentoring program must be connected to the program goals and what peer mentoring is expected to accomplish in your program. One way to think about the organization of a program is to consider everything that happens from identifying needs to recruiting mentors and mentees as program preparation and everything that happens after that as program delivery. Program delivery starts with new mentee orientation or initial mentor-mentee meetings and continues through delivering program content and ongoing mentor training, program evaluation, and the celebration at the end of the program. The following section presents the steps in designing your program.

Developing a Time Line

Because program design is a multifaceted process, it is helpful to develop a time line to make sure you cover all the key design elements while also staying on schedule.

The following is a time line for a hypothetical peer mentoring program for new freshmen scheduled to begin in the fall semester.

1. Identify the need for a mentoring program (including number of potential mentees) and program goals
   Time: one year before start of program
2. Formulate a budget, secure funding, get commitments from stakeholders
   Time: fall semester or term year before program
3. Establish program location
   Time: nine months before beginning of program (January 1 of program year)
4. Hire key staff
   Time: nine months before beginning of program (January 1 of program year)
5. Assemble program content
   Time: nine months before beginning of program (January 1 of program year)
6. Decide on mode(s) of delivering mentee services
   Time: nine months before beginning of program (January 1 of program year)
7. Recruit and hire mentors (includes developing job description)
   Time: six to nine months before beginning of program
8. Design mentor training curriculum
   Time: five months before beginning of program
9. Make initial contact with potential mentees (publicizing the program)
   Time: three to four months before beginning of program
10. Develop program policies and forms, set up a database
    Time: three to four months before beginning of program
11. Conduct informational meetings for mentees (recruitment, commitment, consent)
    Time: two to three months before beginning of program
12. Deliver mentor training (including initial evaluation of mentor training)
    Time: one month before beginning of program
13. Initiate program orientation and kickoff activity for new mentees
    Time: one week before beginning of program or the fall term
14. Coordinate initial mentee-mentor meetings
    Time: first week of classes of fall term or by second week of term

15. Initiate program activities (includes mentor-mentee meetings, all-program activities)
    Time: regularly over the course of the semester/term for the duration of program
16. Hold regular staff and mentor meetings (quality assurance)
    Time: monthly (every two weeks for first month)
17. Provide ongoing mentor training
    Time: integrate into regular staff meetings
18. Collect short-term program evaluation including mentor training evaluation
    Time: end of first semester or term
19. Organize celebration and appreciation ceremony
    Time: end of program year or semester if a shorter duration program
20. Conduct final year evaluation and final mentor training evaluation
    Time: end of program year or semester if a shorter duration program

Developing a Budget and Securing Funding

While all college student peer mentoring programs begin with the admirable goal of helping other students succeed at college, you must keep the question of funding in mind from the very beginning of the program development process to give your program a reasonable chance of succeeding and persisting. Once you have established that there is a need for your proposed peer mentoring program, the next step is to develop a financial plan that includes a budget for your program, along with an estimate of how much funding you will need to start and sustain the program (National Mentoring Partnership, 2005).

Many of the decisions you will need to make about the infrastructure or how you set up specific elements of your peer mentoring program will depend on the available resources. Budgets can evolve as you become clearer about what is possible in your situation. Begin by identifying all the aspects of your program that will require some financial or in-kind assistance:

- Staffing: salaries of workers who will coordinate and supervise the program
- Program space: costs associated with physical space including furniture and computers
- IT: development and maintenance costs associated with online delivery of mentoring (e.g., online resource libraries, discussion groups) including the creation of a program website or Facebook page

- Mentee recruitment: cost of outreach to potential mentees (e.g., postage, printing informational materials and applications), costs associated with initial meetings and mentee orientation, costs associated with printing mentee program materials
- Recruitment and training of mentors: cost of outreach to potential mentors, cost of delivering mentor training including preparing and printing or copying relevant materials, food and beverages (typically lunch plus morning and afternoon beverages), costs associated with printing mentor handbooks
- General program administration: costs associated with telephones, copying, office supplies, printer including print supplies, program completion certificates, developing program database
- Mentee program activities: costs associated with attending on-campus sports and cultural events, costs for catering any social events that bring together mentors and mentees
- Evaluation: costs associated with data collection (e.g., printing forms), storage of evaluation data, and analysis. Online mentoring programs will need to budget additional IT resources for evaluation. Note that externally funded programs will typically require you to hire an independent evaluator and to follow an evaluation plan.
- Mentor compensation: costs range from those associated with tuition remission and stipends to academic credit to textbook scholarships to certificates of participation. You need to decide whether your mentors will be paid before you embark on your recruitment phase.

An associated issue is mentor job expectations. There is a relationship between how you compensate mentors and how much work you can expect them to contribute to your program. Since mentor payment needs to be included in your budget figures, as you seek funding you should consider one or more alternative plans for mentor compensation and related work expectations. Students who agree to be mentors should be fully informed about this issue and the reasons for your decision before they make any commitment (Grove & Huon, 2003). These issues are discussed in greater detail later in this chapter.

Types of Programs
Programs can be categorized based on how they are funded.

Volunteer Programs
A clear distinction must be made between all-volunteer programs and a program with paid staff that relies on volunteer mentors. All volunteer programs

tend to be loosely organized and rely on a pay-it-forward mentality, typically among students from a specific group. Without a paid program coordinator, these programs tend to rely on a shared leadership model with responsibilities diffused throughout the group. Many graduate programs have informal peer mentoring programs where more experienced students are matched with newly admitted students to help them learn the ropes of graduate school. These programs tend to lack clearly defined policies and procedures or systematic program evaluation. Instead of standardized mentor training across cohorts, mentors' common experiences serve as the basis for a level of implied expertise necessary to advise new students. All-volunteer programs tend to only last as long as mentees value the information they are receiving, and the cost to mentors is not onerous enough to interfere with their own studies.

Internally Funded Programs

Internally funded peer mentoring programs rely on institutional support. Sometimes the initial funding for an internally funded peer mentoring program comes from student fees such as the peer mentor program developed and sponsored by the Otis College of Art and Design student activities department (www.otis.edu/student-activities/peer-mentor-program). Many internally funded peer mentoring programs are developed by student affairs units, such as the University of Cincinnati's Center for First Year Experience and Learning Communities peer mentoring program (www.uc.edu/fye/learning_communities.html) and the PSU International Student Mentor Program (www.pdx.edu/international-students/international-student-mentoring-program).

One variety of student-affairs-based programs begins with an individual champion, typically a student affairs professional who recognizes a student need that might be successfully addressed by a peer mentoring program. If the champion makes a successful case for the need of such a program to administrators, the program is initiated with all or part of the champion's full-time-equivalent (FTE) time being assigned to the peer mentoring program. In other cases, administrators provide the initial impetus by recognizing the need for a peer mentoring program to address an issue related to student success.

Internally funded peer mentoring programs that persist and grow do so in large part because they are able to establish effectiveness in supporting students and achieving program goals. These programs can take a variety of forms. In some cases, the college funds the coordinator position and provides program space on campus, and the program uses volunteer mentors and relies on campus collaborations to provide expertise for training. Other more established programs operate with yearly line-item budgets that include a paid coordinator, paid program staff, and mentors who receive stipends or credits for participation. Continuity is a concern, so it is important in these types of programs to have clearly articulated goals and well-thought-out evaluation practices that can build the case that the program is attaining its stated goals.

Externally Funded Programs
Externally funded programs depend on support from contracts from government agencies or grants from foundations. Many peer mentoring programs begin as demonstration projects funded by pilot grants. For example PSU's Students First Mentoring Program (www.friends.studentsfirst.pdx .edu/index.html) began as a demonstration project funded by a grant from the U.S. Department of Education's Fund for the Improvement of Postsecondary Education. Other programs, such as STEM Gateway's Peer Learning Facilitators program (http://stemgateway.unm.edu/documents/ Impact/2013SympPLF.pdf) at the University of New Mexico, are funded through government pass-through money.

Another group of programs is funded by foundation grants. For example, the Bill and Melinda Gates Foundation, in association with Campus Compact, is supporting Connect2Complete (http://compact.org/initiatives/ connect2complete1) which supports more than 4,500 low-income, underprepared students through developmental education courses designed to get them ready for college-level course work at nine community colleges in Florida, Ohio, and Washington.

Externally funded programs typically have more rigorous and extensive evaluation plans and more standardized training and program policies because of their accountability to outside funders. Because many externally funded programs have stop dates for the flow of external support, program staff are required to put additional effort into identifying requests for proposals, gathering appropriate support materials, and developing grant proposals to keep these programs going.

Many peer mentoring programs rely on a combination of external and internal funding. As part of your financial plan, you'll need to determine how long you can expect to receive funding from each source so you can develop new sources before funding runs out.

Getting Support From Administration

Bringing your college administration on board early in the program development process is essential for internally and externally funded programs. Typically you will need to secure an institutional commitment for some degree of funding match, even if this takes the form of in-kind resources, to be considered for external funding. You must be prepared to take advantage of the opportunity to pitch your proposed program to the director of student affairs, college dean, provost, or president.

Begin your presentation by identifying the needs associated with promoting college success of your targeted group of students and why peer mentoring is an appropriate approach for addressing those needs. Clearly articulate the goals of the program and the outcomes you hope to achieve. Next, share your initial budget. It is a good idea to present not only details of the items that will require funding but also the estimated costs associated with each based on experiences from others who have conducted such programs and, where relevant, price quotes from the appropriate sources (e.g., Web page design). In preparation for seeking external funding, explore with your administrators possible areas where the school might be able to provide in-kind support and resources, contingent upon securing the external grant. This is also a good time to identify potential partners on campus who are willing to assist you in setting up and maintaining the proposed program.

Listen carefully to any concerns raised by the administrator; if you are not able to address them immediately, set up a time to provide the administrator with the information she or he requests. While all peer mentoring programs must address fundamental issues of design, delivery, training, and evaluation, variations in the size and degree of institutional support means that what a particular program aims to accomplish and how it goes about doing so may vary with the size of each program.

Establishing Program Location

The issue of program space or venue needs to be addressed at the same time that funding or support is secured. Many times college administrators can provide resources for a mentor project by authorizing the use of space as either part of a support package for an internally funded program or as in-kind matching support for an externally funded one.

Physical Space

There are two important aspects of program space. The first aspect is deciding where the staff that administers the program will be located. In addition to office space for key staff, your program will need to have desks, chairs, and file cabinets. Your school may be able to provide surplus furniture through your college facilities department as in-kind budget items. Similarly, you may be able to secure other in-kind budget items, such as the computers and printer your program needs, through your school's IT department. Your budget also needs to include funds to cover the ongoing costs of telephones. In some situations phone jacks and Internet jacks may need to be added, although most schools have Wi-Fi networks your staff can use for Internet connections. Funds for office supplies and postage are also necessary.

The second aspect of program space is where the delivery of mentoring services will take place. Will your mentors have program-associated space from which to work, or will the mentor-mentee meetings take place at other campus locations? If there is going to be dedicated program space, will you provide telephones and computers? The amount of space you have for your program can have an impact on how your mentoring services are delivered. For example, having program space for mentors to meet with mentees allows drop-in mentoring and increases the ease of face-to-face service delivery. Where will you have your program staff meetings? It is always possible to book meeting space at other campus locations even if you do not have a large enough program space for all your mentors to meet at one time.

Virtual Space

It is also important for your program to have a virtual location. A program website can serve multiple purposes. Your website is an excellent vehicle for increasing awareness of your program among potential mentors, mentees and their families, and the larger campus community. Your virtual space can be used to disseminate program results such as evaluation data and feedback from mentees and mentors who have participated in your program. These testimonials are an excellent way to increase interest in your program and add to the credibility of your ability to achieve program goals (see, e.g., http://mentors.unst.pdx.edu/node/1181).

Peer mentoring program administrators also use social media to establish their virtual program locations. Facebook pages, Twitter feeds, and Flickr pages are particularly useful in connecting with tech-savvy potential recruits and making current participants aware of upcoming activities and social events.[1] Social media is a particularly useful way to have your current mentors and mentees provide their take on the benefits of program participation. You will need to develop program policies about what can be posted on program Facebook pages, particularly any photos involving participants. It is a good idea to obtain written permission from program participants before posting any photos of them on your Facebook page. Many times photographic releases are included with the application materials new program participants fill out when officially joining the program.

Hiring Program Staff

It is important to identify and hire key program staff early in the design process. Often you can find additional low-cost or nonbudgeted program staff to do some of the work setting up your program. Federal work-study students are a great option. Your program pays only 10% of the student's salary, so consider budgeting for a work-study employee. In addition, students who want to eventually go into student affairs may be willing to trade work setting up and maintaining your program for experience and internship credits.

Coordinator

In order to start a peer mentoring program, you minimally need a coordinator at least .5/.6 FTE. The coordinator's responsibilities include supervising the administration and day-to-day operations of your program. The coordinator is also in charge of securing funding, developing a budget, and figuring out how to cooperate with other campus units to provide needed program resources. The coordinator is the public face of your program and needs to be able to deal appropriately with administrators, faculty members, other staff, mentors, and mentees and their families.

Selecting a coordinator is one of the most important tasks in the early planning stages of developing a program. Typically the program coordinator is a student affairs professional, although in some cases a graduate student can successfully manage the role (Grove & Huon, 2003). The success of your program depends in large part on the qualities, skills, and abilities of your program coordinator. Some important personality traits to look for in a potential coordinator include enthusiasm, energy, and a positive attitude. In addition, your coordinator needs to be able to demonstrate organizational and project management skills, the ability to communicate appropriately on different levels, familiarity with and commitment to the mentoring process, knowledge of the issues faced by the students served by the program, and the capacity to inspire and persuade other colleagues about the merits of the program. Additional valuable coordinator skills include technology expertise; knowledge of how your college or university works; available resources; who to reach out to for resolving questions; and experience with data collection, analysis, and report generation.

Program Size and Staffing: The Need for a Mentor Supervisor

Program size can affect staffing decisions. Large programs or those that offer a wide range of mentoring support over a longer duration should reduce the likelihood of coordinator workload overload by hiring a separate mentor supervisor. The mentor supervisor has responsibility for all mentor-related aspects of the program, including recruitment, selection, training, mentor evaluation, and ongoing mentor-mentee supervision and support.

The time line items "deciding on mode of delivery" and "developing program content" are discussed in Chapters 6 and 7.

Recruiting and Hiring Mentors

The ideal ratio of mentors to mentees depends upon the mode of delivery and how mentors are used. Programs that use group mentoring, such as those that match mentors to learning communities, tend to have relatively high mentor-to-mentee ratios. Yet even among learning community–based mentoring programs there is considerable variation. Although Brigham Young University's first-year mentoring program assigns each mentor to work with about 60 mentees, most learning community–based programs tend to have mentor to mentee ratios between 12 and 25 (P. Esplin, personal communication, September 30, 2011). For example, in the University of South Carolina's University 101 program that matches peer leaders with sections of the required class for all incoming freshmen, mentors typically work with 18 to 20 students per class (A. Mojzik, personal communication, November 3, 2011).

Colleges providing individual mentoring may require smaller mentor-to-mentee ratios. In the peer mentoring program for all new incoming freshmen at Alverno College, a considerably smaller institution than either Brigham Young or South Carolina, mentors typically work with between 12 and 18 students (K. Tisch, personal communication, May 14, 2013).

Programs that match mentors with individual students from groups of students with specific identified needs tend to have relatively smaller mentor-to-mentee ratios. For example, in the Lehigh University program for first-year students with diagnosed cognitive learning disabilities or attention deficit disorder, each mentor works with two or three mentees (L. Ruebeck, personal communication, May 10, 2013). Similarly, at Lewis and Clark College, each mentor in the peer mentoring program serving first-year, first-generation, Pell Grant-eligible students of color works with two mentees (J. Stewart, personal communication, May 15, 2013).

Program Size and Mentor Issues

The number of mentees in your program and the services you expect to provide affects the number of mentors you will need to recruit. Consider the anticipated frequency of mentor-mentee meetings as well as how much of a time commitment you expect from each mentor. In programs using volunteer mentors with limits on the amount of time you can expect from each mentor, you will need to recruit a larger number of mentors to serve the same number of mentees compared to the number of mentors required in a program that compensates them. While your program goals, number of students served, types of services provided, and mode of delivery all influence the optimal number of mentors you need to recruit, in the end the resources you have available will determine the actual mentor-to-mentee ratio for your program.

Developing a Mentor Job Description

The group of students you are mentoring and the adjustment issues your program is trying to address will influence your mentor job description. Start by distinguishing between desired mentor qualifications and responsibilities and expectations. Next, group possible qualifications into larger categories.

Serving as a peer mentor will cut into the time a student has to concentrate on her or his own studies. It is important to select mentors who have already demonstrated good study habits and a track record of succeeding at your college or university (Iowa State University, n.d.). Specific academic qualifications include the following:

- GPA: There should be a minimum GPA standard for individuals applying to be a mentor.
- Class standing: Peer mentoring relies upon mentors sharing expertise with their mentees. Do your program goals require mentors of a particular class standing or just mentors who are more experienced than the mentees they are working with? Many undergraduate peer mentoring programs rely on upper-class students for mentors.
- Courses completed: Peer mentoring programs whose mentors are part of a learning community associated with a specific class may need to require potential mentors to have completed the class in question to be able to provide mentees with assistance or tutoring. Other programs require that mentors complete leadership training. For example, in PSU's general education program, University Studies, once a mentor has completed the recruitment interview and been selected to participate in the next year program, she or he must enroll in a four-credit mentor training course offered in the spring. New mentors must successfully complete the course before they can be

hired (http://mentors.unst.pdx.edu/content/mentors-and-mentored-inquiry).

- Major: Some discipline-based peer mentoring programs will limit potential mentors to students majoring in that discipline.
- Educational transition completed: Some peer mentoring programs require mentors to have completed the educational transition that students being served by the program are currently experiencing. For example, programs serving students moving from two-year to four-year colleges and universities should require mentors to be transfer students themselves.

Successful mentor-mentee relationships depend on establishing rapport and shared understandings. Therefore, it may be important to select mentors who share common characteristics or experiences with the group of students your program serves, although specific characteristics and experiences will vary from one program to another. Personal and life-experience qualifications include the following:

- Demographic characteristics: You may want to limit potential mentors to members of a certain group depending on the focus of your program. Programs supporting student veterans need to recruit student veterans who already have college experience to serve as peer mentors. For a program serving first-generation students, it may be important to select mentors from a similar family background. Programs serving returning women students would typically limit mentors to other women. And while there is some discussion about the effectiveness of cross-race mentoring programs in K–12 education, college student peer mentoring programs that serve one particular racial or ethnic group typically limit mentors to students from those same groups.
- Previous residence life experience: Some peer mentoring programs linked to residence-based learning communities may prefer mentors who have already lived in the halls themselves. Possible wording for this quality on a job description might be: Applicants must have lived in the residence halls for at least (__) semester(s) to be considered for this position.
- Language requirements: Mentors in programs serving immigrant, international, or other foreign language students may need to possess specific language skills.

- Communication skills: Potential mentors need to be able to demonstrate strong communication skills because of the importance of communication in establishing mentor-mentee trust and rapport. Requiring potential mentors to include a short essay as part of the application packet is one way to ascertain a student's relative level of writing skills. It is important to explicitly list superior verbal communication skills in the mentor job description if that is one of the criteria used to differentiate mentors in the job interview.
- Interpersonal skills: These are closely linked to communication skills and include empathy, the ability to listen to others, dependability, and willingness to take the initiative and responsibility for one's own actions.
- Ability to work well with others: Your program success depends on your mentors being able to work with and support one another. Therefore it is important that potential mentors can demonstrate that they are comfortable in have experience being part of team.

Technical qualifications include the following:

- Computer skills: You should determine whether to require any computer skills the candidates would need to be successful in your program, particularly being able to locate and appropriately use any online program and campus resources.
- Knowledge of university resources: One important goal of many peer mentoring programs is to help mentees learn which resources are available on campus, what issues each resource might address, and how to appropriately use each resource. Mentors need to have experience and familiarity with using the resources at your school.
- Creative thinking and problem-solving skills: Being an effective mentor requires students to help mentees work out solutions to specific issues, even if it is just referring the student to the appropriate campus resource. Mentors also need to be flexible to accommodate the changing situations their mentees will be dealing with.

Another important part of developing a mentor job description is to explicitly identify what your program expects from mentors. Although different programs may have slightly different work responsibilities for mentors, the following are some general ideas for mentor responsibilities you can adjust to fit your program.

Peer mentors need to

- honor commitments made at the time of hiring and fulfill program obligations;
- spend time wisely;
- participate actively in mentor training;
- remain enrolled as a full-time student and maintain the program's mentor GPA standard;
- interact regularly with mentees whether by e-mail, phone, or in person;
- assist mentees in becoming familiar with university resources;
- follow the college's code of conduct;
- coordinate out-of-class social events and activities;
- assist in program data collection and evaluation;
- serve as a communication link between the program and students;
- attend regular staff meetings;
- develop professional working relationships with mentees, coworkers, and program staff; and
- maintain regular office hours.

As you develop your mentor job description, start by being clear on how much time you expect your mentors to spend working with mentees and other program-related tasks. The mentor time expectations vary between programs. In general, mentors in paid positions are expected to work between 10 hours (e.g., University of Michigan, http://onsp.umich .edu/transfer-connections/about; Utah Valley University, www.uvu.edu/ slss/mentoring) and 20 hours (e.g., Brigham Young University, http:// freshmanmentoring.byu.edu/phoenix/mentoring/index.php; PSU, http:// mentors.unst.pdx.edu/content/mentors-and-mentored-inquiry) per week. Mentors whose responsibilities include being part of a learning community or class typically are asked to work more hours each week. On average, volunteer mentors usually work fewer hours per week.

A critically important element of developing a mentor job description is to be explicit and clear about program expectations concerning mentor-mentee contact. How long do you expect mentor-mentee matches to last? How often should pairs meet in person versus making contact by e-mail or telephone? How long should each mentoring session last? The answers to all these questions really depend on your program goals and what you expect your mentors to accomplish. Ensure that the amount of time you require for mentoring sessions is adequate to accomplish the outcomes you set (National Mentoring Partnership, 2005, p. 18). For example, a program that expects mentors to provide academic support or help mentees navigate the university website as part of helping mentees reach the goal of locating and learning to use campus resources appropriately may need to have mentors schedule 30-minute to hour-long sessions with mentees. On the other hand, a program that emphasizes emotional support and promoting campus connection among mentees may find 15-minute sessions more than adequate. Once your program has been in existence for a year or more, it may be helpful to get input from returning mentors on what they feel are realistic expectations for mentors in your program.

Recruiting Mentors

Example of an Explicit Discussion of Mentor-Mentee Contact: Expectations From the Students First Mentoring Program (SFMP), PSU

Mentors are expected to work between 12 to 15 hours a week, up to 8 to 11 hours of which are dedicated for contact with each mentor's mentees. In addition, each mentor will have a regularly scheduled two-hour block of drop-in coverage, where he or she is available to any student from the program that might have an immediate issue and was not able to reach that student's personal mentor. Mentors also are expected to monitor comments and questions posted by mentees only receiving online mentoring on the "Ask SFMP" section of the website, rotating responsibility every 24 hours.

It is important to allow yourself enough lead time for the mentor recruitment and selection process. In the earlier time line discussion, it was suggested that you begin recruiting potential mentors six to nine months before your program is scheduled to begin. This means that for programs that begin in the fall term or semester, outreach to potential mentors should begin in the winter term or semester of the previous academic year. Initial hiring decisions need to be made in the spring of that same year, particularly if mentor selection depends on candidates having completed a leadership class (http://mentors.unst.pdx.edu/content/mentors-and-mentored-inquiry).

Before you attempt to contact potential mentors, you need to consider the appropriate target pool of potential mentors and how many mentors you would like to recruit. Determining which students are appropriate potential mentors depends on the group your mentoring program is serving as well as the goals of your program. For a mentoring program supporting students in the first year of a particular major, such as civil engineering, the most obvious candidates for potential mentors are more advanced students with that same major. For programs targeting a specific subgroup of students, such as student veterans, first-generation students, or Pacific Islanders, more experienced students at your school who share the same background as the mentees are logical choices. The pool of potential mentors for programs that aim to provide support for all incoming students is naturally larger.

Program Size and Mentor Recruitment

You need to estimate the number of mentees you hope to serve before mentor recruitment so you can have an idea about how many mentors you need to recruit. Keep in mind that the more mentors you require, the more students you will initially need to contact.

There are several different strategies you can use to make contact with potential mentors such as making announcements in upper-division classes; distributing a broadcast e-mail to a relevant target pool; posting on an online campus bulletin board; sending letters to students in the stages of a specific degree program; asking colleagues, faculty, and student affairs professionals for recommendations; and even offering personal invitations to students you may already know.

The University of South Carolina's University 101 freshman year peer mentoring program lays the foundation for mentor recruitment with an extensive campus marketing campaign focusing on the prestige of being a student leader. The mentoring program coordinator initiates the recruitment process by contacting all continuing juniors and seniors with a 3.0 GPA or higher and inviting them to apply for a peer mentor position in the program. The coordinator also asks faculty and staff, particularly those teaching University 101 sections, for mentor nominations. In addition, the program coordinator contacts coordinators of other campus programs, such as minority scholars and other diversity programs, asking for recommendations for potential mentors (A. Mojzik, personal communication, November 3, 2011).

The Alverno College peer mentoring/advising program employs a multifaceted recruiting approach by collecting the names of students who are interested in the peer program at university-wide student involvement fairs in August and January at the beginning of each semester. Program staff also actively seek out recommendations from faculty and staff. In late February, the program participates in a campuswide Student Leadership Fair along with departments and other student affairs units that are recruiting orientation leaders, student activities leaders, and resident hall assistants. At this event more detailed program information and applications are distributed. In addition, any student who was recommended by faculty or indicated an interest in the program is invited to stop by and talk to program staff. Program staff members make a point of letting any student who was recommended know that a faculty member thought the student would be good as a peer mentor or adviser. Often, finding out that they were recommended by a faculty member is enough impetus to get students to apply (K. Tisch, personal communication, May 14, 2013).

One general approach to recruitment starts with an informational session. For example, the Brigham Young University First Year Mentoring program invites mentor candidates to a winter term welcome session in which returning mentors tell potential mentors what it is like to mentor new freshmen. Candidates who express interest in becoming mentors continue on to the interview process (P. Esplin, personal communication, September 30, 2011).

You'll need to get the word out about the upcoming informational session. Produce a flyer announcing your program and the opportunity for students to learn more about becoming a mentor. Provide a link to an online version of the information sheet, the dates and times of program informational meetings, and an e-mail address for more information. The outreach method or methods you decide to use will depend on whether the mentoring program is to be universal or tailored and offered to a discrete group of identifiable students. For example, the veteran's affairs office could pass along recruitment information to potential student veteran mentors. Ethnically focused student groups and clubs (e.g., Las Mujeres, Vietnamese Student Group) might be able to distribute your flyer among club members if your program proposes to serve students from that group.

Potential mentors need to be fully informed about the program and their role in it before they can agree to participate. Therefore you need to develop a program information sheet before you begin the recruitment process. Minimally, the program information sheet should explain

- the goals of the program and the target group of students to be mentored;
- the mentor job description or minimum qualifications to apply for a mentor position;
- the program's expectations for mentors, particularly how much of a time commitment will be required;

- the training requirements for participating in the program along with the dates, times, and general locations of training sessions;
- how the program will provide ongoing support for mentors beyond initial training; and
- the benefits of mentor participation and how mentors' participation will be acknowledged (e.g., a certificate identifying the extent of their participation that could be used for a résumé, academic credit, or payment of a stipend or wages).

Information sessions should be held when the largest number of interested students may be able to attend. Many programs schedule a lunchtime meeting for potential mentors. Distribute the program information sheet to all the students as they arrive at the meeting. The information session should emphasize your program's commitment to making sure students really understand what is involved in taking on a peer mentor role before they decide whether to participate. Students usually appreciate the opportunity to ask questions about your program. It is also a good idea to tell the students a little about how mentors will be selected. Once you have completed the informational presentations and addressed students' questions, invite all those who still believe they are able to make the necessary commitment and want to become a peer mentor to complete a program application form.

The application form must allow you to collect student contact information as well as college-related demographics such as year in school, major, and whether the applicant lives on or off campus. In addition, the form should include a section that asks potential mentors to explain why they want to be a mentor in your program. It might also ask them to identify their skills and experiences they believe will enhance their ability to be effective.

Selecting Mentors

There are two important steps in moving from recruiting to selecting mentors: determining what your program is looking for in its mentors, and the actual selection process. Determining what your program is looking for in a mentor goes back to your mentor job description. It also determines what information you collect on your mentor application form. Consider the academic, personal, and life experiences and the technical qualifications in your program's mentor job description, and include them in your selection process. Use these criteria to make your first cut of prospective mentors.

Mentor selection should always involve at least one interview to make sure that how a student looks on paper actually corresponds to how that student will function as a mentor in your program. Many schools use a combination of group and individual interviews. You can involve mentors with experience in your program at this point in the interview process.

For example, the University of Cincinnati's Center for First Year Experience and Learning Communities program's mentor selection process begins with an online application that includes the student's résumé. Those candidates who do not meet minimum qualifications are eliminated at the first résumé review. The remaining prospective mentors participate in group interviews conducted by program staff and teams of current mentors (see www.uc.edu/fye/learning_communities/pl.html).

For those setting up a new program, at a minimum the program director and mentor supervisor should participate in the group interview. If you are the sole program staff person, it would help to ask another student affairs professional with experience in running a peer mentoring program to help you with the mentor selection process. Remember the interview serves two functions. First, it lets you interact with the potential mentor to better establish the student's appropriateness and commitment to your program. Second, it provides potential mentors with an opportunity to clarify any questions they have about your program.

Regardless of which group of students your program is serving, mentors must

- believe peer mentoring can make a difference in the success of the students you are serving;
- make a commitment to your program and the students you are serving because a desirable mentor should have some understanding of the kinds of issues the mentees may be facing, otherwise the mentor's expertise is of little value to them;
- possess strong communication skills by communicating ideas verbally and in written form at a language level your group of students will understand, and listening actively and with empathy to the issues and concerns of your group of students; and
- demonstrate strong academic skills because even though research shows that the best mentors are not necessarily those with the highest GPAs (Grove & Huon, 2003), prospective mentors need to have established a successful academic history at your school, ensuring that your mentors are providing mentees with strategies for success that actually work while also reducing the possibility that participating in your program might negatively affect your mentors' own academic progress.

Mentor Compensation Issues

Whether and how you compensate your mentors are budget and program philosophy questions. One perspective suggests that the training for and involvement in a mentoring program brings mentors rewards that out-weigh the need for payment. Participating in a program allows mentors to acquire and develop skills that are attractive to potential employers. From this perspective, a certificate of participation or recognition that students can include on their academic curriculum vitae or résumés are a reasonable form of reward (e.g., http://huskyleadership.uw.edu/facultystaff/husky-leadership-certificate-mentor). Another perspective argues that mentors should be financially compensated, either through a stipend, hourly rate wage, tuition, or college credit, for their participation in the mentoring program if they are expected to be committed and conscientious. The philosophical issue centers on the question, Who are the typical mentors in a volunteer program? The answer: Students who can afford to do so. Some students who might make excellent mentors might not be able to participate because of the high cost of college and that many students have to work while attending school.

Because program expectations for peer mentors vary from one institution to another, it is not surprising that mentor compensation varies widely also. At one end of the scale are volunteer programs such as Alverno College's Peer Advising Program (www.alverno.edu/advising/peeradvisingprogram/) and the University of South Carolina's University 101 program (http://sc.edu/univ101/peerleaders/become/description.html) whose peer leaders or mentors volunteer their time to help new students and receive campus acknowledgment for their participation but are not compensated financially. Somewhere in the middle are programs that pay mentors an hourly wage, such as the Western Washington University Mentor Project (www.wwu.edu/sos/mentorproject), the University of Michigan Transfer Student Connections program (http://onsp.umich.edu/transfer-connections), and the University of New Mexico's STEM gateway Peer Learning Facilitators Program (http://stemgateway.unm.edu/documents/Impact/2013SympPLF.pdf), and programs that provide mentors with a flat stipend such as the International Student Mentor Program at PSU (www.pdx.edu/international-students/international-student-mentoring-program) and the University of East Carolina College of Business Peer Mentors program (www.ecu.edu/cs-bus/peermentors.cfm). Other programs, like the Utah Valley University Peer Mentoring program (www.uvu.edu/slss/mentoring) and the PSU University Studies program (http://mentors.unst.pdx.edu/content/mentors-and-mentored-inquiry), provide tuition remission for mentors.

Developing Policies and Procedures

Once you have selected your key program staff, you will need to establish policies and procedures that reflect your program decisions and that everyone in the program will be expected to follow. Having formal policies for your program allows you to document how you want to proceed and facilitates transparency if any of your program-related decisions are questioned.

Program policies fall into four broad areas: policies relating to the larger program, the mentor-mentee pair, program evaluation, and internal program functioning. Though not an exhaustive list, the following are examples of some key policies that should be included in each area.

Policies Relating to the Larger Mentoring Program

This following group of policies needs to be in place at the very beginning of your program to guide your selection process of mentors and mentees:

- How and when mentors are selected, oriented, and trained
- How mentors will be compensated (if this is part of your program)
- How and when mentees are recruited, signed up, and oriented
- How mentors and mentees are matched
- Who supervises mentoring pairs and how often the supervisor is in contact with each mentor
- Where and when mentoring takes place

For example, peer advisers/mentors at Alverno College provide information on mentee meetings through a monthly reflection paper submitted to senior program staff. The reflection highlights contacts mentors have had with students over the past month and asks them to describe an interaction that was particularly meaningful to them. They are also asked to set a goal for the upcoming month. Senior program staff members respond to the reflections, answering any questions and providing feedback (K. Tisch, personal communication, May 14, 2013).

Policies Relating to the Mentor-Mentee Pair

Policies directly relating to the mentor-mentee relationship also need to be clearly articulated early in the life of your program, including the following:

- Expectations for a mentor
- Expectations for a mentee
- The program-preferred method of documenting mentor-mentee contact
- The people a mentor or a mentee should contact when problems arise
- Methods of handling mentee/mentor/staff complaints

- Methods of resolving problems in relationships or bringing relationships to closure

These policies will particularly guide you in how you train your mentors and what is included in mentor training as well as what you share with new mentees in orientation.

Policies Relating to Evaluation

Policies related to evaluation and the internal functioning of your program are very important even if they may be developed a little later in the process of setting up your program. These may include

- the kind of data that will be collected, and
- mentors' roles in collecting evaluation data.

While the details of evaluation are covered in Chapter 9, you need to establish policies about what evaluation data will be collected and how they will be collected before you conduct mentor training because these are an important part of the mentor's job responsibilities.

Policies Relating to Internal Program Functioning

Some policies in relating to the internal functioning of your program, such as how time will be documented, need to be in place before mentor training. Others, such as guidelines for good communication, can be developed with mentor input as part of the training process. These include the following:

- Manner in which mentors will document their time
- Procedure for providing coverage when a mentor is ill or unable to meet with a mentee
- Method of conducting staff meetings
- Guidelines for communicating with other program staff
- Method of documenting what is covered at staff meetings

Setting Up a Program Database and Developing Forms

It is a good idea to get started on setting up your program database several weeks before you actually start delivering mentee support. Use participants' contact information to develop an e-mail list to facilitate regular contact among program staff, mentors, and mentees. The e-mail list can be used to make regular announcements and connect mentees with campus or program resources. While it may seem obvious, for this method to work mentees and mentors need to be encouraged to check their e-mail regularly, to make sure their e-mail address on program records is current, and to notify program staff if their e-mail changes (Grove & Huon, 2003, p. 17).

What Should Be Included in Your Database?

Mentee information could include

- contact information including e-mail, phone, and emergency contact information;
- demographic information including age, sex, major, year in school, and, if it matters for your program, race or ethnicity or citizenship;
- how mentee was recruited, which could help with future recruitment efforts;
- a record of a completed application and the signed mentee contract;
- a record of the signed consent form and photo release form if you want to use photographic images.

Mentor information could include

- contact information including e-mail, phone, emergency contact;
- demographic information including age, sex, major, year in school, and, if it matters for your program, race, ethnicity, or citizenship;
- a record of a signed consent form, mentor contract, photo release.

You will need to submit a proposal to and get approval from your school's institutional review board or Human Subjects Research Review Committee before you start your program if your evaluation plan involves requesting access to sensitive student data like grades and transcripts, or if you plan on ever publishing anything about your program. One aspect of that proposal will be a sample informed consent form.

Development of Key Program Forms

Several forms must be created for any peer mentoring program. For mentors and mentees you will need application, informed consent, photographic release, and mentor-mentee contract forms. You might also need to create forms to document mentor-mentee meetings and data collection.

See Chapter 5 Resources on page 135 for samples of a recruitment letter, mentee application form, mentee enrollment tracking form for database, informed consent, photographic release, peer mentor application forms, and a mentor-mentee contract.

The time line items "mentor training" and "evaluation" (including evaluating mentor training) are discussed separately in Chapters 8 and 9.

Identifying and Recruiting Potential Mentees

An important early design step is to identify the group of students your program plans to serve. In situations where participation in a mentoring program is mandatory (e.g., all incoming freshmen), you do not have to recruit mentees but you will need to make sure they are aware of the mentoring component of the program and the benefits associated with participation. In other situations, such as for programs that target student veterans, your college's registrar's office can provide you with the contact information for all eligible students. For programs that provide mentoring for students on academic warning or facing disqualification, potential mentees may be referred to your program by advisers or concerned faculty members. However, in many situations you will need to decide on the most effective and efficient methods for identifying and contacting the students you hope to serve.

Methods of Making Contact

There are several different ways to make initial contact with potential mentees, each with its own strengths and potential drawbacks.

Sending a letter is probably the most effective approach. *Strength*: A personally addressed letter increases the likelihood the student might actually read it. *Drawback*: An impediment might be the financial cost of postage, paper, and envelopes.

Another good form of outreach is recruitment at orientation or student services fairs. You can set up a recruiting table at regular summer college orientation sessions or at student services fairs immediately before classes begin. *Strength*: Students who are attending are looking for services, and the stress of orientation may help some students realize that mentoring support would be helpful in dealing with the highly stimulating, overwhelming college environment. *Drawback*: The biggest issue is time. Your staff has to attend the tables, and scheduling may become an issue if there are multiple orientation sessions.

You can post announcements about your program on electronic bulletin boards, typically associated with your college e-mail system. *Strength*: There is no cost, and this approach requires little preparation time. *Drawback*: There is no guarantee that the students you are trying to target will actually bother to read the posting. Many new students initially insist on solely relying on their home e-mail system rather than using campus e-mail. An unintended consequence of this choice is that they miss reading e-bulletin board messages only available to those using the campus e-mail system.

You can also post flyers around school or have them distributed with school acceptance materials. All schools have physical bulletin boards located in departments and around campus. Posting flyers in relevant locations rather than in all possible locations is probably a better use of your resources. A good strategy for programs that target a particular subgroup of students, such as student veterans or international students, would be to post recruitment flyers near the offices that provide advising for students from your targeted groups. You should also post recruitment flyers in or near campus student advising and counseling offices as well as ensure that academic support staff are provided with copies of your program's recruitment flyer. Schools with universal mentoring programs should include mentoring program information in the packet of materials sent to students with their acceptance letter. *Strength*: The cost associated with printing flyers is relatively low, and this approach provides the ability to catch the attention of specific subgroups of targeted students. *Drawback*: There is a possibility that the materials may not be read by the students most in need of program participation. Flyers need to be strategically placed, and their effectiveness relies on students reading the notices.

Many programs recruit by making announcements in classes during the first week of the term or semester. *Strength*: This approach is very cost-effective and can also be time effective if you are aware that certain classes are likely to include a high percentage of students from the group you are trying to contact. *Drawback*: Using this recruitment approach means the soonest that you can actually offer mentoring support is during the second week of the term or semester. Yet many students from groups targeted by peer mentoring programs are facing issues that might be better addressed by preparing them before they get too far into their first term classes.

Another excellent way to recruit students for your mentoring program is through outreach to advisers, counselors, and transitioning student support staff at your own college, local high schools, or community colleges. *Strength*: Incoming college students see their high school and community college advisers and counselors as credible sources of information because they have already established relationships with them. A recommendation from one of these insiders generally carries a lot of weight with entering students who may feel overwhelmed and need support. *Drawback*: The biggest cost here will be the time it takes to establish relationships with your colleagues at these other schools. It is a good idea to make initial contact through e-mail or a phone call so you can describe the groups of students your program serves as well as the kinds of services your program provides. One caveat: Because high schools and community colleges are large bureaucratic organizations, sometimes your actual contact person may change from one year to the next. Also, to effectively refer potential participants to your program, high school and community college advisers need information about your program before their students actually transfer or enroll at your school.

Advisers and support staff at your own school need information in advance of your actual recruitment push. These individuals can also refer students to your program during the academic year once students start classes and show up at advisers' offices with college adjustment issues. Advisers are well-placed to spot students who might benefit from participating in a mentoring program. Overall, reaching out to advisers, counselors, and other student support staff is a good investment of your recruitment energies.

You can also post recruiting announcements on your program website or Facebook page. *Strength*: This approach takes advantage of students' increasing use of technology and social media to gather information. You can provide a much wider range of information about your program, including pictures and testimonials from students once your program is established, on a website or Facebook page than you can in a letter, announcement, or flyer. Also, students are comfortable forwarding links to each other, so one student who finds your program interesting might share that information with other students in her or his social network, thus getting your program recruitment information out to a much wider group of individuals than sending one student a letter from your program. *Drawback*: The main expense is IT costs, though these will be relatively low if you have already gone to the trouble of establishing a virtual location for your program in cyberspace. The only additional significant cost is the time involved in putting together recruitment materials on your website or Facebook page.

Informational Meetings With Potential Mentees

Once you have notified students from the group you hope to serve about your mentoring program, the next step is to bring your potential mentees together for one or more informational sessions. It is important for mentees to be fully informed about your program, including the services you will provide, what is expected of them if they agree to participate, and the potential benefits of participating in this program. Ideally, these meetings should happen before classes begin. Many schools have an orientation week before classes that would be an excellent time for an informational meeting. Sometimes it is only possible to have informational meetings during the first week of classes. For colleges and universities that have summer orientation sessions for new students, it may be possible for you to piggyback your informational meetings with the larger college orientation sessions.

Make the most of the limited time you have for your informational meeting by distributing program information in advance to the students who express interest. Program information material should include

- the rationale for the mentoring program, how it came about, and the reasons for its development and implementation including any evidence of its effectiveness;
- program aims, objectives, and basic structure;
- your expectations of participants in the mentoring program; and
- information about the mentors and about the training they undergo to become a mentor (Grove & Huon, 2003, p. 14).

Even though you may have already provided this information to potential mentees as part of your recruitment efforts, make sure to have a handout with the same information on it available for anyone at your informational meeting to refer to.

Although the ideal time for your informational meetings may vary depending upon your circumstances, lunchtime or early evening meetings after individuals leave their jobs work well. After you welcome the students to the informational session, begin by briefly reviewing your materials, particularly what students can expect from the program, the benefits of participating in peer mentoring programs for college success, and what you will expect for them as mentees. Potential mentees must be made aware of the importance of a commitment to regular attendance at mentoring sessions and of your expectation that they will take some responsibility for their conduct in the mentoring relationship.

Next, open the conversation for questions. This is the time to clear up any uncertainties or misconceptions potential mentees might have about your program. Once mentees have had the opportunity to get their questions answered, encourage those who are interested in participating to complete an application form. This form should minimally include their contact information, program qualification information to establish that the student is part of your targeted group, permission to have a mentor contact them, and whatever information you will require to make mentor-mentee matches. This is also a good time to get students who complete an application to read and then sign an informed consent form so you can collect data to evaluate the success of your program as well as a photographic release if your program plans on taking photographs of participants to help document the experience of participating in your program. Students who complete an application and associated forms should be given a handout or card congratulating them on joining your program and providing them with program staff names and contact information as well as an approximate date when they will hear from their mentors.

There is value in setting up your recruitment/information session/application process in a logical step-by-step order. This way, your mentees are clear about their program roles and responsibilities and will have made informed decisions on whether to participate in your program.

Program Year Activities

Program year activities include everything that happens from the initial mentor-mentee meetings through the end-of-program celebration.

Initial Mentor-Mentee Contact

It is helpful to structure your program in ways that explicitly prompt mentors to make sure to take actions that will help your program provide the services you'll need to deliver to reach its goals. Regardless of how much training mentors receive, they will need help in initiating relationships with their mentees.

Many programs have an initial orientation session before the beginning of the term to provide mentors and mentees with a structured opportunity to connect with each other and set up their continuing meeting schedule. Mentors can also use these orientation sessions for informing mentees on how to access online program resources (e.g., directories of on- and off-campus community resources, chat rooms) and encouraging their mentees to participate in upcoming program activities.

Other programs bring mentors and mentees together with a social event rather than a designated program orientation; the goals are the same, only the name is different. For example, the International Student Mentor Program (www.pdx.edu/international-students/mentor-programs) at PSU begins each program year with a preterm overnight retreat for new international students to connect with their mentors and learn about the program while sharing a common experience that includes meals and social activities (J. Townley, personal communication, September 30, 2013). The point of these kinds of initial meeting activities is to connect mentors and mentees, set up a schedule of ongoing mentor-mentee contacts and meetings, and to make both groups explicitly aware of who key program staff are and of program resources available to them in a less threatening, more social context.

However you kick off your program, it is a good idea to provide food for your mentors and mentees at your initial meeting. Psychologists have shown that people eating together are more likely to develop favorable attitudes toward current experiences and each other (Razran, 1938, 1940).

It is also helpful if you can get one of your college's or university's administrators to attend and address the mentors and mentees at your kickoff event. The administrator's presence conveys your school's endorsement of your program's commitment to providing mentoring support for the students served by your program.

Ongoing Program Supervision and Support

Your program's staff must provide mentors with ongoing support and supervision for them to effectively and confidently deliver mentee support. You need to build mentor supervision into your mentor job description and mentor training. Mentors need to understand the importance of participating in supervision sessions when they are hired. You should also explicitly discuss the value of participating in supervision sessions as part of your initial mentor training.

Some of the benefits of ongoing supervision sessions include opportunities for

- mentors to discuss their experiences with mentees, particularly any issues mentees might be having accessing program or campus resources;
- mentors to hear about the experiences of other mentors because mentors learn about possible strategies for dealing with their own mentees by listening to what other program mentors have found to be effective;
- program coordinators to learn about potential mentor-mentee issues before they advance too far as well as to develop and put into action strategies for addressing these potential issues; and
- program coordinators to demonstrate their support for mentors (Grove & Huon, 2003).

Celebrating Your Successful Program and Acknowledging Your Mentors

You have put a lot of energy into preparing your mentors and setting up your program before you even begin to deliver actual support services to mentees. Then, during the program year, you have put additional resources into facilitating mentor-mentee contact, delivering program resources to mentees, and providing ongoing supervision and training for your mentors. When you reach the scheduled end of your peer mentoring program, it is important to celebrate the completion of the program year with a social event for mentors and mentees. This is a good time to invite all the campus personnel and faculty members who contributed in any way to the success of your program to join your mentors and mentees in the celebration. Doing so lets the rest of the campus realize their efforts to support your program have a positive impact and increase the likelihood they will help in the future if asked to do so. Many programs schedule these celebratory events (e.g., a barbecue or luncheon) while school is still in session to increase the likelihood of a high turnout; others do not. Regardless of whether you decide to host social events during or after the term or academic year your program is active, you need to have an initial mentor-mentee social event and final end-of-program celebration to clearly mark the beginning and end of your program.

The end-of-program celebration serves two main purposes. First, it reminds mentees of how valuable participation in your program was for their college adjustment success, and second, this is a good time to acknowledge the contributions of your mentors. Regardless of how you have compensated mentors while they participated in the program, this is an opportunity to recognize all the work they put into making the program a success. All mentors should receive a certificate of appreciation and completion that they can include in their academic or work résumés as a way of demonstrating that the institution values their contributions to the success of mentored students. It should be noted that these certificates are most useful when they actually document some of the key skills the mentors acquired through their participation in your program.

The celebration is an ideal time to have mentees and mentors fill out end-of-program evaluations. Both groups will be reflecting on their experiences in the program at this moment, so it is an ideal time to offer them the opportunity to provide you with feedback on the program. It also will be much easier to collect the data your program needs when all the mentees and mentors are together in one place than trying to get them to respond to individual requests. The celebration is also a good time to take photographs of mentors and mentees that you can share with them after the celebration and also post on your program Facebook page or website as a recruitment tool for the next cohorts of mentees and mentors. Celebrating the end of your successful program year also increases the likelihood that mentors and mentees will favorably recall their experiences in your program in the future and recommend participation to other students.

Size and Design Issues

One of the unique features of this book is the explicit discussion of the inter-action between program size and design. The type of peer mentoring program you envision will affect your program design and, consequently, program size. Let's consider how program size interacts with each of the four dimensions of the peer mentoring program rubric from Chapter 2 (Table 2.1).

Inclusiveness: Universal Versus Tailored

Degree of inclusiveness has an impact on the number of program staff and mentors you'll need, and how you recruit mentors and mentees for your pro-gram. Universal programs typically are larger than tailored ones, although a universal program at a smaller college may be the same size or even smaller than a tailored program at a much larger school. A small or tailored program may have a single individual in both the coordinator and mentor supervisor roles. A universal or larger tailored program will minimally require a program director and a mentor coordinator. The larger the program, the more likely you will need an additional graduate assistant or student assistant to help with data entry and coordinating the program office and online activities.

Universal or larger programs will need more mentors because you are serving more students. This means you need to widen your outreach to potential mentors and allow more time for the process of interviewing and selecting mentors. Tailored programs that emphasize serving a distinct stu-dent population will have to restrict the pool of potential mentors to students who share the common characteristic of the group being served; for example, limiting mentors for a student veteran program to already successful student veterans. This means the identification of and outreach to potential mentors for a tailored program may take longer, although the interview and selection process should be less time consuming.

Universal mentoring programs typically require less effort to recruit mentees, as all of them are being mandated to participate as part of their membership in the university community. Many universal mentoring pro-grams assign mentors to specific learning communities, either in residence halls or as part of freshman experience courses. If your universal program requires you to initially contact mentees outside a learning community set-ting, it should be relatively easier to identify the potential mentees because your registrar can provide you with the contact information for all new stu-dents. Tailored program staff may need to spend more time and strategically use a wider range of mentee recruitment efforts to identify and connect with the students your program aims to serve. The degree of difficulty in identi-fying potential mentees for tailored projects varies by group. Information on international students and student veterans will generally be available through registration. Identifying potential first-generation student mentees may not be as easy unless your school mandates that parents' education levels are included in your college's application form.

Duration: Short Term Versus Long Term

While all programs emphasize the importance of facilitating the initial mentor-mentee bonding, this design issue is particularly important for short-duration programs. Because these programs are designed to last a semester or less, it is imperative for you to schedule some kickoff events to introduce your mentors and mentees before the term begins. Program size becomes important here, as administrators of larger programs have to figure out a timely way to bring groups of mentors and mentees together in small enough groups to facilitate initial bonding. One possibility is to schedule multiple kickoff sessions for small groups of mentor-mentee pairs, either simultaneously at multiple campus locations or distributed over a short period of time. Another possibility would be to have a general everyone-included meeting for a welcome-to-the-program greeting and then break up into smaller groups to promote bonding between the mentor-mentee pairs while not overwhelming mentees. While mentor supervision is critical in all short-duration programs, because time is limited to make changes in mentor-mentee assignments if a relationship does not appear to be working, supervision is even more important in larger programs. Because of their size, large short-duration programs need to budget for and hire separate mentor coordinators because of the greater likelihood of mentor-mentee conflict and the importance of quickly resolving relationship issues in view of the short program participation time period.

Long-term mentoring programs face some different issues. One has to do with maintaining mentor and mentee commitment levels as the program unfolds. Sometimes mentees who actively participated in your program during their first term start to disengage over time. One way to keep mentees and mentors committed to your program is to have social activities (e.g., attending a sporting event, sharing a meal) or community service projects that bring both groups together outside the ongoing academic relationship. Differences in program size make some types of activities easier to coordinate in larger and smaller programs. Some service projects, such as participating in a beach cleanup or helping neighborhood tree-planting programs, are more feasible for larger mentoring programs than smaller ones. Other activities, such as sharing a meal or attending a professional sporting event, might be easier for smaller programs to pull off.

Maintaining mentor commitment is also an issue with long-term programs, particularly if they seek to support students beyond a single academic year. For example, it is difficult for a peer mentoring program that relies on more experienced student mentors to support mentees from the time they enter college as freshmen until they complete their degree. Simply because they are more experienced, mentors will graduate years before their mentees are ready to graduate. Since the mentor-mentee bond is important to the success of a peer mentoring program, administrators of long-term programs need to have a plan in place to maintain that bond if the duration of the program means more than one mentor must support the same mentee. One possible solution is to explicitly discuss this issue with mentors and mentees at the beginning of your program. You might develop a program policy regarding mentor-mentee assignments that explicitly states the pairing will be reviewed and reassigned at the end of each program year but that mentees and mentors who wish to continue their relationship can request to do so. That way, ongoing relationships that are working can be maintained, but program participants are aware in advance that pairings may change during the time the student is in your program. Here again, administrators of larger programs need to budget for and hire an additional staff member, typically a mentor coordinator or student assistant, to review mentor-mentee relationships each term and coordinate ongoing mentee support.

Approach to Addressing Students' Needs: Targeted Versus Developmental

Targeted programs focus their efforts on meeting students' needs at a specific point in time. However, one important part of designing a developmental intervention is the sequencing of program materials and activities. Ideally, mentees will receive relevant program materials immediately before or right at the time they are dealing with specific college adjustment issues. For example, providing mentees with materials on test-taking strategies and stress reduction will be most helpful in the weeks preceding midterm and final examinations. Program size will affect the method by which program materials are delivered to mentees in a timely manner. While smaller programs may have mentors provide support materials to students either in face-to-face meetings or electronically, administrators of larger programs should plan on distributing these same materials via e-mail or online resource repositories.

The support materials sequencing issue has implications for other aspects of putting together your program. As part of your initial needs assessment for the group of students you plan to serve, you need to identify not only potential college adjustment issues these students face but also when these issues are likely needed to be addressed in the time period covered by your mentoring program. You also should put together your program materials in such a way that students are provided with foundational material before they are asked to consider more nuanced issues that typically arise later in the semester or academic year. The developmental nature of your program also has to be built into your mentor training and evaluation efforts.

Nature of College Transition

The college transition or transitions your program focuses on will affect the design issues of how you recruit mentees and how you select mentors. While some methods of recruitment work well regardless of the transition, different transitions require slightly different recruitment approaches. For a high school to college program, high school counselors and advisers can be helpful in recruiting students for your programs. Similarly, community or junior college counselors and advisers can provide recruitment support for programs focusing on the two-year to four-year transition. Administrators of programs serving international students who are making a transition from one educational system to another should form partnerships with your college's department that coordinates international student enrollment to get information about your program to students before they arrive on campus. Department graduate directors can typically facilitate your recruitment process for programs that focus on the undergraduate to graduate school transition.

Size interacts with the nature of educational transition students are making and impacts program design, although the degree of inclusiveness also must be considered. High school to college and two-year to four-year educational transitions involve larger groups of students than programs serving international or undergraduate to graduate students. This means that a universal high school to college program will typically involve a larger number of students and require a larger program staff, more mentors, additional program space, and consideration of how to coordinate mentor-mentee meetings and social activities than a tailored program serving students making the same educational transition. However, a universal international student mentoring program might still be closer in size to a tailored program for students making a different transition, simply because of the relatively lower number of international students enrolling at any given college in a given year.

As noted earlier, in an ideal world the type of peer mentoring program you envision will have an impact on your program design and consequently program size. In reality, many times the size of your program will be based on the amount of resources you have available. However, through thoughtful consideration of the different elements of program design, you should be able to provide your targeted group of students with the mentoring support they need to succeed and in a manner that allows you to make the most of the resources you have at hand.

This chapter provides an overview of the design elements that must be considered when setting up a college student peer mentoring program and walks you through each of the steps in the program development time line, with special attention on budgeting, recruiting potential mentors and mentees, and providing examples of program policies and sample forms. A special feature of this chapter is a discussion of how design elements are affected by program size, and the chapter concludes by illustrating the importance of the size-design relationship using the four dimensions of the peer mentoring rubric from Chapter 2. Chapter 6 continues the size–design discussion in regard to a specific design element, the mode of delivery of mentoring support.

Note

1. See, for example, University of Michigan, Transfer Connection's Facebook page, www.facebook.com/pages/Transfer-Connections-University-of-Michigan/350857308338050?ref=hl; Brigham Young University First-Year Mentoring program's twitter feed, twitter.com/byumentoring; and University of New Mexico Title V Peer Mentor program's Flickr page, www.flickr.com/photos/25314705@N05/.

CHAPTER 5 RESOURCES

Sample Recruitment Letter for a Program Mentoring New Freshmen

Date

Dear [name of student],

Welcome to [insert name of your institution]! Starting college is a very exciting time in your life. However, many new students tell us that they feel anxious, confused, or overwhelmed by the many aspects of college life that are new and different.

You are eligible to participate in a new mentoring program at your [college/university]. The program is called [insert name of your program] and it is being offered free of charge to you. Our mentors are people who just a few years ago were in your shoes and now are successfully completing studies at [insert name of your institution]. They are willing to share their own experiences and college success strategies to help you be successful, too. Our program is designed to help new students make a smoother transition to your [college/university].

We offer new students some strategies to help them adjust to college life easier and faster than they would if they were just trying to do it without any help. If you choose to participate you will be assisted in identifying and using campus resources. You will have access to [specify your program resources] that will help you navigate the [college/university] system.

If this kind of help sounds useful, then the [insert name of your program] may be right for you. This program is being offered to you free of charge and will begin [insert date and year]. [The following is optional.] We will be calling you in the coming weeks to determine your interest in participating in this program. Please take a few moments to read through the enclosed brochure and feel free to call us at [phone number] or e-mail us at [insert your program's e-mail address] with any questions you may have.

We look forward to serving you and wish you a warm welcome to the [insert name of your institution] community.

Sincerely,

Name and signature

_____ Project Coordinator

Sample Mentee Application Form

Name _____ Date: _____

         Last   First   M I

Address _____

City _____ State _____ Zip _____ Home phone _____

Cell phone _____ E-mail _____ Date of birth _____

Name of emergency contact: _____

Relationship: _____ Phone number:_____

Current education status [adapt to the group of students your program will serve]

[For new freshmen] What high school did you graduate from? _____

[For transfer students] What community college did you attend? _____

[For first-generation, student veterans, returning women students, etc.]

How long have you been enrolled at (name of your college)? _____

[For all students]

Year in school _____ Major _____

Cumulative GPA _____ GPA last semester _____

Do you live on or off campus? _____

How did you learn about [insert name of your program]? _____

In what extracurricular activities (clubs, sports, student groups) do you participate?

_____

Do you currently work outside school hours? Yes or No.

If yes, how many hours a week do you work? _____

Student's signature _____ Date _____

Sample Mentee Enrollment Tracking Form for Database

Project ID # ___ ___ ___ ___ [if needed for institutional review board approval]

Name: _____

       Last   First   M I

Address:_____

       Street   Apt. #

_____

     City   State   Zip

Telephone numbers: (_____) home (_____) cell (_____) work

E-mail address: _____

Emergency contact: _____ Relationship: _____

Telephone number: (_____) home (_____) cell

Date of application: Written consent: Photographic release:

___/___/___   ___/___/___   ___/___/___

Year in school: _____ Major: _____

Mentor: _____ Initial meeting with mentor: ___/___/___

Date of enrollment termination: ___/___/___

Reason for termination:

___ Completed program   ___ Academic deficiency

___ Transferred to another school   ___ Student declines further
                                     participation

___ No longer eligible   ___ [your college/university]
                                     enrollment terminated

___ Other: _____

Comments: _____

_____

_____

Sample Informed Consent Form

You are invited to participate in a new [name of your school] mentoring program, the [name of your program], conducted by [name of program director or principal investigator]. The purpose of this project is to determine whether a mentoring program that [describe what your mentoring program is going to do; what follows is an example for a first-generation student program] emphasizes learning how to recognize and respond appropriately to professors' expectations, as well as how to use available campus resources, improve academic performance, college adjustment, and first-year retention rates for incoming first-generation [name of school] students who qualify for financial aid.

You were selected as a possible participant in this project because [describe the criteria for participation in your program; what follows is a description of a first-generation student program] you are an incoming first-generation student at [name of school], and you qualified for and applied for financial aid. If you choose to participate in this project, we will provide you with [describe support services] access to a special telementoring resource website where you can easily identify and learn how to use a wide range of available support services at [school name]. In addition, the website hosts a collection of short films in which already successful first-generation students share their strategies for dealing with a range of college adjustment issues. You also will be signed up for a project listserv where you will receive tips each week to help you adjust to the university. There is also a project chat room where you can post questions that will be answered by project staff.

If you agree to participate, any information that is obtained in connection with evaluating this mentoring program and that can be linked to you or identify you will be kept confidential by the use of a numerical identification coding scheme. Your name will only be used on the consent form, project roster, and personal contact information form. Any published or discussed data will either be presented in a group format or will use the numerical code system.

Participation in this mentoring project is voluntary. If you do decide to participate you can stop at any time without affecting your relationship with [program coordinator or principal investigator] or [name of your college or university]. The primary purpose of this research is to increase knowledge that may help others in the future.

If you have concerns about your participation in this study or your rights as a research subject, please contact the Human Subjects Research Review Committee, Office of Research and Sponsored Projects at [insert the appropriate information from your school].

Your signature indicates that you have read and understood the information and agree to take part in this study. If you are under 18 years of age, please have your parent or guardian also sign this form. [Name of program coordinator or principal investigator] will make a copy of this consent form available for your personal records.

Name (please print): _____

Last   First   M I

Signature: _____ Date: _____

Parent/guardian signature: (if student is under 18 years of age) _____

Sample Photographic Release

I, [full name], do hereby grant full permission to [your name] and [your college/university name] to photograph and/or videotape me and to record my voice to be used in the documentation of program activities for the [name of your mentoring program].

Date: _____ Print name: _____

Signature: _____

Parent/guardian signature: (if student is under 18 years of age) _____

Sample Peer Mentor Application

Demographic Information

Name: _____

Last   First   M I

Address: _____

Street   Apt. #

City   State   Zip

Telephone: Home (_____) Cell (_____)

E-mail: _____

Emergency contact: _____ Relationship: _____

Telephone number: Home (_____) Cell (_____)

Year in school: _____ Major: _____

Last term GPA: _____ Cumulative GPA: _____

[If relevant to your mentoring program] Are you a:

Community college transfer student   _____

Student veteran   _____

International student   _____

Have you previously lived in a [name of your college] residence hall? _____

Peer Mentor Qualifications

Languages you speak (besides English) _____

Please describe any technology-related skills you have (e.g., software, Web design)

_____

What are some qualities you possess that would make you a successful peer mentor?

_____

_____

Describe any courses or educational experiences you have had at [name of your college] that could contribute to your being a successful peer mentor.

_____

_____

Describe any additional experiences you have had that could contribute to your being a successful peer mentor.

_____

_____

Please write and attach a maximum one-half-page essay discussing how becoming a peer mentor would fit with your personal and educational goals and the ways you might benefit from being selected to be a peer mentor in this program.

Please include the name, title, and telephone number of two references.

1.

2.

Name (please print): _____

                   Last   First   M I

Signature:_____

Date: _____

Sample Mentor-Mentee Contract

For mentees

    I agree to actively participate in the [your mentoring program name] at [your college/university name], and I commit to working with my mentor through the duration of the program, [insert program duration date]. I promise to attend all scheduled meetings and maintain regular weekly communication with my mentor. If I am unable to attend a meeting, I will notify my mentor by phone or e-mail to reschedule. In the event that I wish to discontinue my match for any reason, I will first notify the mentor coordinator/program director and discuss this situation before leaving the program.

Date _____

Name (please print): _____

                   Last   First   M I

Signature: _____

For mentors

    I agree to actively participate in the [your program name] Mentoring Program at [your college/university name], and I commit to working with my mentees through the duration of the program [insert program duration date]. I promise to listen empathetically to my mentees, to treat mentees and coworkers with respect, and to convey a sense of safety and support for my mentees at all times. I will maintain regular weekly communication with each of my mentees and be present for all scheduled meetings. If a situation arises when I am unable to keep a scheduled meeting with my mentee, I will notify her or him in advance, either by telephone or e-mail, and reschedule. I commit to attending all mentor training and staff meetings and to fulfill the responsibilities of my position as outlined in the mentor job description. I will notify the mentor coordinator/program director of any potential issues with my mentee(s) and agree to refer mentees to the appropriate campus support services for issues beyond the scope of my job description. In the event that I wish to discontinue my participation as a mentor in the [your program name] Mentoring Program for any reason, I will first notify the mentor coordinator/program director and discuss this situation before leaving the program.

Date _____

Name (please print): _____

                       Last   First   M I

Signature: _____

FIRST-GENERATION STUDENT-FOCUSED PROGRAM

Students First Mentoring Program

Peter J. Collier, Portland State University

TABLE V2.1

Inclusiveness	Duration	Approach to Addressing Students' Needs	College Transition
Tailored: *Designed for a specific audience*	Long term: *More than one semester*	Developmental: *Responds to student needs as they evolve over time*	High school to college *(primary)*
First year at Portland State University, first-generation students who were not in TRIO program	*One year*	*Overall focus on student expertise development*	Two-year to four-year college *(secondary)*

Note. TRIO = combination of federal student support programs including the Educational Opportunity Program, Student Success Services, and Talent Search.

The Students First Mentoring Program (SFMP) was a year-long program for first-generation freshmen who were new to campus and community college

143

transfer students at Portland State University (PSU) from 2005 to 2008. This project was sponsored by the U.S. Department of Education's Fund for the Improvement of Post Secondary Education program.

PSU is located in downtown Portland, Oregon, and offers more than 100 undergraduate, master's, and doctoral degrees as well as graduate certificates and continuing education programs. PSU is the state's only urban university and has a current enrollment of about 30,000 students, 82% of whom are Oregon residents (PSU, Office of Institutional Research, 2013).

Philosophy

The purpose of SFMP was to help low-income, first-generation freshmen and recent community college transfer students increase their relative level of college student expertise in order to improve their academic performance and persistence. The underlying hypothesis was that increasing these students' expertise levels through peer mentoring would result in academic performance and persistence rates approaching those of students from more educated families. SFMP used peer mentoring to help new students learn about what to do in order to succeed at the university, insights into the culture of higher education, and tips on how to become more expert students. Mentors provided students with information about the range of available campus support services, scripts for how to appropriately use specific campus resources, and strategies for key campus interactions, such as how to get a question answered in a large lecture class.

Participants

A total of 253 students participated in SFMP from 2005 to 2008. SFMP was initially designed to serve new freshmen. However, because of increased demand, SFMP was expanded to also serve transfer students starting in the middle of 2005–2006. However, the development of a complementary set of student support resources for transfer students proceeded in a series of steps, and the full set of resources were only available during the 2007–2008 program year. Table V2.2 details the freshmen/transfer student breakdown in program participants over the three years of this program.

Mentors

Mentors were selected based on three criteria related to credibility and PSU expertise. All mentors were first-generation students, and all were graduate

TABLE V2.2

Cohort	Total Students	Freshmen	Transfer Students	Mentee-Mentor Ratio
2005–2006	65	51	14	16:1
2006–2007	104	68	36	21:1
2007–2008	84	46	38	21:1

Note. From "2005–2009 FIPSE Final Report Executive Summary Plus Evaluation Goals," by P. Collier, C. Fellows, & B. Holland, 2009, www.friends.studentsfirst.pdx.edu/files/results.php Copyright 2009 by P. Collier.

students to ensure that mentors had undergraduate student expertise. In addition, all were familiar with the university, as 9 of the 11 had completed PSU undergraduate degrees, and those who had not completed degrees received extra training to provide the necessary foundation knowledge.

Mentors received tuition remissions and monthly stipends. They participated in a week-long, 40-hour mentor training program and continuing training sessions 1–2 times a quarter. During the academic year, mentors were expected to work between 12 and 13 hours a week.

Design

Incoming low-income first-generation freshmen who qualified for but weren't accepted to PSU's federally funded TRIO programs (i.e., Student Support Services [SSS] or Educational Opportunity Program [EOP]) and agreed to participate in SFMP were randomly assigned to two study groups: SFMP online plus in-person mentoring (OLMP) and SFMP online-only mentoring (OLM). In addition, there were three comparison groups: all PSU students, PSU SSS/EOP students, and students who qualified for but chose not to participate in either SFMP or the federal SSS/EOP programs. To determine the stand-alone effectiveness of the online mentoring version of the program, an additional comparison was conducted of the performance and persistence of the SFMP OLM and OLMP students.

Delivery of Mentoring and Frequency of Mentor-Mentee Contact

OLM students received e-mentoring and access to online resources, while OLMP students received a combination of in-person and e-mentoring as

well as access to online resources. All mentees received an in-person orientation. Both groups of SFMP students received weekly e-contact from
mentors via listserv with information about current program and campus
connection opportunities. They also received weekly tip sheets from the
program library about specific student adjustment issues, resources available for addressing those issues, and specific strategies for addressing those
issues.

After the initial orientation, mentors e-mentored the OLM students.
Besides weekly contact from the program listserv, OLM students had access
to program discussion boards where they could post a question, and a program mentor was guaranteed to respond within 24 hours.

After the initial orientation, OLMP students were assigned specific mentors and received weekly contact from mentors. Mentor-mentee pairs were
required to have a minimum of three face-to-face meetings in a 12-week
term and weekly mentor-mentee check-ins by telephone, e-mail, or in person. Mentees could also either make an appointment or drop by the program
office and meet with a mentor.

Program Goals

SFMP had three levels of program goals. At an overarching student success
level, SFMP sought to improve students' first-year academic success, operationalized as GPA, credits earned, and retention. At the foundational student
success level, SFMP aimed to socially and emotionally support mentees and
to help mentees feel connected to other students and involved with the college campus. Program goals at this level included helping mentees to understand important student adjustment issues and when each was likely to occur;
understand the range of available campus resources and how to appropriately
use each one to deal with specific adjustment issues; and how to understand
the college student role, respond appropriately to professors' expectations,
and make higher quality decisions. Finally, on the program delivery level,
SFMP explored the relative effectiveness of two modes of delivering mentor
support: e-mentoring only compared with a combination of in-person and
e-mentoring.

Strategies for Accomplishing Program Goals

Emotional support and validation. Peer mentors provided emotional support
for mentees through regular weekly contact. In addition, mentors validated
mentees as legitimate college students by sharing their own experiences to

help mentees realize that other students had dealt successfully with similar adjustment issues.

Connecting to campus. Mentors helped mentees recognize opportunities to get connected to the campus. Mentors shared their own experiences to illustrate the benefits of participating in campus activities and connecting with other students.

Identifying and prioritizing student adjustment issues. Mentors provided mentees with information on important student adjustment issues. Mentors made mentees aware of the range of adjustment issues mentees were likely to face, when specific adjustment issues must be addressed, and which issues were most important to address first. Online program resources reinforced mentors' efforts.

Identifying campus resources and connecting to specific adjustment issues. Mentors provided information about available campus resources and shared strategies for how to use resources appropriately to address specific adjustment issues. Here again online program resources reinforced mentors' efforts.

Understanding the college student role and using that role strategically. Mentors modeled the college student role for mentees by demonstrating how to act like successful college students as well as sharing with mentees why the mentors acted the way they did. Mentors provided mentees with strategies for addressing specific adjustment issues, such as figuring out professors' expectations and provided mentees opportunities to role-play important interactions. In addition, mentors provided safe environments to help mentees successfully practice acting out the successful college student role.

Making higher quality decisions. Mentors shared their own strategies for success and as a result helped mentees make higher quality decisions. Because mentees considered mentors to be credible sources of information, they followed the mentors' suggestions for how to act in specific decision-making situations. This resulted in quicker, higher quality decisions that then allowed the mentee to spend more time on task, which subsequently improved outcomes.

Program Resources Supporting Peer Mentoring

Additional online mentoring resources were available to all students, and mentors were trained in how to incorporate these resources into their work with their mentees.

SFMP resource website. A program website was developed that complemented the existing university website. The program website consistently presented information about each campus resource in the same format:

name, services offered, location, contact information, and the first three or four steps in how to use the resource appropriately.

Peer mentoring video library. Through the SFMP resource website, students could also access the online video library, a series of five peer mentoring videos on crucial college adjustment issues. A second set of seven transfer-student-specific videos were introduced for use by students in the 2007–2008 SFMP program. In these videos, successful first-generation, low-income students served as voices of experience sharing effective coping strategies for adjusting to the university (see www.youtube.com/channel/UCELw4IEc91euxnND8LlgCnQ). The video library was accessible 24 hours a day, seven days a week from anywhere through the Internet.

Tip sheet library and listserv. The SFMP tip sheet library contained useful strategies for students to use when dealing with a range of pertinent college issues. Students had access to two levels of resources, a foundation-level tip sheet library and a second-tier tip sheet library. Each week all students received one or more foundation-level tip sheets as part of the regular SFMP listserv message. In addition, transfer students received a second-tier tip sheet every second week as part of a message on a separate listserv. Mentors were able to refer to specific tools from the project library when working with their mentees.

Evaluation: How Program Success Was Measured

Overarching level goals. SFMP sought to support students making the transition to college and thereby improve academic success (e.g., GPA, credits earned) and retention. The PSU data warehouse provided data on GPA, credits earned, and retention. The data were collected and analyzed each term (i.e., fall, winter, spring) for SFMP students and comparison groups.

Student-associated foundational-level goals. The goals of feeling emotionally and socially supported and feeling connected to other students were evaluated through the analysis of anonymous online student satisfaction survey data collected at the end of each program year. The goals of understanding important student adjustment issues, understanding the range of available campus resources and how to use them appropriately, and understanding the college student role, how to respond appropriately to professors' expectations, and making higher quality decisions were evaluated based on the analysis of qualitative focus group data. Data were collected at three measurement points over the program year to capture SFMP students' expertise development over time.

In regard to knowledge of adjustment issues, greater expertise was indicated by the ability to articulate a greater number and wider range of issues as well as the ability to articulate some of the subtler nuances of an issue. For the dimension "awareness of campus resources," greater expertise was indicated by the ability to articulate a greater number of resources, the ability to describe in finer detail what can be accomplished using a specific resource, unprompted awareness of and experience in using SFMP program resources, and personal stories of using a resource. In regard to articulation of strategies for addressing adjustment issues (i.e., understanding and using the student role and making better decisions), greater expertise was indicated by the ability to articulate strategies for dealing with specific rather than general issues, the ability to articulate the higher likelihood of success strategies (ones recognized by the student as having a good chance of succeeding), and the ability to articulate strategies promoted in the SFMP program.

Program-level goals. The comparison of modes of delivering mentoring services was evaluated by collecting and analyzing PSU warehouse data on GPA, credits earned, and retention for the two groups of SFMP students for each term (fall, winter, spring) of the program.

Results

SFMP met the overarching student success-level program goals that focused on program effectiveness in regard to academic performance indicators. All three cohorts of mentored freshmen, compared to all new freshmen, demonstrated higher retention, average GPAs, and average credit earned rates (Collier et al., 2009, p. 3).

SFMP met all four foundational student success-level goals. SFMP met the foundational student success-level goals of feeling emotionally and socially supported and feeling connected to other students, as all three cohorts of students rated SFMP favorably in regard to feeling supported and encouraged to connect to other students (Collier et al., 2009, p. 111). The program also met the other three foundational student success-level goals, namely, helping mentees understand important student adjustment issues and when each was likely to occur; understand the range of available campus resources and how to appropriately use each one to deal with specific adjustment issues; and how to understand the college student role, respond appropriately to professors' expectations, and make higher quality decisions (Collier et al., 2009, p. 111).

SFMP met the program delivery-level goal of comparing the relative effectiveness of a hybrid delivery mode with support delivered exclusively through e-mentoring. Both approaches were successful, as three cohorts of mentored freshmen, compared to all new freshmen, demonstrated higher retention rates, average GPAs, and average credits earned. In addition, both methods of delivering mentoring services produced comparable positive results in regard to yearly retention rates, average GPA, and average credits completed successfully during the SFMP program year (Collier et al., 2009, p. 3).

In addition, all three cohorts of SFMP students were highly satisfied with the mentoring services they received in the program. SFMP participants would highly recommend the program to a "student from a similar background [who] is about to start at PSU" (Collier et al., 2009, p. 3).

Mentor Training

Mentors were provided with a five-day, 40-hour training course prior to beginning to work with students. SFMP training consisted of a combination of exercises, readings, group and individual reflection, guest speakers, visits to campus resources, role playing, technical skill training, and opportunities for practicing new skills (see Chapter 8, pp. 268-270, for a sample mentor training curriculum).

Evaluation of Mentor Training

There were two sources of mentor training evaluation data. First, the external evaluator reviewed the mentor training materials to assess the adequacy of the training curriculum. The external evaluator certified the SFMP mentor training curriculum was comparable, and in some cases superior, to the training provided by other college student peer mentoring programs.

Second, information on the adequacy of mentor training was collected using a mentor training satisfaction survey consisting of a series of questions using a 7-point Likert scale format. The program evaluator administered the survey three times: immediately after training, at the end of the first term, and at the end of the program year. All three mentor cohorts rated the training favorably at each measurement point.

Postscript

After external funding ran out in 2008, key elements of the SFMP—for example, the video library, tip sheets, organization of the resource website—were incorporated into the support resources for PSU's Freshman Inquiry program, a general education sequence that serves all incoming freshmen. The SFMP director served as the FRINQ program's faculty in residence for retention during the 2008–2009 transition year.

Reflection: What I Would Do Differently

In hindsight, it would have been helpful to have established a baseline measure of mentor knowledge regarding possible student adjustment issues, appropriate methods to address each issue, and relevant campus resources before we conducted the actual training. That way, a posttraining measure of the same topics could have established that the training increased mentor knowledge in those areas. Satisfaction with the adequacy of training is an indirect measure but not as strong as empirical change data.

6

HOW WILL YOU DELIVER MENTORING SUPPORT AND SERVICES?

How you deliver mentoring support can be as important as the content of the support you provide for the success of the students in your program. Understanding the strengths and limitations of different modes of delivery can help you make informed choices.

Chapter 6

- identifies multiple modes of delivering peer mentoring support to college students,
- reviews peer mentoring benefits to college students shared by e-mentoring and face-to-face programs,
- explores the strengths and limitations of paired face-to-face and group face-to-face delivery of mentoring support,
- examines the strengths and limitations of paired and group e-mentoring delivery of mentoring support,
- investigates the strengths and limitations of hybrid approaches of delivering mentoring support to college students, and
- considers delivery issues related to program size.

> *The medium is the message.*
>
> (McLuhan, 1968)

> *There is a simple way to package information that, under the right circumstances, can make it irresistible. All you have to do is find it.*
>
> (Gladwell, 2000, p. 132)

Chapter 5 walked you through an overview of multiple elements of program design and provided you with a time line for setting up your program. Now it is time to turn our attention to one specific design element: How mentoring services are going to be delivered in your program. Understanding the relative strengths and limitations of different modes of delivery underscores Gladwell's (2000) point that we can make the information we want to deliver to our mentees irresistible if we can find the best way to package that information.

Background: Different Modes of Delivering Peer Mentoring

Chapter 1 established that peer mentoring is associated with a range of positive college student outcomes. This chapter explores the advantages and limitations of five different college student peer mentoring delivery approaches: paired face-to-face, group face-to-face, paired e-mentoring, group e-mentoring, and a hybrid approach.

Paired Face-to-Face Mentoring

Currently the most commonly used method of delivering peer mentoring services is face-to-face. Face-to-face mentoring for college students typically takes place in paired relationships. Mentees are generally more satisfied with fact-to-face mentoring relationships than other delivery methods (Ruthkosky & Castano, 2007).

Group Face-to-Face Mentoring

Group face-to-face mentoring has been found to be an effective way to deliver mentoring support while maintaining the advantages inherent in face-to-face dyadic mentoring relationships. Boyle and Boice (1998) found that graduate students participating in a face-to-face group mentoring program positively rated the support they received and said the program support materials were highly beneficial.

Paired E-Mentoring

E-mentoring is defined as a computer-mediated, mutually beneficial relationship between a mentor and mentee. The mentee receives advice, support, encouragement, important context-relevant information, and problem-solving suggestions while the mentor is provided opportunities for personal and professional development (Bierema & Merriam, 2002, p. 219; Single & Muller, 2001, p. 108). E-mentoring and telementoring are sometimes used interchangeably; however, Single and Single (2005, p. 302) suggest that e-mentoring should be used to describe text-based electronic mentoring communication (e.g., e-mail) to distinguish it from telementoring, which may rely on telephone communications to support the mentoring relationship.

While e-mentoring researchers have established that e-mentoring can provide many of the benefits of face-to-face delivery programs (e.g., Single, 2004), they are also quick to point out that this does not mean they are suggesting that e-mentoring should replace face-to-face delivery of mentoring support. Instead, e-mentoring is better thought of as an alternative mode of delivering support that allows for additional mentoring opportunities that might not otherwise exist (Single & Single, 2005, p. 305).

Group E-Mentoring

Group e-mentoring brings numbers of mentees and mentors together in a virtual forum where they can explore common issues and develop strategies for potentially addressing these issues. E-mentoring typically involves the use of online discussion groups, e-bulletin boards, or chat rooms where both mentors and mentees can post inquiries and receive feedback from others.

Peer Mentoring Benefits Shared by E-Mentoring and Face-to-Face Programs

Many of the program elements that affect the likelihood of success in face-to-face mentoring programs are also critically important to the success of e-mentoring. Well-designed program structures in face-to-face mentoring programs have been associated with program success and mentee involvement and satisfaction (Boyle & Boice, 1998; Single & Muller, 2001). Program structure is even more important in e-mentoring relationships because of the relative lack of contact between mentor and mentee.

Maintaining a regular schedule of mentor-mentee interaction promotes mentee success in face-to-face programs. Similarly, a regular pattern of mentor-mentee e-mail communication is associated with mentee satisfaction in e-mentoring programs (Kasprisin & Single, 2005, p. 61).

There are other similarities between the benefits mentees receive from participating in both types of programs. Programs using each delivery format have been shown to provide mentees with social and informational support.

TABLE 6.1
Benefits Shared by All Four Modes of Delivering Mentoring

Type of Benefit	Face-to-Face Pairs	Face-to-Face Groups	E-Mentoring Pairs	E-Mentoring Groups
Provides social and informational support	X	X	X	X
Promotes new students' integration into their campus academic and social communities (Tinto, 1987)	X	X	X	X
Promotes increased satisfaction with their college experience (Astin, 1984)	X	X	X	X
Increases self-growth (Baxter Magolda, 2009)	X	X	X	X
Provides foreshadowing of important college adjustment issues	X	X	X	X
Promotes an increased sense of self-confidence as well for mentors as skills they believe will benefit them in the job market	X	X	X	X

Table 6.1 details the benefits shared by the four modes of delivering mentoring support. Both face-to-face and electronic delivery promote new students' integration into their campus communities. Within the framework of Tinto's model, increasing campus integration in academic and social systems are important mentoring-related outcomes that have an impact on student success (Hixenbaugh, Dewart, Drees, & Williams, 2006, p. 12). Mentees in both types of programs report increased satisfaction with their college experience, an important mentoring-related outcome in Astin's model (Hixenbaugh et al., 2006, p. 120), and increased self-growth, which is a positive mentoring outcome in Baxter Magolda's self-authorship model (Smith-Jentsch, Scielzo, Yarbrough, & Rosopa, 2008, p. 203). E-mentoring programs, similar to face-to-face delivery programs, have also been shown to provide mentees with a foreshadowing of important college adjustment issues, another

positive mentoring outcome that is associated with increased student success (Kasprisin & Single, 2005, p. 67; Packard, 2003, pp. 56–57). Forewarned is forearmed, particularly when mentors are careful to not only make mentees aware of important adjustment issues but also provide appropriate strategies for addressing these issues in a timely manner.

Strengths of Paired Face-to-Face Mentoring

Paired face-to-face mentoring is typically the most satisfying delivery mode for students, yet this mode of delivery comes with problems in scale (how many students can be served?) and accessibility (if students are not concentrated in the same geographical space, how do they get access to the intervention materials?). Issues of scale and accessibility directly affect the larger issue of intervention cost.

So what is there about paired face-to-face delivery of mentoring support that students find so attractive? Specific strengths include communication, persuasiveness, and commitment.

Communication Advantages

One advantage of face-to-face mentoring support delivery is improved communication. An important aspect of improved communication has to do with message-meaning clarity. The mentee and mentor have access to nonverbal cues, such as sustained eye contact, facial expressions, and gestures (e.g., see Matsumoto & Hwang, 2011, for a discussion of how we read nonverbal behavior to recognize angry and happy emotions in others) that are particularly important when one is trying to communicate interpersonal warmth and emotional support (Smith-Jentsch et al., 2008, p. 195). Because role modeling is a key element of successful peer mentoring it is important that mentees recognize the warmth and support that is part of the mentor's communication efforts, as models have been shown to be more effective when they were perceived as warm and supportive (Grusec & Skubiski, 1970).

In addition, in face-to-face communication, the message sender may be able to read the receiver's nonverbal cues as a way to recognize when the other person may not actually understand what is being said without the other person responding verbally (see Macrae, Quinn, Mason, & Quadflieg, 2005, for a discussion of how we acquire social information about others by reading facial expressions). A final advantage of face-to-face delivery is greater reliability. Because the delivery of mentoring support relies only on the mentor's ability to communicate with the mentee, there is little chance of the communication being disrupted or blocked because of a technical problem with delivery mechanisms such as access to e-mail when a server crashes or the Internet is not accessible.

Persuasiveness Advantage

Persuasiveness is another important element in peer mentoring programs. Mentors try to convince their mentees of the importance of understanding faculty members' expectations and adopting the mentors' suggested strategies for addressing college adjustment issues. Face-to-face delivery of a persuasive message generally has been shown to have a greater impact than the same message delivered in other modes (Petty & Cacioppo, 1981).

Commitment Advantages

The use of public commitment as a social influence technique has been shown to be effective in a variety of settings. Another advantage of face-to-face-based mentoring delivery is the relatively higher level of mentee commitment to the action steps proposed by the mentor that the mentee agrees to engage in. Once face-to-face mentor-mentee relationships have been initiated, it is harder for mentees to disengage from the commitment they made to their mentors and the program (Bierema & Merriam, 2002, p. 221). This sense of obligation to continue the relationship and follow through with the advice offered by the mentor actually leads to more positive outcomes for mentees because the public expression of attitudes serves to increase the performance of behaviors consistent with those attitudes (Single & Muller, 2001, p. 116).

A relatively higher level of mentee commitment also facilitates evaluation in face-to-face-based programs. Mentees are more likely to participate in and complete program evaluations because they feel a commitment to the program and their mentor.

Limitations of Paired Face-to-Face-Based Mentoring

There are some limitations to face-to-face-based mentoring delivery in general. Specific issues include increased physical space needs, mentor-mentee scheduling, the cost of distributed program materials, obtaining candid evaluation responses, and the timeliness of delivery of mentee-support materials.

Physical Space Issues

The issues associated with where mentoring will be delivered in a face-to-face-based delivery program were introduced in Chapter 5. You will need to provide space for your mentors to meet with mentees, either in your program office or at other campus locations. Having dedicated program space for mentors to meet with mentees allows for drop-in mentoring and increases the ease of face-to-face service delivery. However, providing program space for mentors to meet with their mentees brings with it the need for additional resources like telephones, office supplies, and computers. Having mentors meet with mentees at other campus locations like the library is an option; however, there is no guarantee that the space your mentor-mentee pair needs will always be available when wanted.

Scheduling Issues

A major issue in face-to-face programs is scheduling meetings at times that fit with both the mentor's and mentee's schedules. In face-to-face programs where the mentor-mentee pair is expected to meet in the program office, meetings are limited to the days and hours when the program office is open. Weekend and evening meetings may be problematic. Scheduling becomes increasingly difficult as the term progresses and students find themselves increasingly busy and overcommitted. Even when a mentor-mentee pair arranges to communicate by telephone, both parties need to be communicating at the same time even if they are in different locations.

Obtaining Candid Evaluation Responses Issue

Face-to-face-based delivery program mentees' higher levels of commitment to the program and their mentors may make it difficult to obtain candid evaluation responses. When evaluation data are solely collected in face-to-face interactions, mentees may be reticent to respond candidly, particularly when those responses might be interpreted as reflecting negatively on the program.

Mentee Support Materials Delivery Issues

Two issues are associated with the delivery of mentee support materials in face-to-face-based delivery programs. The first has to do with the form support materials must take. In a face-to-face program, mentors provide mentees with copies of support materials during regularly scheduled meetings. There are copying and supply costs to the program for producing hard copies. The second issue has to do with the timeliness of support material distribution. While you may have identified which issues mentees are likely to have to address at different times in the term and when mentees need relevant support materials, mentees may not receive those materials exactly when they need them since materials are only distributed at regularly scheduled mentor-mentee meetings. This timeliness issue is further exacerbated if a mentee misses one or more meetings with a mentor.

Limitations of Paired Mentoring in General

A fundamental question for programs planning to deliver mentoring support through paired mentor-mentee relationships is whether an adequate number of appropriate mentors are available to provide support for all the program mentees. Sometimes not enough individuals are available to provide one-on-one mentoring for all the students who need support. At other times, even if enough potential mentors exist, the program administrator may lack the resources to hire enough of them to meet the mentee demand. Program coordination is also an issue. Often, paired mentoring programs will require an extra program staff person just to coordinate the larger number of mentors in the program. There is also an interaction effect with mentor training. Because paired programs require larger numbers of mentors, mentor training becomes more complicated (see Chapter 8). Group face-to-face mentoring and e-mentoring are two approaches to dealing with these issues.

Strengths of Group Face-to-Face Mentoring

Group face-to-face mentoring has additional strengths compared to paired face-to-face delivery. Potential advantages of group face-to-face mentoring include scalability, the development of a cohort effect, and the potential for mentees to learn from each other and other mentors.

Scalability

The first advantage is scalability; one mentor can work with more mentees than would be possible in a series of dyadic relationships. This means that your program will be able to serve a greater number of mentees with a relatively fewer number of mentors while still retaining the advantages of face-to-face delivery.

Cohort Effect

The second advantage is that this approach can also be used to promote a cohort effect among mentees because they regularly meet to share their issues and questions. While most mentoring programs try to promote a sense of community among mentees, the group face-to-face delivery format uses program structure to facilitate involvement among mentees and increase the likelihood of mentees' commitment to the program (Single & Muller, 2001, p. 16).

Learning Potential

The third advantage is that mentees can learn from each other in the group discussion context. When mentees find out they are not the only student dealing with a specific issue, they realize that this is normal and not a personal issue because of some self-deficit. Helping another student work out a viable strategy of addressing a college adjustment issue is a win-win situation. The mentee in need gets help to address an issue, while the mentee who came up with the strategy gains confidence and an increased sense of self-efficacy. The mentee in need now has more confidence to successfully address his or her own future college adjustment issue, or if unable to do so, knows that he or she can turn to other mentees for help.

Limitations of Group Face-to-Face Mentoring

Group face-to-face mentoring programs share many of the same limitations found in paired face-to-face programs. However, while space will continue to be an issue, a face-to-face group mentoring program will require considerably less mentor office space than a paired program serving the same number of mentees.

Strengths of E-Mentoring

Specific general strengths of e-mentoring include being able to serve students from a larger geographic area, availability of preexisting virtual networks, scalability, increased time and flexibility accommodations, greater timeliness in addressing mentee adjustment issues, facilitating early contact with mentees, several communication-related advantages, avoiding negative labeling of students, and providing benefits to the program administration.

Able to Serve Mentees Located Beyond Immediate Campus

Many current college students are unable to participate in existing peer mentoring programs at their schools even if they are eligible. Geographical location (e.g., colleges with multiple campuses) and time issues (e.g., more and more students spend limited time on campus because of the need to balance work and family obligations) limit students' opportunities to participate in mentoring programs even when they desire to do so.

Virtual Networks Already in Place

The current college context facilitates the use of e-mentoring because virtual networks, necessary for the effective use for this mode of delivery, are already in place. E-mentoring starts with a certain level of acceptance as students are already used to communicating with faculty and each other via e-mail because of the networked nature of academic settings (Single & Muller, 2001, p. 5).

Scalability

Scalability is one of the biggest potential advantages of e-mentoring. This mode of delivery allows a program to provide mentoring support to a larger number of students. Fewer mentors can provide support to a relatively larger number of students than could be served by the same number of mentors in a face-to-face-based delivery program (Packard, 2003, p. 57; Single & Muller, 2001, p. 3).

Time and Flexibility Benefits

Another set of advantages has to do with flexibility issues. E-mentoring is very flexible in terms of location because the mentors and mentees can communicate anytime and anywhere Internet access is available.

E-mentoring allows mentors to be productive in the limited time they have available to work with mentees. E-mentoring can occur at times that are convenient for mentors and mentees (Bierema & Merriam, 2002, p. 220; Kasprisin & Single, 2005, p. 59; Packard, 2003, p. 55). Face-to-face-based delivery programs require the mentor-mentee pair to find a physical location to meet. In addition, both parties need to allow for travel time to reach the location.

E-mentoring also provides scheduling advantages. In face-to-face programs, a mentor may have time to meet with students, but the block of available times might not fit with the mentee's schedule. E-mentoring messages can be sent out whenever the mentor has the time to do so. E-mentoring also allows for asynchronous exchanges between mentors and mentees; both parties do not have to be online at the same time (Single & Muller, 2001, p. 4; Single & Muller, 1999, p. 236). This relates to another advantage: E-mentoring is an effective way to address the problem of deteriorating mentoring relationships that plague face-to-face based programs due to one or both parties failing to meet because of time or space limitations.

Time and flexibility advantages also affect mentor recruitment. This mode of delivery might make it possible for more mentors to participate in programs because it allows mentors flexibility in when and from where they deliver mentoring support. Busy students who would consider being mentors but might initially hesitate to participate because of concerns about fitting face-to-face meetings with mentees into their already busy schedule might now find participation more realistic and possible (Muller, 1997; Smith-Jentsch et al., 2008). The availability of more potential mentors may also allow a program to serve more mentees, depending upon the levels of other resources.

Note that while all e-mentoring programs have a relative advantage in terms of location flexibility, not all programs may enjoy the same level of time flexibility. E-mentoring programs that prioritize real-time communication, such as online chats between mentor and mentee, still must rely on both parties finding a common time to interact.

Timeliness in Addressing Student Adjustment Issues

E-mentoring also has a potential advantage in regard to timeliness in addressing student adjustment issues. Even if a program reserves certain periods in the academic year for mentees to consult with mentors about how to deal with specific issues, it may be difficult for mentors in a face-to-face delivery-based program to schedule timely meetings with mentees. With e-mentoring,

---

E-Mentoring Resource Example: Students First Tip Sheets

Mentees in the Students First Mentoring Program at Portland State University received a weekly e-mail from their mentors accompanied by one or two mentee tools or tip sheets designed to help mentees deal with specific pertinent college issues. The entire 12-week quarter's distribution schedule of tip sheets was planned in advance, and they were scheduled to arrive at the most opportune time of the term to promote student success. Midterm exams typically were scheduled during the sixth week and final exams during the twelfth week of the term.

Week 0 Mapping classes
Week 1 (a) Understanding the syllabus, (b) Goal setting
Week 2 Backward planning
Week 3 Meet your professor
Week 4 (a) Note taking, (b) Using the student tutoring and testing center
Week 5 Exam preparation
Week 6 Adviser scavenger hunt
Week 7 Getting involved with student organizations
Week 8 Schedule planning (for next term)
Week 9 (a) Exploring the Career Center, (a) Choosing a major
Week 10 (a) Test stress, (b) Stress management

Knowing the prearranged schedule of sending tip sheets to mentees each week also gave the mentors a prepared topic of discussion in weekly contacts. (Collier et al., 2008, pp. 59–60)

a schedule of when specific issue-related messages need to be sent out to mentees can be built into the program structure, and the mentors can send out support materials even when mentees are not available to meet face-to-face.

Facilitates Early Contact With Mentees

E-mentoring allows programs and mentors to contact mentees before beginning students' first semester or term on campus. Mentors are able to answer incoming students' questions and start to build supportive relationships with mentees before these students even arrive on campus. For example, Wilkes University in Pennsylvania implemented a new mentoring program designed to aid its incoming class of 560 students in their transition to college by delivering services through an online mentor community (www.hellowilkes .com). One of the unique features of the program is that the mentoring relationship is initiated three months prior to the beginning of the fall semester by providing incoming students with instructions on how to access the online mentoring community, an electronic forum where incoming students and all the mentors can communicate. More than 50% of incoming students reported making contact with mentors prior to beginning the fall term (Ruthkosky & Castano, 2007, p. 6).

Communication-Related Advantages

There are several communication-related advantages to e-mentoring. First, mentees have more time to think about their communication when composing messages on a keyboard rather than in free-flowing conversations in face-to-face situations (Single & Muller, 2001, p. 5). Thoughtful responses are more likely to lead to reflection on the mentor's suggested approach to dealing with an issue or the mentee's experiences in putting mentor advice into action. This type of reflection can lead to scaffolding in which the mentee takes a mentor-suggested approach to dealing with a specific college adjustment issue and applies it to addressing a related issue or even develops a general approach that can be used with a wider range of issues.

Second, the saved e-mails and threaded discussions in online program discussion rooms provide mentees with a record of their conversations with their mentors that they can refer to if questions arise about how to proceed in following the mentor's recommended strategy for addressing a specific issue (Single & Muller, 1999b, p. 2). In face-to-face mentor-mentee interactions, sometimes valuable information is lost or unintentionally distorted when a mentee thinks he or she understands the mentor's recommendation but actually does not. In other instances the mentee may initially understand how to follow the mentor's suggested approach but then lose one or more key steps when trying to recall that information from memory. The saved chain of mentor-mentee e-mails in e-mentoring programs ensures that this should not happen as frequently.

Avoids Negatively Labeling Students

Another advantage of e-mentoring programs is that mentees can participate without experiencing any real or imagined negative labeling as "someone who needs extra help" (Single & Single, 2005, p. 306). College is a developmental stage when young people are particularly sensitive to how others perceive them. A student who might reject participation in a face-to-face program, or initially sign up but then refuse to participate, might be more willing to participate in an e-mentoring relationship because others cannot tell the student is receiving mentoring support.

A related issue is that e-mentoring may lead to more candid mentee-mentor conversations because social markers such as sex, race, and class are not visible. The stereotypes and cultural baggage that accompany these social markers disappear in a virtual context. Students who might be embarrassed to broach a sensitive topic with their mentor in face-to-face interactions might be more willing to do so in an e-mentoring exchange (Bierema & Merriam, 2002, p. 221; Single & Muller, 2001, p. 3). This e-mentoring advantage is even more important in programs where mentors and mentees are not matched on gender or power characteristics (Single & Muller, 1999b, p. 2). This advantage also increases the likelihood that mentees will provide candid evaluation responses as they are already comfortable sharing their honest opinions with their mentors.

Program Administration Benefits

E-mentoring also offers several advantages for program staff, one of which is that e-mentoring programs can be easier to administer than face-to-face-based delivery programs. They do not require the coordination of office space to allow mentors to meet with mentees or the same amount of hard copies of program resources because these can be distributed as virtual resources through downloads from a project website or as attachments to e-mail messages (Hixenbaugh, Dewart, Drees, & Williams, 2006, p. 13).

The current nature of the networked university or college can also facilitate e-mentoring program recruitment. Most universities or colleges already have distribution lists set up based on a range of different group characteristics, such as lists for all new freshmen or students on academic probation. These distribution lists can make it easier to identify and initially contact the group of students your program intends to serve (Single & Muller, 1999a, p. 239).

Limitations of E-Mentoring

At first glance, implementing an e-mentoring program may appear to be much easier than it actually turns out to be. Specific limitations include cost, the need for prerequisite conditions and skills, increased likelihood of miscommunication, unrealistic expectations, and lower commitment levels.

Cost

E-mentoring is not necessarily an inexpensive alternative to the face-to-face delivery of mentoring support. Successful e-mentoring programs require the commitment of IT resources to develop the websites, programmatic features (e.g., Web-based resources), and software required to facilitate data collection, evaluation, and management of these online delivery systems (Single & Single, 2005, p. 315).

Prerequisite Conditions and Skills

Successful e-mentoring depends on students having Internet access as well as at least a foundational level of computer literacy. Access to computers and the Internet have improved for U.S. college students over the past 10 years. According to a Pew Research Internet Project, 94% of community college, 98% of four-year undergraduates, and 99% of graduate students have Internet access (Smith, Rainie, & Zickuhr, 2011). However, program coordinators setting up e-mentoring or hybrid programs need to be aware of the digital divide, that is, the home-computing gap between White or affluent families and Black, Hispanic, and low-income households (Papadakis, 2000). Poorer and minority students are more likely to use their cell phones for Internet access; community college students are 20% less likely than four-year college undergraduates to own a laptop computer (Smith et al., 2011). The type of home Internet connection that students have access to can also be affected by income. White and more affluent individuals are more likely to have home broadband access (Zickuhr, 2013). Not surprisingly, community college students are slightly more than 16% less likely than four-year college undergraduate students to have home broadband access. Students who live in rural areas may only have DSL access to the Internet. A lack of home broadband access could mean that students without this service would have to spend more time waiting to access or download Internet-based program resources. A related issue is emerging as e-mentoring programs try to use webcam capabilities and software programs such as Skype and FaceTime to allow mentors and mentees to make real-time video connections and facilitate virtual face-to-face interactions. The digital divide is also an issue here. All students who have Internet access do not necessarily have capability, which is more likely to be found on computers rather than webcam cell phones favored by poorer students for making Internet connections.

Another implicit assumption underlying e-mentoring programs is that today's college students all possess the requisite level of computer literacy necessary to participate in an e-mentoring program. What constitutes computer literacy continues to evolve because of the incredible rate of change in what is technologically possible (McDonald, 2004). It is one thing to be able to do data entry or retail sales in a work environment and another to demonstrate the academic level of computer literacy needed to format a document, cut and paste text from one document to another, or import data into a spreadsheet, much less be able to effectively search for source documents or download assignments from a project website (Cox, 2009).

Computer literacy issues can particularly affect older first-time and returning students. It is important for programs providing e-mentoring to groups of students who are unfamiliar with higher education or potentially might lack access to technology to budget extra resources for improved access or mentee training (Single & Single, 2005, p. 314).

Increased Likelihood of Miscommunication

In face-to-face interactions, successful communication involves much more than just understanding the words that someone is saying to us. We also pay attention to *nonverbal communication*, defined as the process of sending and receiving messages without using spoken or written words (Nordquist, 2013). Nonverbal communication involves several different types of behavior that are relevant to our understanding of e-mentoring communication issues including paralinguistics (how something is said, the tone, pitch, stress, and speed of speech), kinetics (body language, especially facial expressions), and occulistics (eye language, how much, how often, and with whom one makes eye contact). Nonverbal behavior typically is used to communicate emotion.

There is an increased likelihood of miscommunication because of differences in available information in e-mentoring relationships compared to face-to-face ones (Bierema & Merriam, 2002; Single & Muller, 1999b). Mentees and mentors may question the relative levels of sincerity or depth of emotion in statements of support offered in electronic communication because of the absence of nonverbal behavior-based cues, such as facial expressions of warmth (Smith-Jentsch et al., 2008, p. 195). In one of the few studies that compared the relative effectiveness of face-to-face and e-mentoring among college students, Smith-Jentsch and colleagues found that given the identical amount of contact time, those mentored through electronic chat perceived receiving less psychosocial and career support and also reported lower levels of postmentoring self-efficacy than students in the face-to-face situation (p. 202). E-mentoring's greater potential for miscommunication also affects issues of expectations and commitment.

Another potential source of e-mentoring miscommunication is associated with the relationship between students' attention levels and the length of the e-message. Researchers found that students are more likely to read the entire message if it is no more than one screen in length (Single & Muller, 2001). E-mentors sending messages longer than one screen run a greater risk of miscommunication because of mentees not reading all the information that was sent.

Unrealistic Expectations

Because e-mentoring does not provide mentors and mentees with the kinds of contextual cues in face-to-face interactions, it is very important that clear expectations of how frequently contact will occur are explicitly built into the e-mentoring program design. These expectations need to be clearly communicated to mentees at the beginning of program participation. Providing clear and specific expectations relating to timeliness, frequency of contact, and communication is even more important in e-mentoring programs than in face-to-face-based programs (Kasprisin & Single, 2005).

Unrealistic expectations can work both ways. Because mentors are likely to have continuous Internet access through school and home networks, they may assume that mentees also have the same level of access because mentees have received and responded to earlier program e-mails. Yet some mentees may be relying on their college's computer lab for accessing, downloading, and printing online program resources, particularly if they do not have a home printer. Mentees also can have unrealistic expectations, particularly in regard to the turnaround time mentors take to respond to mentees' requests for information (Bierema & Merriam, 2002, p. 214).

Lower Commitment Levels

Ironically, some of the inherent advantages of e-mentoring can also act as limitations. The ease with which e-mentoring relationships can be initiated unfortunately leads to relatively lower levels of commitment to the e-mentor relationship than is typically present in a face-to-face relationship. Mentors in e-mentoring programs need to be prepared that it may take more time and effort to build the kind of intimate relationship with mentees necessary to keep them committed to and continuing in the program because of the lack of taken-for-granted nonverbal reinforcement cues in face-to-face interactions (Bierema & Merriam, 2002, p. 221; Single & Single, 2005 p.

306). Even when students choose to participate in an e-mentoring program, it is relatively easy for them to not follow through or even ignore mentors' or program staff members' e-mail requests (Kasprisin, 2003; Single & Single, 2005).

Mentees' relatively lower levels of commitment in e-mentoring programs also have an impact on program evaluation. Mentees may feel less obligated to participate in program evaluation if it is only done online.

Addressing Potential E-Mentoring Limitations

Certain design elements, such as matching, developing an explicit format for maintaining mentor-mentee contact, and training mentors and mentees, are even more important in e-mentoring programs than in face-to-face programs. Careful matching of mentors and mentees is very important in e-mentoring programs to facilitate the process of finding a common ground for building an ongoing relationship (Single & Muller, 2001, p. 11). In face-to-face mentoring programs, it is assumed that the initial face-to-face contact between mentoring pairs will help them figure out similarities and shared interests that then serve as the foundation for the ongoing mentoring relationship. E-mentoring programs can promote the development of mentor-mentee relationships by explicitly highlighting commonalities of the pair, as perceived similarity rather than actual demographic similarity has been shown to facilitate relationship development in e-mentoring programs (Ensher, Grant-Vallone, & Marelich, 2002).

As noted in the earlier discussions of communication and commitment issues, the very nature of e-communication can sometimes lead mentees to think they do not have to respond to mentors' inquiries in as timely a manner as they might if the same relationship involved face-to-face interaction. Developers of e-mentoring programs can preemptively address this issue by developing a clear set of communication guidelines and expectations for mentors and mentees, explicitly discussing these with mentees at the initial orientation session, and obtaining a written pledge from mentees and mentors that they will follow the communication protocols during their time in the program.

While development of communication skills is an important element of mentor training and is discussed in more detail in Chapter 9, e-mentoring program administrators should pay additional attention to preparing mentors for potential communication issues. E-mentors need to be aware of the higher potential for miscommunication because of the lack of nonverbal cues that provide more nuanced interpretations of messages in face-to-face interactions. In addition, mentors need to be reminded that using taken-for-granted abbreviated language or emoticons typically used in texting or e-mails may be problematic, particularly when mentors and mentees are not familiar with the same slang or figures of speech such as in intercultural or intergenerational relationships (Smith-Jentsch et al., 2008, p. 204).

E-mentoring programs can facilitate successful mentor-mentee relationships by providing e-mentoring training to both groups (Single & Single, 2005, pp. 315–316). As part of their training, mentors should review all the program's technological protocols and practice explaining them to mentees. Because all mentees do not begin the program with the same level of technological skills, having a mentor review with each mentee how to appropriately use all of the program's online resources and communication protocols can ensure that all participants have the needed information while providing a structured opportunity for building rapport between the mentoring pair.

Strengths of Group E-Mentoring

Group e-mentoring incorporates the advantages of e-mentoring with those of group face-to-face mentoring by bringing numbers of mentees and mentors together in a virtual forum where they can explore common issues and develop strategies for potentially addressing these issues. In preparation for a group e-mentoring program, staff members need to develop multiple discussion boards to provide accessible forums for mentor-mentee communication. Each discussion board should focus on a different mentee adjustment issue. It can be very helpful to involve your mentors in determining which student issues need to be the focus of each discussion board. Inviting mentees to take advantage of the discussion forums is a way to get their questions answered by more experienced peers. Specific strengths of group e-mentoring include the opportunity for mentees to learn from each other, the perceived anonymity of online group discussions, mentor peer support, and being less resource intensive.

Mentees Learn From Each Other

Similar to group face-to-face mentoring, an advantage of group e-mentoring is that mentees learn they are not the only students dealing with specific college adjustment issues. They also benefit from the potential solutions offered by other students who are dealing or who have dealt with similar problems. In addition, some mentees may be more comfortable sharing concerns in an e-discussion group than in face-to-face interactions because of the perceived anonymity of Internet communication (Kasprisin & Single, 2005, p. 63).

Mentor Support From Peers

Another advantage is that mentors can support each other in their work with mentees. Mentors who are experiencing difficulties can benefit from input from other mentors in the network who have dealt with similar issues (Kasprisin & Single, 2005, p. 63).

Less Resource Intensive

Group e-mentoring is less resource intensive than other forms of e-mentoring as one mentor or program staff member can supervise multiple e-discussion groups (Single & Single, 2005, p. 316). Group e-mentoring works well as a complement to pair-based e-mentoring, so an e-mentor-mentee pair struggling with a particular issue can get suggestions for potential strategies from the larger group.

Limitations of Group E-Mentoring

Group e-mentoring shares the general limitations of e-mentoring but also can unintentionally result in an additional issue.

Technology Skills Are Not Evenly Distributed Among Mentees

One limitation of group e-mentoring is that it may reinforce technology-related differences among mentees. Even more than paired e-mentoring, this approach provides the greatest benefits to mentees who are already tech savvy and comfortable networking with others to solve problems. Unfortunately the mentees who could benefit the most from the information available through group e-mentoring are the ones least likely to take advantage of this opportunity.

While it is possible to develop a stand-alone group e-mentoring program, this approach works best in conjunction with other forms of mentoring that are more effective in forging the initial mentor-mentee bond. For example, in a Wilkes University freshman mentoring program that also includes paired mentoring, new students were provided with access to an online community as soon as they were accepted to the university. New students could click on 43 different picture block links to discussion forums including roommate relationships, student activities, time management, study strategies, and new student orientation. The topics were developed by program mentors and student development staff and changed over the course of the academic year (Ruthkosky & Castano, 2007, pp. 6–9). For a side-by-side comparison of the strengths and limitations of various forms of face-to-face and e-mentoring, see Tables 6.2 and 6.3 in Chapter 6 Resources.

Tips for Successful Group E-Mentoring

1. Keep discussion themes focused on mentee-relevant topics.
2. Encourage participation. Have mentors in paired e-mentoring relationships encourage their mentees to participate in group e-mentoring discussions. E-discussion groups need to achieve a certain critical mass to persist over time.
3. Provide facilitation for e-discussion. E-discussion groups require facilitation either by participants (e.g., e-mentors can take turns facilitating discussion threads on a weekly basis) or program staff (e.g., the mentor coordinator).
4. Strive to maintain a *just right* number of e-discussion groups at any one time. Ideally you want a Goldilocks solution. Too many discussion threads could disperse mentees so widely that few of the threads would ever reach the critical mass necessary to last for the duration of the programs. Too few discussion threads may result in mentees' visiting the group e-mentoring chat room without participating because of a lack of interest in the limited set of available topics. While what constitutes a just right number of discussion groups may vary from program to program, one approach would be to start with one or more of group-specific college adjustment issues identified in your initial student needs assessment (see Chapter 3) and then add additional issues based on discussions with mentors in regular staff meetings.
5. Maintain a safe and secure environment for discussions. Students are more likely to participate in group e-mentoring discussions when they feel they can ask obvious questions and express their opinions without feeling judged or belittled for what they don't know. Therefore it is important to explicitly convey a set of communication guidelines to mentees and mentors including the message that flaming (hostile or insulting) or inappropriate responses in e-discussions will not be tolerated (Single & Single, 2005, p. 313).

Hybrid Programs

Interestingly, even though e-mentoring approaches produce positive results, many students still prefer face-to-face communication (Ruthkosky & Castano, 2007, p. 9). This suggests that hybrid programs that combine mentoring with opportunities for face-to-face or the virtual equivalent of face-to-face interaction opportunities for mentees and mentors might be able to have their cake and eat it too.

When e-mentoring for college students was introduced in the 1990s, it was initially viewed as a way to provide students with mentoring opportunities that might not have otherwise existed rather than as a replacement for face-to-face mentoring (Muller, 1997). Nowadays, with college students' increased level of Internet access, more and more hybrid programs are being developed that combine complementary elements from face-to-face and e-mentoring (Packard, 2003, p. 57; Single & Single, 2005). From a learning theory perspective, this makes sense. While there is considerable variation in hybrid programs, interventions that make use of multiple mediums for providing students with information, for example, in person, print, e-mail, video, online, tend to have a greater chance for success just because of differences in students' preferred learning styles (Kolb, 1984).

Hybrid programs, like e-mentoring programs, can produce many of the positive effects of face-to-face mentoring programs. For example Students First Mentoring Program at Portland State University (see Vignette 2, p. 143), compared the relative effectiveness of a hybrid delivery mode (e.g., a combination of in-person and e-mentoring) with support delivered exclusively through e-mentoring. Both approaches were successful as three cohorts of mentored freshmen demonstrated higher retention rates, average GPAs, and average credit-earned rates compared to all new freshmen. In addition, both methods of delivering mentoring services produced comparable positive results in regard to yearly retention rates, average GPAs, and average number of credits completed successfully during the program year (Collier et al., 2008, pp. 1–3).

Bringing the Strengths of E-Mentoring to a Face-to-Face Delivery-Based Program

The limitations of face-to-face delivery-based programs that may be mitigated by incorporating elements of e-mentoring are the cost and ease of distributing mentee support materials, limited flexibility in where and when mentors and mentees meet and communicate, and the timeliness of delivery of specific mentee support materials.

Distributing Support Materials Electronically

Distributing mentee support materials via e-mail and online repositories reduces costs, increases ease of delivery, and improves the likelihood that support materials reach mentees when they actually need them.

Reduces Costs

By incorporating e-mentoring's approach to distributing mentee support materials as e-mail attachments, a face-to-face-based delivery program could reduce costs associated with printing hard copies of support materials as well as increase the likelihood that all mentees would get the materials, as opposed to having mentors distribute materials at their meetings with their mentees. Storing materials in online libraries or repositories students can access when they wish is another e-mentoring approach to delivering mentee support materials that could help face-to-face-based delivery programs. Please note that some of the cost savings in printing may be offset by the increased IT costs associated with setting up the online repository.

Improves Ease and Timeliness of Support Material Delivery

Incorporating online libraries in face-to-face-based delivery programs should probably be used in conjunction with e-mail delivery of mentee support materials because part of the reason students are participating as mentees is that they do not always know what they need or when things are needed. Combining e-mail delivery and online availability allows greater certainty that support materials have reached each mentee and that there is an online library mentors and mentees can access when needed. Incorporating the e-mentoring combination of e-mail delivery and an online resource repository also can help address the relative disadvantage face-to-face programs have in distributing support materials to mentees in a timely manner. E-mail distribution allows mentors in a face-to-face program to get support materials to mentees related to specific issues, such as how to use the tutoring center prior to midterm or final exams, at the time mentees actually could use the materials and not just when the mentor and mentee pair can schedule a meeting to talk about the issue and share support materials.

Increasing Flexibility in Mentor-Mentee Interactions

A related pair of limitations of face-to-face-based delivery programs is finding a suitable location for mentor-mentee sessions to occur and scheduling a time when the mentor and the mentee can both attend a meeting, including prior to the beginning of the program.

Reduces Need for Physical Meeting Places

For face-to-face-based delivery programs, having the physical space to hold mentor-mentee meetings in your program office is an advantage as you do not have to locate a suitable meeting space. However, college and university facilities are not open 24 hours a day, so your space may be available but not at times when it is convenient for the mentor, the mentee, or both to meet in that location.

Facilitates Scheduling Meetings

Scheduling mentor-mentee meetings is another related issue. By incorporating e-mail communication, face-to-face program administrators can address both issues at the same time. E-mentoring provides mentors and mentees with flexibility on where they communicate from. By incorporating e-mail as an alternative means of mentor-mentee communication, travel time to and from the meeting location inherent in face-to-face interaction is eliminated. Incorporating e-mail communication also provides the advantage of asynchronous communication. With this new element, both parties of the mentor-mentee pair do not have to be present in the same place or communicate at the same time for mentoring to take place.

Allows Mentor-Mentee Connection Prior to Beginning of Program

Adding e-mail communication to a face-to-face program also provides an additional advantage by making it easier for mentors to contact mentees prior to the beginning of the program. Early mentor-mentee contact helps build a relationship foundation that will only be strengthened when the mentor-mentee pair meets in person when the new student arrives on campus.

Incorporating this e-mentoring element into face-to-face programs is very easy to do and yet provides significant benefits. The frequency of communication is likely to increase, and mentors and mentees may be more likely to participate in the program if they know in advance about the possible flexibility in when and where they will meet.

Bringing the Strengths of Face-to-Face Delivery to an E-Mentoring Program

The limitations of e-mentoring programs that may be mitigated by incorporating elements of face-to-face-based delivery include relatively lower levels of commitment to action, easier for mentees to leave the program, relatively lower levels of persuasiveness of mentor advice, and increased likelihood of miscommunication because of the lack of nonverbal cues.

Improving Level of Mentor-Mentee Commitment

All these limitations can be traced to relatively lower levels of mentee commitment in e-mentoring programs because the same opportunities mentor-mentee pairs have in face-to-face delivery programs to build a strong relationship foundation through clear initial communication and interaction are not present in an exclusively virtual relationship.

A significant concern for developers of e-mentoring programs is how to address the relatively lower levels of mentee commitment to the program and their mentors with relationships solely based on e-communication. An important aspect of developing commitment in any relationship is a person's recognition that a relationship could be beneficial to that person. People choose to become friends with others based on the process of projecting possible benefits and costs of a relationship (Homans, 1958). An individual's initial decision about whether to pursue a relationship with another person is based on an impression of the other person. Impression formation relies on a combination of information about the person provided by others and the individual and by observing the individual. The person forming the impression tries to detect clues in what the other person says or how he or she presents himself or herself and then uses this impression information to decide whether to pursue a relationship with the other person. When individuals find themselves in situations in which they have limited knowledge, such as new students dealing with college adjustment issues, they tend to rely on social comparison information (Festinger, 1954). Even though a new student may not be sure what kind of advice he or she needs, receiving advice from someone who is similar, comes from the same background, and has dealt with the same issues will be perceived as valuable. E-mentoring programs can address the commitment-level issue by incorporating several elements of face-to-face-based mentoring programs that work to promote relatively higher levels of mentee commitment to their mentors and the program.

Face-to-Face Mentee Orientation
In a face-to-face mentoring program, it is assumed that the initial face-to-face contact between pairs will help them determine similarities and shared interests that serve as the foundation for an ongoing mentoring relationship. E-mentoring programs can reap many of the benefits associated with this aspect of face-to-face delivery by having in-person mentee orientation sessions that include initial face-to-face mentor-mentee meetings. These initial meetings allow mentors and mentees to put faces on their partners and help them identify multiple dimensions of similarity that did not surface from the initial contact via e-mail. Perceived similarity is more important to developing strong e-mentoring relationships than demographic similarity. Initially meeting face-to-face allows the pairs to more easily see their similarities.

The initial mentor-mentee session also allows them to share communication guidelines and allows more accurate communication because they are able to verify or modify messages by relying on nonverbal cues. This platform of accurate communication based on the initial face-to-face interaction should allow the pair to communicate more accurately in the future. If a communication situation arises where one or the other partner could choose between making a negative or positive attribution of the motivations of the other communicator, having a history of accurate, supportive communication from the initial face-to-face meeting should increase the likelihood that they will give each other the benefit of the doubt.

The e-mentoring program that incorporates a face-to-face initial mentee orientation will probably incur increased costs associated with finding appropriate space, providing refreshments, and even time costs in scheduling. However, these costs might prove to be good investments if they lead to relatively higher levels of mentee commitment, making it harder for mentees to leave the program and increasing the likelihood that mentees will follow their mentors' advice. Having seen the mentor in person, the mentee might be more certain the mentor does possess the experiences and associated insights and strategies necessary to offer the mentee useful advice on how to deal with specific college adjustment issues. Knowing that mentors come from similar backgrounds and have walked the path the mentees are now facing should increase mentees' willingness to follow their mentors' advice.

Face-to-Face End-of-Program Celebration
Similarly, adding an in-person final program celebration that brings mentors and mentees together should also have a positive impact on mentee commitment for e-mentoring programs. Just knowing mentees will meet with their mentors face-to-face again at the end of the program increases the likelihood that mentees will stay in the program and take their mentors' advice. Having an in-person end-of-program celebration also provides the opportunity for program staff to acknowledge participants' efforts in the program and to present mentors and mentees with certificates of completion.

The end-of-program celebration could also affect the e-mentoring issue of lower mentee completion of the program evaluation. Higher levels of commitment and the knowledge that mentees will be meeting with mentors and program staff to celebrate the end of the program puts pressure on mentees to complete the evaluation. Attending the celebration and not completing the evaluation is likely to lead to cognitive dissonance among mentees (McLeod, 2014). The mentee reflects, "I am celebrating my effort in completing the program, so if I am the kind of person who completes the program, how can I not participate in the program evaluation?" The two views of self—"I am the kind of person who completes the program" and "I am the kind of person who does not care enough to complete the program evaluation"—are incompatible, and individuals are motivated to reduce this cognitive incompatibility. Of course, costs associated with such a celebration include securing appropriate space, time costs in coordinating and scheduling the event, and possibly refreshments. Again, the costs should be mitigated by the increased rewards because of the increase in mentees' levels of commitment. If a choice has to be made in increasing mentee commitment levels, the initial mentee orientation including the mentor-mentee face-to-face meeting would prob-ably be more worthwhile than the in-person end-of-program celebration.

Using Technology to Replicate Advantages of Face-to-Face Interaction

E-mentoring programs can use technology, specifically Web cams and men-tor videos, as another way to incorporate some of the commitment and com-munication advantages of face-to-face delivery-based programs.

Webcams, Skype, and FaceTime

Using webcams and programs like Skype and FaceTime allows mentors and mentees who are not in the same physical location to communicate more clearly because of the nonverbal cues that can reinforce messages from both parties. But as noted earlier, social class differences and the digital divide come into play here. Unfortunately, all students who have Internet access do not necessarily have webcam capability.

Mentoring Videos

Carefully crafted mentor videos are another technology-based resource that e-mentoring program developers can use to incorporate some of the commitment-building advantages of face-to-face-based delivery programs. A mentor looking directly into the camera and speaking to the mentee as if the two were having a face-to-face conversation can build higher lev-els of mentor-mentee commitment than communication based solely on e-mail messages (for video examples see www.youtube.com/channel/ UCELw4IEc91euxnND8LlgCnQ). This approach was used in a series of short videos created for the Freshman Inquiry program at Portland State Uni-versity. In each video clip, one of the mentors looked directly into the camera and offered specific strategies for addressing one of the adjustment issues along with encouragement that the mentee could effectively use the strategy to succeed. Several of the mentors reported being approached by freshmen in their mentor sections who recognized the mentor from the video, thus prompting the mentors to ask the new freshmen about how they were doing in applying the recommended strategies to their own adjustment issues.

Improving Evaluation by Taking the Best of Both Approaches

Hybrid programs that combine elements of in-person and online delivery may be the best approach when it comes to evaluation. Face-to-face pro-grams are at a disadvantage in obtaining honest, although possibly negative, evaluation responses from mentees. On the one hand, relatively high levels of mentee commitment to the program and their mentors increase the likelihood of mentees participating in evaluation. On the other hand, if the evaluation takes the form of face-to-face interviews or even requiring mentees to fill out program evaluation surveys, that same high level of commitment might make mentees reluctant to make negative comments about the program or the mentor out of concern about being viewed as disloyal.

E-mentoring programs have a disadvantage in regard to collecting evaluation responses from participants because of the relatively lower levels of commitment to the program and the mentor-mentee pair inherent in an e-mentoring approach. However, the format of collecting evaluation through anonymous online instruments increases the likelihood that those mentees who do participate will be more willing to share their honest opinions, even if they might reflect negatively on the mentor or program.

For programs relying on face-to-face-base delivery of mentoring, incorporating the e-mentoring element of anonymous online evaluation collection might make it easier for mentees to provide negative feedback that is also constructive. Because face-to-face delivery programs build and maintain relatively high levels of mentee commitment to the program, asking mentees to provide an anonymous online evaluation should not reduce the overall level of mentee participation in evaluation. As noted previously, for e-mentoring programs, incorporating the face-to-face delivery element of an initial orientation and final celebration is likely to increase the levels of mentees' commitment to the program and their mentors. This higher level of commitment might then increase the chances of mentees' completing the evaluation particularly when mentees know they will be meeting in person with their e-mentor at the completion celebration.

Delivery Issues Related to Program Size

The mode of delivery choices directly affects the potential size of your program, although delivery choice is not the sole determining factor. It is helpful to think about the relationship between mode of delivery and potential program size as a continuum. With the same level of resources, a paired e-mentoring program may be able to hire more mentors than a paired face-to-face program because of reduced costs in office space and coordination of services. With the same number of mentors and the same level of resources, a paired e-mentoring program could accommodate a larger number of mentees than a paired face-to-face program, simply because it would be easier to coordinate mentor-mentee meetings, allowing larger mentor-mentee caseloads, thus resulting in a larger program. With the same number of mentors, group mentoring programs, regardless of whether they are face-to-face or

Example of a Hybrid Program

The Freshman Inquiry program at Portland State University (www.pdx
.edu/unst/freshman-inquiry) uses targeted e-mails and an online library
of strategies for addressing freshman adjustment issues to supplement the
face-to-face mentoring new students received in their first-year general
education classes. The University Studies program uses data from a survey completed by all entering freshmen to identify three groups of potentially at-risk students: those with academic performance concerns, those
with financial concerns, and those whose demographic characteristics
(e.g., first-generation) suggest they might have difficulty in navigating
the university setting and understanding the culture of higher education.
These students then received weekly e-mails tailored to that group of
students' adjustment issues. The mentors working with each class of students are made aware of which of their students fall into each of the three
at-risk categories so that they can follow up with the students as needed.

The Freshman Inquiry program has also created UConnect, an online
library of potential student adjustment issues along with potential strategies for addressing each issue that incorporate text and videos of mentors
and more experienced students sharing their problem-solving strategies.
While UConnect is password protected, here is a link to the Students First
Success System, an earlier iteration that shares the same format and many
of the same resources (http://sfss.stage.rc.pdx.edu/). The site is divided
into three general categories, academic preparedness, Portland State University people and places, and financial and overall well-being. Sample
topics under each category are shown in the following table:

Academic Preparedness	Portland State University People and Places	Financial and Overall Well-Being
Communication with professors	Getting to know the campus	Student health and counseling
Picking classes	How to use the book-store	Financial aid
Importance of the syllabus	Writing center	Managing money
Studying for success	Joining a student group	Managing time
Dealing with procrastination	Using the library	Campus recreation

e-mentoring programs, should be able to accommodate a larger number of mentees than paired delivery-based programs because of the relatively larger case load in the number of students served for each mentor. Finally, with the same number of mentors and the same level of resources, a group e-mentoring program could accommodate a larger number of mentees than a group face-to-face program because of the coordination and scheduling advantages discussed earlier. These advantages should allow larger mentor-mentee case-loads that would result in a larger program.

This chapter focuses on issues associated with choices in how your program will deliver mentoring support to participants. It explores in detail the advantages and limitations of five different college student peer mentoring delivery approaches: paired face-to-face, group face-to-face, paired e-mentoring, group e-mentoring, and a hybrid. Reflecting the growing trend in the use of hybrid delivery approaches, this chapter offers suggestions on how incorporating e-mentoring elements into face-to-face-based delivery programs might address specific limitations of face-to-face programs and vice-versa. The chapter concludes with a discussion of how mode of delivery choices has an impact on the potential size of a program. The next chapter explores elements of program content that are common in college student peer mentoring programs.

CHAPTER 6 RESOURCES

Table 6.2 and Table 6.3 are visual aids to help you more easily compare the strengths and limitations of various forms of face-to-face and e-mentoring. Table 6.2 summarizes program-level strengths and limitations for each delivery format. Table 6.3 summarizes mentor-mentee interaction-level strengths and limitations for each delivery format.

Your final decision on which delivery format or formats you will use in your program should balance the specific issues you are trying to address with your available resources.

TABLE 6.2
Comparative Mode of Delivery Strengths and Limitations: Program-Level Issues

	Face-to-Face Pairs	Face-to-Face Groups	E-Mentoring Pairs	E-Mentoring Groups
Program administration	1. Coordinating physical space L. Will require the most effort to coordinate mentor-mentee meetings 2. Distributing mentee support materials L. Resource issue as program incurs costs associated with providing hard copies of resources for mentees	1. Coordinating physical space L. Will require some effort to coordinate mentor-mentee meetings, need large rooms, less effort than face-to-face pairs 2. Distributing mentee support materials L. Resource issue as program incurs costs associated with providing hard copies of resources for mentees	1. Coordinating physical space A. Do not have to coordinate physical space for mentor-mentee meetings 2. Distributing mentee support materials A. Mentee resources can be distributed as e-mail attachments or downloaded from virtual repositories 3. Costs L. Not a low-cost alternative; requires IT resources to develop the websites, Web-based resources, and software to facilitate data collection, evaluation, and management of online delivery systems 4. Matching L. Even more important in e-mentoring relationships to facilitate finding common ground to build relationships	1. Coordinating physical space A. Do not have to coordinate physical space for mentor-mentee meetings 2. Distributing mentee support materials A. Mentee resources can be distributed as e-mail attachments or downloaded from virtual repositories 3. Costs L. Not a low-cost alternative; requires IT resources to develop the websites, Web-based resources, and software to facilitate data collection, evaluation, and management of online delivery systems 4. Matching L. Even more important in e-mentoring relationships to facilitate finding common ground to build relationships

Program participation		
	5. Mentor training N. Need to practice teaching mentees how to use e-resources, need to prepare mentors to notice and respond appropriately to possible miscommunication issues, need to make mentors aware that use of abbreviated words and emoticons typically used in e-mail or texting may be problematic	5. Mentor training N. Need to practice teaching mentees how to use e-resources, need to prepare mentors to notice and respond appropriately to possible miscommunication issues, need to make mentors aware that use of abbreviated words and emoticons typically used in e-mail or texting may be problematic
	1. Facilitate early contact A. Allow early/preterm contact with mentees	1. Facilitate early contact A. Allow early/preterm contact with mentees
	2. Minimize negative labeling A. Can participate in mentoring relationships without negative labeling	2. Minimize negative labeling A. Can participate in mentoring relationships without negative labeling
3. Learn from others in program A. Mentees can learn from other mentees and other mentors, find out they are not the only students dealing with specific issues		3. Learn from others in program A. Mentees can learn from other mentees and other mentors, find out they are not the only students dealing with specific issues
		4. Encourage sharing concerns A. Some students may be more comfortable sharing concerns in relative anonymity of an e-discussion group as opposed to face-to-face or e-communication with personal mentor

(Continues)

Table 6.2 (Continued)

	Face-to-Face Pairs	Face-to-Face Groups	E-Mentoring Pairs	E-Mentoring Groups
				5. Works best for tech-savvy students L. Students who could benefit the most from info provided by group e-mentoring program are less likely to take advantage of opportunity because of lower level of comfort with technology
Availability of qualified mentors	1. Number of mentors L. Need larger number of mentors, limit potential number of mentees in program because of lack of qualified mentors	1. Number of mentors A. Need fewer mentors to serve same number of mentees	1. Number of mentors L. Need larger number of mentors, however this is less of an issue than in face-to-face program	1. Number of mentors A. Need fewer mentors to serve same number of mentees
			2. Interaction with scheduling flexibility A. Potential mentors with time constraints might still feel they can participate in e-mentoring program	2. Interaction with scheduling flexibility A. Potential mentors with time constraints might still feel they can participate in e-mentoring program
	3. Interaction with program size L. Need for larger number of mentors affects space, resources, mentor training, and program coordination		3. Interaction with program size L. Need for larger number of mentors affects space, resources, mentor training, and program coordination	
Scale		1. Serve more mentees A. Can serve larger number of mentees with fewer mentors		1. Serve more mentees A. Can serve larger number of mentees with fewer mentors

		2. Serve mentees beyond immediate campus A. Provides opportunity for peer mentoring for students in geographic locations where face-to-face programs are hard to get started
Availability of virtual networks	1. Students used to using existing networks A. Start with certain level of acceptance as virtual networks are already in place on college campuses and students are used to using them	1. Students used to using existing networks A. Start with certain level of acceptance as virtual networks are already in place on college campuses and students are used to using them
Location flexibility	1. Mentor from multiple locations A. Can communicate from any location where Internet access is available	1. Mentor from multiple locations A. Can communicate from any location where Internet access is available

Note. A = advantage; L = limitation; N = neutral but important point.

TABLE 6.3

Comparative Mode of Delivery Strengths and Limitations: Mentor-Mentee Interaction-Level Issues

	Face-to-Face Pairs	*Face-to-Face Groups*	*E-Mentoring Pairs*	*E-Mentoring Groups*
Communication	1. Nonverbal cues A. Can read nonverbal cues that convey warm and emotional support	1. Nonverbal cues A. Can read nonverbal cues that convey warm and emotional support	1. Nonverbal cues L. Increased likelihood of miscommunication because of lack of available information	1. Nonverbal cues L. Increased likelihood of miscommunication because of lack of available information
	2. Tech-based miscommunication A. Reduced chance of miscommunication because of tech-associated transmission error	2. Tech-based miscommunication A. Reduced chance of miscommunication because of tech-associated transmission error	2. Tech-based miscommunication L. Increased chance of miscommunication because of tech-associated transmission errors such as messages misidentified as spam or systems that are out of service	2. Tech-based miscommunication L. Increased chance of miscommunication because of tech-associated transmission errors such as messages misidentified as spam or systems that are out of service
			3. Asynchronous communication A. Both parties don't need to be online at the same time to communicate	3. Asynchronous communication A. Both parties don't need to be online at the same time to communicate
			4. Flexibility in terms of timing of communication A. Messages can be sent whenever mentor or mentee has the time to do so	4. Flexibility in terms of timing of communication A. Messages can be sent whenever mentor or mentee has the time to do so
			5. More candid communication A. Mentees may be more open as social markers, e.g., sex, race, class, are not visible	5. More candid communication A. Mentees may be more open as social markers, e.g, sex, race, class, are not visible

	8. Duration of attention A. Using nonverbal cues like eye contact and head nodding that serve to maintain conversations and hold mentees' attention	8. Duration of attention A. Using nonverbal cues like eye contact and head nodding that serve to maintain conversations and hold mentees' attention	6. More time to think about response A. Composing message on keyboard allows more thoughtful responses that are associated with reflection and scaffolding 7. Provides record A. Mentees have record of communication they can refer back to 8. Duration of attention L. Students may skim or ignore messages that are longer than one page 9. Unrealistic expectations L. Lack of contextual cues may lead to unrealistic expectations about how quickly responses should be received. Similarly, mentors' easier access to Internet may lead to misattribution of mentees' slow response time
			6. More time to think about response A. Composing message on keyboard allows more thoughtful responses that are associated with reflection and scaffolding 7. Provides record A. Mentees have record of communication they can refer back to 8. Duration of attention L. Students may skim or ignore messages that are longer than one page 9. Unrealistic expectations L. Lack of contextual cues may lead to unrealistic expectations about how quickly responses should be received. Similarly, mentors' easier access to Internet may lead to misattribution of mentees' slow response time
Persuasiveness	1. Greater persuasiveness A. Shown to produce a greater impact than same message delivered in other modes	1. Greater persuasiveness A. Shown to produce a greater impact than same message delivered in other modes	

(Continues)

Table 6.3 (Continued)

	Face-to-Face Pairs	Face-to-Face Groups	E-Mentoring Pairs	E-Mentoring Groups
Commitment	1. Commitment to action A. Produces relatively higher level of mentee commitment to mentor-proposed action steps	1. Commitment to action A. Produces relatively higher level of mentee commitment to mentor-proposed action steps		
	2. Breaking ties to program A. Harder for a mentee to disengage from the commitment (effect strongest in pairs)	2. Breaking ties to program A. Harder for a mentee to disengage from the commitment	2. Breaking ties to program L. Informal nature of e-mail communication makes it easier for mentees to disengage and leave program	2. Breaking ties to program L. Informal nature of e-mail communication makes it easier for mentees to disengage and leave program
		3. Cohort effect A. Promote cohort effect among group of mentees, increasing commitment		
			4. Interaction with communication, nonverbal cues L. Takes more time and effort to build relationship necessary to keep mentees committed to program because of lack of nonverbal reinforcing communication cues	4. Interaction with communication, nonverbal cues L. Takes more time and effort to build relationship necessary to keep mentees committed to program because of lack of nonverbal reinforcing communication cues
	5. Interaction with evaluation A. Higher commitment makes it harder for mentee to refuse to complete evaluation L. Mentees may be less willing to share negative feedback on program or mentor	5. Interaction with evaluation A. Higher commitment makes it harder for mentee to refuse to complete evaluation L. Mentees may be less willing to share negative feedback on program or mentor	5. Interaction with evaluation L. Easier for mentee to decline evaluation A. May be easier to get mentees to share negative feedback about program or mentor	5. Interaction with evaluation L. Easier for mentee to decline evaluation A. May be easier to get mentees to share negative feedback about program or mentor

Timeliness of addressing student adjustment issues	1. Delivery of time-sensitive information to mentees regardless of meeting schedule A. Mentors can follow a schedule of when specific issue-related messages need to be sent out to mentees regardless of when next mentor-mentee meeting is scheduled	1. Delivery of time-sensitive information to mentees regardless of meeting schedule A. Mentors can follow a schedule of when specific issue-related messages need to be sent out to mentees regardless of when next mentor-mentee meeting is scheduled
Prerequisite skills	1. Requires a foundational level of computer literacy L. Not all students possess same levels of computer skills	1. Requires a foundational level of computer literacy L. Not all students possess same levels of computer skills
	2. Depends upon students having Internet access L. Not all students have home Internet access, could make them campus dependent, which reduces e-mentoring flexibility advantages	2. Depends upon students having Internet access L. Not all students have home Internet access, could make them campus dependent, which reduces e-mentoring flexibility advantages
	3. Interaction with social class L. Poorer students more likely to use phones for Internet access, harder to download resources, slower downloads (DSL versus cable; less likely to have Web cams and capacity to use video conferencing software like Skype)	3. Interaction with social class L. Poorer students more likely to use phones for Internet access, harder to download resources, slower downloads (DSL versus cable; less likely to have Web cams and capacity to use video conferencing software like Skype)

Note. A = advantage; L = limitation; N = neutral but important point.

Vignette 3

TRANSFER STUDENT-FOCUSED PROGRAM

Transfer Connections Program

Phil Larsen, Lydia Middleton, and Adam Baker, University of Michigan

TABLE V3.1

Inclusiveness	Duration	Approach to Addressing Students' Needs	College Transition
Tailored: *Designed for a specific audience* *New transfer students in College of Literature, Science, and Arts*	Short term: *One semester or less* *First semester*	Developmental: *Responds to student needs as they evolve over time*	Two-year to four-year college *(primary)* Four-year to four-year college *(secondary)* One educational system to another *(secondary)*

Transfer Connections is a year-long peer mentoring program that provides incoming transfer students with support and guidance during their critical first year at the University of Michigan (U-M), a highly selective, academically challenging institution. The program is coordinated by the Office of New Student Programs.

Located in Ann Arbor, U-M consists of 19 schools and colleges with emphasis on liberal arts and science, technology, engineering, and mathematics. U-M offers nearly 250 degree programs as well as master's, doctoral, and professional degrees. Undergraduate student enrollment as of fall 2013 was 28,283. Roughly 60% of U-M undergraduate students are from the state of Michigan.

Participants

Transfer Connections initially targeted community college transfer students entering U-M's College of Literature, Science, and the Arts (LSA). However, it became clear that LSA transfer students from four-year institutions and international students were also interested in participating in this program. There is an application and evaluation process for participants to enter the program. Each summer and fall semester we begin the recruitment, application, and admissions processes. We use Qualtrics survey software (Qualtrics, 2013) to collect basic demographic information (e.g., age, residency, previous institution attended, expected major/minor), as well as short-answer question responses to gain an in-depth understanding of each applicant. Sample short-answer questions include, What are you most excited about/most concerned about as a transfer student? and How do you think Transfer Connections will enable your success at the University of Michigan? This is a highly competitive program; Transfer Connections had an estimated 42% acceptance rate for fall 2013. To fairly evaluate each applicant, we focus on the following key variables:

1. Demonstrated need for Transfer Connections. Is student first generation or underrepresented minority? Is student transferring from similar or significantly different university/environment compared to U-M?
2. Effort and thought put forth in application. Did student take time to thoughtfully answer application questions?
3. Evidence of commitment and continued participation in program. Does student anticipate being involved in extracurricular activities? Did student mention future involvement as a mentor?

Our participant cap has steadily increased throughout the program with an initial 31 participants for fall of 2008 to a high of 84 students matched in fall 2012. The application is also used to match the student with our Transfer Connections Mentors (TCMs).

TCMs

TCMs are hired for the academic year (fall and spring semesters) and are paid $9.50 per hour. Work hours are defined as office time, typically six to eight hours per week, and individual monthly meetings with mentees, the length of which can vary widely between semesters. The program started with four TCMs but that number was increased to the current level of six because of increased demand for the program. TCMs must be recent transfer students, academically successful, personable, welcoming to students of diverse backgrounds, and knowledgeable about campus resources and the obstacles transfer students face. TCMs are selected by a process that includes reviews of a written applications and individual interviews.

What Transfer Connections Attempts to Address

The overall goal of Transfer Connections is to facilitate student success in the rigorous academic climate at U-M. In Transfer Connections, we define *academic success* as academic retention past the first semester, along with increased knowledge of campus resources and feelings of belonging on campus. Transfer Connections provides opportunities for new U-M transfer students to connect with peer mentors to ease the transition process. Transfer Connections provides support and guidance and helps students build new relationships on campus. All TCMs have experienced acclimating to the same academic, social, and cultural environments the mentees now face. The role of our mentors is to share what they have learned along the way.

Evolution of Transfer Connections

Transfer Connections was initially funded by a grant through the Jack Kent Cooke Community College Transfer Initiative at U-M. The idea of Transfer Connections came from U-M transfer students themselves. Planning for the program started in December 2007 with an anticipated rollout in fall 2008. Group mentoring and events were at the center of the model. Mentors were to communicate, offer resources, and plan activities in their individually assigned groups. One-on-one mentor-mentee meetings were not mandatory.

Program activities mainly consisted of social events and small-group talks with the mentors.

Participation rates were extremely low during the program's first semester, especially for the coffee-hour style group-facilitation events designed to be the main socialization and mentor interaction opportunities. The group and mentor interactions, designed to organically occur, were not happening as frequently as anticipated.

As the program progressed in subsequent years, the group facilitation events were replaced with a series of structured interviews, the topics of which were determined in advance by the program manager. These interviews were adapted from a program originally developed at the University of South Carolina's First Year Experience and Students in Transition program, and further refined at Arkansas State and Ohio State Universities. At these interview sessions, each TCM and his or her mentees would talk about current concerns and then have a semidirected discussion on topics such as social integration and campus involvement, academic aspirations and achievement, campus resource direction, and personal responsibility.

When the Student Success Initiative (SSI), a tool designed to serve the needs of transfer students, was integrated into Transfer Connections in 2009, the program emphasis shifted from group mentoring to one-on-one delivery of mentoring support (for an example of an SSI, see Chapter 8, pp. 273–274). Mentors were asked to meet one-on-one with their mentees once a month throughout the semester, during which time mentors followed the SSI as an outline to their meetings. This ensured that key transfer student transition points were being highlighted and discussed throughout the regular one-on-one meetings. These motivational interviews serve as the core element of Transfer Connections today and are regularly adapted to meet incoming students' needs. In addition, Transfer Connections provides additional mentoring at academic and social events. Each month the program hosts events ranging from coffee-hour style socials, to more academic and structured events, such as a how not to waste your first summer at U-M workshop. This event is cohosted by our partner program, University Mentorship, which provides resources and guidance for summer employment as well as volunteer and internship opportunities.

Evaluation: How We Measure Program Success

Program success is measured in several different ways. Almost all the students who begin Transfer Connection complete the full year program. However we do not track retention data after the program ends as the program is designed to support transitions from students' former institutions to the University of Michigan during their first year only.

One program-emphasized dimension of student success is knowledge of campus resources. Transfer Connection mentees complete entrance and exit resource-knowledge surveys. Comparisons of the data from the two surveys consistently find improved postprogram levels of resource knowledge compared to where they were when students began the program. Program success is primarily measured by the testimonials we receive from students in focus groups and discussions. Mentees are also asked in the exit surveys whether the experience of Transfer Connections has specifically addressed their needs as transfer students. Mentee evaluation of their program experiences is very favorable. In addition, we examine the effectiveness of particular program elements by a series of satisfaction surveys sent out after each workshop, social event, or group activity. Mentee satisfaction survey responses are generally positive, and activities that receive poor evaluations are either dropped or modified in subsequent years.

Program supervisors review and assess the mentor-compiled motivational interview notes. Mentors also submit postevent reflection pieces for each group activity they develop and lead, including the results of the online mentee satisfaction surveys. The reflection is a way to record relevant details about the event, as well as the mentor's learning process over the course of the assignment.

With the entrance and exit surveys, postevent reflections paint a full picture of the kinds of services Transfer Connections delivers and whether they are useful to participants. The straightforward individual feedback in the surveys allows us to measure change in their knowledge over time and the extent to which Transfer Connections has affected their ability to navigate campus resources and student life.

The first year of a Transfer Connections postprogram focus group was in 2014. All mentors along with several mentees were invited to participate in a group dialogue that allowed them to offer honest and direct feedback about their experiences. The main suggestion that emerged from the 2014 group was that the program should develop an alumni network of former Transfer Connections mentees who could offer support and additional informal mentoring for current mentees.

The program manager stores and reviews all feedback with the Office of New Student Program (ONSP) Mentorship Programs director and collaboratively determines the ways this information will be incorporated in training sessions, planning, and overall development of Transfer Connections. Over the years, the evaluations have become benchmarks for creating a program that adapts to each incoming group of mentees and is influenced by the unique perspectives and experiences of our mentors and mentees.

Preparing Successful TCMs

The TCM Trainings are interactive workshops led by the program manager that prepare TCMs for their roles not only as mentors but also as program coordinators and ONSP staff. Trainings occur in spring and fall. Trainings begin by making mentors-to-be aware of their specific program responsibilities. They are asked to reflect on their role as mentors, respond to scenarios as a problem-solving activity, and set goals for their work with mentees in the fall. Prior-year mentors share advice, tips for success, and strategies for effective mentoring in the context of working with transfer students. The Transfer Connections program manager supervises mini workshops on effective communication, resource finding, and active listening. This is also an opportunity for mentors to get to know one another and begin to work together as a team.

Mentor Training Evaluation

Transfer Connections' mentor training evaluation is mainly formative assessment. The program staff solicits mentor feedback at multiple junctures during the semester about the effectiveness of training and any additional resources or training elements that should be included in subsequent years. The program manager and ONSP mentorship programs director collaborate to use one year's mentor feedback to develop an appropriate curriculum for the next year's training.

The Road Ahead for Transfer Connections

In the future, Transfer Connections plans to expand to accept all transfer students so that students enrolled in 12 other undergraduate schools and colleges (e.g., music, theatre and dance, nursing, kinesiology, pharmacy, Ross School of Business) will also have the opportunity to apply. The only exception will be the School of Engineering, which has its own program for incoming transfer students. We began promoting and giving special consideration to students coming from community colleges starting in 2014 to further diversify and expand the program. We are also working to develop specific programming for international transfer students.

We hope to collaborate with the International Center and our experienced international transfer mentees and mentors to create a workshop that explores ways to support international students beyond traditional socializing and resource-finding activities. Finally, we are considering ways to offer programs, activities, and mentoring specially designed for first-generation students, of whom many are also transfer students. In this way, we hope a wider population of nontraditional students may access Transfer Connections.

Transfer Connections will also work to improve the experiences of our TCMs. Moving forward, we plan to put more emphasis on staff development. We could use the TCM position to provide students with opportunities to improve and enhance their skillsets through trainings, activities, and reflection. It is hoped that the skills TCMs acquire over the course of their employment will further their own intrinsic and extrinsic goals after graduation.

7

WHAT CONTENT MATERIALS WILL YOU SHARE WITH MENTEES?

While there are some universal content elements, others are program specific. Regardless of the focus of your program, you should organize the content you provide in ways that facilitate retention, recall, and future high-quality mentee decision making.

Chapter 7

- explores three essential program content areas—universal content, content shared by programs that all serve the same group of students, and program-specific content;
- identifies communication issues related to whom to contact to get key questions answered, when the best time is to contact faculty, and choice of the appropriate communication medium;
- reviews standpoint theory and considers how differences in perspective affect students' understanding of identical issues;
- considers the value of service-learning and providing mentees with opportunities to "pay it forward";
- discusses methods of organizing information to facilitate mentee recall;
- shares how to organize college student adjustment issue information to facilitate better mentee decision making; and
- reflects on the benefits of sequencing program content to mirror mentee development.

If you can't explain it simply, you don't understand it well enough.

(Einstein, 2015a)

Knowledge is of no value unless you put it into practice.

(Chekhov, 2015)

All college student peer mentoring programs draw from several common content areas. However, the details of the material in each content area may vary significantly from one program to another. Some universal content areas are consistent across programs, such as understanding fundamental college student adjustment issues, cross-cultural sensitivity and diversity issues, and the value of service. Another set of content areas is group specific. The same content is consistently found among programs that all serve the same group of students such as returning women, first-generation and international students, and student veterans. Group-specific content typically includes materials relating to that group's college adjustment issues, such as helping international students understand U.S. faculty members' class participation expectations. This type of content also includes resources for locating and appropriately using group-specific resources, such as assisting student veterans in learning about veterans' center services. A final group of content areas tends to be program specific, such as what to expect in the mentor-mentee relationship and how to appropriately use program resources. Figure 7.1 shows how these three types of content overlap.

Figure 7.1   Venn Diagram of Content

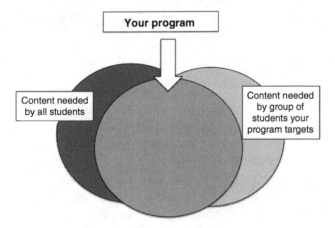

Content Areas That Are Consistent Across Programs

The usual content in all peer mentoring programs includes fundamental student adjustment issues such as negotiating the campus bureaucracy; identifying and appropriately using resources; and developing communication skills, cross-cultural sensitivity, and material on the value of service. For ideas about additional possible universal content materials, see Chapter 7 Resources, page 216.

Fundamental College Student Adjustment Issues

Chapter 3 discusses several fundamental adjustment issues all college students must address. The act of participating in a mentoring program helps mentees feel more connected to others at your college and increases their sense of belonging. Program activities discussed in Chapter 5, such as regular meetings with mentors, shared meals, and social events for students in the program, all contribute to increasing your mentees' sense of belonging and connection to your program and your college. The amount of emphasis your program puts on some issues, such as financial situations or poor precollege preparation, depends on the goals of your program and the educational transition the students you serve are experiencing. However, all students, regardless of the educational transition they are negotiating, need program support related to universal adjustment issues such as time management, maintaining personal well-being, understanding the culture of the university, and identifying and appropriately using relevant campus resources. Finding campus resources and understanding the culture of the university are particularly important.

Understanding the culture of the university content elements includes learning how to negotiate the campus bureaucracy and how to be a successful college student.

Negotiating the Campus Bureaucracy

Mentees need reliable and up-to-date information on how to successfully navigate their colleges' bureaucracies, regardless of which educational transition they are experiencing. Specific elements of negotiating the campus bureaucracy include securing appropriate advising, developing an educational plan, registering or withdrawing from classes, determining how to check academic records, managing financial aid awards, and learning how to complete important forms (e.g., Free Application for Federal Student Aid forms, scholarship applications) as well as meeting form submission deadlines.

Learning how to be a successful college student is a multifaceted process. Mentees need help deciphering professors' expectations, learning how to take personal responsibility for their own education, and figuring out where to turn for help. It is important to note that what it takes to be a successful student varies from one context to another. That means even when your program serves relatively more experienced students (e.g., transfer students, new graduate students) they will still need help recognizing and responding appropriately to the new standards associated with their current transition.

It can be very difficult for students to let go of strategies associated with previous understandings of the student role that once worked as opposed to adapting to new expectations. International students moving from one educational system to another can be very resistant to U.S. university expectations of class participation and critical thinking. Some may retreat to preferring the way their home educational system works without acknowledging that they are no longer in their home system. Many community college transfer students insist on trying to use the standards of their previous school, even after they've transferred to the university. Similarly, many new graduate students try to hold on to the undergraduate standard of judging academic progress based on course grades, even when the timeliness of completing a thesis or dissertation is the more appropriate criterion of graduate program progress.

Mentors can facilitate transitioning students' efforts to deal with these changes in several ways. First, they can help mentees recognize the new expectations by explaining how and why the standards are different. In addition, mentors can encourage mentees to put aside old problem-solving strategies for more appropriate ones.

Identifying and Appropriately Using Relevant Campus Resources

Content areas associated with finding and using campus resources appropriately include learning how to identify which resources are available, how to know where to look for this information, and how to use each resource. There is also an overlap with understanding college adjustment issues as mentees need to learn which campus resources are appropriate for addressing specific college adjustment issues. There is also an overlap with learning the college student role in that mentees need to learn which strategies are most appropriate to employ when using a specific campus resource to address a specific college adjustment issue.

A good exercise to help your mentees connect specific campus resources with different student adjustment issues is a campus resource treasure hunt. Explain to your mentees that the treasure they are trying to find is a collection

Exercise 7.1   Campus Resource Treasure Hunt

Preparation

Step 1. Create a list of campus resources you've identified as important for your mentees.

Step 2. Develop a series of short scenarios that ask mentees to address specific student adjustment issues using campus resources. It is a good idea to ask your mentors to help develop scenarios specific to the campus resources you've identified as important for your mentees to be familiar with.

Step 3. With your mentors, develop program-recommended appropriate strategies for using campus resources to address the issue presented in each scenario.

Working With Mentees

Step 4. Have each mentor pick one scenario and share it with his or her mentee. The mentor then asks the mentee how he or she would proceed to address the issue and which campus resource might be used to do so.

Step 5. Have each mentor-mentee pair discuss the mentee's response to the issue presented in the scenario. It is important that mentors reinforce mentees' appropriate problem-solving responses as well as provide input when mentees propose less-than-optimal solutions. This is also an opportunity for the mentor to discuss with the mentee how the proposed solution might also apply to solving other issues.

Step 6. Repeat for as many of your program-developed scenarios as the pair has time to complete. The following are some sample scenarios you can modify and use:

- In one of your classes, you are assigned to write a 25-page research paper that is *the* major project that will determine your grade for this term. Your teacher has given you a list of guidelines but you are not sure how to begin. What are *two* places where you could get help?
- You need to access a computer to print out your paper that is due for your next class. Where would you go to find out where

> computer labs are located and which one is the least busy at this moment?
>
> - Your mother, who has been watching your four-year-old son while you are in classes, has gotten a new job out of town and has to move. How can you use the resources available here on campus to resolve your child care issue? If there is more than one option, what are the differences between them?
> - You went to community college in another part of the state, and you loved to go kayaking and white-water rafting with your friends whenever you had any time off. Now you are at the university, you don't know anyone who kayaks or rafts, and you don't have your own equipment. Where would you go to connect with other students who enjoy the same things you do? How would you go about getting equipment?

of campus resources that can help them deal with important student adjustment issues.

This exercise can be repeated at different times throughout the program to coincide with when you think mentees need resources to address specific issues. For example, assisting mentees with finding resources to help plan their schedules for next year probably belongs near the end of the program year rather than when mentees are just beginning the program.

Communicating Effectively

Program content needs to be designed to support mentees in regard to several different communication-related issues. Mentees need information to help them understand when to communicate with professors and other university personnel. They also need to understand what office hours are for and how to prepare to make the most of the opportunity to communicate one-on-one with their professors. Mentees should be encouraged to ask their professors for clarification of course assignments rather than relying on other students who may or may not correctly understand the assignment.

You can facilitate this process by providing mentees with starting questions to break the ice in conversations with faculty members. The following are useful starting questions: Could you explain this section of the syllabus to me? Do you have examples of this assignment from past classes that I could look at? and Do you have any tips for me about things I could do to improve my chances of doing well in your class? When mentees initiate a conversation with a professor with an appropriate question, it reinforces the mentee's claim of being a legitimate college student.

Mentees need to know whom they need to communicate with to address different adjustment issues or get specific questions answered. Programs need to provide mentees with information about when is it appropriate to try to get a question answered by a professor, mentor, university staff member, or another student. This information needs to be linked to larger program-level discussions about the best way to address specific adjustment issues. When it comes to getting help with a family crisis or a substance-abuse-related problem, a counselor from student health services is a much more appropriate source of information than either a faculty member or a mentor.

Another communication-related content element has to do with helping mentees understand which is the most appropriate way to communicate in different situations. This is part of understanding the university culture. Program content should help mentees understand, for example, when face-to-face interaction with a professor is required and under what conditions it is optional.

Mentees also need help in figuring out how to appropriately address the individuals teaching their classes. A mentor told the following story.

> A first-generation student approached his young female professor in an introductory class and tried to use what he thought was the most politically correct language he could think of. He began his question, "Excuse me, Ms. Johnson," to which the professor replied, "That's *Doctor* Johnson." Embarrassed, the student left without ever asking the question. When he complained to his mentor about the rudeness of the professor, the mentor explained to him that there is still a lot of sexism in higher education and that young female professors many times have to use their professional title (Doctor or Professor) in interactions with students or some male students will not treat the professor with the respect that they would normally show to a male professor.

The student had made an incorrect interpretation of the professor's behavior. The mentor used this as a teachable moment and also provided the mentee with a strategy to reduce the likelihood of that disturbing situation happening again. The mentor advised her mentee to "address every person who is teaching your class as Professor or Doctor unless that person indicates they prefer to be addressed differently." That way, if the person teaching the class is a graduate student or instructor without a PhD, he or she will probably be flattered and then politely correct the student. Even more important, the mentee is not perceived as rude when he did not intend to be. Encouraging mentees to use this strategy eliminates the problem of misidentifying a professor as a nonprofessor simply because of the person's age. New students may correlate age with seniority of position, but in higher education that is not always so.

Cross-Cultural Sensitivity or Diversity Issues

Diversity issues involve understanding marginalization and privilege. Depending on the group of students your program targets, your mentees may be very aware of feelings of marginalization associated with group membership (e.g., social class, race or ethnicity, first generation, immigrant, returning veteran) in higher education and the larger community. Sometimes they may be aware of feelings of marginalization associated with experiences outside school but have not yet experienced the same feelings of inequality at their colleges and universities. However, your mentees may be much less aware of the privilege they enjoy compared to different groups and how that privilege affects their own and other students' college experiences.

Perspective is crucial to unpacking and understanding privilege. Kathy Kelly (2011) notes, "What we see depends on where we stand." This is an example of what has been called the Rashômon effect (Roth & Mehta, 2002). The famous Japanese director Akira Kurosawa's 1950 film *Rashômon* explores four different accounts of the fatal attack on a Japanese nobleman and the subsequent rape of his wife. The viewer is asked to decide which of the narrators is telling the truth and even if a single objective truth exists. Kurosawa makes it clear these are not necessarily completely self-serving accounts as each narrator implicates himself or herself as the murderer. Yet all the narrators somehow convince themselves that their own account represents an objective truth.

Standpoint theory (Harding, 1987; Smith, 1987) offers a helpful framework for understanding the ways memberships in various identification groups situate individuals to perceive the world. Feminist sociologist Dorothy Smith (1987, 2005) contends that the only way we can understand the world is through the social lens provided by group membership. The three main elements to standpoint theory are, first, there is no objective knowledge; second, no two people have exactly the same standpoint because even if they belong to the same groups, they have not had the same experiences; and third, individuals should not take their standpoint for granted, since everyone else does not view the social world in the same way (Barnett, 2009, pp. 186–187). Standpoint theory draws attention to the ways individuals are empowered and privileged through their membership in certain groups (i.e., occupying agent status) as well as the ways the same individuals lack privilege and access to power because of their membership in other groups (i.e., occupying target status). Individuals can occupy agent and target statuses at the same time.

It is important for your program to help mentees recognize that regardless of how they feel marginalized by first-generation, nondominant group, immigrant, transfer, or nonnative student status, they still enjoy privileged social locations in other dimensions. Mentors can use one-on-one and group discussions along with written reflection exercises to help mentees imagine how other groups experience higher education. It is helpful for mentees when they realize students from other groups share some of the same issues they do but also face issues the mentees have not even considered as problems. When students adopt the unquestioned position their perspectives are true and appropriate for everyone else regardless of the situation, they risk imposing biased solutions on others even though their agent or target status may be different from that of the other students. Mentoring programs can help mentees better understand the complexities of higher education and build social connections by helping mentees move beyond focusing on their disadvantages to interacting with other students in the same way they wish to be treated (for a more in-depth discussion of the application of standpoint theory to college students see Cress, Collier, & Reitenauer, 2013, pp. 81–91).

The Value of Service

Another important program content area involves helping mentees understand the value of service. As a pedagogical approach, service-learning is often linked to academic courses. However peer mentoring programs and other extracurricular activities can be very appropriate vehicles for providing students with the benefits associated with service-learning. Compared to volunteerism that solely focuses on meeting community needs, service-learning meets community needs while at the same time empowering students and providing them with opportunities to apply their knowledge and skills in real-world settings (Kretchmar, 2001; Prentice & Garcia, 2000; Schmidt, Marks, & Derrico, 2004).

Identified benefits of service-learning participation include

- improving student satisfaction with college and the likelihood of graduation (Eyler, Giles, Stenson, & Gray, 2001),
- promoting active learning that increases students' motivation to learn and engagement in the learning process (Gray, Ondaatje, Fricker, & Geshwind, 2000, p. 31),
- affecting students' sense of personal efficacy, interpersonal development, and ability to work well with others (Cress et al., 2010; Eyler et al., 2001),
- improving critical thinking and communication skills (Cress et al., 2013, p. 17; Eyler et al., 2001),

- reducing stereotypes and facilitating cultural and racial understanding (Cress et al., 2013, p. 17; Eyler et al., 2001), and
- acquiring broader life skills needed for effectively making the transition into adult roles and responsibilities (Cress et al., 2010; Eyler, Giles, & Braxton, 1999; Fenzel & Peyrot, 2005).

In addition, working with community partners makes students reevaluate their abstract ideas about societal and political problems (Cress et al., 2013, p. 18).

An example of integrating service-learning into a peer mentoring program is the Student Mentors Inspiring Latino Excellence (SMILE) program at Portland State University (PSU) (2007–2010). This program connected college, high school, and middle school students and exemplified how program design allowed mentees to benefit on multiple levels from serving as mentors to others. Initially the SMILE project director mentored a group of college students. Then the college students mentored Latina/Latino high school students who then mentored Latina/Latino middle school students. The overarching goal of SMILE was to create a web of support to keep middle and high school students in school and to encourage them to attend college while providing leadership opportunities for high school and college students. Community service activities (e.g., community art and neighborhood cleanup projects) were built in at each level of the program as part of an effort to connect students at all levels with the larger community and to provide an avenue for students to pay forward the support they received in the program to others in their communities (J. Padin, personal communication, April 17, 2014).

Another example of the benefits of service for college student mentees involved students in the Louis Stokes Alliance for Minority Participation (LSAMP) program at PSU. Starting in the summer and fall of 2011, LSAMP mentees went to local high schools to mentor underrepresented high school students and help them work on original science research projects. The completed projects were subsequently entered in the Intel-sponsored Northwest Science Exposition System regional science fair. In addition to helping the high school students, LSAMP scholars benefited by applying skills and concepts learned in their LSAMP mentoring workshop, building bridges between their PSU course work and a science classroom, and getting to share community and opportunity with students like themselves. The LSAMP students visited the high schools once or twice a week, and wrote reflections on their mentoring experiences (L. Tran, personal communication, April 18, 2014).

The skills and knowledge about college adjustment issues mentees are acquiring in your program make them ideal candidates to mentor students who are anticipating making the same educational transition that your program focuses on. Mentees who are participating in a program to help community college students make the transition to the university are excellent spokespeople for reaching community college students considering transfer who have not yet made that transition. First-year graduate students who are being mentored by more experienced graduate students are credible sources for how to succeed in graduate school for undergraduates preparing to enroll in graduate school the next year. International students who are completing an international student–focused mentoring program are perfect mentors for the next wave of new international students.

Your mentees have acquired skills and cognitive capacities in your program. You can strengthen the depth of their learning by offering them opportunities to apply those skills and knowledge. Mentees might like an opportunity to give back to others. Providing students with opportunities where they can help others may make it easier for them to accept and act on the help they need from their mentors. For service-learning exercises and activities you can adapt to use in your program, see Cress et al., 2013.

Content of Programs That Serve the Same Targeted Groups

Shifting to the level of shared content among programs that target the same specific subgroups of students (e.g., first-generation students, student veterans), one important element is providing mentees with information about the adjustment issues particularly relevant to their group.

Identifying Group-Relevant Campus Resources

You can identify group-specific issues by referring to the research you did on your targeted groups' issues before you proposed your mentoring program, the issues discussions in Chapter 3, and the issues identified in your program needs assessment (see Chapter 4). However, it is not enough just to identify these issues. Your program content should also provide your mentees with enough background information so they can understand which college adjustment issues are common to all incoming students and which ones are more important for them and other students from their group to understand how to address appropriately.

Appropriately Using Group-Relevant Campus Resources

You should approach finding and using campus resources appropriately in a similar manner. Programs serving targeted groups of students need to help their mentees identify, find, and appropriately use the same key campus resources (e.g., tutoring center, library) that all students need to be familiar with. However, in addition, targeted programs need to familiarize mentees with campus resources that are valuable for dealing with their group's particular college adjustment issues (e.g., helping student veterans locate and connect with the VA office).

Program-Specific Content

Program-specific content areas include helping mentees learn how to use program resources appropriately, ensuring mentees understand program expectations for mentees and mentors, and instructing mentees in how to participate in evaluation efforts.

Using Program Resources

Mentees need information about how to access and apply program materials that explain how to use campus resources appropriately. Many e-mentoring and hybrid programs store mentee support resources related to locating and using campus resources in online libraries or repositories. Your program content should include information on accessing resource-related materials regardless of whether you create your own library of materials or plan on using existing campus resources. Program content should also include instructions on how to use resources that deal with specific issues as well as how to access the needed support materials. This resource-related content could take the form of tips on how to navigate the program library or more detailed instructions about where to find relevant campus resources on the university's website. Either way, you must assume that your mentees do not understand why each resource is relevant to dealing with specific issues or how to use those resources.

You need to not only link resources to specific adjustment issues, but also provide mentees with information about when they are most likely to encounter the corresponding issues. Just telling mentees that a certain resource is important to use when addressing a particular issue and how to use it is not enough. Your program needs to provide mentees with exercises that allow them to practice using the identified resources. Practice makes perfect.

Understanding Program Expectations

Communicating expectations for mentees is an important program-specific content element. Plan on reinforcing some of the materials you introduced during mentee orientation. Clearly spell out role rules for mentors and mentees.

Example of Program Expectations for Mentees

Mentees are expected to do the following:

1. Communicate in a regular and timely manner.
2. Honor your word, follow through on your commitments.
3. Be personally engaged in your education, take responsibility for your own learning.
4. Keep up with the work in your classes. Plan on studying at least two hours for every hour of seat time.
5. Use program resources to address issues.
6. Treat your mentor with respect.
7. Be honest in dealing with mentors, program staff, and other mentees.

Mentors also need to explicitly state what they will and will not be able to do for the mentee.

Mentors and mentees should role-play key campus interactions, such as meeting with a professor during office hours for the first time, planning a schedule with an adviser, or finding help locating materials at the library. Mentors should also practice with mentees how to access online resource websites or videos.

You also need to provide some program-specific communication guidelines. Mentors and mentees should exchange contact information and discuss which mode of communication (e.g., in person, e-mail, or phone) might work best under which conditions. It is important for mentees to know how to contact their mentors if unexpected issues arise. At the same time, the mentees must clearly understand the communication expectations of their mentors, which might include making weekly contact at a specific day of the week and time, giving advance notice if a meeting will be missed, or sending a courtesy text or calling if the mentee is running late for a scheduled mentor appointment. Some programs include these communication-related expectations in the mentor-mentee contract discussed in Chapter 5.

Participating in Evaluation

A final program-specific content area has to do with preparing your mentees so they can participate in your scheduled evaluation activities. It is important to impress upon mentees the importance of doing their part in regard to program evaluation.

If you plan to collect mentees' reflections on different experiences in your program, then part of program content needs to help them understand the value of reflection and how to do it meaningfully. Mentors could initially guide mentees to reflectively consider recent experiences through a series of verbal prompts as part of their regular meetings. Then mentees could be asked to follow a similar series of questions on their own to reflect on subsequent experiences.

In the same way, a program that uses a pre- or postprogram online survey exploring mentees' strategies for addressing specific adjustment issues might prepare mentees for end-of-program evaluation activities through specific program activities. One approach might be to have mentors work out strategies for what-if scenarios with their mentees at regular meetings. Another possible approach for online or hybrid programs might be to send out regular issue-specific materials on good, better, and best strategies as part of the regular program e-mail listserv.

In the end, it is important that identified mentee needs, program goals, and the content you share with mentees are conceptually and practically connected. For example, imagine that a major need of the group of students you serve is that they are at a relative disadvantage in recognizing college adjustment issues and responding appropriately. One of the program goals, then, is to help mentees better understand their important adjustment issues and respond in ways that maximize their likelihood of success. Program content would emphasize recognizing important adjustment issues, useful campus resources, and the best strategies for addressing each issue. Content would also include information about when each issue would most likely need to be addressed. This then would connect with your mentor training (see Chapter 8) and how you evaluate whether your program actually met this goal (see Chapter 9).

Content Packaging Strategies

Regardless of the content presented to mentees in your program, it is important to consider the organization of that material. How material is packaged and presented can facilitate or limit student learning and the application of information.

Organizing Information About Campus Resources

You can use the process of organizing content for better recall when you share information on campus resources with your mentees. Almost every college student peer mentoring program includes an aspect of helping mentees identify important campus resources. While some campus resources are important for all students, the value of other resources differs depending on the group of students your program serves and the issues they are facing. As the program developer, you can package important pertinent information about a campus resource in a way that facilitates recall and subsequent memory searches.

It is helpful to organize information about each resource in the same way. For example, the discussion of each campus support service on the resource website for PSU's Students First Mentoring Program (see Vignette 2) was organized using the same six questions.

What is the name of the resource?
What kinds of support does this resource provide?
Which adjustment issues is this resource helpful in addressing?
Whom do I contact?
Where is it located? It is helpful to identify the location on a campus map?
How do I use this resource appropriately? (Collier et al., 2008, p. 62)

Organizing your resource-related information in this manner actually primes your mentees to do more effective searches when they try to learn about additional campus resources or deal with another adjustment issue. Because most campus resource sites contain multiple pages of information, the "what, which, who, where, and how" structure cues mentees to focus on finding the important information on the site without being distracted by the sheer volume of information.

Organizing Information About Adjustment Issues

Content organization can also help students in their efforts to address specific college adjustment issues, such as how to write a college-level paper or how to find assistance with financial aid issues. You can help mentees make quicker and higher quality decisions by organizing your program information in ways that facilitate the organized storage and easy retrieval of that information.

Psychologists use the term *schema* to describe cognitive organizing structures that help individuals organize and connect different bits of information to facilitate retrieval and usage of the information in problem definition and decision making (Deaux & Wrightsman, 1988; Markus, 1977; Stryker & Serpe, 1994). Schemas are like cognitive closet organizers. An important way that more expert or experienced students differ from students new to the university has to do with how each group categorizes and organizes college-relevant information. More expert students' cognitive closets of how-to scripts for college success tend to be more extensive and much better organized than those of university novices. More experienced students' better organized systems of college student success scripts help in decision making as experts have been shown to be able to more quickly recognize, categorize, and apply schema-relevant new information (for a discussion of schemas and decision making, see Collier & Callero, 2005, pp. 47–48).

Most of the information we share with mentees involves providing them with plans based on the experiences of more expert students for how to address specific adjustment issues. A helpful program developer can package this program content in the form of how-to-do scripts or issue adjustment event schemas, which are lines of action designed to successfully address specific college adjustment issues (see Figure 7.2).

There are three elements in each issue-adjustment event schema (Collier, 2011), the first of which is the specific adjustment issue or college success task. Second, the schema includes one or more strategies for dealing with that specific issue based on the experiences of more expert students. Third, the schema also includes relevant campus resources that are useful for putting the strategy into action to appropriately address the issue.

Figure 7.3 shows an example of how to package information relating to the adjustment issue of how to write a college-level paper.

As a program developer, you should present content to your mentees in ways that can influence how they store that information in their memories. Organized information is easier to recall. So if you explicitly link each issue to appropriate strategies and resources, you will decrease the cognitive clutter they face and facilitate quicker decisions. Linked cognitive information tends to be easily recalled.

This approach is analogous to helping young people learn to make better quality clothing decisions by encouraging them to think of clothing as outfits in the form of coordinating shirts, slacks, socks, and shoes rather

Figure 7.2   Issue Adjustment Event Schema

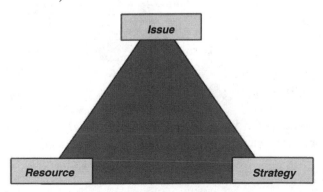

Figure 7.3   Writing a College-Level Paper

than requiring them to make a separate decision when selecting each item of attire. After being mentored to think of a wardrobe as a smaller number of outfits, when that individual faces a choice of what to wear today, he or she only has to choose from among five or six outfits. This is much simpler than looking through all the slacks and picking one, then all the shirts and picking one, then repeating the process for socks and shoes before finally trying to determine if the selected items really go together. Helping mentees learn this information-chunking process will reduce the time it takes them to make decisions compared to searching through all the decision-relevant information that they have stored in an unorganized fashion (for a discussion of a study that demonstrated schema formation leading to faster decision time, see Collier & Callero, 2005, pp. 50–54). Mentees will also tend to make higher quality decisions by following the strategies offered by more expert mentors rather than trying make a decision based on their limited college experience. And, as we learned in Chapter 4, higher quality decision making is associated with higher levels of college student success outcomes.

Another way to understand the benefit of presenting mentees' college student role information in this format is to think of each of these issue-adjustment event schemas as scripts for successfully enacting the college student role in addressing one specific issue. The mentee internalizes the three elements of the event schema—the issue, the strategy to address it, and the relevant campus resource—as a linked set. The more of these specific scripts a mentee internalizes, the more the mentee acquires greater mastery of the role and increased likelihood of his or her college success. When the student next encounters that specific situation, he or she does not just recall knowledge about the issue, the student also recalls the linked content, a workable strategy using a relevant campus resource.

This should lead to better decision making in two ways. First, the relative speed of decision making improves. The mentee automatically knows how to proceed with addressing this issue because the preferred problem-solving strategy is stored with the basic information about the issue. Second, the quality of the decision should also be relatively higher because the mentee automatically uses a strategy with a high likelihood of success developed by a more expert, more experienced college student who developed the linked strategy part of the schema by working through the problem in the past. In addition, these how-to-do program elements act as scaffolds for students' further understanding of why the actions in the script have a better likelihood of producing student success. Over time, these *why* messages about the reasons for enacting a specific issue-related strategy generalize into strategies that can be used for addressing other college student adjustment issues.

Sequencing When Content Is Introduced

The discussion in Chapter 5 about designing peer mentoring programs that incorporate a developmental approach to addressing mentees' needs noted that mentees should ideally receive program materials right before they have to deal with specific college adjustment issues. Sequencing program content in the order in which mentees are introduced to material is important regardless of whether you are putting together a targeted or developmental program. Mentees need to be provided with foundational material, such as locating their classes or making sense of a syllabus, before they are asked to consider more nuanced issues, such as setting up the subsequent years' schedule of classes, that typically arise later in the semester or academic year. Sequencing program content facilitates mentees' successful role-playing by providing them with knowledge about and appropriate behaviors for addressing a limited initial set of important adjustment issues. Once mentees have successfully addressed the initial set of adjustment issues, a second wave of program content prepares them to appropriately address another set of important adjustment issues that typically occur later in the program year. Sequencing program content contributes to mentees' development of college student role mastery by chunking information in digestible bites that are manageable yet not overwhelming.

This chapter identified three distinct yet at times overlapping areas of program content: universal content, content shared by programs that all serve the same group of students, and program-specific content. It makes the case that all programs need to include content that helps mentees understand college communication issues, realize how differences in perspective affects individuals' understanding of different college student adjustment issues, and recognize the value of service to others regardless of the group of students each program serves. This chapter also introduced the issue-adjustment schema as a way to organize pro-gram content relating to appropriately using campus resources and addressing specific student adjustment issues to facilitate mentee recall and higher quality decision making. The next chapter focuses on how to design and implement effec-tive mentor training.

CHAPTER 7 RESOURCES

The following source material can be used for program content and mentor training.

College Persistence Models

Astin, A. (1984). Student involvement: A developmental theory for higher education. *Journal of College Student Personnel, 25*, 297–308.

Chickering, A. W., & Reisser, L. (1993). *Education and identity*. San Francisco, CA: Jossey-Bass.

Tinto, V. (1993). *Leaving college: Rethinking the causes and cures of student attrition* (2nd ed.). Chicago, IL: University of Chicago Press.

Reflection

Collier, P., & Williams, D. (2013). Reflection in action: The learning-doing relationship. In C. Cress, P. Collier, & V. Reitenauer (Eds.), *Learning through Serving: A Student Guidebook for Service-Learning and Civic Engagement Across Academic Disciplines and Cultural Communities* (2nd ed., pp. 95–110). Sterling, VA: Stylus.

Peet, M. R., Walsh, K., Sober, R., & Rawak, C. S. (2010). Generative knowledge interviewing: A method for knowledge transfer and talent management at the University of Michigan. *International Journal of Educational Advancement, 10*(2), 71–85.

Professors' Expectations and Expertise Development

Benner, P. (1982). From novice to expert. *The American Journal of Nursing, 82*(3), 402–407.

Collier, P., & Morgan, D. (2008). Is that paper really due today? Differences in first-generation and traditional college students' understandings of faculty members' class-related expectations. *Higher Education, 55*(4), 425–446.

Dreyfus, H., & Dreyfus, S. (2005). Peripheral vision: Expertise in real world contexts. *Organizational Studies, 26*(5), 779–792.

Cross-Cultural Sensitivity

Reitenauer, V., Cress, C., & Bennett, J. (2013). Creating cultural connections: Navigating difference, investigating power, unpacking privilege. In C. Cress, P. Collier, & V. Reitenauer (Eds.), *Learning through Serving: A Student Guidebook for Service-Learning and Civic Engagement Across Academic Disciplines and Cultural Communities.* (2nd ed., pp. 77–94). Sterling, VA: Stylus.

Value of Service

Cress, C. M., Burack, C., Giles, D. E., Elkins, J., & Carnes Stevens, M. A. (2010). Promising connection: Increasing college access and success through civic engagement. Boston, MA: Campus Compact.

The following is useful content from this book for helping mentees understand relevant adjustment issues.

Chapter 3, pp. 48–51, "What Are Some Important Issues Faced by All College Students?"

Chapter 3, pp. 51–55, "What Are Important Student Adjustment Issues Associated With Specific Higher Education Transitions?"

Chapter 3, pp. 55–62, "What Are Some Important College Adjustment Issues for International Students, First-Generation Students, and Student Veterans?"

Vignette 4

STUDENT VETERAN– FOCUSED PROGRAM

VETS to VETS Program

Elizabeth Erickson, Sacramento State University

TABLE V4.1

Inclusiveness	Duration	Approach to Addressing Students' Needs	College Transition
Tailored: Designed for a specific audience	Short term: One semester or less	Developmental: Responds to student needs as they evolve over time	Returning to college after military service (Primary)
Student veterans	One semester	Overall focus on leadership development	Two-year to four-year college (Secondary)

Sacramento State is one of 23 campuses in the California State University (CSU) system and serves 28,500 students. Located five miles from the capital of California, Sacramento State is an urban campus with 72% of its students from Sacramento or one of five surrounding counties. The university offers 58 undergraduate majors, 41 master's degrees, 6 postbaccalaureate certificates, and 2 doctoral degrees. The student body is quite diverse: 40% of the students are White/Anglo, 21% Asian/Pacific Islander, 19% Latino, 6% African American, 2% foreign, 1% American Indian, and 11% other.

The city of Sacramento is situated near several military installations, including Travis and Beale Air Force Bases. Sacramento State prides itself on being a veteran-friendly campus. The university serves 800 veteran students, the second largest number of veterans in the CSU system. In the fall of 2013 the Veteran Success Center, an office in Student Affairs where staff assist veterans in obtaining their needed benefits, and the academic Department of Recreation, Parks, and Tourism Administration formed a partnership to create a leadership and mentorship program for veterans. This program is housed in a course titled RPTA 122 and serves as a general elective upper-division writing-intensive course, a requirement for all students for graduation. Only veterans may register for this particular section of this course. The curriculum is specifically designed for student veterans entering Sacramento State. During the semester, each new student veteran receives one-on-one peer mentoring from a student who participated in the course during a prior semester.

The majority of the student veterans who attend Sacramento State are transfer students, typically from one of five community colleges surrounding the university. Most of these students have already completed the majority of their general elective requirements upon entering and start taking courses that relate to their major degree plan when they arrive. The average student veteran is 28 years old, far older than the typical 19- or 20-year-old entering the university from high school. The majority of the veterans entering Sacramento State served in Operation Enduring Freedom, Operation Iraqi Freedom, and Operation New Dawn; although, on occasion, a Vietnam veteran will take courses at the university. The student veterans have served in all the service branches including the Army, Marines, Air Force, Navy, Coast Guard, and the National Guard. The students have had varied and vast experiences traveling worldwide; some served on the front line or assisted those on the front line. Snipers, airplane mechanics, truck drivers, medics, linguists, technicians, soldiers, and chefs are just a few of the roles these students had during their years of service. In other words, these students have had worldly experiences that often far surpass those of a typical student coming out of high school.

The leadership/mentorship program has multiple goals. The program is designed to help student veterans develop their leadership skills in preparation for their transition to the civilian workforce postgraduation, get students involved in campus life, assist in the transition to being a student at the university, achieve academic success, educate the students about available university resources, help them build professional networks, and create a supportive veteran community at Sacramento State.

Program Description

The structure of this program came about as a result of revising a more stand-ard peer mentor program in which student mentors were hired and paid to mentor new student veterans entering Sacramento State. After one academic year (2012–2013) using this initial structure we found that money did not necessarily motivate the student veterans to mentor others since they had access to GI Bill benefits. Furthermore, because individuals who served in the U.S. Armed Forces were often taught to adapt to new situations as they arise and to be fairly self-sufficient, new students did not always welcome being mentored. The staff at the Veteran's Success Center, the students involved in the mentorship program, and faculty with the Department of Recrea-tion, Parks, and Tourism Administration identified what students needed—a general elective upper-division writing-intensive course. Using an existing course taught by the Department of Recreation, Parks, and Tourism Admin-istration, the professor adapted the curriculum to the needs of the veterans, coupling leadership development with a mentorship program.

During the first semester of the program, we recruited 22 students to enroll in the course. Any student who was a veteran was welcome to take the course. One half of the students enrolled in the first semester were new students, while the other half were returning Sacramento State students. Because we did not have students who had taken the course before, we did not have any mentors for the new student veterans. Consequently, student veterans who were near graduation were hand selected by the faculty member and the director of the Veteran's Success Center to serve as mentors. Vice presidents and faculty members also volunteered to initially serve as mentors. This first semester, the mentors were required to meet with the mentees four times per semester. The mentors served purely on a volunteer basis.

The curriculum of the course focused on leadership and work/recrea-tion life balance. It incorporated program offerings situated within the uni-versity so students would be aware of what was available to them during their educational journey. For example, students were required to take one of five outdoor trips (e.g., white-water rafting, sea kayaking, backpacking in Yosemite National Park, zip-lining in the redwoods in Sonoma County) offered by Peak Adventures, an organization that offers students outdoor trips at a reduced fee. Students were also required to participate in an all-day Ropes Course Challenge and to join a club on campus (preferably one associ-ated with their major) in addition to participating in the Veteran's Student Organization. The ropes course and 50% of the fee for the outdoor trip were paid for by the Veteran's Success Center. The Career Center helped student veterans learn how to write the war into their résumés.

The leadership curriculum was based on the Leadership Initiative, a series of four leadership certificates from Student Affairs in the Office of Student Organizations and Leadership. Because this was a writing-intensive course, the student veterans were required to write at least 2,500 words during the semester. Students kept weekly journals in which they answered personal questions that required profound self-reflection. Finally, the new student veterans were required to see their assigned mentor four times during the semester and write about their experiences. At the end of the course, the students received two of the four Leadership Initiative Certificates and a challenge coin.[1]

We had a pool of 12 students from the group that took the course the first semester who wanted to serve as mentors for the students who would take the course the next semester. These students were required to fill out an application at the end of course if they wanted to serve as a mentor for the incoming class. In the application, they explained why they wanted to serve as mentors, their branch of service, number of years served, GPA, and their level of current student involvement at Sacramento State. A GPA of at least 2.5 was preferred in addition to a high level of student involvement and dedication to and belief in the Veteran's Leadership and Mentorship Program. During the second semester, we recruited 27 students to enroll in the course. We promoted this mostly to new student veterans entering the university; however, returning Sacramento State student veterans also enrolled in the class. Only the new student veterans were required to have a mentor.

The mentors had already received leadership training and familiarization with university resources in the prior semester's class. In addition to this, new mentors received one to two hours per week of supplementary training during the semester they worked with mentees. They also were given additional leadership training using a curriculum based on the last two leadership certificates offered by the Office of Student Organizations and Leadership. They received instruction on event design and implementation and how to create an e-portfolio. By the end of the semester, the mentors were required to meet with their mentees five times throughout the semester, design an e-portfolio, and create a fund-raising event to help financially sustain the program. In return, the mentors received the last two leadership certificates offered by the university, a second challenge coin, and a scholarship of $500 from the Veteran's Success Center.

One of the biggest difficulties in creating a program based on a writing-intensive course was that the students were required to take and pass a writing proficiency exam before they could enroll in the course, a requirement for all students at Sacramento State. This was an initial impediment to enrolling new students in the class because they would not have taken this exam prior to entering Sacramento State. In addition, it was imperative to get the students enrolled as soon as possible so that they could apply for GI benefits. For a student veteran to wait for the exam results would simply delay needed funding for the student to attend the university. To help alleviate this obstacle, the vice president of Academic Affairs, faculty in the English department (that facilitates the exam), staff at the Veterans Success Center, and staff working with the Office of Student Orientation helped create an e-mail that was sent to all new student veterans introducing the course, explaining that they needed to take the exam prior to entering the university should they want to enroll. Furthermore, a special June orientation was created specifically for student veterans so a faculty member could recruit student veterans for the course and explain that they would have to take the exam scheduled in July. Most important, the vice president of Academic Affairs instituted a new policy stating that if a student veteran said that he or she intended to take the exam, that student could sign up for the course. This amounted to bending a university policy that students must pass the writing exam before signing up for an upper-division writing-intensive course. It goes without saying that having the support of the upper administration helped in the creation of this program.

For the fall semester 2014, we had two sections of the Veterans Leadership and Mentorship Program with 30 students each. Almost all were new students. We had a class of 14 students who served as mentors for the fall semester and hired a student assistant for the faculty member. Because we now have more students than mentors, each mentor will have two to four students and must meet with each student four times during the semester. Based on the program history, we have found no magic number of contacts that works perfectly. Instead we are basing this number on what we perceive is reasonable for the mentors to take on in addition to their job and schoolwork.

Evaluation

The evaluation of this program is currently being developed. For the course itself, the students are required to fill out a course evaluation that is quantitative and qualitative. The students in the first semester also fill out a questionnaire from the director of the Veterans Success Center. The students who have completed the year-long program are required to participate in a focus group with the director of the Veteran's Success Center to recap what went well in the program and where work is needed for program improvement (a one-on-one meeting is available if a student desires). These data are purely qualitative. One indicator of success is the high number of program students who continue to participate in the Veteran's Student Organization. Currently a more formal pre- and posttest are being created for the students enrolled in the academic course and for those who participate in the year-long program.

To measure the effectiveness of the program, qualitative and quantitative methods were used. Upon completion of the course, students completed a course evaluation that provided rich information on the program's effectiveness. When asked whether the course was valuable to their transition into the university, 100% of respondents agreed or strongly agreed with the statement, "The course was valuable to your transition into Sacramento State." In addition, 92.3% of veterans in the course considered the course effective and a valuable part of their education. When asked what was most enjoyable about the course one student said, "The course was a great way for me to open up without feeling pressured." Others noted that the class was important because it allowed them to reflect on their past military experiences in a safe environment. The most common statement throughout the evaluations was that the students appreciated spending time with other veterans they could feel comfortable with and who they knew understood their situation. The unintended consequence of creating this program is that these students experienced camaraderie similar to what they experienced at the platoon-level in the service. This brotherhood/sisterhood that is developed within a platoon is often greatly missed by the servicemen and servicewomen when reentering the civilian world but can be somewhat recaptured in a program like VETS to VETS.

In addition to the course evaluation, a focus group was held for those who had served as mentees and then mentors in the year-long experience. The overwhelming majority of participants found the program instrumental to their transition into the university. One participant said, "I don't think I would have made it past the first semester without the program." Another stated, "This experience has allowed me to experience the same level of camaraderie I had in the military." Ultimately, in both groups, the camaraderie was what helped the students more than anything else that was offered in support of their transition to the university.

Note

1. A challenge coin is a small medallion or coin that bears the emblem of an organization. They are often given to show membership in a particular organization; in the military, unit commanders often distribute these to individuals as an award for meritorious achievements. Challenge coins are now used in organizations beyond the military to recognize group members' accomplishments (Lammie, 2012).

HOW ARE YOU GOING TO TRAIN YOUR PEER MENTORS?

Mentor training must be informed by your program goals, design, and what mentoring is supposed to accomplish. Regardless of the duration, mentor training must mirror your program content so that mentors are appropriately prepared to work with their mentees.

Chapter 8

- presents six fundamental questions to consider when designing a mentor training curriculum;
- reflects on the characteristics of a good mentor training program;
- discusses a set of universal mentor training elements, including understanding the mentor role, developing communication skills, mentee adjustment issues, differences in learning styles, cross-cultural sensitivity, the importance of service, and identifying campus resources;
- identifies practical skill development training elements, such as boundary setting and problem solving;
- explores important subgroup training elements, such as group-specific adjustment issues, school policies that affect the students your program serves, and relevant campus resources;

- reviews program-specific training elements including expectations, policies, protocols, and how to do the job;
- provides more than 20 mentor training exercises; and
- considers sequencing issues.

We learn by practice. Whether it means to learn to dance by practicing dancing or to learn to live by practicing living, the principles are the same.

(Graham, 2015)

Practice isn't the thing you do once you're good. It's the thing you do that makes you good.

(Gladwell, 2008, p. 42)

As you develop your mentor training curriculum, it is important to understand how training connects with program content to achieve your program goals.

Getting Started

The following six fundamental questions should be considered to help you determine how you should organize your mentor training and what you should include:

What do you want to accomplish with the training? Developing your mentor training curriculum starts with your program goals. Next, consider what mentoring is supposed to accomplish in your program. If there are program goals that you do not expect to meet through peer mentoring (e.g., integrating your program into your schools' network of student support services), then materials relating to those goals should not be emphasized in mentor training.

What kind of time line are you operating on? This question relates to the duration and extensiveness of your mentor training. Underlying this question are several related issues similar to the "Which comes first, the chicken or the egg?" conundrum. These issues have to do with two different aspects of program design. The first issue is "What you are asking your mentors to do?" The more extensive, detailed, or sophisticated the expectations you have of your mentors (e.g., helping teach a class as opposed to providing social support), the more extensive and typically longer your mentor training must be. You also must address a second issue, "How will mentors be compensated?" (see Chapter 5, pp. 118–119, for a discussion on mentor compensation). Program administrators who rely on volunteer mentors will typically not expect them to participate in extensive preterm mentor training compared to programs that compensate mentors. In addition, you must consider a third related issue, "How much time do you have available for mentor training?" Time constraints will limit how much material can be covered in your mentor training.

What information should be covered in your training? It is important to consider which materials, not just how much material, will be included in your initial mentor training. Triage your potential training materials in terms of importance. Divide potential content into materials mentors must know, should know, and could know. Make must-know materials your primary learning targets and organize your initial training accordingly. If you have additional training time, incorporate some or all of the should-know material. Any of the should-know material not covered in your initial training may be shared with mentors in mentor development workshops throughout the program year.

What resources will be necessary to carry out the training? This can include handouts, supplies for exercises, food and beverages, and physical space (see the discussion of budgets and in-kind resources in Chapter 5, pp. 102–103).

Will you need assistance from other campus or community offices, programs, or trainers? Because many programs conduct mentor training prior to the beginning of the fall term or semester it is helpful if you can develop your training curriculum before the end of the previous spring term. That way you can identify people from other campus units who might be useful to include in your training. You will have a better chance of securing a commitment to participate in your training from those individuals by speaking with them in advance. For example, as part of the regular mentor training, Wilkes University's freshman peer mentoring program includes workshops on sexual harassment and violence offered by a local community victims' resource center.

Will current or past mentors and mentees be included in the training? The University of Cincinnati's Center for First Year Experience and Learning Communities program mentor training regularly includes a session where veteran mentors talk about the peer mentor role as part of the new mentor training (P. Person, personal communication, October 11, 2011). If you decide to include current or previous mentors or mentees in your training, it is helpful to secure a commitment from these individuals as early as possible.[1]

The Purpose of Mentor Training

When conducted appropriately, mentor training

- clarifies understanding of the peer mentor role;
- communicates your program's goals, desired outcomes, policies, and procedures;
- provides mentors with information on your mentees' needs and potential adjustment issues;
- gives mentors insights into common issues they may face;

- allows mentors to practice important program-specific skills;
- reduces risk, potential problems, and program liability; and
- instills trust in mentors that your program staff will be there to support them (Arévalo, Boggan, & West, 2004; North & Sherk, 2002).

Ideally, mentor training is an ongoing process. Mentors acquire additional, more nuanced information on effective mentoring practices as the program unfolds over time. It is unrealistic to imagine that you will be able to completely provide your mentors with all the information and skills they need in an initial mentor training session, regardless of how long it is. What your initial training can do is provide mentors with a foundational set of skills, information, and experiences they can build on as they work with their mentees over the duration of your program. The initial mentor training session can also establish your program staff as a valuable resource that mentors can trust to be available to provide guidance and support when issues arise.

Characteristics of a Good Mentor Training Program

Effective mentor training programs share several characteristics. First, the training must cover the materials needed to do the job, must be comprehensive but not overwhelming, and should be presented at a level appropriate for the group being trained. Second, the training needs to be interesting and dynamic to engage the trainees. Effective training incorporates a variety of learning approaches and involves the trainee in activities and not just information pitch and catch. Third, effective mentor training promotes reflection. Successful programs are designed with frequent, regular reflection exercises that encourage trainees to think about and articulate concerns and issues within a supportive setting. Linking a series of reflections over time can also help trainees recognize their personal accomplishments by providing a record of the trainee's understanding of the program and his or her confidence in effectively doing the job at different points in time. Effective training programs build trainees' confidence by allowing them to practice key job activities in simulated or real-life situations. Fourth, successful training programs promote connections within groups of trainees and facilitate the development of mentor group support networks.

The Information-Connection-Application Model of Mentor Training

It is helpful to think about the process of mentor training as a three-step model consisting of information presentation, connection, and application with reflection being the glue that connects the three elements together. In the information-connection-application (ICA) model, Step 1 in any mentor training element is presentation of information. This can take the form of either trainer-shared content or some form of mentor experience. The material on Chickering's (1969) student development theory (introduced in Chapter 3) is an example of a trainer-shared content presentation suitable for all college student mentoring programs. An assignment that has mentors locating and collecting information about three campus resources they think could be useful for promoting student success is an example of information acquired through mentor experience.

In Step 2, connection, mentors try to link the newly acquired information to past personal experiences. Mentors could be asked to reflect and consider their own college adjustment experiences and how knowing or not knowing how to use different resources affected their college success.

In Step 3, application, mentors use their bundles of newly acquired information and relevant personal experiences to imagine the kinds of issues their mentees might encounter. Mentors then should be asked to reflect on and discuss what they would do to help their mentees use specific resources in appropriate ways to address some of these issues.

Mentor reflection (discussed in more detail in the section "Universal Areas of Training Content," p. 230) can take place in several formats: individual reflection in a journal or written assignment, small-group discussion, or large-group discussion. You can structure your training so that mentors shift from one format to another. Start out by asking mentors to individually reflect on how the new information connects to their own experiences. Next, have trainees form small groups where mentors share their experiences with each other. The group then brainstorms the projection stage by asking the following: How might the issues associated with this information or experience play out for their mentees? What strategies would mentors use to help mentees address the identified issues using the knowledge gained from the training? In the final step, the small groups form a single large group and discuss strategies for helping mentees address specific issues.

Duration

There is tremendous variation in the duration of mentor training. Initial mentor training sessions can vary from two or three hours (Lehigh University, L. Ruebeck, personal communication, May 10, 2013; Auburn University, www.auburn.edu/cosam/departments/diversity/mentor) to multiple full-day sessions (University of Ottawa, http://sass.uottawa.ca/en/mentoring/student-mentoring/become-mentor) to weekend trainings (Western Washington, www.wwu.edu/sos/mentorproject) to regular attendance in semester- or term-long courses (PSU University Studies, http://mentors.un st.pdx.edu/content/mentors-and-mentored-inquiry; San Jose State, http://

peerconnections.sjsu.edu/; Utah Valley State, www.uvu.edu/slss/mentoring) because of differences in program goals and available resources. Many programs provide ongoing mentor training (Bunker Hill Community College, www .bhcc.mass.edu/learning-communities/bhccacementors/; Humboldt State www2.humboldt.edu/cps/info/faculty-staff-resources/residential-academic-mentoring-program-ramp-now-hiring) in online (Brigham Young University, P. Esplin, personal communication, September 30, 2011) and face-to-face formats (University of Michigan, www.onsp.umich.edu/transfer_students/ mentorship). In the end, the goals of your program and what you expect peer mentoring to accomplish will determine the duration of your mentor training, the content you include, and how or if content is divided between initial and ongoing mentor training sessions.

Size-Associated Training Issues

The "how" of mentor training is pretty much the same up to a certain threshold. However, large mentoring programs may face some size-related training issues that are not issues for smaller programs. Building a sense of community among mentors in a small program may occur relatively easily, while achieving that same sense of common purpose and solidarity in a larger group may require a different approach. Training activities performed at a single time with the entire group of mentors in a small program may have to be organized into a series of smaller groups at multiple times for a large program. And while all the mentors in both programs may get to participate in the same activity, the sense of community and belonging to a cohort that arises naturally in the training for a smaller program may not emerge in the same way in the training for a larger program.

Many times discussion of mentor training seems to be based on an implicit assumption that all peer mentoring training programs should include the same material; for example, communication skills and sensitivity to diversity. This book takes a different and more nuanced approach to what needs to be included in mentor training by differentiating between the elements all college student peer mentoring programs should include in their training and elements that might be idiosyncratic for specific programs. While there are many shared elements across programs, the design and program goals determine what must be included in mentor training. Every mentoring program will not be able to include every recommended element or go into the same level of depth for specific elements in their mentor training because of differences in program goals, expectations of mentors, and available resources. Regardless of your program goals, mentor training needs to mirror the content provided to mentees. It is beyond the scope of this book to provide detailed content for each element of mentoring training.

Instead, this chapter provides an introduction of the topic and one or more training exercises for each topic. See Chapter 8 Resources, p. 265, for some relevant source materials and links to extended discussion of topics in earlier chapters of this book.

Universal Areas of Training Content

Universal training elements should provide mentors with the information, tools, and skills they'll need to do their job effectively. The first group of training elements concerns understanding mentoring and the mentor role.

What Is Mentoring?

Every training program should begin by developing a program-specific definition of *mentoring*. Even if your trainees have mentoring experience in other programs, developing a shared understanding makes sure everyone is on the same page. Exercise 8.1 can also serve as an icebreaker for trainees who do not know each other.

Exercise 8.1. What Is a Mentor?

Purpose: Develop a shared understanding of what a mentor is.
1. Ask mentors to list all the words and images that come to mind when they think of the term *mentor*. Write them down on one side of the flipchart or whiteboard.
2. Ask mentors to turn to the person next to them and tell them about someone whom they consider to have been a mentor in their life.
3. Once the first person has finished, switch roles.
4. After the individual sharing, bring the group back together. Now ask group members to tell you all the images, thoughts, feelings, and words that came to mind when they thought about their own and heard about their partners' personal experiences with mentors. Write them down on the other side of the flipchart.
5. Ask mentors if they see any differences or similarities between the words that were written about the idea of a mentor and their actual experiences of a mentor.
6. Develop a shared program definition of *mentor*. (Based on Arévalo et al., 2004, p. 96)

See Chapter 8 Resources, page 265, for additional variations of this exercise.

Enacting the Mentor Role

Every training program should also include material on program expectations for how mentors will enact the mentor role. While many aspects of acting in the mentor role are program specific, common elements include facilitating group work, being a leader, learning how to be reflective, and helping mentees with being reflective.

Exercise 8.2 is another excellent icebreaker that encourages mentors to work together to accomplish a common goal. It also provides valuable insights into working in groups that mentors can apply to their subsequent work with mentees.

Exercise 8.2. Marshmallows and Spaghetti

Purpose: Help mentors reflect on processes of working in groups and team building.

Create teams of mentors (no more than five per group). Each group receives one package of spaghetti and one package of marshmallows. (You may also want to cover the floor with newspaper.) The goal is to build the tallest tower possible out of the marshmallows and spaghetti. Allow about 15–20 minutes for the exercise.

Afterward, explore the following questions together:

- How well did the team work together?
- What helped the group pursue its goal?
- What roles did you observe group members playing as you constructed your tower?
- What would you do differently if you could begin again? (Collier & Voegele, 2013 p. 53)

Leadership

Many programs, like Sacramento State's VETS to VETS and Utah Valley University's University Student Success, make material on understanding leadership and developing mentors' leadership skills a central part of initial training. The purpose of Exercise 8.3 is to encourage trainees to consider how past leadership experiences might help them as they work with mentees in your program.

Exercise 8.3. You as a Leader (Individual Reflection)

Purpose: Help mentors become more aware of their past leadership experiences and skills they developed in those experiences that might be useful in working with current mentees.

Think about your own leader experiences in different areas of your life: home, school, sports, work, and volunteering.

- Describe the best leadership experience you ever had.
- What effective strategies did you use in this leadership experience?
- What personal qualities do you think contributed to your success as a leader in this situation? Explain how each quality contributed to your leadership success.
- How might the effective strategies you used in this situation be used in your current work with the mentees in this program? (Collier, 2013a, p. 125)

See Exercises 9.7a and 9.7b (pp. 306–307) for a two-step variation of this exercise.

Reflection
Reflection is defined as a person's intentional and systematic consideration of an experience and how that person and others are connected to that experience. In the context of peer mentoring programs, this process usually involves experiences in a college or university context and is framed in terms of particular student success objectives (Collier & Williams, 2013, p. 96). Pragmatist philosopher John Dewey (1933) argued that reflection is the key to whether an experience actually involves learning. Reflection connects the world of observations and facts with the world of ideas. Reflection is the process that connects current experiences with prior knowledge and past experiences to achieve specific goals, such as adjusting to college.

Helping mentors understand the value of reflection should be an element that occurs relatively early in your training. Exercise 8.4 should help mentors gain insights into the value of reflection.

You can build on this initial understanding of reflection to help mentors learn how to facilitate mentee reflection and the subsequent problem-solving process through the new Johari window.[2]

Exercise 8.4. Telling the Tale: The Value of Reflection

Purpose: Demonstrate the value of reflection, and consider how mentors might assist mentees in reflecting on and better understanding their college experiences.

Note: You can use this exercise as a follow-up to any group training exercise. This is written as a follow-up to Exercise 8.2: Marshmallows and Spaghetti.

1. Pair up with another mentor who was not in your "Marshmallows and Spaghetti" group. In two minutes tell your partner the story of your building a structure out of marshmallows and spaghetti experience. In a follow-up two-minute period, answer any questions your partner might have about your experience.
2. Switch roles. Now let your partner describe his or her experiences. In the follow-up period, ask as many clarifying questions as you can think of so that you have as deep an understanding of his or her experiences as possible.
3. In an additional two-minute period, discuss how answering your partner's questions helped clarify your own experiences for you.
4. Bring all the pairs back together into a single large group.

Discuss the following:

- What types of questions did you find most helpful in understanding your own experience?
- How could what you've learned in this exercise affect how you work with your mentees? What types of reflection questions might be particularly effective in helping your mentees understand their experiences? (adapted from Collier & Williams, 2013, p. 109)

Mentoring and Reflection: The New Johari Window
The format of the new Johari window is useful for demonstrating how the combination of mentoring and reflection can work together to increase mentee knowledge of how to be successful in a particular mentoring context (e.g., first year of college, making the transition from a two-year to a four-year college).

In this model, reflection affects the open and hidden cells, while mentoring affects the missing and oblivious cells (see Table 8.1).

TABLE 8.1
The New Johari Window

| | Who Knows What? | |
	Things Mentee Knows	Things Mentee Doesn't Know
Information mentee has	**Open:** *Things mentee knows she or he knows*	**Hidden:** *Tacit knowledge the mentee does not realize that he or she knows, either because the mentee takes knowledge for granted or because it is some key action that has become automatic because the mentee does it so often that he or she has separated the instrumental function of the task—getting the work done—from the actual skills involved in doing the tasks*
Information mentee does not have	**Missing:** *Things mentee knows that he or she does not know*	**Oblivious:** *Information that is relevant to success in this domain or role that the mentee does not even include in his or her current understanding of minimum level of competencies needed to be successful in this domain*

Open cell (information mentee has that he or she is aware he or she possesses). To tap into relevant knowledge the mentee already has, the mentor encourages mentee reflection through direct questioning:

- Tell me the kinds of things you will need to be able to do in order to succeed in doing X.
- How adequate do you feel your skills are in each of the things you identified as necessary to be able to successfully perform X?

Hidden cell (information mentee has that he or she is not initially aware he or she possesses). To tap into a mentee's relevant tacit knowledge, a mentor should encourage reflection that helps the mentee uncover knowledge and skills the mentee might not initially think he or she possesses. Two reflection techniques that promote the retrieval of tacit knowledge by mentees are Thinking by Analogy (see Exercise 8.5) and Generative Interviewing (Peet, 2010; see Exercise 8.6). Thinking by Analogy is a reflection approach a mentor can use to help the mentee recognize that skills from an apparently nonrelated area could be adapted to address an issue in the current environment (e.g., college).

Missing cell (*information the mentee is aware exists but does not possess*). Mentoring is the key to helping a mentee gain the information the mentee knows he or she does not possess. For an example, a mentee may recognize that the professor may be the best source of clarification on how to prepare for an exam, but at the same time the mentee may not be sure about the best or most appropriate way to approach the professor. The mentor has already worked out effective strategies for addressing this issue because of greater college experience. By sharing these strategies, the mentor helps the mentee move from knowing there is important information missing and not knowing how to go about acquiring it to actually acquiring that information.

Oblivious cell (*important information the mentee does not possess and is not even aware of its importance*). The mentee does not know he or she is missing key information that is very important to college student success. Because the mentee is oblivious to the importance of this information, it is not even included in his or her current understanding of the minimum level of competencies needed to be a successful college student.

This is another situation where mentoring can help. The mentor starts by identifying the issue as important, offering appropriate strategies that have a high likelihood of success, and sharing any available resources that may help, all of which are based on the mentor's previous college experience. Many times it is most helpful for mentees when mentors share their own stories about how they learned to successfully address the same issue that mentees are currently facing. By accepting the mentor's advice, a mentee swaps a potential strategy (i.e., trial and error) that has a poor likelihood of success for dealing with an important but poorly understood issue for a strategy that has a high likelihood of success and proven to be effective for addressing that issue. Through mentoring, the complex process of decision making involving multiple alternatives is replaced with a simple judgment: Is the mentor trustworthy?

Exercise 8.5. Thinking by Analogy

Purpose: Make mentors aware of how problem-solving techniques from other areas of life may be applied to dealing with current college adjustment issues. This can be done as an individual or a group training exercise.

This reflection technique involves three steps:

Step 1: Identifying an issue

Prompt: What is your issue?

Group training: Prepare a list of relevant issues before the training exercise. Divide mentors in small groups (two to three people to a group is ideal). Assign each group one issue.

For individual work: Pick one of the following issues to use in this exercise, or identify another issue related to your current mentoring program.

For a new college freshman: How to figure out professors' expectations for assignments

For a recent transfer student: How to feel more connected to a new campus

For a returning student veteran: How to find support resources for student veterans

Step 2: Identifying other potentially similar experiences

Prompt: Explain the process underlying your issue.

Example:

- Issue: How to figure out professors' expectations for assignments; process: getting directions
- Issue: How to feel more connected to new campus; process: connecting with others
- Issue: How to find support resources for student veterans; process: getting questions answered

Prompt: Drawing from your own experience, explain how you see issues involving the same process playing out in one or more other areas of your own or the mentee's life.

Example:

- Issue: How to figure out professors' expectations for assignments; process: how to acquire the directions for doing something you do not know how to do
- Issue: How to feel more connected to new campus; process: how to make friends in a new context
- Issue: How to find support resources for student veterans; process: whom to talk to in order to find needed services in the military

Step 3: Probing and connecting

Prompt (probing): Drawing from your own experience, what problem-solving strategies did you use in dealing with similar issues in the other areas you identified in Step 2?

Prompt (connecting): Explain how your problem-solving strategies in other areas could be used in trying to address your issue.

For individual work: Reflecting on this exercise, write a paragraph about how you might be able to use this in your work with your mentees.

For a group: Re-form large group. Ask those in the previous small groups to report on their issues and the strategies they used from other areas of their experience to address this issue (Collier, 2013b, p. 117).

Remind mentors that the thinking by analogy approach will work best if the mentor initially models the process for the mentee and then walks the mentee through the process using a different college issue. Mentors can refer to this Thinking by Analogy exercise in helping mentees develop strategies for other issues that might surface over their time in the program. Generative interviewing is discussed in the next section.

Communication

It is helpful to provide mentors with opportunities to improve their listening and verbal communication skills as part of your training curriculum. Active listening and generative interviewing are two approaches to helping mentors develop better listening skills. Active listening is a rapport-building technique that involves paying attention to the meaning of what is being said along with nonverbal cues and taking into account the speaker's intention and the context in which the communication occurs. Active listening typically involves providing feedback through paraphrasing or asking clarifying questions.

In generative interviewing the mentor or interviewer prompts the mentee to tell stories about specific learning, work, or life experiences. The types of stories depend on the purpose of the reflection. From these stories, the mentor or interviewer identifies an initial set of patterns and themes that reflect the mentee's tacit knowledge. These patterns and themes are shared with the mentee and validated, and then tested against additional stories. Exercise 8.6 is an excellent way for mentors to practice listening to what their mentees are actually saying to them.

Exercise 8.6. Generative Interviewing and Active Listening: Engagement in Learning

Purpose: Help mentors learn to actually listen to mentees, and help mentees recognize capacities they might not realize they possess.

1. Ask mentors to individually write in as much detail as possible about a personal experience where they felt they were particularly engaged in their own learning. Ask them to consider the following: What was the context? What were you doing, and why was it engaging? Describe an aha! moment or something that was challenging. What was the result of this experience? (5–10 minutes)

2. Divide group into pairs. Designate one person to be the speaker and one to be the listener. Have the speaker tell a story while the listener takes notes. When the speaker is finished, ask the listener to provide feedback. Encourage the speaker to write down any strengths or skills identified by the listener, particularly those the speaker had not really noticed before. (10–15 minutes)

3. Reverse roles and repeat process. (10–15 minutes)

4. Bring the entire group back together and discuss the experience from the perspective of the listener and then from the perspective of the speaker. Ask about strengths the listener identified. How did the speaker feel about feedback about strengths? How could this exercise inform how mentors work with mentees? (15 minutes)

Instructions for the Speaker

1. Tell your story from the beginning. Include details about who was there, what happened, how you felt.
2. Speak slowly; do not go too fast or the listener will not be able to keep up while taking notes. Remember, the feedback is what will be valuable for you.

Instructions for the Listener

1. Let the speaker finish his or her thoughts before asking questions.
2. This is the speaker's story, not yours. Try to follow along without getting emotionally invested or sharing your own thoughts verbally or through body language. For example, do not show agreement or disagreement, disgust, and so on. You can nod to show you are listening.

3. Listen for recurring themes for the speaker's story. Jot them down as the speaker is talking.
4. Assist the speaker in giving you details:
   a. Ask about the context: How did you end up speaking at the training?
   b. Ask about the people involved: Who else was there? What are the other people like?
   c. Ask the speaker to explain how she or he felt at the time: When the other person got mad at you, what were you feeling?
   d. Ask about the speaker's goal: What were you trying to accomplish?
5. Ask the speaker to explain his or her use of common phrases. For example, if the speaker says, "I was in charge of the whole thing," you may ask what being in charge means, what or who the speaker was responsible for, what the speaker learned about himself or herself, or ask for an example to illustrate what was involved with being in charge.
6. Listen for general adjectives or adverbs such as *interesting, frustrating,* or *fun,* and prompt the speaker to provide more detail about what each of these meant in the context of the story.
7. Pay attention to key verbs the speaker uses to describe the experience and ask for a description of a particularly memorable moment. For example, if the speaker says, "I was there to support my group," ask for a description of a moment when the speaker supported the group.
8. Describe to the speaker what you heard the speaker say after hearing part of the story.
9. Share your own insights on the story, focusing on what you grasp as the speaker's strengths or capacities and find out if the speaker agrees. (adapted from Shattuck, 2011)

Mentors also need to practice communicating with mentees in language the mentees can understand. Sometimes what a mentor considers to be simple directions turns out to not be quite as simple as the mentor initially thought (see Exercise 8.7).

Mentee Needs

Your trainees need information on mentees' needs and opportunities to practice appropriate ways to work with mentees on addressing those needs.

Understanding Adjustment or Development Issues
Providing mentors with information on student adjustment issues involves familiarizing them with theories of student development and college

Exercise 8.7. Giving Directions

Purpose: Help mentors practice giving, receiving, and following directions. Involves work at home.

Part 1: Distribute instructions the session before you want to conduct the in-class exercise. Provide students with the following prompt: Consider how you might give directions for a relatively simple task. How do you begin? What assumptions do you make about the person seeking directions? How detail oriented are you in your attempt to explain the task clearly? What do you find helpful in directions you read or are read to you?

Assignment: Create a set of directions for a relatively simple task, such as mailing a letter, making a sandwich, or drawing a flower. Assume you are writing this set of directions for a typical undergraduate.

From beginning to end, the task should take about three to five minutes to complete. Type your directions and at the very least include 12 detailed steps. You can generate more than 12 steps for this task if it demands additional steps. Depending on the task, you may want to include a title for the activity, comprehensive materials list, drawings, or examples.

Think about all the factors that will increase the success of the person reading and following your directions, and try to integrate those elements. Consider what helps you to follow directions.

Come to the next training session with your typed step-by-step set of directions of at least 12 detailed steps and all the supplies (not props) needed to complete your simple task.

Do not under any circumstances procure any directions or suggestions for directions from an Internet search of resources. This assignment is intended to tap into your creativity and your attention to detail.

In-Class Exercise Directions
1. Divide mentors into pairs. One individual giving directions, gives the written directions and any supplies to the other individual who then tries to follow the directions and complete the task. The direction giver may not speak or offer any additional information during the time his or her partner is completing the task. (5 minutes)
2. Have the pair switch roles and complete the exercise following directions for the second direction giver's task. (5 minutes)

3. Have the pair discuss their experiences in trying to follow the other person's directions and in watching someone try to follow the directions. (5 minutes)
4. Have the entire group of mentors discuss their experiences. Ask the participants to reflect on how what they learned from this experience might affect the way they work with their mentees. (C. Gabrelli, personal communication, May 15, 2013)

persistence (see Chapter 2). For example, Alverno College's Peer Advising Program training focuses on helping mentors understand student development theory, particularly Chickering and Reisser's work on developmental vectors, because this program serves all incoming students (K. Tisch, personal communication, May 14, 2013). Exercise 8.8 uses the generative learning framework from Exercise 8.6 to help mentors frame addressing adjustment issues as an intersection of challenges and assets.

Exercise 8.8. Active Listening and Generative Interviewing Adjustment Issues

Purpose: Help mentors use past experiences to think about addressing adjustment issues as an intersection of challenges and assets, and prepare them for using this approach in their subsequent work with mentees.

1. Ask mentors to each write in as much detail as possible about a personal experience in which they discovered they had to deal with a specific college adjustment issue, how they felt when they realized they had to come up with a way to address this issue, and how they solved the problem. (5–10 minutes)

Follow the remaining directions for Exercise 8.6.

Differences in Learning Styles
Your mentors may or may not be able to articulate their own preferred learning styles. However, they all should be able to share their experiences in classes where professors' instructional approaches seem to be at odds with the ways students felt they learned best. It is helpful to provide mentors with training on differences in learning styles, potential signs that might indicate a mentee

is experiencing difficulties in a class because of a learning style conflict, and a vocabulary and strategies for working with mentees who are experiencing these kinds of issues (see Exercise 8.9).

Exercise 8.9. Autobiography of a Learner

Purpose: Help mentors identify their own learning styles. This should be used as a follow-up to an information presentation on learning styles. Have mentors complete Part 1 outside training and bring it to the training session.

Part 1: Directions

1. Write a brief autobiography describing your progression as a learner. This does not have to be a scholarly essay; feel free to use phrases, words, drawings, whatever will portray you as a learner.
   - Discuss one of your earliest memories of learning. When? Where? What were you learning? Create images or scenes of those learning experiences.
   - Work your way through childhood up into high school. Discuss something you learned that was important to you. Don't limit yourself to school-based learning. Consider family, friends, employers, organizations, clubs, and so on.
   - Now think about your experiences in college. Discuss something you learned that was important to you.

Part 2: Directions

1. In a group format (if training a large number of mentors, have multiple small groups) have each person discuss his or her learning history. Then ask the group participants to discuss what they noticed in patterns of similarities and differences in learning experiences.
2. Follow-up: Have mentors discuss how information from this exercise might have an impact on their work with their mentees. How would a mentor recognize a mentee who was having learning style issues? How would the mentor explain the issue to the mentee? What strategies could be given to the mentee about how to address this issue? (A. Driscoll, personal communication, June 15, 2005)

Understanding Expectations

An important part of college success involves students' figuring out what professors expect of them in their classes. Students typically refer to the syllabus for explicit, clearly articulated information about some of the professors' expectations such as when assignments are due and which textbooks are required. But there is a second set of professors' expectations that are not explicitly stated. Instead, professors take it for granted that all students understand these implied expectations, such as the value of visiting a professor during office hours. These implicit expectations are what Polanyi (1996, pp. 3, 7) describes as tacit knowledge, knowledge brought into play as part of a process in which a person searches out clues from proximal information to make sense out of a larger body of not immediately accessible information. Professors take it for granted that by looking at the present situation, students can locate their class within a larger universe of classes they have completed, and by doing so know what the professor wants and what it will take to succeed in this class. Exercise 8.10 is a useful activity to help mentors turn implicit assumptions into explicitly stated information that could be shared

Exercise 8.10.   Figuring Out Professors' Expectations

Purpose: Help mentors recognize professors' implicit and explicit expectations as well as make explicit mentors' tacit knowledge relating to meeting these expectations. This exercise combines content with a modeling process mentors can use in their work with mentees.

1. Divide mentors into several smaller groups. Provide each group with a syllabus from a different class. Ask each group to look at the syllabus, develop a list of explicit and implicit professor expectations, and suggest how students would appropriately respond to each expectation.
2. Re-form into a single large group and have a representative from each small group identify (and provide examples of) (a) explicitly stated expectations from the group's syllabus and (b) implicit expectations from the same syllabus.
3. After participants in each group have shared their lists of explicit and implicit expectations, discuss the similarities in expectations among the different syllabi and the difficulties mentors had in recognizing and responding to professors' expectations.
4. Next, shift to projecting what kinds of difficulties relating to understanding professors' expectations mentors think their mentees might have. (A. Kneppler & C. Gabrelli, personal communication, May 15, 2013)

with a mentee. Assign mentors to read an article about differences between professors' expectations and students' understanding of those expectations as preparation for this exercise (see the section in Chapter 7 Resources titled Professors' Expectations and Expertise Development, pp. 216–217).

Understanding professors' expectations is an important step in getting students to take responsibility for their own learning. The following are tips from an experienced mentor for helping your mentees take more responsibility for what they learn at college.

> I try to start a dialogue, either face-to-face or in an assignment, about a student's goals in order to promote students taking responsibility for own learning. I ask the student to consider "why are you attending college?"
>
> If the answer to that question is some form of "To learn more about X" or "To become a Y" the next question is, "How is this going to happen?" It may take several more questions but eventually we get to the level of "is learning something someone is going to do *to* or *for* you, or is it something you will have to do for yourself?" Framed like that, most students have to acknowledge that they need to be responsible for their own learning.
>
> If the answer to my initial question is some form of "To get a degree so I can get a job and be Z" then the dialogue may take a couple of extra steps. e.g. "Do you think it is the degree or the skills associated with the degree that will help you get and keep this job?" However soon we're back to "How is this going to happen?" and eventually "Is learning something someone is going to do *to* or *for* you, or is it something you will have to do for yourself?"
>
> I believe we do students a favor by explicitly linking their goals with choices they have to make like whether or not to take responsibility for one's own learning. And then the next step is to discuss what "taking responsibility for your own learning" would look like in terms of specific actions. Implied choices and actions that may seem obvious to faculty or more experienced students may not be quite as clear for your mentees. This is where mentoring can prove invaluable. (M. Balshem, personal communication, April 15, 2012)

Developing Student Expertise

It is not just what information a mentor shares with a mentee that is important, it is also how that information is packaged. A mentee can be totally turned off when a mentor uses language that is over his or her head or offers an explanation of a situation that is too complex and provides too much detail. Patricia Benner (2004) has adapted Dreyfus and Dreyfus's five-stage model of expertise development to suggest ways to work with learners with different levels of expertise. The five stages in the model are novice, advanced beginner, competent, proficient, and expert, but the first three stages are

TABLE 8.2

Tips for Working With Mentees Who Have Different Levels of Expertise

Novice	Advanced Beginner	Competent Learners

• Mentor provides mentee with key content and process information
    For example, "This is what is important, and here is how to do it."
• Mentor provides rules that mentee can apply in any context
    For example, "Always stay for the full class period and take complete notes."
• Mentor shows mentee safe starting points for tasks and relationships
    For example, "Unless you are told otherwise, address your teacher as 'Professor.'"
• Mentor identifies good informants in mentee's immediate environment
    For example, "If you need help using the library ask any of the librarians." Or,
    "The person at the career center who can help you figure out your major is —"
• Mentor provides mentee with insights into others' expectations
    For example, "When a professor says to 'write' a paper, it should be typed, not handwritten."
	• Mentee starts to separate the relevant from the irrelevant information
	    For example, "The syllabus is a better source of information about how strict a grader a professor is than how formally or casually he or she is dressed."
	• Mentee starts to become more aware of additional factors that influence outcomes (beyond those covered by novice's context-free rules)
	• Important for mentor to validate student's successes because the advanced beginner is becoming more aware of how much she or he does not know
	    For example (after proofreading mentee's paper), "You've developed a clear topic sentence and there is a logical flow to your argument, although you might work on making smoother transitions between sections."
	• Important to provide feedback; mentor is a coach; watch for mentee overload
		• Mentee now starts to develop perspectives (based on meta-level rules) as well as learn to use specific perspectives appropriately
		    For example, "If the assignment is a term paper, then always use *APA* or *MLA* citation formating; however, if the assignment is in-class writing, then identifying the source is sufficient."
		• Mentee can become frustrated while seeking new meta-level rules, but these are much harder to come by
		• Mentee has new emotional issue to deal with: "Can't duck responsibility for outcomes." As novice or advanced beginner, if the choice of following a rule leads to a poor outcome, the mentee can deflect self-criticism by claiming, "I wasn't provided with a rule that worked."
		    Now because the strategy employed is based on the perspective employed, and the competent

TABLE 8.2
(Continued)

Novice	Advanced Beginner	Competent Learners
	• Mentee may need help prioritizing as everything seems to be an important factor that needs to be considered	learner is the one to select the perspective, that means the learner must take responsibility for successes and failures alike

most relevant for mentor training. Most of your mentees will be novices and advanced beginners, though some may progress to the competent learner stage in regard to college student expertise.

The Stage 1 novice learns to recognize interpretation-free features. A novice driver learns to recognize speed by observing the speedometer and drives by context-free rules; for example, shift to second when the speedometer needle points to 10 miles an hour.

The advanced beginner in Stage 2 begins to note examples of other meaningful aspects of the situation. The advanced beginner driver, using (situational) engine sounds as well as (nonsituational) speed in the gear-shifting rules, learns the maxim, "Shift up when the motor sounds like it is racing and down when it sounds like it's straining." Unlike a rule, a maxim requires one to already have some understanding of the domain the maxim applies to.

In Stage 3, competent, with more experience, the number of potentially relevant elements the learner is able to recognize becomes overwhelming. To cope with this overload and to achieve competence, people learn to devise contingency plans (if this happens, adopt strategy A, but if that happens, adopt strategy B). Choosing a specific strategy acts like a filter that identifies which elements of the situation should be treated as important and which ones can be ignored, thereby making decision making easier by restricting attention to only a few of the vast number of possibly relevant features and aspects (Dreyfus & Dreyfus, 2005, pp. 783–786).

Table 8.2 adapts the first three stages of this model to a higher education context by identifying key elements of how a mentor might work with and effectively communicate with a mentee at each stage of expertise.

Training can help mentors learn to craft effective messages that are appropriate for your program mentees' relative levels of college student expertise. Exercise 8.11 allows mentors to practice working with mentees who have different levels of college student expertise.

Exercise 8.11. Crafting Expertise-Level-Appropriate Messages

Purpose: Provide mentors with the opportunity to apply learning tools and develop expertise-level-appropriate messages for mentee problem solving.

1. Divide training group into pairs of mentors. Initially assign one person from each pair to be the mentor and the other to be the mentee.
2. Have the mentor assist the novice-level mentee in solving the problem of one of the following scenarios (feel free to develop your own scenarios). After the pair role-plays the first scenario, switch roles and repeat the novice-level exercise with another scenario from the following list or others you've developed on your own.

   - Help a mentee figure out what a professor expects when the professor states: "You can take any position you choose on this topic, but you will need to be able to support your chosen position."
   - Have the mentee imagine he or she is the more experienced student helping a novice: "Can you tell us about a time when you did not get the grade you expected on your paper? When you started getting As on your papers, what had changed? What did it take to raise your papers up to a higher level?"

3. Repeat the role-playing exercise for the advanced beginner mentee using one of the following scenarios or others you've developed on your own.

   - Help a mentee figure out the steps to take in writing a term paper.
   - Help a mentee figure out how to put together a class schedule that helps balance school work and family responsibilities.

4. Repeat the role-playing exercise for a competent mentee using one of the following scenarios or others you've developed on your own.

   - Help a mentee who has developed a successful relationship with a professor in one class figure out an approach to developing successful relationships with professors in other classes.

- Help a mentee who wants to attend a graduate program in a specific area at a particular graduate program strategize about how to best prepare to be a strong candidate for admission to that program.

5. Bring the entire training group back together and discuss any insights or issues resulting from the exercise.

Identifying Campus Resources

Preparing your mentors to help mentees locate and appropriately use campus resources is another important training element. While many mentors begin training assuming they already know about important campus resources, Exercise 8.12 provides opportunities for mentors to clarify their resource knowledge and to explicitly link resources to specific mentee adjustment issues.

Exercise 8.12.   Building Your Campus Resource Tool Kit

Purpose: Help mentors learn about available campus resources and understand which specific resources might be helpful in addressing different student issues.

Directions: Build yourself an initial resource tool kit through direct contact with your campus resources, choosing a set from the required and additional options (or by identifying new ones):

1. Visit in person (and view online) the three required resources: the Writing Center, Academic Skills Resource Center (replace with the name of your school's tutoring center), and campus library, even if this means going in person to learn more about their resources, meet the staff, and find cards or brochures for your own reference as a mentor.
2. Visit in person (and online) three more different campus life or student resource centers or offices. Gather brochures, cards, information, Web info, and learn about how these services might help the students your program serves address specific college adjustment issues. Also inquire how you might make appropriate referrals for your mentees while respecting their needs, confidentiality, and dignity.

Examples may include the Disability Resource Center, Multicultural Student Center, Residence Life, Queer Resource Center, Women's Resource Center, Student Legal Services, Student Health and Counseling, Student Recreation, Office of Information Technology, International Student Office, and many, many more.

3. Create a visual map (one page) along with a brief narrative (one page) of the six resources you visited, dates of your visit, and interconnections you can draw among them to show the students how they may use them to address specific student adjustment issues. On your map show all the resources you visited and visually note the relationship or relationships you see for students and their mentors in the diagram or tool kit you have illustrated. Get creative in your format for this one. (D. Lundell, personal communication, October 17, 2011)

Mentors also need opportunities to practice giving clear directions to be able to help mentees appropriately use campus resources (see Exercise 8.13).

Exercise 8.13.   Giving Directions for Using Campus Resources

Purpose: Help mentees appropriately use campus resources to address specific college adjustment issues.

Preparation: Have the training group develop a list of specific student issues (e.g., writing a term paper, getting help with a financial aid issue, dealing with health issues) and possible campus resources for addressing each issue. Note: If you are providing mentor training over multiple days, have the group develop the list of issues and linked possible resources on one day and have them complete Exercise 8.13 at home and bring it to the next training session.

Assignment

1. Create a set of directions for addressing a specific mentee adjustment issue using an appropriate campus resource. As you build your response to this assignment assume you are writing this set of directions for a typical student this program serves.

Note: If you are using this as a follow-up to Exercise 8.7, make sure to include this additional instruction: Follow the same logic and steps you used in Exercise 8.7.

2. Type your directions and include at least 10 detailed steps. Feel free to generate more than 10 steps if the task demands additional steps.
3. Think about all the factors that will bolster the success of the person who is reading and following your directions, and try to integrate those elements in your directions.

In-Class Directions

1. Ask the mentors to pair off. One individual, the person giving directions, gives the written directions and any supplies to the other person who then tries to follow the directions and complete the task. The direction giver may not speak or offer any additional information during the time his or her partner is completing the task. (5 minutes)
2. Have the pair switch roles and complete the exercise again with the second person now giving directions for a task. (5 minutes)
3. Have the pair discuss their experiences trying to follow the other person's directions and watching someone try and follow the directions they each gave. (5 minutes)
4. Have the entire group of mentors discuss their experiences. Have them reflect on how what they learned from this experience might affect the way they work with their mentees. (Carol Gabrelli, personal communication, May 15, 2013)

Cross-Cultural Appreciation or Diversity

If your program goals include increasing mentees' awareness of and ability to deal with diversity issues, then your training should be structured accordingly. Exercise 8.14 provides mentors with opportunities to improve their appreciation of the different perspectives they will encounter as they work with mentees.

Value of Service

Chapter 7 notes several benefits that college students gain from participating in service-learning projects. If you plan on incorporating a service-learning element into your program, then your training must prepare mentors to be able to help mentees get the most out of that service activity. Exercise 8.15

Exercise 8.14.   Who Are You?

Purpose: Prepares mentors to work with mentees who share perspectives or who bring different perspectives to the mentor-mentee relationship.

Step 1. Who are you? Describe who you are in regard to age, race, gender, socioeconomic class, spirituality, physical appearance, sexual orientation, and important groups you see yourself as part of (e.g., sports fan, political party, neighborhood).

Reflection Prompts

- Are some of these identities more important to you than others?
- Which ones? Why?

Note that each of these identities comes with its own perspective and way of making sense out of life experiences.

Step 2. Your identity and this program. Think about how your current understanding of your multiple identities might affect your experiences working with your mentees and other mentors in this program. Use the following prompts to focus your thinking about who you are in relation to the others you will be working with.

- How do your multiple identities affect the way you perceive your university?
- How does your identity affect the way you think about the students who attend your college or university, the students your program serves, or the other mentors you will work with in this program?
- How does your identity orient you toward effective interactions with others, and how does it challenge effective interactions?
- How might you use your perspective to create effective working relationships with your mentees and the other mentors in this program?
- How might you learn from the perspectives of others? What particular perspectives would be valuable for you to encounter?

This reflection typically takes the form of a written essay, but you also can be creative and write a poem or a dialogue, or make a drawing or a collage. Try to be as honest as possible in this reflection even if it means you record negative or contradictory thoughts and feelings as well as positive and clear ones (developed from Reitenauer, Cress, & Bennett, 2013, p. 80).

Exercise 8.15.   Active Listening and Generative Interviewing Service-Learning

Purpose: Help mentors use past experiences with service-learning as practice for their subsequent work with mentees.

Follow the directions for Exercise 8.6, substituting the following: Step 1.

1. Ask mentors to individually write up, in as much detail as possible, a college/high school service-learning experience or a personal experience where they engaged in community service, how they felt when they realized they had to come up with a way to address this issue, and how they solved the problem. (5–10 minutes)

Follow all the remaining directions for Exercise 8.6.

Note: If your mentors have the necessary background, this exercise would be most useful if they describe a college or high school service-learning experience as this is likely to be closer to what mentees will experience at college.

provides mentors with the opportunity to consider past service experiences and how what they learned can facilitate their work with mentees in the service-learning element of your program.

For a more in-depth discussion on how to help mentors and mentees make the most of service-learning experiences, see Chapter 8 Resources, p. 265.

Enacting the Mentor Role Revisited: Interpersonal Skills

The earlier discussion of training elements associated with enacting the mentor role focused on leadership and the importance of reflection. Your training curriculum should also include opportunities for mentors to develop additional interpersonal skills, particularly setting boundaries and recognizing and solving mentee problems.

Setting Boundaries

Setting boundaries is important for mentors and mentees to know their roles. Clear boundaries reduce unanticipated problems. Exercise 8.16 allows mentors to role-play and develop possible strategies for dealing with a range of potential mentor-mentee interactions.

Recognizing Potential Problems and Managing Conflict

Including material on recognizing and solving typical mentee problems in your training curriculum can serve two purposes. First, you provide mentors

Exercise 8.16.   Helping Mentors Set Boundaries

Purpose: Make mentors aware of potential mentee boundary issues and help develop possible strategies for appropriately addressing those issues.

Preparation: Develop a set of mentor-mentee scenarios and write them on index cards.

(Ask your own experienced mentors, if available, along with directors and experienced mentors from other programs to suggest scenarios; see Chapter 8 Resources, p. 265, for an additional source of possible scenarios.)

1. Split mentors into small groups of four or five. Give each group a different scenario and ask its members to be prepared to role-play it for the larger group. Give them 15 minutes to discuss the scenario and develop their role-plays, and then bring the group back together.
2. Performance: Bring the larger group back together and have each small group role-play its scenario and discuss what participants felt the boundary issue was, how they decided to resolve the issue, and the significance they felt it had on the mentoring relationship. Get input from others who were not part of that group on how they might have handled it differently and why. (30 minutes)
3. Discussion: Ask the larger group to discuss the common threads they noticed across all scenarios. What are some suggestions for setting boundaries that could be useful across situations?

with a shared set of program-recommended problem-solving strategies. Second, including this material reassures mentors that they are prepared to work with their mentees and that if problems arise your program staff will be there to support them (see Exercise 8.17).

Subgroup-Specific Areas of Training Content

The discussion on universal mentor training elements (pp. 230–253) is relevant for any type of college student peer mentoring program. However, developing a training curriculum for programs tailored to serve specific subgroups of students requires a slightly different approach. You will need to customize some of those universal elements so that your training prepares mentors for working with mentees from that specific subgroup.

Exercise 8.17.   What If?

Purpose: Prepare mentors to deal with potential issues, understand differences of quality in possible solutions, and realize that other mentors and program staff are available for support.

Directions

1. Have the group develop a list of potential issues a mentor might encounter: What if this happens? What if my mentee does or says such and such? Encourage brainstorming; really try to imagine every possible scenario. Develop an extensive list of "what ifs" on a clipboard or chalkboard.

2. Divide mentors into pairs or trios; try to keep groups small so everyone actively participates. Assign each mentor pair or trio one important "what if" and give each pair a different colored marker.

   • Ask the pair or trio to make a list of five possible coping strategies for addressing that issue. (About 5 minutes)

   • Ask each pair or trio to prioritize their ideas using a numerical scale, with (1) for the best idea, (2) for the next best idea, and so on. (About 5 minutes)

   • Next ask the pairs or trios to exchange lists. Have each group review the ideas of the other group, add more ideas (in their colored marker), and then prioritize or rank the new list, either agreeing or disagreeing with the previous pair's rankings. You can repeat this process until all pairs or trios have reviewed all lists, until momentum runs out, or you're out of time.

Discussion

1. To emphasize the value of support, ask mentors to reflect on what happened during this exercise. Prompt: What did you notice? What if you had handled those "what ifs" all by yourself? Or you had to respond on the spot?

2. To emphasize the value of experience or expertise in problem solving, ask mentors to reflect on what makes one strategy better than others in dealing with a specific "what if." How might this relate to their work with their mentees?

Adjustment Issues Particular to Specific Subgroups of Students

The issues mentors need to be prepared to help their mentees deal with are different for different groups of students. For example, training for an international student mentoring program might prepare mentors for dealing with group-specific issues such as helping mentees with F-1 visas who live outside the United States register for classes or helping set up an international wire transfer to pay their account balances. On the other hand, training for a program serving student veterans needs to prepare mentors to help mentees address a different set of issues, including accessing GI Bill benefits, negotiating the steps for turning American Council on Education certification or service-related education or experiences into college credit at your school, or connecting with veteran-sponsored post-traumatic stress disorder support groups.

Understanding Your University's Group-Relevant Policies

An important part of preparing mentors to help mentees deal with group-specific adjustment issues is making mentors aware of your school's policies that directly affect the group of students your program serves. Mentors need to be aware that while financial aid issues are critical for all students, your mentees may have specific financial aid issues not necessarily experienced by the typical student at your school. You can help mentors learn more about the typical issues your mentees face along with providing some recommended approaches on how to address those issues by including presentations by financial aid office staff in your mentor training.

Locating Group-Relevant Campus Resources

For tailored programs, the training element "developing mentors' knowledge of campus resources" should be customized in the same way as the training material on adjustment issues so that it focuses on your mentees' needs. Use the issue adjustment event schema information organizing tool, introduced in Chapter 7 (pp. 211—213), to explicitly connect specific issues and relevant campus resources. Provide mentors with opportunities to practice developing appropriate strategies for using campus resources to address specific mentee adjustment issues.

Although Exercise 8.18 is presented so that it can be used in any college student mentor-training curriculum, it can easily be modified for use in tailored programs. It is valuable to allow mentors to brainstorm possible strategies linked to specific campus resources and collectively decide on which ones might be most effective under which conditions. This is an excellent way to build a common mentor perspective while developing strategies that should work well for your group of mentees.

Exercise 8.18.   Campus Resource Treasure Hunt

Purpose: This mentor version of Exercise 7.1 allows mentors to role-play helping mentees identify how to use specific campus resources to address specific adjustment issues and to help mentors share their knowledge about the most effective strategies for addressing specific issues using campus resources.
Preparation

- Develop a series of short scenarios that ask mentees to address specific student adjustment issues they face using campus resources. Ask your mentors to help develop scenarios specific to the issues and campus resources they learned about in mentor training. For examples see Exercise 7.1.
- Have mentors develop program-recommended appropriate strategies for using campus resources to address the issue presented in each scenario.

Step 1. Divide mentors into pairs; assign one to be the mentor and one to be the mentee. Ask the role-playing mentor to present one scenario to the role-playing mentee, asking the mentee how he or she would proceed to address the issue and which campus resource(s) might be used to do so.
Step 2. Have the mentor discuss with the mentee the mentee's response and the mentor's recommended response to the issues presented in each scenario.
Step 3. Reverse roles and repeat the exercise with a different scenario until each trainee has had two or three opportunities to play both roles.
Step 4. Bring the large group together and discuss the exercise. What issues did mentors experience trying to share recommended strategies with mentees? What issues did mentees notice? How can mentors use what they've learned in this exercise in their work with mentees?

Program-Specific Areas of Training Content

It is helpful to integrate program-specific elements throughout your actual training. An early element of any training curriculum needs to be an explicit discussion of your program's goals and objectives. Before your mentors begin trying to understand the mentor role, they need a clear picture of what the program is trying to accomplish.

Mentor and Mentee Expectations

After your mentors progress through curriculum elements like understanding mentee adjustment issues, identifying important campus resources, and developing communication skills, it is a good idea to shift the focus back to the program level. Go back and review the materials you introduced in the hiring process about the mentor job description and expectations for mentors and mentees. A useful exercise is to have mentors review the initial mentor-mentee contract and then look at the contract expectations in more depth. Expectations that initially seemed simple may now seem more complex in light of the training they have already received.

Program Policies and Procedures

The middle of your training is a good time to review important program protocols and policies, particularly those relating to documenting mentor-mentee contact and evaluation. The following is an example from the Transfer Connections Program described in Vignette 3 of how mentoring training provides mentors-to-be with opportunities to practice helping mentees develop action plans. The action plans serve as records of regular mentor-mentee contact and as a source of evaluation data.

This is also an appropriate time to introduce more specific program protocols that might not have meant as much to mentors before they had a clearer view of the actual program and how they would do their job.

Developing an Action Plan Using a Student Success Initiative (SSI) Interview

SSIs are motivational interviews used by Transfer Connections mentors in one-on-one sessions with mentees as a means of developing action plans to meet specific needs of incoming transfer students. One part of mentor training involves preparing mentors to effectively use SSIs in their work with mentees. Completing an SSI provides mentees with a practical plan for success in any academic department, and mentors will have a record of their mentee's progress and the ability to refer to their specific monthly goal (Phil Larson, Lydia Middleton, Adam Baker, The University of Michigan Transfer Connections Program, personal communication, January 28, 2014). See Chapter 8 Resources (p. 272), for a sample SSI.

Mentor Communication Guidelines

We want to be very explicit about our program's mentor communication expectations.

1. Mentors are expected to take *responsibility* for communicating any questions or issues to the program manager and the program director (see point No. 2). Specifically, we need you to communicate clearly and in a timely manner when

- you do not understand an assigned task or request,
- you feel you cannot do an assigned task or request,
- you are finished with an assigned task and now are ready for more work (remember this position involves on average [number of] hours a week),
- you cannot be reached through normal means (e.g., when you are out of the area, when your normal communication options aren't working such as if your cell phone is broken or you are someplace where you cannot get e-mail), or
- you know you will be missing a staff meeting or an assigned work task.

2. Mentors are expected to communicate with the *appropriate* person.

- For all program business, including issues with mentees, other mentors, outside work conflicts, and scheduling issues, contact the program manager and send a copy to the program director.
- If you have an issue you are not comfortable discussing with the program manager, then contact the program director directly.
- If you need someone to cover work or responsibilities that have been assigned to you (and you cannot fulfill), first contact other mentors and work out some sort of trade in which you take on someone else's work and that person covers for you. Then contact the program manager, let him or her know your plans, and make sure the manager agrees that the arrangement you have made fits with other program goals and work assignments.

3. Mentors are expected to communicate in an *appropriate* manner.

- Generally the best manner of communication is to talk to us either in person or by phone. The next best manner of communicating would be e-mail, as long as you are able to regularly check your e-mail messages (even off campus) so that if we have questions we can get them answered. Leaving a voicemail message is not the best way of communicating on program issues and should only be used as a last resort (see next point).
- Your responsibility for communication does not end until you get confirmation that your message was received and we have the opportunity to respond with any questions about your message or plan. Example: If you leave a voicemail message, you need to follow-up until you get confirmation that the message was received and we can communicate any concerns or questions to you. The same principle holds true for e-mail. Just sending an e-mail requesting something, asking a question, or asking permission is not a complete communication.

The most basic communication rule is: If you're not sure what is expected of you, *ask*. (Collier & Fellows, 2006)

How to Do the Job

The later stages of training are a good time to emphasize the specifics of how to do the actual mentor job. This should include role-playing working with mentees, practicing program-related skills, and discussing potential problems and possible solutions. It can be a valuable teachable moment when mentors identify issues they are not sure how to address. Program staff should be prepared to work with mentors to develop shared solutions that might be effective.

If possible, it is valuable to end your training with a celebration. Review with your mentors how much they have learned in training. Reassure them that they are not supposed to be perfect or experts on everything, they just need to be able to direct mentees to appropriate resources and others on campus who can provide the needed information. Also remind them that program staff will be available to support them throughout their work with mentees. Regardless of the duration of the training or even the specific

Exercise 8.19.   Packing Your Mentor Bag

Purpose: Remind mentors about the collective vision of what constitutes an effective mentor that they have developed in training and how valuable a resource they will be to their mentees.

Preparation: Write "Mentor Bag" in large letters on brown paper grocery bags so you have one for each mentor in training and the trainer.

1. Distribute the bags to mentors the day before they are to complete the in-class exercise.

Instructions: You are asked to pack one bag to take with you as you go out to work with mentees in our mentoring program. Think about all the things we have learned about the skills, tools, and qualities of an ideal mentor. Use your imagination to figure out the essential knowledge and skills your mentees could use and that you could pack in your bag. These can be symbolic or literal resources.

Note: The trainer should bring out one or two sample items as examples to show the trainees (e.g., "I included a ruler in my mentor bag so that mentees can realize how much they have grown over their time in the program.").

In-Class Exercise

2. Mentors bring their packed bags to the next day's training. Ask one mentor to share something from his or her bag with the rest of the group and explain why it was included. Ask if anyone else included the same item or something close to it, and if so, ask the person to share any additional comments with the group. Continue through the group with one person at a time sharing an item from the mentor bag until all participants have displayed all the items they brought with them.

3. Discuss the different contents of the mentor bags, any commonalities of items, and whether any important elements are missing. (Amy Driscoll, personal communication, June 24, 2005)

---

content covered in your curriculum, it is very important to have mentors reflect on their experiences. Exercise 8.19 provides mentors with an opportunity to creatively reflect on what they've learned.

Sequencing and Integrating Different Elements of Mentor Training

It is finally time to consider the organization of your mentor training. After you have decided what material you want to include in your training, there are still three important questions you'll need to answer.

How Will Materials Be Presented?

When you consider how materials will be presented in your training, it is important to carry over what we've learned about differences in learning styles. Keep in mind that different mentors will likely prefer different learning styles, so it is important to employ multiple approaches. Incorporating multiple learning styles may include having mentors listen to presentations (i.e., auditory learning), view Web videos and slide shows (i.e., visual learning), and write reflections and do activities (i.e., kinetic learning). You can also introduce variety into your training by using multiple learning formats: individual work, pairs, small groups or teams, and the entire group of mentors.

Who Should Present Specific Training Elements?

It is also important to consider the selection of the appropriate person to conduct each specific element of training. This boils down to an issue of balance. On the one hand, you can add interest and novelty to your training by having different facilitators present content or lead different activities. For example, covering material on engaging mentees in their own learning by involving faculty members, staff from important campus offices like financial aid, and community experts can help hold your trainees' interest more than if that same material was presented by a single speaker.

On the other hand, trainees may view individuals who are experts or who have had similar experiences as those of your mentors or the mentees they'll be serving as more credible and trustworthy. Having mentors who worked in your program in previous years share their experiences with trainees tends to be much more effective than if the program director provides the same information. It seems to mean more coming from someone who has already done the job your mentors-to-be are training to do. Similarly, mentors can gain confidence in their ability to make a difference by hearing an advising professional talk about how his or her office has noticed the positive effect of peer mentoring on the students who participated in programs like yours.

How Will Training Materials Be Sequenced?

Another important element to consider is timing or sequencing. You must consider the most appropriate times to present different training materials. Some sequencing decisions are based on logical steps needed to build trainees' knowledge bases. For example, mentors for a program tailored to serve returning women students need information about college adjustment issues shared by all incoming students before being presented with the specific challenges faced by the students their program serves. However, your most fundamental sequencing decision has to do with figuring out how to best combine the different elements of your training in ways that provide trainees with the knowledge and skills they need to do their jobs in an engaged learning environment within the time you have available. A helpful analogy is to think of sequencing mentor training like putting together a multicourse formal dinner. Appetizers, soup, and salad are typically served before the entrées, and subtler entrees, like fish or pasta, are served before heavier, more full-flavored ones like beef or pork. Sometimes intermediate elements, like sorbet, are served between courses to cleanse the diners' palates. Putting together the menu for your mentor training is quite similar. Too many content presentations in a row can overload your mentors; you need to provide them with opportunities to cleanse their palates by varying your training elements. One good rule to consider is to follow any content presentation with an activity to energize your trainees and involve them in their own learning.

The following is an example of the possible sequencing of activities in a single day of a multiple-day mentor training session along with an explanation why the elements are ordered in the way they are. Mentors are typically not highly energized right at the beginning of a training session. Therefore it is useful to begin with a relatively low-energy element, such as a 10–15 minute small-group discussion of assigned readings related to program content with the trainer moving from group to group to gauge progress and encourage involvement. Then the entire group is brought together, and each small group reports on its discussion. Starting the discussion in small groups increases the likelihood that more students will participate than if you started the same discussion in a single large group. After this initial content discussion (auditory learning), it is time for a mentor exercise or activity, ideally something that connects with either the content discussed in the earlier small-group discussions or will be covered in a subsequent presentation. The activity should be something that gets trainees out of their seats and moving, such as Exercise 8.2. The next training element should be a more formal content presentation (e.g., differences in learning styles) from the program staff followed by a break for trainees to use the restroom and stretch. It is not a bad idea to actually build stretching exercises into your training, particularly if the sessions will last more than a couple of hours.

When the trainees come back from their break, involve them in a second activity that shifts the format between paired work to larger group discussion and relates to the content presentation, something like Exercise 8.9. Finally, before the lunch break, have a second content presentation, ideally something less theoretical and more practical such as having a campus staff person from advising, financial aid, or the tutoring center tell your trainees about the range of services their offices provide and how mentees can contact that office and its services. It would be helpful if they could explicitly link those services to specific adjustment issues. Allow an hour for lunch, and encourage mentors to informally discuss their impressions of the experiences in the morning training.

After lunch is another low-energy time, so this is a good place to take your mentors out of your training room and walk to a campus resource where they could hear from the director of the office what that office provides. Note that in this example mentors are learning about campus resources in two different formats, in-class presentations and walking to offices, which allows them to know how to direct mentees to that service. When you return to your training room, it is time for another content presentation by program staff or a faculty expert on a program-important content topic like student adjustment issues. Follow this presentation with a related mentor exercise or activity that has them linking campus resources to specific student adjustment issues, such as Exercise 8.13. After this, the mentors-in-training need another break.

When they come back, have a nuts-and-bolts content presentation by program staff on program protocols, policies, procedures for documenting work with mentees, and mentors' roles in program evaluation. After the presentation, group the trainees into pairs and have them practice or role-play using program resources, filling out mentor-mentee session forms, and any other program-specific parts of the mentor role. Allow at least 30 to 45 minutes at the end of the day of training for debriefing and reflecting on the day's activities. This is an opportunity for you to collect some data if that is part of your evaluation plan. The final element of the day's training is to prepare mentors for the next day's assigned readings and activities.

See Chapter 8 Resources, (p. 268), for a sample curriculum.

This chapter began with an overview of the fundamental issues you need to consider when setting up your mentoring program. Because it is imperative that mentor training mirrors program content so mentors are prepared to work with mentees, this chapter shares a parallel structure with Chapter 7: program content. Chapter 8 identifies three areas of training elements: universal, elements shared by programs serving the same subgroup of students, and program-specific elements. The chapter also provides more than 20 training exercises along with suggestions for the best way to sequence training elements in your curriculum. The next chapter focuses on evaluation, including the evaluation of mentor training.

Notes

1. This section was adapted from Arévalo, Boggan, and West (2004, p. 6).
2. The Johari window, named after the first names of its inventors, Joseph Luft and Harry Ingham (1961), is a model for describing the process of human interaction. A four-paned window is used to divide personal awareness into four types and is a model for describing the process of human interaction. The four types of personal awareness are represented by the four quadrants of the window:

   • Open: things I know about me and you also know about me
   • Hidden: things I know about myself that you do not know
   • Blind: things you know about me that I am unaware of
   • Oblivious: things I do not know about myself and that you do not know either

   The lines dividing the four panes serve as window shades, which can move as the interaction progresses and previously unrevealed knowledge of self is made public. The window is used as a metaphor to explain how a person's self-awareness increases through interaction. The goal is to increase the size of the open pane of the window, thus increasing meaningful interaction with others (Collier, 2013b, p. 115).

CHAPTER 8 RESOURCES

There are four sections in the resources for Chapter 8: additional exercises, a sample training curriculum, additional source material, and a step-by-step guide for using an SSI to develop a mentee action plan.

Additional Exercises

What Is a Mentor?

Exercise 8.20. Characteristics of Successful Mentors

Purpose: Develop an explicit understanding of characteristics or behaviors of successful mentors. Connect to materials on what mentoring can accomplish from the literature.

1. Ask mentors-in-training to sit in small groups (if number of trainees is small, have them work in pairs). For a larger group of trainees a good group size is four to five individuals to ensure everyone participates. Ask each group to pick someone to be the secretary and someone to be the presenter.
2. Ask mentors-in-training to think about, discuss, and list positive and negative experiences they've had as mentees.
3. After everyone has spoken, ask the group to come up with the three most positive characteristics of successful mentors or, if they prefer, the top three characteristics of ineffective mentors.
4. Bring the groups back together and have each group representative share with the larger group.
5. Debrief by highlighting the characteristics of successful mentors as shown by research. (developed from Arévalo et al., 2004, p. 97)

Exercise 8.21.   Understanding the Mentor Role

Purpose: Develop a shared understanding of *mentorship* and reflect upon what being a mentor might look like in your program. Connect this exercise to training materials on mentor expectations (see Chapter 8, p. 257).

Note: The first five steps can be done as an individual written reflection exercise or as a group training exercise. The sixth step must be a group exercise.

1. Ask mentors-in-training to list all the words and images that come to mind when they think of the word *mentor*. Group exercise: Write them down on one side of the flipchart or whiteboard.

2. Group exercise: Ask mentors-in-training to turn to the person next to them and tell them about someone they consider to have been a mentor in their own life. Individual written reflection: Write a paragraph describing one important relationship in your own life when you were mentored by some else.

3. Group exercise: After the individual sharing, bring the group back together. Now ask them to describe to you all the images, thoughts, feelings, and words that came to mind when they thought about their own personal experience with a mentor. Write them down on the other side of the flipchart.

4. Group exercise: Ask mentors-in-training if they see any differences or similarities between the words that were written about the idea of a mentor and their actual experiences of a mentor. For individual written reflection: Compare the list of mentor-related words and images with your description of your personal mentoring experiences. Write a paragraph about the similarities and differences between the list of terms and your personal mentoring experiences.

5. Group exercise: Develop a shared program definition of *mentor*. For individual written reflection: Develop your personal definition of *mentor* and bring this to your group discussion.

6. Keeping this definition of *mentor* in mind, discuss how this might inform their work with the mentees your program serves. Ask mentors-in-training to describe specific behaviors in working with their mentees that would exemplify this definition of *mentor*.

The sixth step is very important as it moves mentors-in-training from an abstract conceptualization of mentor to how they would act as mentors working in your program. This is an excellent place to introduce Exercise 8.16 (p. 253), on setting boundaries and discuss what is and is not appropriate for a mentor to do when working with mentees. For example, the University Studies Program suggests not giving your cell phone number to your mentees. (A. Kneppler & C. Gabrelli, personal communication, May 15, 2013)

Differences in Learning Styles

Exercise 8.22.   How Do You Learn?

Purpose: Help mentors-in-training reflect on personal learning styles and how differences in mentees' learning styles might affect the mentor-mentee relationship.

1. Present the following scenario to mentors:
    Imagine you just bought a new 8G cell phone (update to reflect the most advanced current technology) with all the bells and whistles, along with a host of apps that came with it. How do you go about learning how to use it?

Do you do any of the following:

- Read the instruction manual cover to cover trying to absorb all the new features so you can understand how each feature is going to improve your phone's overall communication capacity?
- Base your understanding of how to use this phone on your last phone since if you know how to use one phone you can use any phone?
- Read the quick start guide at the beginning of the manual and then figure out the rest of the features as the need arises?
- Look around at other people using their phones until you find someone who has the same type of phone and then copy how that person operates the phone? Figure it out based on observation of users?
- Ask your friends, younger siblings, or children to explain how the phone operates?

Ask participants to discuss their responses. (10 minutes)
2. Present material on learning styles (see additional source material later in Chapter 8 Resources).

3. Have mentors-in-training take a learning style inventory
4. Discussion: Ask mentors-in-training to reflect on how what they have learned about differences in learning styles might affect how they share material with mentees. What kinds of advice might a mentor offer a mentee who appears to be having classroom issues related to differences in learning styles?

This could also be an opportunity to role-play interaction.

Sample Training Curriculum for a First-Generation Student Mentoring Program

The following is from Collier and Fellows (2006).

Day 1 Think Like a Learner
Preparation: Write an autobiography of yourself as a learner (see Exercise 8.9, p. 242)

0900–0930	Introductions, overview of project goals and intentions, design, and roles of project staff
0930–1030	Pair interviews, development of group profile Analysis of major themes of group
1030–1200	Understanding the expertise model

For each level of model: description and examples, self-analysis, and processing activities

1200–1230	Lunch
1230–1400	Campus resource exploration walk and processing
1400–1430	Preview of day 2—do you think first-generation students develop through the expertise model? How can we support them? Assign reading for next day.
1445–1545	Technical skills—exploring Web resources
1545–1630	Reflective processing/assessment Reflect on the day—what did you experience as a learner?

Day 2 Walking in the Shoes of First-Generation Learners
Preparation: Read article(s) about first-generation learners. Reflect on the previous day's question.

0900–0930	Shared reflections on assigned readings

| 0930–1100 | Processing descriptions of first-generation learners in terms of assets, issues, transitions, and challenges (needs) in pairs |

Consider what strategies first-generation students will need to be successful in relation to each category

1100–1200	Understanding first-generation students through prose, poetry, and digital stories
1200–1230	Lunch
1230–1400	Campus resource exploration walk and processing
1400–1430	Preview of Day 3–with all the information about first-generation learners in mind, write a prescription for your role as mentor to support the students
1445–1545	Exploring technical skills—reviewing program videos, exploring the program tip sheet library, and mentor responsibilities for regular e-mail connections with mentees
1545–1630	Reflection/assessment

Day 3 Becoming a Mentor
Preparation: Read assigned article(s) on mentoring

0900–0915	Continuum of mentor expertise—using the Dreyfus and Dreyfus (2005) model to place students on continuum from novice to expert mentor
0915–0930	Review Day 2 reflection—discuss prescriptions for selves as mentors
0930–1000	Pair interviews exploring mentor assets and potential challenges. Develop group profile of mentor assets and challenges
1000–1015	Finding connections in the mentor group for matching assets with challenges
1015–1130	Role-plays of scenarios of mentoring first-generation students using categories of information from previous day and group profile of assets and challenges
1130–1200	A day as an effective mentor—drawing posters of ideal days, group sharing
1200–1230	Lunch
1230–1400	Campus resource exploration walk and processing
1400–1430	Brainstorm your greatest fears, dreaded issues, problems of worry, and so on
1445–1545	Technical skills—using the website

1545–1630	Reflect on your day as a mentor learner—locate self on expertise continuum, what influenced growth and change, continuing needs

Day 4 Mentoring in Context
Preparation: Pack mentor bag with supplies for new role (see Exercise 8.19, Part 1, p. 260)

0900–1015	Presentation on conceptual foundations of intervention
1015–1115	Limitations of mentors recognizing boundaries—why/ why not?
1115–1230	Unpacking our mentor bags—lunch
1230–1400	Campus resource exploration
1400–1430	Coming attractions—advice for orientation of mentees: identifying potential problems
1445–1530	Technical skills—practicing mentee orientation
1530–1630	Processing—resources to respond to potential problems, needs, issues

Day 5 Are We Ready? Are We Mentors Yet?
Preparation: Literature on mentoring issues for review by mentors

0900–1100	Consider potential problems and work with consultant on approaches
1100–1200	Synthesis of guidelines for mentoring (assessment)
1200–1300	Lunch and Reflection
1300–1430	Resource—mentor office (practice entering data from forms)
1430–1530	Quiet review and reflection—self-assessment (assessment)
1530–1615	Planning/design of mentee orientation Advice/suggestions from mentors (assessment)
1615–1630	Review and rate daily schedules for effective and ineffective training activities (assessment)
1630	Celebration

Additional Source Material (also see Chapter 7 Resources)

What Is Mentoring?

Crisp, G., & Cruz, I. (2009). Mentoring college students: A critical review of the literature between 1990 and 2007. *Review of Educational Research, 50,* 525–545.

Eby, L. T., Rhodes, J. E., & Allen, T. D. (2007). Definition and evolution of mentoring. In T. D. Allen & L. T. Eby (Eds.), *The Blackwell handbook of mentoring: A multiple perspectives approach* (pp. 7–20). Malden, MA: Wiley-Blackwell.

Leadership

Komives, S., Lucas, N., & McMahon, T. (2006). *Exploring leadership: For college students who want to make a difference* (2nd ed.). San Francisco, CA: Jossey-Bass.
Lipman-Blumen, J. (2000). *Connective leadership: Managing in a changing world.* Oxford, UK: Oxford University Press.
Wheatley, M. J. (2006). *Leadership and the new science: Discovering order in a chaotic world.* San Francisco, CA: Berrett-Koehler.

Learning Styles

For material on Kolb learning styles, see the following:
Bixler, B. (2014). *Learning style inventory.* Retrieved from http://www.personal.psu.edu/bxb11/LSI/LSI.htm
David Kolb's learning styles model and experiential learning theory. (2013). Retrieved from http://www.businessballs.com/kolblearningstyles.htm
McLeod, S. (2013). *Kolb learning styles.* Retrieved from http://www.simplypsychology.org/learning-kolb.html

Communication Skills

Grohol, J. M. (2007). *Becoming a better listener: Active listening.* Retrieved from http://psychcentral.com/lib/become-a-better-listener-active-listening/0001299
Pachucki, D. (2014). *Games that will develop the listening skills of college students.* Retrieved from http://everydaylife.globalpost.com/games-develop-listening-skills-college-students-14355.html

Service-Learning

Cress, C., Collier, P., & Reitenauer, V. (2013). *Learning through Serving: A Student Guidebook for Service-Learning and Civic Engagement Across Academic Disciplines and Cultural Communities* (2nd ed.). Sterling, VA: Stylus.

Setting Boundaries

University of Victoria Teaching and Learning Center. (2011). *DVD 7: Teaching assistant issues.* Available from http://ltc.uvic.ca/servicesprograms/criticalincidents/tadvd.php

University of Michigan Transfer Connections Program's Step-by-Step Guide for Developing an Action Plan Using a Student Success Initiative Interview

The following is from a personal communication from P. Larson, L. Middleton, & A. Baker, January 28, 2014.

After your initial meeting with each of your mentees, offer to work with them to develop an action plan for the next month to guide the mentees' first semester at the University of Michigan (U-M). The Student Success Initiative Interview (SSI) offers a unique peer-to-peer way to help students identify their transitional goals. The themed, guided discussions are there to help you be a good coach and mentor.

The three action plans cover the following:

- Expectations of the U-M
- Campus involvement
- Mid-semester goals and academic success
- Semester self-evaluation and plans for winter semester

SSI action plans are tailored to supplement each interview. This sheet contains a series of questions that ask the student to think about the topics you just discussed with them. It asks them to think about where they see themselves as part of the campus community and where they would like to be at the end of the semester. These questions should be used to guide further conversations between the mentor and mentee.

When the questions have been discussed, work with the mentee to fill in the goals and steps that the mentee will take to reach those goals. Help mentees be realistic and detailed about the goals they commit to. Come up with an action plan that includes steps they will take to reach those goals. Again, specifics and how reasonable these steps are will be the key to success.

The interview guide contains academic resources that may be helpful in student success. Go over the resources with the mentees to help them decide which resources best meet their needs. Use your knowledge of the campus to provide any additional resource you think may be helpful.

Your most important role is listening, taking notes, and initiating discussion.

Follow up with the progress the students are making with their action plan by e-mail and subsequent conversations. Keep track of what mentees discuss and are interested in exploring.

Encourage but *do not* insist! The SSI is a resource for your mentees, but do not sacrifice your relationship with the student just so they will fill out an action plan. Judge the student's willingness to talk about an issue or share information. If mentees do not fulfill their goals or find the goals too out of reach, it is okay. Simply have them fill out a new action plan or modify the one they have by both of you setting reachable goals.

Sample SSI

Transfer Mentee Interview: First Meeting (September)
Adaptation, Involvement, and Academics
Use this page as a guideline for asking questions. Use the next page to take notes.
I. Mentor-Mentee Conversation Warm-Up
Explain why you became a mentor and what your role is.

- Describe benefits of being involved on campus and in leadership opportunities.
- Discuss the transitions and differences between high school and college.
- Discuss time management between homework, involvement, work, social life, and so on.

II. How have you adapted to campus life?
Consider asking the following:

- Why did you choose to come to U-M?
- What do you think of U-M so far?
- How do you like your residence hall/place you live?
- What was the most difficult thing about coming from another university? What was the easiest?

Resources available: M planner, campus map, residence hall activities, Magic Bus website: http://mbus.pts.umich.edu/arrivals/routeView.php

III. What are you involved in so far?
Consider asking the following:

- Did you attend Festifall?
- What activities or student organizations interest you?
- Are there activities I can do that you would be interested in (suggest some)?
- I'm involved in _____ and found out about it through _____.

Resources available: Maize Pages (http://uuis.umich.edu/maizepgs), Center for Campus Involvement

IV. How do you define success in college?
Consider asking the following:

- Describe your study habits at your previous institution. How do you think they will change?
- What was the easiest thing about your past institution? What was most difficult?
- What was the classroom environment like there, and how is it different from U-M?
- What is your major?
- Tell me about your classes; are you taking any courses in your major? If so, what are they?
- What are your academic goals for this semester? Do you have a plan to make that happen?
- What courses do you think you will do well in or find more difficult? (Encourage the use of academic labs or programs on campus.)
- Do you know about C-Tools? Have you considered using a tutor? Why? Why not?

Resources available: http://academicsupport.umich.edu, the M Planner
Note-taking prompts

How have your mentees adapted to college life (one to two examples)?

What organizations or groups are they involved in so far, or interested in finding out about?

What impression do they have about academic life at U-M? What transition issues, if any, have they expressed?

What academic goals have they identified? What steps will they take this month to achieve these goals?

UNDERGRADUATE TO GRADUATE SCHOOL TRANSITION-FOCUSED PROGRAM

The Project for New Mexico Graduates of Color and Integrity in Graduate Training

William L. Gannon, Stephanie Sanchez, and Felipe Amaral,
University of New Mexico

TABLE V5.1

Inclusiveness	Duration	Approach to Addressing Students' Needs	College Transition
Universal: *Open to all students*	Long term: *More than one semester*	Developmental: *Responds to student needs as they evolve over time*	Undergraduate to graduate school

With just over two million people, New Mexico is the first majority-minority U.S. state of the lower 48 (U.S. Census Bureau, 2011). New Mexico stands out as a source for training and development of students traditionally

We thank Julie Coonrod, dean of graduate studies, for her enthusiastic and continuous support of our graduate programs at the University of New Mexico. We also thank Tomás A. Arciniega and anonymous reviewers for improvements to earlier versions of this vignette.

underrepresented in research, graduate-level education, and university enrollment in general.

The University of New Mexico (UNM), founded in 1887, is a public, four-year, PhD-granting, research university located in Albuquerque. UNM's main campus total student enrollment is 29,056 (48.6% are minorities), undergraduate enrollment is 20,936 (54% are minorities), and graduate student enrollment is 4,522 (30% are minorities; UNM, 2012–2013). UNM is one of only two Carnegie research/doctoral intensive institutions in the United States that are also Hispanic-serving institutions. New Mexico is among the 24 National Institute of Health Institutional Development Award Program states and is a National Science Foundation Experimental Program to Stimulate Competitive Research state.

Like many academic and research institutions, UNM administrators recognize the challenge of fostering a culture of academic integrity among a diverse population of graduate students while nurturing the cultural identity of students who are traditionally underrepresented in graduate school. UNM has a long-standing commitment to these types of programs and supports initiatives that help guide students toward degree completion and pursuing successful careers. To this end, UNM has embraced programs that foster success of students of color while encouraging all graduate students to become aware of ethics and integrity tools using mentoring as a foundational component.

In 2010 new federal regulations required research institutions to provide content on the responsible conduct of research (RCR) to postdoctoral and graduate students as well as undergraduate students who are supported by federal funds (National Science Foundation, 2014). RCR-related content areas today include research misconduct, the use of humans and other animals in research, conflicts of interest, data management and reproducibility, ethical peer review and publication, whistle blower ethics, financial management of funded awards, collaborative research, and scientists as responsible members of society, using responsible mentoring as a means to deploy RCR content. RCR guidelines emphasize mentoring relationships between graduate students and their faculty advisers. However, they also include peer mentoring, responsibility to other members of the lab group, and the relationship of undergraduates and postdoctorates. For the National Science Foundation and other federal funders, mentoring at the graduate level is considered critical and central to successful conduct of research and other academic scholarly activities as well as fostering academic integrity and a willful adoption of research ethics by these professionals in training.

Research institutions are increasingly providing resources to graduate students in regard to research ethics and mentoring. A series of workshops through the university's Professional and Academic Workshops (PAW) portal is offered each semester for RCR certification (see http://grad.unm.edu/

resources/paw.html). This same PAW series has workshops and other sessions that provide information for student success including writing camps, grant funding information, and wellness seminars for graduate students of color. Also, ethics content is being blended with research methods courses traditionally established to bring disciplinary expectations and vocabulary into the graduate student consciousness. While attention to raising ethical awareness is increasing in the general graduate student culture, mentoring is seen as a way to help culturally diverse cohorts of entering graduate students feel that their experiences and successes are equally important to the university community.

Institutional Context

In 2002 the Project for New Mexico Graduates of Color (PNMGC) was formed at UNM with the idea that through mentoring, students underrepresented in graduate school could support one another in achieving academic success. As Kalichman (2001) notes,

> The enterprise of science depends on effective communication not just about the science, but about the practice of science, standards of conduct, and ethical and social responsibility. Taking an active role in helping to train the next generation of scientists should not be optional. And scientific trainees have a complementary responsibility to take an active role in their own development and seek mentors.

At UNM, many groups that support graduate student education share these responsibilities. The PNMGC, in particular, promotes the idea of academic integrity and thoughtful research design through discussions with mentees and as a general principle. Although the program does not host workshops on ethics in particular, PNMGC does conduct workshops on community-based participatory research and the ways research should be approached in a variety of fields. PNMGC plays an important role in making sure students from groups typically underrepresented in graduate school research receive the training and guidance they need to conduct research in responsible and ethical ways within and across fields.

Program Description

Peer mentoring is the foundation of the PNMGC. In 2003 several graduate students created Peer Mentoring for Graduates of Color, a student organization that provided UNM graduate students of color with the opportunity to mentor one another and share experiences and strategies for success in graduate school and beyond. PNMGC envisions peer mentoring as a mutually beneficial and nonhierarchical relationship in which partners or cohorts, often comprising peers in different stages of postsecondary education, provide one another with support, guidance, and the necessary tools to navigate academia.

This program works to build partnerships that meet the individual, academic, and cultural needs of graduate students. The matching process allows students to select specific criteria for pairing with other students, such as one's native language, cultural background, gender, or academic association. Once in the program, participants have a number of opportunities to attend workshops, social mixers, or special activities with their mentor or other mentored students, many of who come from similar cultural backgrounds. The UNM has collaborative resources in the form of the Global Education Office that provides additional support to non-U.S. students and scholars coming to UNM, coordinates opportunities for UNM students to study overseas, and offers intensive English language programs to students interested in studying in the United States. PNMGC staff believe that mentorship can occur in informal and formal spaces and through various forms of communication. Participants are encouraged to interact with their mentoring partner or other students in the program through any communicative process that involves and benefits the parties involved.

PNMGC's Peer Mentoring Program is distinct from other more traditional mentoring models in that it is specifically aimed at providing mentorship for diverse populations, including first-generation college students, ethnic or cultural minority students, students from low economic status, and any other group that feels underrepresented in a field. This mentoring model is a holistic approach to academic success that focuses on students' wellness, sense of community and belonging, and ability to grow as leaders, which in turn positively influences their educational experiences and attainment.

Although it remains a student-based organization, PNMGC is affiliated with UNM's Graduate Studies as it works to build community among students historically underrepresented in graduate school. PNMGC is funded primarily by student fees. PNMGC program staff consists of hired project assistants who manage the program and typically are graduate students with a special commitment to social and educational justice issues. PNMGC also has an advisory board made up of staff, faculty, graduate, and undergraduate students who collaborate in shaping PNMGC programming.

Evaluation

It is important to note that PNMGC project assistants also serve as key resources to address issues and provide guidance to both mentors and mentees. They monitor the mentoring relationships and collect feedback throughout the semester. This feedback is collected formally through evaluations and essays and informally through routine contact and conversations with mentors and mentees. Informally, mentoring partners often comment on successful shared meetings or social activities as well as strategies for overcoming obstacles within the relationship. Feedback from these conversations is incorporated into the PNMGC program and influences the information provided in subsequent activities, orientations, and question-and-answer sessions.

All mentors and mentees receive an online survey at the end of each semester to help them reflect on their mentoring experience and provide feedback on the strengths and weaknesses of the program. A reflection essay is also required of all those who wish to apply for the peer mentoring scholarship, which is intended as an incentive to foster commitment to a mentoring partnership and is also used as an additional way to provide feedback for evaluation purposes.

Peer mentoring program evaluations provide information on the types of mentoring practices students most appreciated, such as opportunities to participate in sponsored community or social activities and continued networking opportunities, particularly outside their established social groups or disciplines. Spring 2014 mentor partners also expressed an appreciation for the mentoring experience and for the mutually supportive space that was provided outside their departments. Mentors, in particular, reflected on their previous experiences in being mentored and how this spurred their desire to give back to others. Other students reflected on specific projects or goals that guided their mentoring experiences and partnerships, such as writing letters of intent, working on graduate school applications or posteducational plans, and navigating final theses or dissertation projects.

Training

PNMGC's mentoring program begins with a Meet and Greet that serves as a recruitment and general information session for potential participants. It is also an opportunity for new and returning participants to connect or reconnect with one another. The Meet and Greet also helps facilitate mentor-mentee matches. Once accepted to the program, students are required to attend one orientation session that covers program basics including best practices, ethics, obstacles, behaviors to avoid, partner and program expectations, and additional resources. This information is also contained in the PNMGC Peer Mentoring Handbook, which is provided to each participant and is available from PNMGC upon request. Question-and-answer sessions throughout the semester also allow students to discuss and learn from their collective experiences. For example, in one session mentors shared with each other their strategies for time management and overcoming communication issues with their mentees. The PNMGC program is set up so that different forms of peer mentoring can take place between mentors and mentees, amid mentors, and among project assistants and participants.

Reflection

Felipe Amaral, one of this vignette's authors, found that getting involved with PNMGC and helping revamp the peer mentoring program opened his eyes to all the resources and advocacy activities that were available at UNM. Although he started his graduate studies without a mentor, he so appreciated the PNMGC program support that he now serves as a mentor for current graduate students so they don't have to go through the same challenges he faced without knowledge and support. Student-to-student mentoring is important because things often sound different when coming from a peer. Talking to someone who has experienced the same or similar issues the new student is experiencing is comforting, and the mentor's advice also allows new students to be more efficient in their studies. Unlike the relationship with an academic adviser, there is no hierarchy, which allows the mentor relationship to be mutually beneficial. It is very rewarding to be a PNMGC mentor, an experience that has changed and enriched Felipe's life.

Conclusion

Graduate school is a time when students begin or change their careers by joining a professional discipline. In addition to becoming a recognized expert in a specific discipline, one goes to graduate school to succeed and to acquire tools that will result in professional success. This is especially important for students who are traditionally underrepresented in graduate school. Providing these students with research ethics training is one important way to assist them in not only doing what's ethical but also engaging in their research and scholarly activities in a fully professional manner. Peer mentoring validates and reassures graduate students that they are legitimate scholars and that they can work through problems communally and confidently. The PNMGC sets a high bar for student success and prepares students for successfully addressing the challenges that may confront them as they move through their professional and private worlds.

HOW WILL YOU EVALUATE THE IMPACT OF YOUR PEER MENTORING PROGRAM?

> What, how, and when you evaluate should be based on your program design, goals, and theoretical foundation along with what mentoring is supposed to accomplish in your program.

Chapter 9

- introduces the evaluation plan and explains why it is crucial to your program success;
- reviews the three-step model of evaluation;
- explores several kinds of evaluation designs;
- identifies different types of evaluation data;
- examines a range of data collection tools;
- provides examples of how to measure common program goals including satisfaction, engagement in learning, knowledge of campus resources, and awareness of adjustment issues; and
- discusses appropriate ways to analyze and present different forms of data.

True genius resides in the capacity for evaluation of uncertain,
hazardous, and conflicting information.

(Churchill, 2015)

Not everything that can be counted counts, and not everything that counts can be counted.

(Einstein, 2013)

Program evaluation can serve several purposes: It can provide information on your mentors' and mentees' experiences as well as which specific aspects of your program are working and which ones might need to be reviewed and adjusted.

Summative Versus Formative Evaluation

It is important to distinguish between summative and formative evaluation. The purpose of summative evaluation is to evaluate mentee or mentor knowledge and behaviors by comparing them against some standard or benchmark (Eberley Center for Teaching Innovation, 2014). The general goal of formative evaluation is to collect detailed information that can be used to improve program content, delivery, and student learning while it's happening. What makes evaluation formative is not what is measured or the way that an instrument is designed as much as how the evaluation data are used.

Formative evaluation lets you gain feedback from mentees and mentors about whether the different elements of your mentoring program that you think are positively contributing to mentee success are actually working as planned. You can go directly to your mentees for the information you seek. The problem here is that mentees lack the expertise to be aware of the important adjustment issues they must face at specific times, much less which issues are not covered in your program materials. That is why your mentors are valuable for collecting formative evaluation information. They are in an excellent position to learn mentees' perceptions of how useful program resources are, issues mentees are struggling with, the strategies that work or do not work, and the activities that are particularly rewarding.

Your regular weekly meeting with mentors is an excellent time to collect formative evaluation information. Once mentors have identified program resources that need to be clarified or additional issues to be addressed, use part of your staff meeting time to brainstorm the best ways to address these issues or clarify program resources. Also consider whether mentees need additional resources or mentors need supplemental training to address these issues. It is important that you capture what is discussed in your staff meetings. This will be the record of the issues identified during formative evaluation and of how you responded to the issues identified in the feedback you receive. While formative evaluation is typically not part of your evaluation plan, it is an essential element in ongoing program development. During mentor training, make sure to share your expectations for mentors to facilitate formative evaluation.

You will need to conduct summative and formative evaluation in the course of developing and maintaining your program. The remainder of this chapter focuses on summative evaluation.

Establishing Program Success

I want to emphasize again that it is important to connect program goals, design, content, and mentor training to evaluation as you move from designing to implementing your program. You need be clear about your program's objectives and how you are going to measure them so that you can tell whether they have actually been achieved.

Three-Step Evaluation

It is helpful to think about program evaluation in three steps. The first step is to represent the key characteristics of your program using descriptive data. Important characteristics include demographic information, number of mentees and mentors, frequency of mentor-mentee contact, and number of students who enroll in or complete the program.

The second step is to gather institutional data on your mentees' college success. Typical academic success indicators are degree completion, retention, GPA, and number of credits earned. Academic success can be operationalized several ways. Degree completion is an excellent way to operationalize student success if your program design allows you to mentor students until graduation. You can get these data from your school's institutional research unit. The time to collect degree completion rates would be when students are awarded their degrees. A simple way to analyze and present these data would be using a percentage of mentees who complete their degrees within a given period of time (e.g., 78% of mentees completed their BA/BS degrees within three years of transferring). Later in this chapter I discuss how the strength of your claims can be improved through the use of additional comparison standards.

Given that many student support programs are not available to students over their entire time in college, and that persistence data (has the student remained in college even if he or she transfers to another school?) may be hard to obtain, you may have to settle for retention (has the student remained in your school?) as your measure of student success. Your school's institutional research unit will be able to provide you with retention data.

The timing of data collection becomes very important here. Many colleges use year-to-year data as their institutional measure of retention. However, this approach will not differentiate between students who only attend one semester a year but enroll in fall term two years in a row from students who consistently attended school during that time. Your program will be better served by collecting retention data on a semester-by-semester basis to identify risk and possible intervention points for mentees. Identifying the percentage of mentees who reenrolled from one year to the next or who were consistently enrolled for the entire program year are good ways to present retention data for a one-year program. You could present data for a one-semester program in a similar manner by focusing on the percentage of mentees who complete the program semester and reenroll the subsequent fall.

However, simply reporting mentee retention data for a one-semester or one-year program does not adequately make the case that your program promotes student success. While it reflects well on your program that your mentees continue in school, they also need to maintain GPAs that will keep them off academic probation and avoid academic dismissal. If the program is longer than a semester, term GPA and cumulative GPA would be additional indicators to support the claim that your program promotes mentee success. GPA data would also be provided from your school's institutional research unit and should be collected at the end of each term or semester. GPA data are typically presented as your total group of mentees' mean value. You could also present the data in the form of the percentage of mentees who earned a GPA above a certain criterion value. For example, mentees earned a 2.89 fall term GPA, with 72% earning GPAs of 3.1 or higher.

If you stop here you may not be capturing the full picture of student success. Educational research has established a relationship between the number of credits a student completes in a semester, term, or year, particularly the first year, and subsequent degree completion (Chen & Carroll, 2005; Miller & Spence, 2007). So another good indicator of success would be the number of credits your mentees successfully completed while they were in your program. Here again your school's institutional research unit should be able to provide you with data, ideally collected at the end of each semester or term. These data are typically presented as a mean value for the group of mentees. By the end of Step 2 you've operationalized student success into several measureable indicators: degree completion, GPA, retention, and number of credits earned.

The third step involves developing measureable goals that explain how participating in your program contributed to mentee college success. These goals will be linked to the theoretical and conceptual foundations of your program.

As you consider which program outcomes you want to evaluate and how you will do so, also keep in mind the benefits peer mentoring has been shown to provide for college students, including providing social support, increased knowledge of campus resources and services, increased campus connection, increased engagement in learning, improved decision making, and increased understanding of expectations. Each of these has been associated with students' academic success.

If the reason you believe peer mentoring will promote retention and student success is based on Astin's (1977, 1984, 1993) work, and you have operationalized his theory in your program design, then one program goal would be to facilitate students' engagement in their own learning. You can go to the literature and find other studies that used Astin's model to see how they operationalized engagement. Keep in mind that the way you operationalize engagement will affect the types of data you collect. Your claim of success rests on the argument that through participation in your program and the peer mentoring they received, mentees met academic success indicators because of your program.

As you plan your data collection approach, consider the information you'll need, who will collect it, by what means, and when and how it will be analyzed to provide answers to questions about whether your program has attained specific goals. Involve your mentors in the data collection when appropriate, as their rapport with mentees should increase participation rates. Mentors will also benefit. The information they collect about students' issues and current strategies will be useful in helping mentees develop action plans for addressing specific adjustment issues.

The timing of data collection is also important here. You may want to collect change-over-time data to capture the impact of program participation. If so, you'll want to get a baseline measure as early in the program as you can. Ideally this would occur during program orientation or at the first mentor-mentee meeting. The second measure should occur as late in the program as possible, perhaps at the end-of-program celebration. Change data are typically presented as a comparison of the group's average scores at the two times or as a percentage of mentees whose scores improved during their time in the program. For more information on research design, see Chapter 9 Resources (p. 311).

In summary, making the claim that your program is associated with mentees' college success is a three-step process. First, describe your program. Second, establish that your mentees performed well on your indicators of college success; that is, degree completion, retention, GPA, and credits completed. Third, collect, analyze, and present data that confirm mentees met midlevel program goals associated with different arguments about how peer mentoring promotes college success. You'll need an evaluation plan to make this happen.

You Need an Evaluation Plan

If you are applying for federal or foundation funding you will be required to develop an evaluation plan. Programs receiving this level of support typically hire an outside evaluator to conduct the evaluation. I propose that you need to develop an evaluation plan regardless of how your program is funded. Done correctly, an evaluation plan will link program goals or objectives with specific design elements and appropriate measurement instruments in ways that will provide clear information about whether your program is actually accomplishing what it was intended to accomplish.

Your evaluation plan must start with your program goals. You then need to operationalize your goals so that each is measurable and can be expressed

Figure 9.1 Excerpts From Students First Mentoring Project Evaluation Plan Worksheet

> Goal 1: Improve retention rates for first generation freshmen college students who qualify for federal TRIO programs (EOP, SSS) but cannot be currently accommodated

> Goal 1A: Promote student retention and academic success
> control groups: all students, TRIO students, non-mentored first-generation students

EQ1. Did program students show higher retention rates than control groups during each year?
Data source: Banner data from PSU Data Warehouse
Data collection: collected at the end of each term by means of Hummingbird Bi-Query
Data analysis: comparison of group mean values

EQ2. Did program students successfully complete more academic units than control groups?
Data source: Banner data from PSU Data Warehouse
Data collection: collected at the end of each term by means of Hummingbird Bi-Query
Data analysis: comparison of group mean values

EQ3. Did program\students earn higher grade point averages than control groups?
Data source: Banner data from PSU Data Warehouse
Data collection: collected at the end of each term by means of Hummingbird Bi-Query
Data analysis: comparison of group mean values

> Goal 1B: Develop an innovative mentoring program for first-generation students

Project element: (note: evaluation of additional project elements included peer videos and discussion groups)
1. Resource Website
EQ1a. Did the program generate a website that provided comprehensive access to student services at PSU?
Data source: existence of resource website
Data collection: observation
Data analysis: comparison with current PSU website. Evaluation criteria: equal or greater # student services links

EQ1b. Did students and mentor-advisors rate the website positively?
Data source: student satisfaction surveys
Data collection: anonymous on-line survey end of each program year
Data analysis: average score higher than "4" on 7-point Likert scale

2. Graduate Student Mentor-Advisors
EQ2a. Were the graduate student mentor-advisors adequately trained?
Data source: mentor training satisfaction survey
Data collection: anonymous mentor training satisfaction survey at three points: immediately after training, at end of 1st term, at end of program year
Data analysis: average score higher than "4" on 7-point Likert scale

Figure 9.1 (Continued)

EQ2b. Did the students rate the mentor-advisors positively?
Data source: student satisfaction surveys
Data collection: anonymous on-line survey end of each program year
Data analysis: average score higher than "4" on 7-point Likert scale

3. Expertise development
EQ1. Did students' knowledge of potential adjustment issues increase over their time in the program?
Data source: focus group data
Data collection: mentee focus groups held in the 4th and 5th weeks of fall, winter and spring terms
Data analysis: average number of adjustment issues discussed in spring compared to fall term focus groups

EQ2. Did students internalize program-promoted strategies for dealing with specific adjustment issues?
Data source: focus group data
Data collection: mentee focus groups held in the 4th and 5th weeks of fall, winter and spring terms
Data analysis: greater number of program-promoted issue adjustment strategies discussed in spring compared to fall term focus groups

4. Satisfaction
EQ1. Did the program students rate the Students First program positively?
Data source: student satisfaction surveys
Data collection: anonymous on-line survey end of each program year
Data analysis: average scale score higher than "4" on 7-point Likert scale

Goal 2 Disseminate program to other colleges and universities

EQ1. Did program establish a dissemination website where program results were available for review?
Data source: dissemination website
Data collection: review by evaluator
Data analysis: criteria: does the site exist?

Goal 3 Promote the institutionalization of Students First Program at PSU

EQ1. Did the Students First program receive continued support from PSU-after the completion of the grant?
Data source: PSU budget documents
Data collection: electronic files provided by PSU financial officer
Data analysis: examination of budget document. Inclusion of program operating expenses in post-grant operating budgets of PSU deemed evidence of institutional commitment

as one or more evaluation questions. Next you need to describe the data you will use, explain how and when you will collect these data, and discuss how you are going to analyze the collected data to establish that your program has achieved that goal. One important part of analyzing data is stating in advance the criteria you will use to determine that a goal has been attained. Figure 9.1 illustrates how the parts of an evaluation plan fit together.

This project has three top-level goals, one of which has two subgoals.

- Goal 1: Improve retention rates for first-generation freshmen who qualify for federal TRIO programs (e.g., Educational Opportunity Program, Student Success Services) but cannot be currently accommodated
  - Goal 1A: Promote student retention and success
  - Goal 1B: Develop an innovative mentoring program for first-generation students
- Goal 2: Disseminate program to other colleges and universities
- Goal 3: Promote the institutionalization of the Students First program at PSU

Evaluation questions (EQs) for each goal and subgoal amount to operationalizing the goal in a measureable way. Note that for subgoal 1A: Promote student retention and academic success, relevant comparison groups were identified in the evaluation plan. Data sources, data collection methods, and analysis approaches for each evaluation question are also specified.

For example, subgoal 1B, "Develop an innovative mentoring program for first-generation students" is operationalized into sets of EQs associated with different program elements. In regard to the resources website program element, EQ1B asked, "Did students and mentor-advisors rate the website positively?" The associated data source was student satisfaction data, collected by an anonymous online survey at the end of the program year. In regard to data analysis, the program was said to have met this goal if the group of mentees' mean satisfaction score was greater than 4 on a 7-point Likert scale.

Develop your evaluation plan as you develop your program. Start by operationalizing your program goals as a set of evaluation questions you need to answer to demonstrate program success. This will provide you with a much better idea about what services your program needs to provide to meet those goals, the kinds of content you need to share with mentees, and some key points you'll need to emphasize in mentor training. We will return to your evaluation plan later in the chapter.

Setting the Stage

Setting the stage refers to several questions you need to consider before you begin your actual data collection. These include evaluation design, types of information you'll need, institutional data, and the respective value of quantitative and qualitative data.

Evaluation Design

The design of your evaluation affects subsequent data collection, analysis, and presentation choices. A *descriptive* evaluation design provides valuable and essential information to the reader about your program. It paints a picture of your program by drawing attention to important characteristics, such as how many mentees you serve and the frequency of mentor-mentee contact. All programs collect and report descriptive data about program characteristics.

Some programs also use a descriptive approach with outcomes: 2% of program participants reenrolled the subsequent fall term, mentees earned a 2.72 GPA for fall semester, or 42% reported participating in two or more campus events or activities during their program participation term. You are limited in the program success claims you can make with a descriptive design. You can strengthen your success claim by stating a criterion for what constitutes success before you begin your program: Program satisfaction will be established if mentees' mean satisfaction score is above 4 on a 7-point Likert scale.

A *comparative* evaluation design uses a different referent, another group of students, to make a claim of program success. You do not learn as much from the absolute value of a measure like GPA as when you compare it to another relevant group of students' score for the same measure. A program in which mentees take five years to complete a BA or BS will not seem effective if the average time to degree completion for all students at the same school is four years. On the other hand, the same program seems very effective when the campus average for years-to-degree-completion is six. These other groups are called *comparison groups*. You need to have a hypothesized relationship between your mentees' outcomes and those of the control group students.

For example, based on the literature and past research, you would expect first-generation students to complete fewer credits during the first year and be retained at lower levels than students from families who are more familiar with the norms of higher education. You then could claim your mentoring program is a success if your mentees achieve the same level of those outcomes as students from more educated families. Similarly, based on the literature, you would expect mentored students to be more successful than nonmentored students from the same group. Therefore your program would be seen as effective if your first-generation or student veteran mentees complete their degrees in less time than it takes for a nonmentored group of similar students.

The element of comparison can be one group of students with other control groups of students, one location with another location, or one approach to delivering mentoring services with another. For example, Rodgers and Tremblay (2003, p. 13) examined the effect of peer mentoring on the relationship between anxiety and motivation. They found that high-anxiety peer-mentored students had grades comparable to those of their low-anxiety counterparts, while high-anxiety control group students did significantly worse than low-anxiety control group students.

A change-over-time evaluation design represents a special kind of comparative approach. Here the comparison is between the same mentees' responses to a particular measure at two different points in time. This is an excellent way to establish the added value of your program. For example, if an overarching goal of your program is to promote students' academic success through improved problem solving, and you believe knowledge of campus resources and how to use each appropriately are important for better problem solving, then a change-over-time measure is the right approach. First you must establish that your mentee's levels of academic success, in this example time to degree completion, match your preestablished criteria. You decide to use the criterion *students will be considered academically successful if they complete their degrees in five years or less* since the current campuswide average time to degree completion is five and a half years. Satisfactory progress toward earning a degree in five years requires 36 credits a year or 12 credits a term. Based on institutional data, you confirm that your mentees' average credits earned for the year are 37.5. Your mentees' performance matches your standard for satisfactory progress.

Next you need to link that performance to something that happened in your program. Otherwise a critic might question whether your mentees' success was because of prior skills, maturation, or some other factors besides participating in your program. Your program is built upon two foundational assumptions. The first is that greater knowledge of campus resources and how to use them appropriately will lead to high-quality problem solving and academic success. Second, the peer mentoring support your program delivers will help mentees acquire this important information. So you set up your measure of change over time in regard to level of knowledge and how to use resources appropriately by collecting a baseline measure of your mentees' knowledge on this topic as soon as they begin your program. Then you use the same instrument to remeasure the same group of mentees at the end of the program. Change in mentees' mean resource knowledge scores from time one to time two demonstrates that mentees' resource knowledge increased over the time they participated in your program. Since their academic success performance also met the preestablished criterion, you can claim participating in your program is associated with mentees' academic success.

However, the same critic asks how you know that your students' demonstrated improvement in resource knowledge is any different from the knowledge they might have increased on their own if they were not part of the program. So you bring in a relevant comparison group, demographically similar but nonmentored students. Now you measure mentored and nonmentored students' level of resource knowledge at the beginning of your program and again at the end of the program. When your mentees' resource knowledge scores increase over the time in the program, and that change is greater than what occurred among nonmentored but similar students, you have made a very strong case that your mentees' making satisfactory progress toward degree completion was associated with participation in your program rather than another explanation such as maturation.

So we end up with three standards for evaluating a midlevel goal like resource knowledge:

1. Silver standard: Measure knowledge of resources at the end of your program. Present your mentees' end-of-program score. Without a measure of preprogram resource knowledge you infer that knowledge increased over time in the program and did so because of program participation.
2. Gold standard: Use change-over-time measure. Present your mentees' pre- and postprogram participation resource knowledge scores. Change in mentees' scores over time establishes resource knowledge increased over time in your program, and you infer this was because of program participation.
3. Platinum standard: Use change-over-time measure with a relevant comparison group. Present your mentees' and control group students' time one and time two resource knowledge scores. Comparing the change in your mentees' scores over time with the scores of the control group students establishes that your mentees' resource knowledge improved over time and demonstrates that the mentees' rate of change was greater than the rate of a nonmentored comparison group. This then makes the strongest argument that program participation is associated with your mentees' academic success.

The scope and depth of your evaluation efforts depend on the purpose of your evaluation and the level of available resources. Externally funded projects will typically use the platinum standard of evaluation to make as strong a case as possible to funders that the program was successful. In many other situations, using a gold or even a silver standard is more realistic. Many times it is difficult to get comparison group data for specific measures of program goals. However, with some forethought, you may be able to get useful comparison group data for academic success indicators from your college's institutional research unit.

Institutional Data

It is important to think about the parameters of the categories of potential comparison group students you may want to include in your evaluation before requesting data from your Office of Institutional Research. You need to make sure you are comparing apples with apples, instead of apples to oranges. While your institutional research unit should be able to provide you with collegewide outcome data for all undergraduate students, you still need to be aware of important distinctions.

One important parameter is the distinction between full-time and part-time students. If your program requires mentees to maintain a full-time schedule then make sure your comparison groups only include full-time students. You should write out all the decision rules you use to guide your evaluation so you can include them when writing your program evaluation. The following is an example from the decision rules used to guide the evaluation for the Students First Mentoring Program:

> In order to be considered full time, a student was required to be registered for at 9 or more credits. This decision matches the federal financial aid distinction between half-time and full time (https://studentaid.ed.gov/sites/default/files/funding-your-education.pdf) and the PSU definition of a half-time student as taking between 6 and 8 credits (http://pdx.edu/finaid/disbursement.html). (Collier et al., 2009, p. 151)

Accessing institutional data for smaller, more specific subgroups of students requires planning and cooperation from your institutional research unit. If your program serves low-income students, you need to once again set up parameters in your data request for comparison group students. The following is another example from the same project:

> "Low Income status" was determined based on whether the student qualified for the national needs based Pell grant. The data field, RNVAND0_PELL_AWARD, lists the amount that the student was granted. By selecting all students who were granted more than $0 we were able to be sure that all students in the comparison cohort met, at the least, federal low-income status. (Collier et al., 2009, p. 151)

Sharing the details of your evaluation plan with the director of your institutional research unit while the plan is still in the development stage will give you a better idea of what is possible with the current institutional data. For example, while your first-generation student peer mentoring program can require family information confirming first-generation status before accepting students to your program, if your school does not collect information about parents' educational levels on its application form, you will have a hard time identifying a comparison group of nonmentored first-generation students. Ultimately, the information that is possible to access will strongly affect your decisions about which comparison groups might be realistically possible to use.

What Types of Data Should You Use?

Quantitative data refers to anything that can be expressed as a number, ranked, or empirically measured (McLeod, 2008). *Qualitative data* are descriptive data that are not in numerical form. Qualitative data are almost always interpretive and attempt to understand individuals' experiences from their own perspective (Marshall & Rossman, 2010).

Lofland (1995) differentiates between questions of frequency, magnitude, causes, and consequences, which he saw as best answered using quantitative methods, and questions of type, structure, process and agency, which he argued are best suited for exploration with qualitative methods. Examples of quantitative data would be institutional data like GPAs and retention rates, scores on achievement tests, or the number of times a mentor-mentee pair met over one term. Examples of qualitative data would be reflection responses, open-ended questionnaire responses, or focus group data. Ultimately which type of data you collect will depend on what you are measuring. For example, quantitative data are much more appropriate for capturing academic success indicators such as retention, GPA, and credits successfully completed. On the other hand, qualitative data are more appropriate for understanding mentors' and mentees' experiences. You will probably want to collect both quantitative and qualitative data.

Data Collection

Now that you've figured out the design of your evaluation and the types of information you will be collecting, it's time to consider what kinds of data collection instruments you will use.

Instruments for Measuring Common Program Goals

Following are six data collection instruments with an example of how each could be used to measure a different program goal.

Frequencies or Counts

Frequencies or counts are simple but useful evaluation data. This information is typically collected through open-end questions, such as, "How frequently did mentors and mentees meet?" or "How many mentees completed the program?"

While stand-alone frequency data have some value, that value is dramatically increased when counts are compared to some relevant standard. For example, you can compare actual frequencies of mentor-mentee meetings with the levels you suggested in your program proposal or explicitly stated in the mentor job description. Counts of the frequency of mentor-mentee contact, when compared with a relevant standard, can serve as evidence of your program attaining the goal of providing mentee support.

If one of your program goals is to encourage mentees to become active in campus activities, counts can be used to measure campus connection. You can collect this frequency information several ways. One way would be through direct observation. Your program could sponsor or recommend that mentees attend a variety of campus events, and you could count the number of mentees attending each event. A second way would be through self-reports. You could use a short-answer question that asked mentees to list how many campus activities they participated in during their time in the program or provide mentees with a list of activities and ask them to indicate which ones they attended.

Attitude Ratings or Scales

Attitude ratings, whether for an individual question or a set of questions as in a summated rating scale, are another common and useful instrument for collecting evaluation data (Kerlinger, 2011, pp. 453–456). Likert-scored items are the type of subjective rating most frequently used in educational assessment. This format is useful for capturing the intensity of respondents' reactions. The individual is presented with a statement followed by a continuum of possible choices ranging from strongly agree to strongly disagree. Respondents' scores place them at different places along the continuum of intensity. Averaging the individual scores produces a group intensity value for that item. This approach can be used with a single question or as a scale made up of the respondents' scores for a set of related items.

You will need to determine in advance how many different values you will have along your continuum of intensity. There is an element of forced choice in using Likert-scored questions in that respondents are limited to the values you provide (e.g., strongly agree, agree, neutral, disagree, strongly disagree; see Exercise 9.1). You need to decide if you want to use an odd or even number of values. I recommend using an odd number just to provide an option for a respondent who may feel that choosing between agree and disagree does not reflect his or her personal attitude toward the question.

There are benefits to short and long versions of the intensity continuum. If you believe that the majority of your mentees are going to rate a question very positively or negatively, then a five-value continuum will allow you make claims like "73% of respondents either support or strongly support question eight." On the other hand, if you are trying to capture as much variation as possible, then a seven-value continuum will be of more use to you, particularly if your analysis plan calls for using a test to determine if differences between group scores are statistically significant.

Exercise 9.1. Likert Scale Items From PSU Students First Mentoring Program End-of-Year Survey

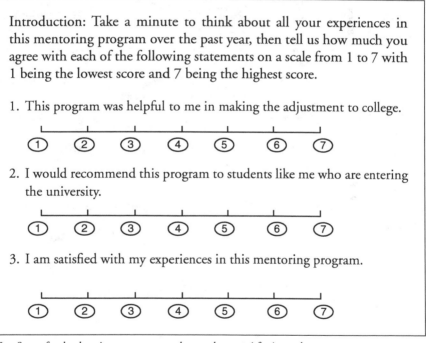

Note: Scores for the three items were averaged to produce a satisfaction scale score.

Short-Answer Surveys

A survey or interview soliciting short-answer responses is another common form of evaluation data collection. It addresses a problem with multiple-choice response questions where a mentee might use the metaprocess of eliminating unlikely responses to figure out which response is correct. A short-answer question requires the respondent to come up with an answer based on his or her own knowledge (see Exercise 9.2).

Exercise 9.2. Examples of Short-Answer Survey Questions From PSU International Student Mentee Program Orientation Quiz

---

1. When can you see your immigration adviser?
2. How many credits are undergraduate students required to take and successfully complete each term?
3. Who should you contact if you have questions about health insurance?
4. Where do you go to get an ID card?

Short-answer responses are relatively straightforward. You develop an answer key, and typically there is not a lot of possible variation in correct answers.

Open-Ended Interview Questions

Open-ended responses are typically collected using an interview. An interview is preferred to a self-administered survey because the interviewer can probe deeper after incomplete responses or ask more specific follow-up questions. This approach is useful when you do not know all the possible answer categories in advance, or when you are interested in learning what your mentees think are the appropriate answer categories.

Exercise 9.3. Examples of Open-Ended Interview Questions From University of Michigan Transfer Connections SSI

---

1. What was the most difficult thing about coming from another university? What was the easiest?
2. Describe your study habits at your previous institution. How do you think they will change?
3. What are your academic goals for this semester? Do you have a plan to make that happen?

Notice in Exercise 9.3 that each question is accompanied by a follow-up question. Open-ended interview responses are much more varied than short-answer responses. There is no single correct answer. Instead, you are trying to understand each mentee's individual experiences from his or her perspective along with commonalities across mentees' experiences.

Reflection
While reflection data can take many different forms (see Collier & Williams, 2013, pp. 106–108), written reflection exercises or journals are used many times to capture individuals' personal understandings of how program participation affected them. As mentioned in the discussion of program content, it is important for your mentor training to prepare mentors to reflect on their own experiences so that they can help mentees do likewise. Therefore it is not surprising that reflection is frequently used to collect data on the impact of program participation on mentors (see Exercise 9.4). Collecting data through a mentor reflection journal can be extremely valuable because program impacts are not always visible to an observer, or an observed mentor's actions may mean one thing to the mentor and another to the observer.

Exercise 9.4. Using Reflection Data to Capture the Development of Mentor Leadership Skills From PSU's International Student Mentoring Program

---

As part of the end-of-program evaluation, mentors were asked to reflect on the question, "How have your leadership skills and abilities grown as a result of your experiences in this program?"

Seven themes were identified in the mentor reflection data using thematic content analysis (discussed in detail under "Analysis and Presentation of Results," p. 300):

- Developed the leadership skill of listening
- Learned to appreciate diverse cultural perspectives
- Realized student possessed more leadership skills than previously acknowledged
- Developed improved intercultural communication skills
- Increased knowledge of campus resources that are important for international students
- Learned how to encourage others
- Became more engaged in the campus community

The following are some additional sample reflection questions to elicit mentor reflection on the development of leadership skills:

- Tell me a story of an incident working with your mentees when you realized you were putting the program material on leadership skills into action.

- How have your experiences as a mentor in this program affected other areas of your life?

Focus Groups

Focus groups are another useful way to collect qualitative data for program evaluation by retrieving data through group interaction on a topic determined by the researcher (Morgan, 1997). You pick the topic or topics, but the actual data come from the interaction among participants in the group. The essence of focus groups is listening to people, in this case your mentees. This approach allows participants to give their accounts about why things are the way that they are, and how they got that way. A strength of focus groups is that participants share and compare their experiences with each other. In a focus group, your mentees want to understand each others' shared experiences. Their efforts to reach a common understanding can provide valuable evaluation data. Focus groups are typically recorded and transcribed to facilitate evaluation. You will need to collect a separate informed consent form from focus group participants. The sample informed consent form in Chapter 5 Resources (pp. 138–139) can be modified to serve this purpose.

For example, the program described in Vignette 2 on p. 143 conceptually drew on the two-path model that proposed mentoring could provide first-generation students with cultural capital in the form of college student expertise and have a positive impact on students' academic success and persistence. One goal of the program was to improve first-generation students' levels of college student expertise; that is, the ability to identify important issues and then use strategies that have a high likelihood of success to address issues using appropriate campus resources.

A series of focus groups were conducted early in the fall term when students had not yet been exposed to the majority of program material on effective problem solving and then again in the spring term after mentees had participated in the program for more than two terms. For this measure, mentees' expertise levels were defined as increasing if in the second wave of focus groups they were (a) able to identify a wider range of potential adjustment issues and (b) recall program-promoted strategies for using campus resources to address specific issues.

Once the recorded focus group is transcribed, you now have the group discussion as a form of qualitative data, ready to be analyzed. For more information on focus groups see Exercise 9.5 and Chapter 9 Resources (p. 311).

Exercise 9.5. Using Focus Groups to Collect Expertise Data

This section of the focus group was designed to get students talking about the adjustment issues they were facing and how they were addressing them. Students initially brainstormed a list of the biggest adjustment issues they faced. This example will use the issue "trying to understand professors' expectations," a topic that came up in every focus group.

Moderator: I noticed one area of adjustment issues that we came up with has to do with trying to understand professors' expectations. I'd like to hear your stories about your experiences with trying to understand professors' expectations. I know it is only halfway through the first term, but I suspect you've all had to deal with this issue by now. These don't all have to be success stories. Maybe you have run into problems and looking back now you wish you'd done things differently. Also, you might know other people who've run into these same issues, and we're interested in hearing about it. Who can tell us a story about your experiences in trying to understand professors' expectations?

(Instructions for moderator: After the first mentee shares his or her story and others in the group pick up on it and start to tell their own stories, let them continue. If no one jumps in, then you probe further.)

Moderator: What about some of the rest of you?

(Instructions for moderator: After a mentee tells his or her history, ask follow-up question.)

Moderator: Tell me how you dealt with this issue in this situation.

(Instructions for moderator: After as many mentees who want to tell their stories and associated strategies have spoken, ask follow-up question).

Moderator: We heard several stories about trying to understand professors' expectations and how different students dealt with that issue. Can any of you think of additional strategies for dealing with this issue?

(Instructions for moderator: Repeat this line of questions for as many topics or issues as possible in the time available.)

Analysis and Presentation of Results

It is not enough to analyze your data; you have to present your results in a manner that makes the outcomes clear to the reader.

Frequency, Attitude Ratings, and Short-Answer Data

You can present these kinds of quantitative data in several forms:

Group average or mean score. For example, the group of 32 mentees reported an average satisfaction score of 6.2 (out of 7.0 maximum positive value) at the end of their semester of program participation.

Percentage of responding mentees who reported engaging in a behavior at a specific level. For example, 82% of mentees reported participating in five or more campus activities during the program semester.

If you are using a pretest/posttest model of data collection, you can present change-over-time data in several ways.

Change over time: comparison of the preprogram average with postprogram average values. For example, mentees correctly identified an average of 24 out of 30 campus resources at the end of the program semester compared to only 18 out of 30 at the beginning of the program.

Change over time: absolute numbers. For example, mentees reported engaging in five more engagement activities postprogram than they reported for the time before joining the program.

Change over time: percentage increase. For example, mentees' mean score increased by 42% postprogram participation.

Change over time: percentage of mentees whose frequency score improved over time. For example, 72% of mentees demonstrated an increase in the number of campus resources they could use appropriately over the semester they participated in the program.

Qualitative Evaluation Data

Qualitative data are typically analyzed using thematic content analysis (Boyatzis, 1988). This approach involves looking for important ideas or themes that are present or repeated in individuals' responses. It is also helpful to capture direct quotations to illustrate those themes. Qualitative data will provide very rich information, but it will take a longer time to analyze than other forms of data.

I illustrate the idea of theme using mentor reflection journal data from the PSU International Student Mentoring Program's (described in Vignette 6) assessment of the effects of participation on the development of mentor leadership skills. The following are excerpts from four mentors' responses to the question, "How have your leadership skills and abilities grown as a result of your experiences in this program?"

Mentor 1: I have continued to work on the act of listening, having an open mind, and trusting in myself as a leader.

Mentor 2: Through the mentor program I have learned how to better listen to all different personalities and people.

Mentor 3: I was able to expand my way of thinking and was able to grow in my listening skills as a leader.

Mentor 4: During my time as a mentor, I have developed many leadership skills. First of all, I have learned how to listen effectively. I have learned how to listen to my mentees and get feedback from them.

A common theme in all four reflection essays is that participating in the program helped mentors develop the leadership skill of listening. Since one of the program goals is to facilitate the development of mentor leadership skills, this outcome could be reported as follows:

One recurrent theme from the mentor reflection essays is that participating in the program helped mentors develop the leadership skill of listening. As one mentor noted, "During my time as a mentor, I have developed many leadership skills. First of all, I have learned how to listen effectively. I have learned how to listen to my mentees and get feedback from them."

Your most important themes are the ones that occur most frequently in your mentees' or mentors' responses. The key is the number of different individuals who report the same theme, not the absolute number of times a theme occurs. You can claim consensus or agreement on importance if the same theme occurs in the responses of all or most of your respondents. I recommend you limit the number of important themes you identify from any qualitative data source to three or four. It is helpful to provide a direct quote that illustrates any important theme you identified. Additional secondary themes can be listed without accompanying quotes. For more information on thematic content analysis see Chapter 9 Resources (p. 311).

Examples of Linking Specific Program Goals, Indicators, and Appropriate Data Collection

The previous section on data collection instruments provided examples of ways to measure campus connection, program satisfaction, strategies for addressing specific adjustment issues, academic goals, mentor leadership skill development, and expertise. Now let's look at some other examples of how you might link program goals, indicators or evaluation questions, data sources, and data collection.

Engagement in Learning
This could be an indicator for Astin's (1977, 1984, 1993) concept of engagement; it could also capture Tinto's (1975, 1987, 1993) concept of academic connection.

Goal: Increasing Engagement in One's Own Learning

Evaluation questions or indicators:
Did mentees exhibit engagement in their own learning during their time in your program?
Data: the number of times mentees visited professors during office hours, asked professors questions, or participated in campus activities during the time they participated in your program.
Collect data: (a) mentor records of mentees' activities collected by interview during regular contact, (b) self-reported responses on survey, combination of predetermined questions (e.g., How many times have you visited your professors during office hours this term?) and open-ended ones (e.g., Please list all the campus events you attended this term.).

One important key here will be how you operationalize *engagement in one's own learning*. You need to establish whether this will be measured by the number of office hour meetings, number of questions asked of professors, involvement in major department activities, or any combination of possible markers.

Decision Making
This is an excellent indicator of expertise development and very important for programs serving students who are unfamiliar with college. See page 303 for an example.

Resiliency
Resiliency is the ability to bounce back from life's adversity, cope with stresses, and deal with these stresses in healthy ways. The development of resiliency attitudes has been associated with higher levels of college adjustment, retention, and GPA. Higher levels of resiliency have been associated with lower risks for development of post-traumatic stress disorder (Markel, Trujillo, Callahan, & Marks, 2010). This is a very important indicator for programs serving student veterans and other groups trying to cope with stress in healthy ways. See page 303 for an example.

Goal: Improving Decision Making

Evaluation questions or indicators:
Did the quality of mentees' decision making improve during their time in your program?
Data: pre- and postprogram participation measure of students' strategies for dealing with specific college situations
Collect data: Interview or survey asking mentees, What would you do in this situation?
Again an important key will be how you measure high-quality decision making. One option would be to provide some program-recommended strategies for dealing with specific issues that mentors gave mentees as part of program content. Higher quality decision making would be indicated by how many program-recommended strategies for dealing with specific issues mentors adopted.

University of Arizona's Supportive Education Programs for Returning Veterans[1]

Goal: Promoting Resiliency Among Student Veterans

Evaluation questions or indicators:
Did the mentees' self-reported measure of resiliency improve during their time in your program?
Data: preprogram, midterm, and end-of-program responses in resiliency survey
Collect data: used Reivich & Shatté's (2002) Resiliency Quotient test.

Evaluating Mentor Training

It is important to evaluate the effectiveness of you mentor training, although this is not typically included as an explicit program goal. There are two important aspects to mentor training assessment: the appropriateness of the curriculum and the mentors' evaluations of their experiences.

Curriculum

One of the best ways to establish that your training curriculum is appropriate is by comparing it to curricula from similar programs, either those you are aware of through experience or those in the literature. For example, in response to the Students First Mentoring Program EQ, "Were the graduate student mentor-advisers adequately trained?" the mentor training curriculum was deemed appropriate if upon review the evaluator found it was similar to curricula in the literature designed for similar programs. Although you may not have an independent evaluator, you can still make the claim that your training curriculum is sufficient if it mirrors key elements of curricula from other mentoring programs.

Another way to establish the adequacy of your curriculum is by establishing that your mentors are being provided with background information and experience in delivering the services that are important for the academic success of the students you serve. For example, one of the goals of PSU's International Student Mentoring Program is to help mentees learn to use campus resources appropriately, particularly those important for international student success. Therefore an important part of initial training involves making sure mentors know how to use key campus resources appropriately. The program uses a 37-item survey to evaluate the effectiveness of this aspect of mentor training. Mentors complete this survey at the beginning and at the end of the resource training. For the 2013–2014 training, 90% of mentors demonstrated higher levels of knowledge of relevant campus resources over time, and there was a 27% increase in the average number of relevant campus resources mentors could identify posttraining. These data support the claim that the training curriculum is adequate because mentors demonstrated posttraining improvements in levels of resource knowledge, a factor that has been linked to international students' success.

Mentors' Experiences

The mentors' experiences aspect of training evaluation can be captured using many of the data collection approaches discussed earlier. For example, from the Students First Mentoring Program evaluation plan, the adequacy of mentor training was determined by data collected using an anonymous mentor training satisfaction survey at three measurement points: immediately after training, at the end of the first term, and at the end of the program year (see Exercise 9.6).

Mentors used a self-selected numeric code so the evaluator could link their multiple surveys but their anonymity was still maintained. The five Likert-scored items were combined into a single training satisfaction scale score for each mentor for time one (fall), time two (between fall and winter), and time three (end of program year). Training was deemed satisfactory if the mentors' average scale score exceeded 4 on a 7-point Likert scale.[2]

When to collect mentor training satisfaction data is important. Collecting your data immediately after the training is the best way to capture whether mentors learned the material presented in the training. While that is important, you might also be interested in how effective mentors feel the

Exercise 9.6. Students First Mentor Program Satisfaction Survey

Please tell us how much you agree with each of the following statements, using a scale from 1 to 7 with 1 being the lowest score and 7 being the highest score.

Based on the mentor training I received in the mentor training program

1. I am prepared to recognize and respond to the challenges and needs of the first-generation students in this program.

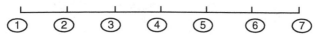

2. I am prepared to use and navigate the resource website.

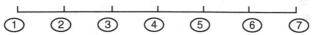

3. I am prepared to help students use program-based scripts in appropriate situations at college.

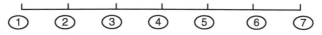

4. I am prepared to use the mentor session log form for online data collection.

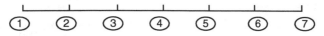

5. I know how to find and access a range of campus resources to meet the needs of my student mentees.

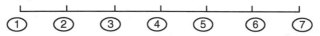

6. Tell us about two of the most important ways that the Students First Mentor Program prepared you for your work with student mentees.

7. Tell us about the two greatest concerns you have relating to how well the mentor training program prepared you for your work with student mentees.

8. Do you have any suggestions about ways that we might improve the mentor training program in the future?

training was in preparing them to work with their mentees. This information is better collected after mentors have been working with their mentees for some time, so collect it at the midpoint and end of your program. The midpoint data are useful for identifying and addressing mentor concerns about issues that may have come up after the initial training.

You could also consider using an exit interview to collect mentors' perceptions of their experiences in the program. However, this will require several trade-offs. One advantage of anonymous training evaluation is that mentors might feel freer to express concerns or issues with training than they might if they felt their responses could be linked to them directly. In a face-to-face interview, mentors might feel they need to be loyal to the program and tell you what they think you want to hear. Qualitative interview data will typically provide more in-depth information as the interviewer can probe any unclear or incomplete responses. The trade-off is that qualitative data will take more time to analyze.

Integrating Evaluation Into Mentor Training Activities

I urge you to consider how you might incorporate evaluation of mentors' experiences into your mentor training. For example, the following two-step understanding leadership exercises are useful for mentor training and evaluation. Exercise 9.7a typically would be done during the initial mentor training, and Exercise 9.7b at the end of the term or program.

Exercise 9.7a. You as a Leader

> Purpose: Help mentors reflect on their understanding of what it means to be a mentor.
>
> Ask each mentor to write out a one-paragraph (no more than two to three sentences) personal definition of *leader*. Ask mentors to place their definitions in separate envelopes, seal the envelopes, and write their name on the outside. Collect the envelopes and put them away until it is time for Exercise 9.7b.

Exercise 9.7b. You as a Leader Revisited

> Purpose: Help mentors reflect on how their understanding of what it means to be a mentor changed or did not change postprogram participation.

1. As part of the end-of-program reflection, ask each mentor to write out a one-paragraph (no more than two to three sentences) personal definition of *leader* based on their experiences working with mentees and other mentors in this program.
2. Return the envelopes from the initial mentor training exercise to each mentor and have them read the definitions they wrote then.
3. Have each mentor answer the following reflection questions in writing: Did your definition of *leader* change over the time you participated in this program? How has your understanding of yourself as a leader changed over the time you participated in this program? What are some specific examples of situations in which you felt you demonstrated leadership qualities?

Training evaluation: Collect both definitions and reflections from each participant. Compare how close each definition is to the one you have explicitly promoted in your program. The training would be deemed effective if the mentors' end-of-program definitions more closely matched the program's definition than the in-training definitions. Thematic content analysis could be used to identify common themes in the individual end-of-program reflections.

Exercise 9.8, which uses the same before-and-after training evaluation format, explores the impact of training on mentors' understanding of *the students your program serves* and *college success*.

Exercise 9.8. Definitions and Growth

Purpose: To make tacit knowledge or assumptions explicit; help mentors in training understand how the training has changed their understandings.

1. On the first day of training, take five minutes and have each mentor write a definition of the students your program serves (*student veterans, returning women students*, etc.) and a definition of *college success*. Place the submissions in envelopes, one for each mentor, and label the envelopes with mentors' name.
2. At the end of the training, ask the mentors to write the two definitions again. Then ask each mentor to open his or her envelope and compare definitions.

3. Next, assign a written reflection in which mentors discuss how their definitions have changed, how the training affected these changes, and how these changes in understanding might have an impact on their subsequent work with mentees.

Thematic content analysis could be used to identify common themes in the individual reflections. (Amy Driscoll, personal communication, June 15, 2005)

Figure 9.2 Sample Evaluation Plan Worksheet

How will you determine student success (e.g., degree completion, retention, GPA, credits earned)?	Data source	How and when will data be collected?	How will data be analyzed? What criteria will be used to establish the goal has been met?
A. Sample evaluation question: Did mentored students reenroll in school for the term or year after program participation? B. C.			
How will you establish that program participation affects student success (program goal plus evaluation question)?	Data source	How and when will data be collected?	How will data be analyzed? What criteria will be used to establish the goal has been met?
1. Sample goal plus evaluation question: Goal: Provide social support EQ: Were students satisfied with their experiences in mentoring program?			
2. Sample goal plus evaluation question: Goal: Increase student expertise level EQ: Can students appropriately use important campus resources?			
3.			
4.			

Evaluation Plan Revisited

I proposed earlier in this chapter that every program needs an evaluation plan. Developing an evaluation plan allows you to operationalize program goals so that they are measurable and can be expressed as evaluation questions. In addition, your plan connects your goals with specific design elements and appropriate data collection tools that will support your claim that your program actually accomplishes what it is meant to accomplish. Figure 9.2 is a sample worksheet you can use to start your evaluation plan.

The first part of the worksheet asks you to indicate how you will determine student success. You will typically use institutional data for this part of the plan. The academic success indicators you use will depend on the length of your program and the data available to you.

The second part of the worksheet focuses on how you will establish that program participation has an impact on student success. I recommend including an evaluation question for each goal. Turning a goal into a relevant evaluation question makes your abstract goal measureable. Before you operationalize key concepts in the evaluation questions, think about what type of information it would take to capture the essence of that concept. For example, in the PSU Students First Mentoring Program *college student expertise* is defined as the ability to identify important issues and then use strategies with a high likelihood of success to address specific issues using appropriate campus resources. Evaluation of expertise development then required data on mentees' knowledge of adjustment issues, knowledge of campus resources, and strategies for using resources to address adjustment issues. A change-over-time evaluation design seems appropriate. Pre- and postparticipation measures could be used to capture any changes in expertise that might occur during the time students participated in the program.

Several data collection approaches are possible. A short-answer survey could be used to measure mentees' level of campus resource knowledge at the beginning of the program and at the end of the program. Focus groups could be used to produce qualitative data on mentees' knowledge of adjustment issues along with preferred strategies for dealing with specific issues. Collecting focus group data at the beginning and end of the program year would provide opportunities to examine if participants' awareness of issues and strategies for addressing them changed over the time in the program.

The resource knowledge data could either be presented as a comparison of group average scores or as the percentage of mentees whose scores increased over the time in the program. The qualitative adjustment issues and strategies data would be presented first as a comparison of themes and then as an examination of the two sets of groups discussions to see if the linking of issue, resource, and strategy, promoted by the program, occurred more frequently in the second set of focus groups. The program would be deemed to have met the goal if mentees' resource knowledge score improved over time, and there were a greater number of linked issue-resource-strategy elements in the end-of-program focus groups.

Taking the time to develop a well-thought-out evaluation plan will pay dividends in the long run. Your plan will expedite the process of identifying, collecting, analyzing, and presenting data in ways that make the case that your program facilitated your mentees' college success.

Making an effective claim that your program promotes student success requires connecting program goals, design elements, data collection, analysis, and presentation into a plan that will then guide all aspects of the evaluation process. Chapter 9 examines some differences in evaluation design and identifies three essential types of evaluation information. This chapter reviews a range of data collection tools and provides examples of how those tools could be used to measure common program goals like social support, satisfaction, campus connection, engagement in learning, decision making, knowledge of campus resources, and expertise development. Particular attention is paid to ways to best present evaluation data to make the strongest possible argument for program effectiveness. Establishing the effectiveness of your program will be particularly important for addressing the issues discussed in the next and final chapter.

Notes

1. For a detailed discussion of research on the positive impact of resiliency training on student veterans' readjustment to college, see Markel et al., 2010.
2. All three cohorts of mentors rated the training favorably, and scores increased over the program year (e.g., for 2005–2006, scores were 6.2 in the fall and 6.5 at program completion).

CHAPTER 9 RESOURCES

Research Design

Creswell, J. W. (2013). *Research design: Qualitative, quantitative, and mixed methods approaches*. Thousand Oaks, CA: Sage.

Focus Group Methodology

Krueger, R. A. (2009). *Focus groups: A practical guide for applied research*. Thousand Oaks, CA: Sage.

Morgan, D. L., Krueger, R. A., & King, J. A. (1998). *The focus group kit* (Vols. 1–6). Thousand Oaks, CA: Sage.

Thematic Content Analysis

Braun, V., & Clarke, V. (2006). Using thematic analysis in psychology. *Qualitative Research in Psychology, 3*(2), 77–101.

INTERNATIONAL STUDENT–FOCUSED PROGRAM

The International Student Mentoring Program

Paul Braun and Jill Townley, Portland State University

TABLE V6.1

Inclusiveness	Duration	Approach to Addressing Students' Needs	College Transition
Tailored: *Designed for a specific audience* *International students who are new to Portland Statue University*	Short term: *One semester or less* *One term or quarter*	Targeted: *Addresses student needs at one point in time* *Overall focus on dealing with first-term issues*	One educational system to another

Portland State University (PSU) is located in downtown Portland, Oregon, and offers over 100 undergraduate, master's, and doctoral degrees, as well as graduate certificates and continuing education programs. PSU is the state's only urban university and has a current enrollment of about 30,000 students including nearly 2,400 international students (see www.oirp.pdx.edu/source/port1213/all_all.pdf).

The International Student Mentor Program (ISMP) began in 2005 as an opt-in, one-term program for incoming fall-term international PSU students. In 2009, ISMP was changed from an optional to a mandatory one-term program and now serves cohorts of new international student mentees admitted during fall, winter, spring, and summer terms.

In 2005 staff consisted of a .6 FTE international student life adviser whose primary responsibility was to create and maintain this mentoring program. By 2008 the initial adviser position was increased to .8 FTE and a second adviser was hired to provide a wider range of services for international students and support the growing mentor program. The ISMP leadership team has continued to grow and now includes a third adviser as well as front office support staff.

ISMP operated without a budget from 2005 to 2008, relying on in-kind support from other campus student support programs. In 2009, ISMP began receiving funding from PSU's Office of International Affairs and Enrollment Management and the Office of Student Affairs as part of increased campuswide retention efforts.

Philosophy

ISMP's philosophy is that peer mentoring can help international students build strong connections to PSU and ease their transition to a new type of educational system and a new country. Peer mentoring is particularly effective during this transition time, as new international students are more likely to be comfortable seeking peer rather than faculty or staff support because of their home cultural beliefs that dictate a greater power distance between themselves and faculty or staff than with student peers.

Participants

In the fall of 2005, 20 ISMP mentors were matched with about 80 new student mentees, a 4:1 mentee-to-mentor ratio. By fall 2013, 45 mentors were matched with 310 mentees, for an approximately 7:1 mentee-to-mentor ratio. There are several reasons for the dramatic increase in participation over the past eight years. First, PSU's international enrollment rates grew substantially over this period. Second, the university changed ISMP from an opt-in to a mandatory participation program.

In view of the diversity among the international student population, ISMP participants can range from first-time freshmen to doctoral students, and demographics of the group can change dramatically from term to term. Indian students are currently the largest group of ISMP mentees, making up nearly 25% of the fall term 2013 mentee cohort. Japanese, Chinese, Vietnamese, and Korean students make up another 25% of fall term ISMP mentees.

Mentors

Mentor selection is based on several different criteria. First, ISMP mentors are likely to have experience working, volunteering, or participating in other student leadership programs at PSU. A second important criterion is knowledge of international student concerns. The selection team looks for potential mentors who can articulate international student college adjustment needs. Experience as a PSU student is a third selection criterion. Potential mentors can be undergraduate or graduate students but must have completed at least one full year of PSU courses not counting terms spent in the Intensive English Language Program. Finally, mentor selection is influenced by students' majors and year in school so mentors and mentees can be matched according to programs of study and undergraduate-graduate student status. Mentors are selected in spring term for the subsequent year's program.

In 2013 the ISMP introduced a new mentor leader position with additional formalized leadership responsibilities that include assisting with developing and presenting training materials, leading social activities, and facilitating mentor trainings. Eight mentor leaders were hired for the 2013–2014 academic year.

Mentor compensation has varied throughout the program, depending on the level of university support and the size of the program. From 2005 to 2008, the program relied on campuswide collaborations to provide small ($100–$200) stipends for the mentors. Each mentor also received a certificate of completion and participation in the program, a tradition that still continues. In 2009 when ISMP operated with a budget for the first time, the stipend for mentors doubled to $400. Currently, mentor stipends are highest in fall term, then reduced in winter and spring terms because of lower workloads. With the introduction of the mentor leader position, there are now two levels of stipends with leaders receiving $500 and mentors receiving $400.

While ISMP does admit students during the summer term, mentor participation is purely voluntary because of budgetary constraints. Summer mentor responsibilities are dramatically reduced, with mentors only being asked to help during orientation and communicate regularly with mentees via e-mail.

Delivery and Frequency of Contact

ISMP delivers support through a combination of face-to-face and e-mentoring. E-mail remains the primary means of communication throughout much of the program. Mentor-mentee pairs are matched several months before international students' arrival in the United States. Mentors are expected to check in with their mentees at least once a week starting late summer and throughout the fall. However, because this is a mandatory program, not all incoming international students choose to participate at the same level. Typically the amount of mentor-mentee contact varies with each mentee's needs. Once mentees arrive in the United States they are given the option to meet with their mentors before International Student Orientation; however, many times the initial meeting takes place at orientation. After orientation, mentors continue to check in weekly through e-mails and set up face-to-face meetings with their mentees upon request. Mentors are expected to encourage their mentees to attend the Organization of International Students Welcome Party as well as program events such as a Halloween Party. Fall term social activities culminate with a large ISMP-sponsored Thanksgiving dinner.

Program Goals

While ISMP is part of a larger university-wide effort to increase international student retention and success at PSU, program goals are much more specific. ISMP has four mentee-related program goals. The first goal is to provide incoming international students with a social support network during their first term at PSU. Mentors provide a first point of social contact for their mentees. Prearrival e-contact is an important aspect of ISMP because international students often feel confused and concerned about how things work before they arrive.

The second goal is to facilitate incoming international students' transition to PSU by helping them become involved in their program of study or major and with the larger university. Mentors are available to address incoming international students' immediate adjustment questions and concerns and help mentees understand the value of engagement in campus activities. Mentors also model engaged student behavior by joining their mentees in attending campus- and ISMP-sponsored events or participating in service opportunities hosted by the ISMP or campus partners.

The third goal is to help new international students understand the expectations of a U.S. university and of PSU professors. Mentors recount their own cultural adjustment experiences at PSU during International Student Orientation. In addition, mentors share strategies for addressing issues such as how to approach professors appropriately when trying to clarify course expectations.

The fourth goal is to make incoming international students aware of important campus resources and how to use those resources appropriately. Mentors are trained to anticipate which college adjustment issues new students are likely to face during their first term on campus as well as which resources are most useful for addressing specific issues. Mentors link new international students to important academic support services, such as department advisers and tutors, as well as needed campus housing and community resources.

In addition, ISMP has two mentor-specific program goals, the first of which is to develop a strong mentoring community to support mentors. ISMP mentors provide a support network for each other. This sense of community is particularly valuable for mentors dealing with challenging mentee issues.

The second goal is to provide peer mentors with opportunities to develop their own leadership skills. This desire to ensure that mentors have the opportunity to develop skills throughout their participation in the program was one of the driving forces in the creation of the mentor leader position.

Program Resources That Support Peer Mentoring

ISMP includes two elements intended to support peer mentoring. The first is the regular bimonthly mentor meetings with the International Student Life Team. These meetings provide opportunities for the program team to answer and address mentor concerns, as well as to troubleshoot possible solutions and suggest further resources.

A second program resource is a Facebook group created for each mentor cohort. This online resource provides an additional forum where mentors can ask for and receive help from each other and staff when necessary.

Evaluation: How Was Program Success Measured?

Prior to the 2013–2014 academic year, the majority of program evaluation focused on two ISMP goals. The mentee-specific goal of providing incoming international students with a social support network during their first term at PSU was assessed using program satisfaction data from an end-of-fall-term survey. The majority of this data was collected at the program-sponsored Thanksgiving dinner. The other initial evaluation focus related to the mentor-specific goal of providing a strong mentoring community to support mentors. This was also evaluated using program satisfaction data from the end-of-fall-term survey. In addition, mentors provided feedback to program staff through their reflective journal postings. This feedback was used to revise the subsequent year's mentor training and program activities. In 2013–2014 a more holistic and comprehensive evaluation plan was initiated after increased university pressure to validate the effects of the program. The first step in this new plan was ensuring that program goals were clearly articulated and measurable. The assessment plan shifted from solely focusing on mentee and mentor satisfaction to trying to assess mentor and mentee program participation-associated knowledge gains. This involved changing when data were collected as well as the kinds of data that were collected.

The first mentee goal, to provide incoming international students with a social support network during their first term at PSU, was assessed based on mentee satisfaction data from the end-of-term survey. For 2013–2014, overall program satisfaction was very high, with a majority of comments highlighting mentees' positive experiences with their mentors. In addition, 76% of mentees noted that having an ISMP mentor eased her or his transition to the university.

The second mentee goal, to help incoming international students become engaged in their major programs and the larger university, was assessed based on mentee engagement data from the end-of-term survey. Almost 50% of 2013–2014 mentees noted that having a mentor encouraged the mentee to be more involved in campus activities during the program term.

The third goal, to help students understand U.S. university and PSU professors' expectations, was assessed based on the comparison of postorientation and end-of-term mentee survey data on knowledge of issues. Very few of the 2013–2014 mentees could identify potential campus adjustment issues at orientation, much less how to address them. By the end of the program term all mentees could explain how to access health services, register for classes, and get immigration questions answered. However, there was much more variation in their knowledge of how to address other issues.

The fourth goal, to make incoming students aware of important campus resources, was assessed based on comparisons of preorientation, postorientation, and end-of-term mentee survey data on resource knowledge. Eighty-eight percent of 2013–2014 mentees showed an increase in knowledge of campus resources over their time in the program. The fact that all four mentee-focused goals were met makes a strong case that the ISMP program was successful in promoting international students' transitions to Portland State.

The ISMP also had two mentor-focused program goals. The first, developing a strong mentoring community to support mentors, was assessed based on mentor satisfaction data from the end-of-term survey. The 2013–2014 mentors unanimously reported that they felt well supported by the program staff and other mentors. Many volunteered that they would recommend ISMP to another student from a similar background. The second goal, providing peer mentors with opportunities to develop their own leadership skills, was assessed based on qualitative reflection data from mentors. While all 2013–2014 mentors reported personal and professional development associated with participating in ISMP, 33 out of 36 mentors explicitly reported improved leadership skills. Mentors showed they valued their ISMP experiences.

Mentor Training

Mentors are hired in spring term and attend a series of trainings throughout the summer and fall terms. Mentors receive four full days of preprogram training during the summer and four two-hour continuing training or check-in sessions throughout the fall term.

The three-part summer training begins with a weekend off-campus retreat. The first part focuses on understanding cultural adjustment issues, building cross-cultural awareness and communication skills, and creating a sense of community among the mentoring team. The second part of summer training focuses on the policies and ground rules of the program. The final training component helps mentors build their knowledge of PSU and community resources. Fall term continuing trainings include leadership and communication skills development and problem solving current mentee issues.

The ISMP leadership skills trainings focus on gaining the skills necessary to be a successful mentor, such as leading small groups, facilitating conversation among students with different communication styles and cultural identities, and practicing personal leadership. There are also supplemental trainings and activities such as service-learning projects for mentors who continue beyond the fall term.

Evaluation of Mentor Training

ISMP mentor training evaluation traditionally involved data collection via a survey that focused on general feelings of mentor program satisfaction. These evaluations have been almost universally positive, with mentors often commenting on their growth as a leader or sharing transformative program experiences.

In 2013–2014, program administrators added the first full evaluation of the effectiveness of the mentor-training element that focuses on knowledge and appropriate usage of PSU and community resources. An initial measurement of resource knowledge was conducted at the start of formal training and a second at the end of training to capture the effect of mentor training on knowledge levels. For the 2013–2014 training, 90% of mentors demonstrated higher levels of relevant campus resource knowledge, and there was a 27% increase in the average number of relevant campus resources that mentors could identify posttraining.

Reflection

In hindsight, the greatest lesson we learned was that it is critically important to create a cohesive assessment plan that captures measures of mentee learning and growth as well as mentor and mentee feedback during their time in ISMP. Ideally, this assessment plan should be created while you are developing your program. Not surprisingly, we found implementing changes while running a peer mentoring program was a more challenging process.

The changes to the ISMP have come with time and through trial and error. Peer mentoring coordinators must be willing to learn from what works and doesn't work, and grow with each program year. As student numbers and demographics change, budgets fluctuate, and communication and assessment tools evolve, program leaders must be willing to shape their programs accordingly.

10

HOW WILL YOU CARE FOR AND MAINTAIN YOUR PEER MENTORING PROGRAM?

> Maintaining a successful peer mentoring program requires activities following the program year that include revising program elements, disseminating results, and making the case to administrators and funders that your program is worthy of ongoing support.

Chapter 10

- introduces three elements in the care and maintenance of your program,
- examines how reviewing program evaluation data can facilitate between-year program revisions,
- discusses the value of getting the word out about your program success to different audiences,
- identifies important steps in approaching administrators with requests for ongoing program support, and
- reviews the central argument of this book.

The road to success is always under construction.

(Tomlin, 2015)

Persistence is incredibly important. Persistence proves to the person you're trying to reach that you're passionate about something, that you really want something.

(O'Donnell, 2015)

So far you've conceptualized your college student peer mentoring program, developed its theoretical foundation, designed the program, gathered and delivered content, appropriately trained mentors, and implemented and evaluated your program, and it was a success. Your mentees did well in regard to academic success indicators, demonstrated improvement in meeting program goals, and reported being highly satisfied with their experiences in your program. In addition, your program received very favorable reviews from your mentors. So now what?

Your program is like a bare-root rosebush. It started out as a stark collection of stalks and roots when you planted it, but it grew into a leafy bush, covered with beautiful and fragrant blossoms. The rosebush looks good now, but it will not keep that lovely appearance for very long, much less be a healthy plant next year, without ongoing care and maintenance. The care and maintenance of your program involves three elements: review and revision, getting the word out, and negotiating ongoing support. You will draw heavily from your evaluation data, in different ways, to address each element.

Review and Revision

Review and revision is similar to formative evaluation in many ways; the biggest difference is when each takes place. As noted in Chapter 9, formative evaluation involves collecting data or feedback on program experiences while they are happening. The goal of formative evaluation is to provide feedback about whether or not mentees understand program content, how mentees experience program activities, and whether or not mentees interpret those experiences as intended in the initial program design. Review and revision also involves the use of feedback and other evaluation data to inform programmatic decisions; however, this process typically occurs after a one-year or one-semester program has finished and before the next program begins.

One of the uses of evaluation data discussed in the previous chapter is to provide information about which program aspects are working as planned and which ones require revision. If you discover one or more program elements are not working or not working as effectively as you planned, I suggest you begin by reconsidering the conceptual and theoretical foundation for each element. It is rare for program administrators to totally change an initial theoretical foundation. For example, if you developed your initial program on the belief that improving campus connection is related to student success, you are not likely to entirely abandon that perspective. However, if mentee and mentor feedback suggests that other factors like engagement in student's own learning complement the effects of campus connection, then reconceptualizing your program foundation may be in order. This theoretical reconceptualization would necessitate adding program goals relating to promoting mentees' engagement in their own learning.

Adding new goals is like dropping a big rock in a pond; the ripples extend out in all directions. New goals require new content along with considerations of how it will be delivered. New goals and associated content will then require additional mentor training; changes to your evaluation design; and the ways you collect, analyze, and present your data. The logical argument that supports your claim of success will also have to change.

Sometimes end-of-program feedback might not require changes in goals but still might lead you to change design elements such as when you recruit mentees, the size of group orientation, or the number or frequency of mentor-mentee meetings. Your mentors' feedback can be particularly valuable. Did they notice that some content elements did not seem to engage mentees? Were there program policies and procedures that unintentionally made unnecessary work for mentors? Mentors may be able to suggest useful modifications based on their work with mentees during the program year.

I recommend reviewing your evaluation plan even if you decide not to change it. Did the hypothesized relationships between your mentored students and any initial control groups prove accurate? If not, where is the issue? The ways and times you collect data may also need to be modified. For example, if you are getting relatively low response rates with an anonymous online mentee satisfaction survey, you might consider collecting the same data when all students are present for an activity such as an end-of-program celebration. This is also the time to consider if the initial way you presented your data makes the strongest case.

The end of the program year is a good time to review mentor training with your mentors. Use your mentor training evaluation data to keep elements that work and replace those that do not.

I want to be clear that revision after end-of-year review is a shared characteristic of high-quality programs. Because mentoring programs tend to be developed in silos without a lot of communication with people from other programs, it may not be widely known that most successful programs go through several iterations before they end up in their current working state. For examples, see Vignettes 3 and 4.

Getting the Word Out

Getting the word out involves sharing your results with several different audiences, and your campus community is one important audience. Take every available opportunity to share the story of how your program promotes student success including open houses; meetings with departments, units (e.g., Student Affairs), or subunits (e.g., Campus Housing); on-campus conferences; alumni groups; and presentations at new student orientations or department chair meetings. Contact your school's public relations unit and provide information its staff can use to stir up interest in your program and its accomplishments in the community and local media. Offer to be interviewed by your school's student newspaper or radio station. When you get media requests for interviews it is very helpful to have one or more mentors and mentees willing to join you and share their experiences. For this first important audience, emphasize that your program provides peer mentoring that helps students succeed in regard to academic success indicators. You want the campus community to know that your program works, what students your program serves, how departments and units could identify students who might benefit from your program, and how to refer students to the program.

A second important audience is the advisers, counselors, and administrators from the schools or programs (e.g., secondary schools, community colleges, veteran transition offices, international student brokers) that feed students to your program. Many of these outreach efforts will target smaller audiences or even single individuals. Take advantage of any chance to directly share the story of your program's success with soon-to-be college students who would qualify for your program.

With this second audience, you again want to make sure to emphasize your students' success in meeting specific academic success indicators. However, students' testimonials of the benefits they received from participating in your program (e.g., satisfaction, fun, and connections to other students) carry a lot more weight here.

The third important audience is the larger professional community. Take advantage of opportunities to give presentations at local, regional, and scholarly professional meetings. For faculty members, these can be groups in specific academic disciplines like national and regional sociology and psychology meetings or the American Educational Research Association. There are also student affairs professional groups such as the National Academic Advising Association, Consortium for Student Retention Data Exchange, the National Collegiate Honors Council, Utah Valley University's Student Leadership and Mentoring Conference and Minority Male Mentoring program, or the University of South Carolina's annual conference on the first-year experience. In addition, there are cross-disciplinary mentoring-focused conferences such as the University of New Mexico's Mentoring Institute's annual meetings. A professional audience will want more than your data on whether students met your academic success indicators. These folks want to hear about your program-specific goals that establish the effectiveness of the conceptual and theoretical underpinnings of your mentoring intervention. They are particularly interested in best practices. Presentations to this audience provide great opportunities for you to network with other scholars who share your interests. Connections that you make presenting to this audience may lead to possible future collaborations. At the very least you will get feedback on how others outside your school view your efforts. Sometimes other professionals are more impressed by your program's success than your local community.

Ongoing Support and Institutionalizing Your Program

In the discussion on differences in funding programs in Chapter 5, I pointed out that some externally funded programs apply for a follow-up grant even while the initial grant is still active. However, most programs that are initially successful look to internal institutional support to continue. This means you will need to approach campus administrators for new or ongoing support. Here, again, your evaluation data are important.

Administrators will be most interested in your academic success data. You have to make a strong case that your program is associated with improved student success before mentioning your data about whether the program achieved specific goals. How you interpret your data is critical here. To make a case that your program is worth an investment, or a continuation of investment, you need to start by identifying the academic success indicators that are most important to the administrators you are presenting your materials to. Those are the criteria you want to explicitly emphasize when you present your program data. All administrators will initially pay attention to academic success indicators such as degree completion and retention, but some will also pay more attention to certain additional indicators than others. An administrator with a student veterans' program would certainly care about retention but might also prioritize participant satisfaction. Similarly, the administrator who supervises an international student program might focus less on GPAs beyond a certain minimum level that keeps students off probation and more on how connected students feel to the host school.

Administrators are busy, so keep your presentation short and to the point. Repeat your most important arguments about why funding this program will promote student success more than once, typically at the beginning and end of your presentation. If you are able to generate the cost per student, it makes a powerful case when you compare this to the cost to the university if a student drops out before completing a year, the term, or a degree (see the discussion on the issue of degree noncompletion in Chapter 2). Make sure you provide a concrete budget that details the amount of support you are requesting as well as how those funds will be allocated. Come prepared with handouts you can leave with the administrator that demonstrate your program success and detail your support request.

In the best of all worlds, your school's administration will recognize the value of your program and agree to fund it in the upcoming year. Sometimes, programs that are initially funded externally will require more support to continue after the grant funding ends than the administrators are willing to commit. One option would be to see if you could get a commitment for partial support dependent upon your securing outside funding.

Another road to institutionalization involves incorporating all or part of your program into already existing student support programs at your school. For example, after federal grant funding for the Students First Mentoring Program (Vignette 2) ran out, and budget shortfalls made continuing it as a free-standing program unfeasible, the director of PSU's University Studies program offered to incorporate key elements of the first-generation student mentoring program into University Studies, which provides mentoring support for all incoming freshman and sophomore general education students. The peer mentoring videos and online library of problem-solving tip sheets became the foundation for the UConnect virtual resource (http://uconnect.unst.pdx.edu/), which then was available for all first- and second-year students and their mentors in PSU's general education program. The Students First program director served as faculty in residence for retention during the transition year to coordinate the development of the virtual resource system. If you are faced with this kind of dilemma—choosing between letting your program expire or combining your work with existing programs—think about the reasons you initially began this journey to develop a mentoring program. Keep in mind that the ultimate goal is promoting student success through peer mentoring, not perpetuating any one program.

Putting All the Pieces Together

As I near the end of this book, I want to summarize my argument that you can develop a college student peer mentoring program that works by explicitly connecting key content elements from the different chapters of this book.

Peer mentoring can help address the educational crisis of degree noncompletion by facilitating college student academic success. Chapters 1 and 2 explain why it is nationally, locally, and institutionally important for students who begin college to complete their higher educational journeys and that peer mentoring can help address this issue. These chapters review what we already know about the impact of peer mentoring on college student success, introduce multiple models of traditional and nontraditional college student persistence, and discuss how peer mentoring might affect each model.

Preparation facilitates program development and implementation. Chapters 2, 3, and 4 review important steps you need to take before you begin the actual nuts and bolts of program development. At the most basic level, you need to understand the key college adjustment issues all students and your specific group of students must address to succeed at college. Chapters 2 and 3 discuss important transitions into and within higher education and identify issues associated with specific transitions. Chapter 3 explores group-specific adjustment issues for student veterans, first-generation, and international students, and provides several issue identification tools. Chapter 4 connects what peer mentoring can accomplish with different adjustment issues and introduces the adjustment issue and a peer mentoring matching tool to help you realistically determine the feasible goals for your program.

Design is the bridge that connects program goals with students' program experiences and outcomes. Chapter 5 introduces the planning and structural choices you will need to make as you develop your program, including timing, funding, recruiting, and developing policies and procedures. Chapter 6 explores the relative strengths and limitations of different modes of program delivery. Design and delivery choices are shaped by your understanding of what facilitates student success at college, the issues your students face, and how peer mentoring may be able to affect those issues. Design also connects to content, particularly in regard to the sequencing of content materials.

Program goals must inform content and mentor training. Chapter 7 distinguishes among three essential program content areas: universal content, content shared by programs that all serve the same group of students, and program-specific content. Chapter 8 introduces six fundamental questions that will help you determine how you should organize and what you should include in your mentor training. Regardless of your program goals, mentor training needs to mirror the content provided to mentees.

The quality of your evaluation has a direct impact on your program's likelihood of success. Chapter 9 describes evaluation as a three-step process: using descriptive data to capture key program characteristics, using institutional data to establish your mentees' college success, and measuring operationalized program goals in ways that produce data that can be analyzed to determine whether goals have been realized. In addition, the chapter introduces three standards of evaluation quality and proposes an evaluation plan to link program goals with specific design elements and appropriate measurement instruments to provide clear information about whether your program is accomplishing what it was intended to accomplish. Chapter 10 reaffirms the importance of evaluation quality because of the important role program outcome data play in each of the three elements of program maintenance: review and revision, getting the word out, and negotiating ongoing support.

Program size affects design, delivery, evaluation, and mentor training. One of the unique features of this book is the explicit consideration of how program size has an impact on the development and implementation of your peer mentoring program. Chapter 5 explores how program size affects program design in each of the four dimensions of the peer mentoring rubric: degree of inclusiveness, duration, approach to addressing students' needs, and educational transition. That chapter more specifically discusses how differences in program size can affect recruiting, mentee orientation, staffing, how materials are delivered to mentees in a timely manner, mentor training, and coordinating program activities. Chapter 6 explains how program size interacts with the strengths and limitations of different delivery choices. With the levels of resources held constant, group-mentoring-delivery-based programs typically can accommodate more students than paired-delivery-based ones. Similarly, e-mentoring programs can serve greater numbers of students than face-to-face programs. That chapter also reviews the trade-offs that accompany size-related delivery choices. Chapter 8 examines size-associated mentor training issues including coordinating training exercises and building a sense of community among mentors. Finally, Chapter 9 considers how differences in program size could influence data collection and presentation choices.

A Closing Thought

It is my hope that this book will provide you with the tools you'll need to develop and implement a new peer mentoring program or refine an existing one. As you move forward, I'd like to share a quote from Vincent Tinto (2008) that has inspired my work: "Access without support is not opportunity."

Peer mentoring is the ideal vehicle for providing college students with social, academic, and cultural support. Your programs will provide the students you serve with opportunities to turn college access into college success. You can do it. The next step is up to you.

Act on fact: Using data to improve student success. (2006). Retrieved from http://www.ccsse.org/publications/CCSSENationalReport2006.pdf

Adelman, C. (2006). *The toolbox revisited: Paths to degree completion from high school through college*. Washington, DC: U.S. Department of Education.

Ajzen, I., & Fishbein, M. (1970). The prediction of behavior from attitudinal and normative variables. *Journal of Experimental Social Psychology, 6*(4), 466–487.

Allen, T. D., & Poteet, M. L. (1999). Developing effective mentoring relationships: Strategies from the mentor's viewpoint. *The Career Development Quarterly, 48*(1), 59–73.

Allensworth, E., & Easton, J. (2007). *What matters for staying on-track and graduating in Chicago public high schools: A close look at course grades, failures, and attendance in the freshman year*. Chicago, IL: University of Chicago Consortium on Chicago Schools.

Allum, J., Bell, N., & Sowell, R. (2012). *Graduate enrollment and degrees: 2001 to 2011*. Retrieved from http://www.cgsnet.org/graduate-enrollment-and-degrees-2001-2011

Al-Sharideh, K. A., & Goe, W. R. (1998). Ethnic communities within the university: An examination of international students. *Research in Higher Education, 39*(6), 699–725.

American Council on Student Financial Assistance. (2005). *The student aid gauntlet: Making access to college simple and certain*. Retrieved from http://www.ed.gov/about/bdscomm/list/acsfa/edlite-gauntlet.html

Angelique, H., Kyle, K., & Taylor, E. (2002). Mentors and muses: New strategies for academic success. *Innovative Higher Education, 26*(3), 195–209.

Arévalo, E., Boggan, D., & West, L. (2004). *Designing and customizing mentor training*. Folsom, CA: Center for Applied Research Solutions.

Armsden, G. C., & Greenberg, M. T. (1987). The inventory of parent and peer attachment: Individual differences and their relationship to psychological well-being in adolescence. *Journal of Youth and Adolescence, 16*(5), 427–454.

Arnstein, R. L. (1980). The student, the family, the university, and transition to adulthood. *Adolescent Psychiatry, 8*, 160–172.

Aschaffenburg, K., & Maas, I. (1997). Cultural and educational careers: The dynamics of social reproduction. *American Sociological Review, 62*(4), 573–587.

Astin, A. (1977). *Four critical years*. San Francisco, CA: Jossey-Bass.

Astin, A. (1984). Student involvement: A developmental theory for higher education. *Journal of College Student Personnel, 25*, 297–308.

Astin, A. (1993). *What matters in college? Four critical years revisited*. San Francisco, CA: Jossey-Bass.

Awayaa, A., McEwana, H., Heylerb, D., Linskyc, S., Lumd, D., & Wakukawac, P. (2003). Mentoring as a journey. *Teaching and Teacher Education, 19*(1), 45–56.

Bachelor's degree attainment in the United States and OECD countries, 1940 to 2011. (2012). *PostSecondary Opportunity*, 238, 1–16. Retrieved from http://www .postsecondary.org/last12/238_412pg1_16.pdf

Bagalman, E. (2011). *Suicide, PTSD, and substance use among OEF/OIF veterans using VA health care: Facts and figures*. Washington, DC: Congressional Research Service, Library of Congress.

Barker, T. (2013, February 5). Meet the transfers: They are academic nomads. *St. Louis Post Dispatch*. Retrieved from http://www.stltoday.com/news/local/education/meet-the-transfers---they-are-academic-nomads/article_075d610e-dc58-5686-abfe-61c803e18594.html

Barnett, M. B. (2009). From theory to classroom: Some practical applications of standpoint theory. *Feminist Teacher, 19*(3), 186–194.

Bartlett, T., & Fischer, K. (2011, November 3). The China conundrum: American colleges find the Chinese-student boom a tricky fit. *Chronicle of Higher Education*. Retrieved from http://chronicle.com/article/Chinese-Students-Prove-a/129628/

Baxter Magolda, M. B. (2001). *Making their own way: Narratives for transforming higher education to promote self-development*. Sterling, VA: Stylus.

Baxter Magolda, M. B. (2004). Learning partnerships model: A framework for promoting self-authorship. In M. B. Magolda & P. M. King (Eds.), *Learning partnerships: Theory and models of practice to educate for self-authorship* (pp. 37–62). Sterling, VA: Stylus.

Baxter Magolda, M. B. (2009). *Authoring your life: Developing an internal voice to navigate life's challenges*. Sterling, VA: Stylus.

Baxter Magolda, M. B., & King, P. M. (2008). Toward reflective conversations: An advising approach that promotes self-authorship. *Peer Review, 10*(1), 8–11.

Beatrice, J., & Shively, P. (2007). Peer mentors target unique populations; increase use of campus resources. *E-Source for College Transitions, 4*(5), 1–4.

Becker, H. (1963). *Outsiders: Studies in the sociology of deviance*. New York, NY: The Free Press.

Bedsworth, W., Colby, S., & Doctor, J. (2006). *Reclaiming the American dream*. Boston, MA: The Bridgespan Group.

Beebe, S. A., Beebe, S. J., Redmond, M. V., & Geerinck, T. M. (2004). *Interpersonal communication: Relating to others*. Toronto, CA: Pearson/Allyn and Bacon.

Bell, A. G. (2015). *Alexander Graham Bell quotes*. Retrieved from http://www .brainyquote.com/quotes/quotes/a/alexanderg387728.html

Benner, P. (1982). From novice to expert. *The American Journal of Nursing, 82*(3), 402–407.

Benner, P. (2004). Using the Dreyfus model of skill acquisition to describe and interpret skill acquisition and clinical judgment in nursing practice and education. *Bulletin of Science, Technology & Society, 24*(3), 188–199.

Bierema, L., & Merriam, S. (2002). E-mentoring: Using computer-mediated communication to enhance the mentoring process. *Innovative Higher Education, 26*(3), 211–227.

Billson, J. M., & Terry, M. B. (1982). In search of the silken purse: Factors in attrition among first-generation students. *College and University, 58*(1), 57–75.

Bixler, B. (2014). *Learning style inventory.* Retrieved from http://www.personal.psu.edu/bxb11/LSI/LSI.htm

Black, K. A., & Voelker, J. C. (2008). The role of preceptors in first-year student engagement in introductory courses. *Journal of the First-Year Experience & Students in Transition, 20*(2), 25–43.

Boyatzis, R. E. (1998). *Transforming qualitative information: Thematic analysis and code development.* Thousand Oaks, CA: Sage.

Boyle, P., & Boice, R. (1998). Systematic mentoring for new faculty teachers and graduate teaching assistants. *Innovative Higher Education, 22*(3), 157–179.

Bouquillon, E. A., Sosik, J. J., & Lee, D. (2005). "It's only a phase": Examining trust, identification and mentoring functions received across the mentoring phases. *Mentoring & Tutoring: Partnership in Learning, 13*(2), 239–258.

Bourdieu, P. (1973). The forms of capital. In J. G. Richardson (Ed.), *Handbook of theory and research for the sociology of education* (pp. 241–258). New York, NY: Greenwood Press.

Bourdieu, P. (1984). *Distinction: A social critique of the judgment of taste* (R. Nice, Trans.). Cambridge, MA: Harvard University Press.

Brack, G., Gay, M. F., & Matheny, K. B. (1993). Relationships between attachment and coping resources among late adolescents. *Journal of College Student Development, 34*(3), 212–215.

Brancu, M., Straits-Tröster, K., & Kudler, H. (2011). Behavioral health conditions among military personnel and veterans. *North Carolina Medical Journal, 72*(1), 54–60.

Braun, V., & Clarke, V. (2006). Using thematic analysis in psychology. *Qualitative Research in Psychology, 3*(2), 77–101.

Brown, M. C., Davis, G. L., & McClendon, S. A. (1999). Mentoring graduate students of color: Myths, models, and modes. *Peabody Journal of Education, 74*(2), 105–118.

Bui, K. V. T. (2002). First-generation college students at a four-year university: Background characteristics, reasons for pursuing higher education, and first-year experiences. *College Students Journal, 36*(1), 3–11.

Bulthuis, P. (Ed.). (1986). The foreign student today: A profile. *New Directions for Student Services, 36*, 19–27.

Bunting, B., Dye, B., Pinnegar, S., & Robinson, K. (2012). Understanding the dynamics of peer mentor learning: A narrative study. *Journal of the First-Year Experience & Students in Transition, 24*(1), 61–78.

Burke, P. J., & Stets, J. E. (2009). *Identity theory.* New York, NY: Oxford University Press.

California Climate Action Registry. (2001). *Registry design charette.* Retrieved from http://www.climateregistry.org/tools/member-resources/past-events.html

California State University. (2013). *The California State University graduation initiative.* Retrieved from http://graduate.csuprojects.org/home?noCache=162:1372436416

Callero, P. L. (1994). From role-playing to role-using: Understanding roles as resources. *Social Psychology Quarterly, 57*(3), 228–243.

Campbell, T. A., & Campbell, D. E. (1997). Faculty/student mentor program: Effects on academic performance and retention. *Research in Higher Education, 38*(6), 727–742.

Carey, K. (2010). *U.S. college graduation rate stays pretty much exactly the same.* http://www.quickanded.com/2010/12/u-s-college-graduation-rate-stays-pretty-much-exactly-the-same.html

Cerna, O., Platania, C., & Fong, K. (2012). Leading by example: A case study of peer leader programs at two Achieving the Dream colleges. New York, NY: MDRC.

Chekhov, A. (2015). *Anton Chekhov quotes.* Retrieved from http://www.brainyquote.com/quotes/quotes/a/antonchekh119058.html

Chen, C. P. (1999). Common stressors among international college students: Research and counseling implications. *Journal of College Counseling, 2*(1), 49–65.

Chen, X., & Carroll, C. (2005). *First-generation students in postsecondary education: A look at their college transcripts* (Postsecondary Education Descriptive Analysis Report, NCES 2005-171). Washington, DC: National Center for Education Statistics.

Chickering, A. W. (1969). *Education and identity.* San Francisco, CA: Jossey-Bass.

Chickering, A. W., & Reisser, L. (1993). *Education and identity.* San Francisco, CA: Jossey-Bass.

Choy, S. P. (2001). *Students whose parents did not go to college: Postsecondary access, persistence, and attainment* (NCES 2001-126). Washington, DC: National Center for Education Statistics.

Churchill, W. (2015). *Winston Churchill quotes.* Retrieved from http://www.brainyquote.com/quotes/quotes/w/winstonchu144998.html

Coleman, J. S. (1988). Social capital in the creation of human capital. *American Journal of Sociology, 94*, S95-S120.

College continuation rates for recent high school graduates, 1960 to 2012. (2013). *PostSecondary Opportunity,* 251, 1–13. Retrieved from http://www.postsecondary.org/last12/251_513pg1_13.pdf

Collier, P. J. (2000). The effects of completing a capstone course on student identity. *Sociology of Education, 73*(4), 285–299.

Collier, P. J. (2001). The differentiated model of role identity acquisition. *Symbolic Interaction, 24*(2), 217–235.

Collier, P. J. (2011, April). *Building blocks of identity: Event schemas and role mastery.* Paper presented at the 82nd annual meeting of the Pacific Sociological Association Convention, Oakland, CA.

Collier, P. J. (2013a). Leadership and service-learning. In C. Cress, P. Collier, & V. Reitenauer, *Learning through Serving: A Student Guidebook for Service-Learning and Civic Engagement Across Academic Disciplines and Cultural Communities* (2nd ed., pp. 123–136). Sterling, VA: Stylus.

Collier, P. J. (2013b). Mentoring, relationship building for empowerment. In C. Cress, P. Collier, & V. Reitenauer, *Learning through Serving: A Student Guidebook for Service-Learning and Civic Engagement Across Academic Disciplines and Cultural Communities* (2nd ed., pp. 113–122). Sterling, VA: Stylus.

Collier, P., & Callero, P. (2005). Role theory and social cognition: Learning to think like a recycler. *Self and Identity, 4*(1), 44–58.

Collier, P., & Fellows, C. (2006). *Students first: Improving first-generation student retention and performance in higher education: Final report of program activities: 2005–2008* (148–158). Retrieved from http://drpeterjcollier.com/approach.htm

Collier, P., Fellows, C., & Holland, B. (2008). *Students first: Improving first-generation student retention and performance in higher education: Final report of program activities: 2005–2008.* Retrieved from http://drpeterjcollier.com/approach.htm

Collier, P., Fellows, C., & Holland, B. (2009). *2005–2009 FIPSE final report executive summary plus evaluation goals.* Retrieved from http://drpeterjcollier.com/approach.htm

Collier, P., & Morgan, D. (2008). Is that paper really due today? Differences in first-generation and traditional college students' understandings of faculty members' class-related expectations. *Higher Education, 55*(4), 425–446.

Collier, P., & Voegele, D. (2013). Groups are fun, groups are not fun. In C. Cress, P. Collier, & V. Reitenauer, *Serving and learning: A student workbook for community-based experiences across the disciplines* (2nd ed., pp. 51–76). Sterling, VA: Stylus.

Collier, P., & Williams, D. (2013). Reflection in action. In C. Cress, P. Collier, & V. Reitenauer (Eds.), *Learning through Serving: A Student Guidebook for Service-Learning and Civic Engagement Across Academic Disciplines and Cultural Communities* (2nd ed., pp. 95–112). Sterling, VA: Stylus.

Colvin, J. W., & Ashman, M. (2010). Roles, risks, and benefits of peer mentoring: Relationships in higher education. *Mentoring & Tutoring: Partnership in Learning, 18*(2), 121–134.

Cook, B. J., & Kim, Y. (2009). *From soldier to student: Easing the transition of service members on campus.* Retrieved from ERIC database. (ED505982)

Cosgrove, T. J. (1986). The effects of participation in a mentoring-transcript program on freshmen. *Journal of College Student Personnel, 27*(2), 119–124.

Cox, C. (2009). *The digital divide: Information competency, computer literacy, and community college proficiencies.* Retrieved from Academic Senate for California Community Colleges website: http://www.asccc.org/content/digital-divide-information-competency-computer-literacy-and-community-college-proficiencies

Cress, C., Burack, C., Giles, D., Elkins, J., & Stevens, M. (2010). *A promising connection: Increasing college access and success through civic engagement.* Boston, MA: Campus Compact.

Cress, C., Collier, P., & Reitenauer, V. (2013). *Serving and learning: A student workbook for community-based experiences across the disciplines* (2nd ed.). Sterling, VA: Stylus.

Creswell, J. W. (2013). *Research design: Qualitative, quantitative, and mixed methods approaches.* Thousand Oaks, CA: Sage.

Crisp, G., & Cruz, I. (2009). Mentoring college students: A critical review of the literature between 1990 and 2007. *Review of Educational Research, 50*, 525–545.

Cuhls, K. (2003). From forecasting to foresight processes: New participative foresight activities in Germany [Special issue]. *Journal of Forecasting, 22*(2/3) 93–111.

Davidson, M., & Foster-Johnson, L. (2001). Mentoring in the preparation of graduate students of color. *Review of Educational Research, 71*(4), 549–574.

Deaux, K., & Wrightsman, L. S. (1988). *Social psychology.* Monterey, CA: Brooks.

Del Monte, B. (2006). *Charettes: Smoothing the process to LEED certification.* Retrieved from http://www.facilitiesnet.com/green/article/Charettes-Meeting-of-the-Design-Minds--3918#

De Tocqueville, A. (1840). *Democracy in America* (Vol. 3). New York, NY: Penguin Classics.

Dewey, J. (1916). *Education and democracy.* New York, NY: MacMillan.

Dewey, J. (1933). *How we think: A restatement of the relation of reflective thinking to the educational process.* Lexington, MA: Heath.

Doran, G. T. (1981). There's a S.M.A.R.T. way to write management's goals and objectives. *Management Review, 70*(11), 35–36.

Dreyfus, H., & Dreyfus, S. (2004). The ethical implications of the five-stage skill-acquisition model. *Bulletin of Science, Technology & Society, 24*(3), 251–264.

Dreyfus, H., & Dreyfus, S. (2005). Peripheral vision: Expertise in real world contexts. *Organization Studies, 26*(5), 779–792.

Dumais, S. A. (2002). Cultural capital, gender, and school success: The role of habitus. *Sociology of Education, 75*(1), 44–68.

Duru, E., & Poyrazli, S. (2007). Personality dimensions, psychosocial-demographic variables, and English language competency in predicting level of acculturative stress among Turkish international students. *International Journal of Stress Management, 14*(1), 99–110.

Eberley Center for Teaching Innovation. (2014). *What is the difference between summative and formative evaluation?* Retrieved from http://www.cmu.edu/teaching/assessment/basics/formative-summative.html

EBI MAP-Works. (2013). *Making achievement possible.* Retrieved from http://www.webebi.com/mapworks

Eby, L. T., Rhodes, J. E., & Allen, T. D. (2007). Definition and evolution of mentoring. In T. D. Allen & L. T. Eby (Eds.), *The Blackwell handbook of mentoring: A multiple perspectives approach* (pp. 7–20). Malden, MA: Wiley-Blackwell.

Edgcomb, M. R., Crowe, H. A., Rice, J. D., Morris, S. J., Wolffe, R. J., & McConnaughay, K. D. (2010). Peer and near-peer mentoring enhancing learning in summer research programs. *Council on Undergraduate Research Quarterly, 31*, 18–25.

Education and training pay 2013. (2013).Retrieved from http://www.postsecondary.org/archives/Posters/Education_and_Training_Pay.pdf

Einstein, A. (2015a). *Albert Einstein quotes.* Retrieved from http://www.brainyquote.com/quotes/quotes/a/alberteins383803.html

Einstein, A. (2015b). *Albert Einstein quotes.* Retrieved from http://www.brainyquote.com/quotes/quotes/a/alberteins162052.html

Ehrich, L. S., Hansford, B. & Tennent, L. (2004). Formal mentoring programs in education and other professions: a review of the literature, *Educational Administration Quarterly, 40*(4), 518–540.

Engle, J. (2007). Postsecondary access and success for first-generation college students. *American Academic, 3*, 25–48.

Engle, J., Bermeo, A., & O'Brien, C. (2006). *Straight from the source: What works for first-generation college students.* Washington, DC: Pell Institute for the Study of Opportunity in Higher Education.

Engle, J., & Tinto, V. (2008). *Moving beyond access: College success for low-income, first-generation students.* Washington, DC: Pell Institute for the Study of Opportunity in Higher Education.

Ensher, E. A., Grant-Vallone, E. J., & Marelich, W. D. (2002). Effects of perceived attitudinal and demographic similarity on protégé's support and satisfaction gained from their mentoring relationships. *Journal of Applied Social Psychology, 32,* 1407–1430.

Eraut, M. (2000). Non-formal learning, implicit learning and tacit knowledge in professional work. In F. Coffield (Ed.), *The necessity of informal learning* (pp. 12–31). Bristol, UK: The Policy Press.

Eyler, J., Giles, D. E., Jr., & Braxton, J. (1999). The impact of service-learning on college students. In M.C. Sullivan (Ed.), *Service-learning: Educating students for life* (pp. 19–39). Harrisonburg, VA: Institute for Research in Higher Education.

Eyler, J., Giles, D. E., Jr., Stenson, C. M., & Gray, C. J. (2001). *At a glance: What we know about the effects of service-learning on college students, faculty, institutions, and communities, 1993–2000.* Retrieved from http://www.compact.org/wp-content/uploads/resources/downloads/aag.pdf

Falchikov, N., & Blythman, M. (2001). *Learning together: Peer tutoring in higher education.* New York, NY: Psychology Press.

Family income and unequal educational opportunity 1970 to 2011. (2012). *PostSecondary Opportunity, 245,* 1–20. Retrieved from http://www.postsecondary.org/last12/245_1112pg1_20.pdf

Fenzel, L. M., & Peyrot, M. (2005). Comparing college community participation and future service behaviors and attitudes. *Michigan Journal of Community Service Learning, 12*(1), 23–31.

Ferrari, J. R. (2004). Mentors in life and at school: Impact on undergraduate protégé perceptions of university mission and values. *Mentoring & Tutoring: Partnership in Learning, 12*(3), 295–305.

Festinger, L. (1954). A theory of social comparison processes. *Human Relations, 7*(2), 117–140.

Fischer, K. (2011, May 29). Colleges adapt to new kinds of students from abroad: Younger, sometimes less-experienced students require more academic and social support. *Chronicle of Higher Education.* Retrieved from http://chronicle.com/article/Colleges-Educate-a-New-Kind-of/127704/

Fisher, S., & Hood, B. (1987). The stress of the transition to university: A longitudinal study of psychological disturbance, absent-mindedness and vulnerability to homesickness. *British Journal of Psychology, 78*(4), 425–441.

Ford, D., Northrup, P., & Wiley, L. (2009). Connections, partnerships, opportunities, and programs to enhance success for military students. *New Directions for Student Services, 126,* 61–69.

From goal to reality: 40-40-20. (2012). Retrieved from http://www.oregon.gov/Gov/OEIB/Docs/nnOUSReport.pdf

Furnham, A. (1988). The adjustment of sojourners. In Y. Y. Kim & W. B. Gudykunst (Eds.), *Cross-cultural adaptation: Current approaches* (pp. 42–61). Newbury Park, CA: Sage.

Furnham, A., & Alibhai, N. (1985). The friendship networks of foreign students: A replication and extension of the functional model. *International Journal of Psychology, 20*(6), 709–722.

Fusch, D. (2011a, April 14). Helping veteran students succeed. *Academic Impression: Higher Education Impact.* Retrieved from http://www.academicimpressions.com/news/helping-veteran-students-succeed

Fusch, D. (2011b, October 10). Steps to Support International Student Success. *Academic Impression: Higher Education Impact.* Retrieved from http://www.academicimpressions.com/news/steps-support-international-student-success

Fusch, D. (2012). The transition in: Setting international students up for academic success. Retrieved from http://www.academicimpressions.com/news/transition-setting-international-students-academic-success

Garvey, B., & Alfred, G. (2000). Educating mentors. *Mentoring & Tutoring: Partnership in Learning, 8*(2), 114–126.

Girves, J. E., Zepeda, Y., & Gwathmey, J. K. (2005.) Mentoring in a post-affirmative action world. *Journal of Social Issues, 61*(3), 449–479.

Gladwell, M. (2000). *The tipping point: How little things can make a big difference.* Boston, MA: Little, Brown.

Gladwell, M. (2008). *Outliers: The story of success.* Boston, MA: Little, Brown.

Gloria, A. M., & Robinson Kurpius, S. E. (2001). Influences of self-beliefs, social support, and comfort in the university environment on the academic nonpersistence decisions of American Indian undergraduates. *Cultural Diversity and Ethnic Minority Psychology, 7*(1), 88.

Good, J., Halpin, G., & Halpin, G. (2002). Retaining Black students in engineering: Do minority programs have a longitudinal impact? *Journal of College Student Retention: Research, Theory and Practice, 3*(4), 351–364.

Graham, M. (2015). *Martha Graham quotes.* Retrieved from http://www.brainyquote.com/quotes/quotes/m/marthagrah117263.html

Gray, M. J., Ondaatje, E. H., Fricker, R. D., Jr., & Geschwind, S. A. (2000). Assessing service-learning: Results from a survey of learn and serve America, higher education. *Change, 32*(2), 30–39.

Grohol, J. M. (2007). *Becoming a better listener: Active listening.* Retrieved from http://psychcentral.com/lib/become-a-better-listener-active-listening/0001299

Grove, J., & Huon, G. (2003). *How to implement a peer-mentoring program: A user's guide.* Sydney, Australia: University of New South Wales.

Grusec, J. E., & Skubiski, S. (1970). Model nurturance, demand characteristics of the modeling experiment, and altruism. *Journal of Personality and Social Psychology, 14,* 353–359.

Guers, K. (Producer). (1997). *Pooh's grand adventure: The search for Christopher Robin* [Motion picture]. United States: Walt Disney Corporation.

Guesstimate. (n.d.). *In Merriam-Webster's online dictionary* (11th ed.). Retrieved from http://www.merriam-webster.com/dictionary/guesstimate

Guiffrida, D. A. (2006). Toward a cultural advancement of Tinto's theory. *The Review of Higher Education, 29*(4), 451–472.

Habley, W., Valiga, M., McClanahan, R., & Burkum, K. (2010). *What works in student retention: Public four-year colleges and universities.* Iowa City, IA: American College Testing.

Hall, R. (2006). Peer-mentoring program eases transition to university and increases retention. *E-Source for College Transitions, 4*(2), 7–9.

Harding, S. (1987). Introduction: Is there a feminist method? In S. Harding (Ed.), *Feminism and methodology* (pp. 1–14). Bloomington: University of Indiana Press.

Harper, M. S., & Allegretti, C. L. (2009). Transition to university: An adjustment and retention program for first-year students. *E-Source for College Transitions, 6*(4), 10–12.

Hastie, R. (2001). Problems for judgment and decision making. *Annual Review of Psychology, 52*, 653–683.

Health insurance coverage for people 18 years or older by type of coverage by educational attainment 2008. (2009). Retrieved from http://www.postsecondary.org/archives/Posters/healthins.pdf

Hitchcock, S. (2015). Shawn Hitchcock quotes. Retrieved from http://mediarelations.illinoisstate.edu/identity/1213/nov/Hitchcock.asp

Hixenbaugh, P., Dewart, H., Drees, D., & Williams, D. (2006). Peer e-mentoring: Enhancement of the first year experience. *Psychology Learning and Teaching, 5*(1), 8–14.

Hoffman, A. J., & Wallach, J. (2005). Effects of mentoring on community college students in transition to university. *Community College Enterprise, 11*(1), 67–78.

Homans, G. C. (1958). Social behavior as exchange. *American Journal of Sociology, 63*(6), 597–606.

Hopkins, K. (2012, August 29). 6 challenges for international students in college. *U.S. News and World Report.* Retrieved from http://www.usnews.com/education/best-colleges/articles/2012/08/28/6-challenges-for-international-students-in-college

Horn, L. (2009). *On track to complete? A taxonomy of beginning community college students and their outcomes 3 years after enrolling, 2003–04 through 2006.* Washington, DC: National Center for Education Statistics.

Hovland, C., Janis, I., & Kelley, H. (1953). *Communication and persuasion.* New Haven, CT: Yale University Press.

How to limit opportunity for higher education 1980–2011. (2011). *PostSecondary Opportunity, 230*, 1–16. Retrieved from http://www.postsecondary.org/last12/230_811pg1_16.pdf

Humboldt State University Institutional Research & Planning. (2012a). *Fast facts fall semester 2012.* Retrieved from http://www.humboldt.edu/irp/fast_facts.html

Humboldt State University Institutional Research & Planning. (2012b). *Retention report 2012.* Retrieved from http://www.humboldt.edu/irp/downloads/RetentionReports/RETENTION_REPORT_2012_FINAL.pdf

Humboldt State University Institutional Research & Planning. (2013). *Retention and graduation rate initiative report 2013.* Retrieved from http://www.humboldt.edu/irp/Reports/Retention_Report/RETENTION_REPORT_2013.pdf

Hurtado, S. (1994). Latino consciousness and academic success. In A. Hurtado, E. E. García, & R. Buriel (Eds.), *The educational achievement of Latinos: Barriers and successes* (pp. 17–56). Santa Cruz, CA: Regents of the University of California.

Hurtado, S., & Carter, D. F. (1997). Effects of college transition and perceptions of the campus racial climate on Latino college students' sense of belonging. *Sociology of Education, 70*(4), 324–345.

Hurtado, S., Kurotsuchi, K., & Sharp, S. (1996, April). *College entry by age groups: Paths of traditional, delayed-entry, and nontraditional students.* Paper presented at a meeting of the American Educational Research Association, New York, NY.

Institute of International Education. (2012). *Fast facts open doors 2012* [Data file]. Retrieved from http://www.iie.org/en/Research-and-Publications/Open-Doors

Iowa State University. (n.d.). *Learning community peer mentor supervisor's manual.* Retrieved from http://www.lc.iastate.edu/pdfs-docs/PMSupervisors%20Manual.pdf

Ishiyama, J. (2007). Expectations and perceptions of undergraduate research mentoring: Comparing first generation, low income White/Caucasian and African American students. *College Student Journal, 41*(3), 540–549.

Jackson, A. P., Smith, S. A., & Hill, C. L. (2003). Academic persistence among Native American college students. *Journal of College Student Development, 44*(4), 548–565.

Jacobi, M. 1991. Mentoring and undergraduate academic success: A literature review. *Review of Educational Research, 61*, 505–532.

Jefferson, T. (1894). *The writings of Thomas Jefferson: 1781–1784* (Vol. 3). GP Putnam.

Johnson, W. B. (2002). The intentional mentor: Strategies and guidelines for the practice of mentoring. *Professional Psychology: Research and Practice, 33*(1), 88–96.

Johnson-Bailey, J., & Cervero, R. M. (2004). Mentoring in black and white: The intricacies of cross-cultural mentoring. *Mentoring & Tutoring: Partnership in Learning, 12*(1), 7–21.

Jones, D. J., & Watson, B. C. (1990). *High-risk students and higher education: Future trends.* Retrieved from ERIC database. (ED321726)

Juarez, K., & Thompson-Grove, G. (2003). *The charrette: Overview.* Retrieved from http://www.nsrfharmony.org/system/files/protocols/charrette_0.pdf

Kalichman, M. (2001). *Mentoring.* Retrieved from http://research-ethics.net/topics/mentoring/

Kasprisin, C. A., & Single, P. B. (2005). Identifying essential elements of successful e-mentoring programs through needs assessment. In F. K. Kochan & J. T. Pascarelli (Eds.), *Creating successful telementoring programs* (pp. 51–71). Greenwich, CT: Information Age Press.

Kelly, K. (2011, 5 August). *Kathy Kelly in Afghanistan, Pakistan & Iraq: The costs of war, the price of peace* [Speech]. Portland Community College, Portland, OR.

Kerlinger, F. N. (2011). *Foundations of behavioral research, 1986.* New York, NY: Holt, Rinehart and Winston.

Kerr, C. (1991). *The great transformation in higher education, 1960–1980.* New York, NY: SUNY Press.

Kim, C. Y., Goto, S. G., Bai, M. M., Kim, T. E., & Wong, E. (2001). Culturally congruent mentoring: Predicting Asian American student participation using the theory of reasoned action. *Journal of Applied Social Psychology, 31*(11), 2417–2437.

King, P. M., & Baxter Magolda, M. B. (2005). A developmental model of intercultural maturity. *Journal of College Student Development, 46*(6), 571–592.

Kolb, D. A. (1984). *Experiential learning: Experience as the source of learning and development* (Vol. 1). Englewood Cliffs, NJ: Prentice Hall.

Kolb learning styles: David Kolb's learning styles model and experiential learning theory. (2013). Retrieved from http://www.businessballs.com/kolblearningstyles.htm

Komives, S., Lucas, N., & McMahon, T. (2006). *Exploring leadership: For college students who want to make a difference* (2nd ed.). San Francisco, CA: Jossey-Bass.

Kram, K., E. (1983). Phases of the mentor relationship. *Academy of Management Journal, 26*(4), 608–625.

Kram, K. E. (1985). *Mentoring at work: Developmental relationships in organizational life.* Glenview, IL: Scott Foresman.

Kram, K., & Isabella, L. (1985). Mentoring alternatives: The role of peer relationships in career development. *Academy of Management Journal, 28*(1), 110–132.

Kretchmar, M. D. (2001). Service learning in a general psychology class: Description, preliminary evaluation, and recommendations. *Teaching of Psychology, 28*(1), 5–10.

Krueger, A., & Lindahl, M. (2001). Education for growth: Why and for whom? *Journal of Economic Literature, 39,* 1101–1136.

Krueger, R. A. (2009). *Focus groups: A practical guide for applied research.* Thousand Oaks, CA: Sage.

Kurosawa, A. (Director). (1950). *Rashôman.* Japan: Daiei Motion Picture Co.

Lacina, J. G. (2002). Preparing international students for a successful social experience in higher education. *New Directions for Higher Education, 117,* 21–27.

Lammie, R. (2012). *A brief history of challenge coins.* Retrieved from http://mentalfloss.com/article/12630/brief-history-challenge-coins.

Larose, S., & Boivin, M. (1998). Attachment to parents, social support expectations, and socioemotional adjustment during the high school-college transition. *Journal of Research on Adolescence, 8*(1), 1–27.

Lev, L., Kolassa, J. & Bakken, L. (2010). Faculty mentors' and students' perceptions of students' research self-efficacy. *Nurse Education Today, 30,* 169–174.

Lewis, M. (1990). Self-knowledge and social development in early life. In L. A. Pervin (Ed.), *Handbook of personality* (pp. 277–300). New York, NY: Guilford Press.

Lipman-Blumen, J. (2000). *Connective leadership: Managing in a changing world.* Oxford, UK: Oxford University Press.

Livingston, W. (2009). *Discovering the academic and social transitions of re-enrolling student veterans at one institution: A grounded theory.* Available from ProQuest Dissertations and Theses database. (UMI No. 3355150)

Lofland, J. (1995). Analytic ethnography: Features, failings, and futures. *Journal of Contemporary Ethnography*, *24*(1), 30–67.

Lokken, J. M., Pfeffer, D. S., McAuley, J., & Strong, C. (2009). A statewide approach to creating veteran friendly campuses. *New Directions for Student Services*, 126, 45–54.

Luft, J., & Ingham, H. (1961). The Johari window: A graphic model of awareness in interpersonal relations. *Human Relations Training News*, *5*(9), 6–7.

Macrae, C. N., Quinn, K. A., Mason, M. F., & Quadflieg, S. (2005). Understanding others: The face and person construal. *Journal of Personality and Social Psychology*, *89*(5), 686–695.

Markel, N., Trujillo, R., Callahan, P., & Mark, M. (2010, September). *Resiliency and retention in veterans returning to college.* Paper presented at the Veterans in Higher Education Conference: Listening, Responding, Changing for Student Success, Tucson, AZ. Retrieved from http://files.eric.ed.gov/fulltext/ED526337.pdf

Markus, H. (1977). Self-schemata and processing information about the self. *Journal of Personality and Social Psychology*, *35*(2), 63–78.

Marshall, C., & Rossman, G. B. (2011). *Designing qualitative research* (5th ed.). Thousand Oaks, CA: Sage.

Matsumoto, D., & Hwang, H. S. (2011, May). *Reading facial expression of emotion.* Retrieved from http://www.apa.org/science/about/psa/2011/05/facial-expressions.aspx

Mattanah, J. F., Hancock, G. R., & Brand, B. L. (2004). Parental attachment, separation-individuation, and college student adjustment: A structural equation analysis of mediational effects. *Journal of Counseling Psychology*, *51*(2), 213–225.

McDonald, D. S. (2004). Computer literacy skills for computer information systems majors: A case study. *Journal of Information Systems Education*, *15*(1), 19–33.

McDougall, M., & Beattie, R. S. (1997). Peer mentoring at work: The nature and outcomes of nonhierarchical developmental relationships. *Management Learning*, *28*, 423–437.

McGinnies, E., & Ward, C. (1980). Better liked than right: Trustworthiness and expertise as factors in credibility. *Personality and Social Psychology Bulletin*, *6*, 467–472.

McLean, M. (2004). Does the curriculum matter in peer mentoring? From mentee to mentor in problem-based learning: A unique case study. *Mentoring & Tutoring: Partnership in Learning*, *12*(2), 173–186.

McLeod, S. (2008). *Quantitative qualitative.* Retrieved from http://www.simplypsychology.org/qualitative-quantitative.html

McLeod, S. (2013). *Kolb learning styles.* Retrieved from http://www.simplypsychology.org/learning-kolb.html

McLeod, S. (2014). *Cognitive dissonance.* Retrieved from http://www.simplypsychology.org/cognitive-dissonance.html

McLuhan, M. (1968). *The medium is the message.* Retrieved from http://marshallmcluhanspeaks.com/sayings/1968-the-medium-is-the-massage.php

Mead, George H. (1934). *Mind, self, and society.* Chicago, IL: University of Chicago Press.

Mee-Lee, L., & Bush, T. (2003). Student mentoring in higher education: Hong Kong Baptist University. *Mentoring & Tutoring: Partnership in Learning, 11*(3), 263–271.

Meris, M., & Webley, R. (2012). *Dissecting diversity at HSU 2008–2012: A retrospective.* Retrieved from http://www.humboldt.edu/diversity/report_2012.html

Miller, H., & Spence, S. (2007). *Lessons learned: Places—and faces—that foster student success.* Indianapolis, IN: Lumina Foundation for Education.

Milne, A. A. (2015). *A. A. Milne quotes.* Retrieved from http://www.brainyquote .com/quotes/quotes/a/aamilne121656.html

Minor, F. D. (2007). *Building effective peer mentoring programs.* Retrieved from http://www.evergreen.edu/.../lcsa4building.pdf

Moreno, T. (2014). States without an income tax. *About Money.* Retrieved from http://taxes.about.com/od/statetaxes/a/tax-free-states.htm

Morgan, D. L. (1997). *Focus groups as qualitative research* (2nd ed.). Thousand Oaks, CA: Sage.

Morgan, D. L., Krueger, R. A., & King, J. A. (1998). *The focus group kit* (Vols. 1–6). Thousand Oaks, CA: Sage.

Muller, C. B. (1997, November). *The potential of industrial "e-mentoring" as a retention strategy for women in science and engineering.* Retrieved from http://fie-conference.org/fie97/papers/1268.pdf

National Center for Education Statistics. (2011). *Graduation rates of first-time postsecondary students who started as full-time degree/certificate-seeking students, by sex, race/ethnicity, time to completion, and level and control of institution where student started: Selected cohort entry years, 1996 through 2007.* Retrieved from http://nces .ed.gov/programs/digest/d11/tables/dt11_345.asp

National Center for Education Statistics. (2012a). *The condition of education 2012* (NCES 2012-0450). Retrieved from http://nces.ed.gov/pubs2012/2012045.pdf

National Center for Education Statistics. (2012b). *Total fall enrollment in degree-granting institutions, by control and level of institution: 1970 through 2011.* Retrieved from http://nces.ed.gov/programs/digest/d12/tables/dt12_223.asp

National Center for Education Statistics. (2013). *Nontraditional undergraduates: Definitions and data.* Retrieved from http://nces.ed.gov/pubs/web/97578e.asp

National Mentoring Partnership. (2005). *How to build a successful mentoring program using the elements of effective practice.* Retrieved from http://www.mentoring.org/ downloads/mentoring_413.pdf

National Science Foundation. (2014). *Responsible conduct of research.* Retrieved from http://www.nsf.gov/bfa/dias/policy/rcr.jsp

Newell, A., & Simon, H. (1972). *Human problem solving.* Englewood Cliffs, NJ: Prentice Hall.

Nguyen, M. (2012). *Degreeless in debt: What happens to borrowers who drop out.* Retrieved from http://www.educationsector.org/publications/degreeless-debt-what-happens-borrowers-who-drop-out

Nonmarital births for women who have had a child in the last year, 2004. (2005). Retrieved from http://www.postsecondary.org/archives/Posters/nonmaritalbirths. pdf

Nordquist, R. (2013). *Nonverbal communication*. Retrieved from http://grammar .about.com/od/mo/g/Nonverbal-Communication.htm

Nunez, A. M., Cuccaro-Alamin, S., Nuñez, A. M., & Carroll, C. D. (1998). *First-generation students: Undergraduates whose parents never enrolled in postsecondary education* (NCES 98-082). Washington, DC: National Center for Education Statistics.

O'Donnell, N. (2015). *Nora O'Donnell quotes*. Retrieved from http://www.brainyquote .com/quotes/quotes/n/norahodon536440.html

Olaniran, B. A. (1996). Social skills acquisition: A closer look at foreign students on college campuses and factors influencing their level of social difficulty in social situations. *Communication Studies, 47*(1/2), 72–88.

Olaniran, B. A. (1999). International teaching assistants (IGTA) workshop as seen from an eye witness perspective. *College Student Affairs Journal, 18*(2), 56–71.

Oldfield, K. (2007). Humble and hopeful: Welcoming first-generation poor and working-class students to college. *About Campus, 11*(6), 2–12.

Olivas, M., & Li, C. (2006). Understanding stressors of international students in higher education: What college counselors and personnel need to know. *Journal of Instructional Psychology, 33*(3), 217–222.

Pachucki, D. (2014). *Games that will develop the listening skills of college students*. Retrieved from http://everydaylife.globalpost.com/games-develop-listening-skills-college-students-14355.html

Packard, B. W. (2003). Web-based mentoring: Challenging traditional models to increase women's access. *Mentoring & Tutoring: Partnership in Learning, 11*(1), 53–65.

Packard, B. W. (2004). Mentoring and retention in college science: Reflections on the sophomore year. *Journal of College Student Retention, 6*(3), 289–300.

Pagan, R., & Edwards-Wilson, R. (2002). A mentoring program for remedial students. *Journal of College Student Retention, 4*(3), 207–226.

Papadakis, M. C. (2000, March). *Complex picture of computer use in home emerges* (National Science Foundation Division of Science Resources Studies Issue Brief). Retrieved from http://www.nsf.gov/statistics/issuebrf/sib00314.htm

Pascarella, E. T., & Terenzini, P. T. (1991). *How college affects students: Findings and insights from twenty years of research*. San Francisco, CA: Jossey-Bass.

Pascarella, E. T., & Terenzini, P. T. (2005). *How college affects students: A third decade of research*. San Francisco, CA: Jossey-Bass.

Peet, M. (2010). The integrative knowledge portfolio process: A program guide for educating reflective practitioners and lifelong learners. *MedEdPORTAL Publications*. Retrieved http://dx.doi.org/10.15766/mep_2374-8265.7892

Peet, M. R., Walsh, K., Sober, R., & Rawak, C. S. (2010). Generative knowledge interviewing: A method for knowledge transfer and talent management at the University of Michigan. *International Journal of Educational Advancement, 10*(2), 71–85.

Perez, M. (2010). *Agile code reviews: The charrette protocol*. Retrieved from http:// www.nearsoft.com/blog/agile-code-reviews-the-charrette-protocol.html

Petty, R. E., & Cacioppo, J. T. (1981). *Attitudes and persuasion: Classic and contemporary approaches.* Dubuque, IA: Wm. C. Brown.

Pitney, W. A., & Ehlers, G. G. (2004). A grounded theory study of the mentoring process involved with undergraduate athletic training students. *Journal of Athletic Training, 39*(4), 344–351.

Pizzolato, J. E. (2008). Advisor, teacher, partner: Using the learning partnerships model to reshape academic advising. *About campus, 13*(1), 18–25.

Polanyi, M. (1966). The logic of tacit inference. *Philosophy, 41*(155), 1–18.

Pornpitakan, C. (2004). The persuasiveness of source credibility: A critical review of five decades' evidence. *Journal of Applied Social Psychology, 34*(2), 243–281.

Portland State University, Office of Institutional Research. (2013). *Student profile total enrollment fall 2012, 4th week.* Retrieved from http://www.oirp.pdx.edu/source/port1213/all_all.pdf

Poyrazli, S., & Lopez, M. D. (2007). An exploratory study of perceived discrimination and homesickness: A comparison of international students and American students. *The Journal of Psychology, 141*(3), 263–279.

Poyrazli, S., & Kavanaugh, P. R. (2006). Marital status, ethnicity, academic achievement, and adjustment strains: The case of graduate international students. *College Student Journal, 40*(4), 767–780.

Provasnik, S., & Planty, M. (2008). *Community colleges: Special supplement to the condition of education 2008* (NCES 2008-033.) Washington, DC: National Center for Education Statistics.

Putnam, R. (2000). *Bowling alone: The collapse and revival of American community.* New York, NY: Simon & Schuster.

Qualtrics (Version 37.892) [Computer software]. Provo, UT: Qualtrics.

Quinn, F., Muldoon, R., & Hollingworth, A. (2002). Formal academic mentoring: a pilot scheme for first-year science students at a regional university. *Mentoring & Tutoring: Partnership in Learning, 10*(1), 21–33.

Ragins, B. R., & Cotton, J. L. (1999). Mentor functions and outcomes: A comparison of men and women in formal and informal mentoring relationships. *Journal of Applied Psychology, 84*(4), 529–550.

Raisman, N. A. (2009). *Retain students retain budgets: A primer for colleges and universities.* Retrieved from http://www.universitybusiness.com/article/retain-students-retain-budgets-how

Rajapaksa, S., & Dundes, L. (2002–2003). It's a long way home: International student adjustment to living in the United States. *College Student Retention, 4*(1), 15–28.

Razran, G. H. (1938). Conditioning away social bias by the luncheon technique. *Psychological Bulletin, 35*(9), 693–695.

Razran, G. H. (1940). Conditional response changes in rating and appraising sociopolitical slogans. *Psychological Bulletin, 37*(7), 481–493.

Reitenauer, V., Cress, C., & Bennett, J. (2013). Creating cultural connections. In C. Cress, P. Collier, & V. Reitenauer (Eds.), *Learning through Serving: A Student Guidebook for Service-Learning and Civic Engagement Across Academic Disciplines and Cultural Communities* (2nd ed., pp. 81–91). Sterling, VA: Stylus.

Reivich, K., & Shatté, A. (2002). *The resilience factor: 7 essential skills for overcoming life's inevitable obstacles.* New York, NY: Broadway Books.

Rendon, L. I. (1994). Validating culturally diverse students: Toward a new model of learning and student development. *Innovative Higher Education, 19*(1), 33–51.

Rhodes, J. E., Grossman, J. B., & Resch, N. L. (2000). Agents of change: Pathways through which mentoring relationships influence adolescents' academic adjustment. *Child development, 71*(6), 1662–1671.

Richardson, R. C., & Skinner, E. F. (1992). Helping first generation minority students achieve degrees. *New Directions for Community Colleges, 80,* 29–43.

Roberts, L. W., Clifton, R. A., & Etcheverry, E. (2001). Social capital and educational attainment: A study of undergraduates in a faculty of education. *Alberta Journal of Educational Research, 47*(1), 24–39.

Rodger, S., & Tremblay, P. F. (2003). The effects of a peer mentoring program on academic success among first year university students. *Canadian Journal of Higher Education, 33*(3), 1–17.

Roth, W., & Mehta, J. (2002). The Rashomon effect combining positivist and interpretivist approaches in the analysis of contested events. *Sociological Methods & Research, 31*(2), 131–173.

Ruthkosky, P., & Castano, S. (2007). First-year peer mentoring helps ease student transition to college. *E-Source for College Transitions, 5*(1), 6–9.

Sachs, R. (2008). Valuing veterans. *Inside Higher Education.* Retrieved from https://www.insidehighered.com/views/2008/06/12/c2c

Saenz, V., Hurtado, S., Barrera, D., Wolf, D., & Yeung, F. (2007). *First in my family: A profile of first-generation college students at four-year institutions since 1971.* Los Angeles, CA: Foundation for Independent Higher Education.

Sanchez, R. J., Bauer, T. N., & Paronto, M. E. (2006). Peer-mentoring freshmen: Implications for satisfaction, commitment, and retention to graduation. *Academy of Management Learning & Education, 5*(1), 25–37.

Sands, R. G., Parson, L. A., & Duane, J. (1991). Faculty mentoring faculty in a public university. *Journal of Higher Education, 62*(2), 174–193.

Santovec, M. L. (Ed.). (1992). *Building diversity: Recruitment and retention in the '90s.* Madison, WI: Magna.

Schmidt, M. E., Marks, J. L., & Derrico, L. (2004). What a difference mentoring makes: Service learning and engagement for college students. *Mentoring & Tutoring: Partnership in Learning, 12,* 205–217.

Schneider, M., & Lu, Y. (2011). *$4.5 billion in earnings, taxes lost last year due to the high U.S. college dropout rate.* Retrieved from http://www.air.org/news/index.cfm?fa=viewContent&content_id=1405

Schultheiss, D. P., & Blustein, D. L. (1994). Contributions of family relationship factors to the identity formation process. *Journal of Counseling & Development, 73*(2), 159–166.

Self-concept. (2003). *Collins English dictionary* (6th ed.). Glasgow, Scotland: HarperCollins.

Selvadurai, R. (1992). Problems faced by international students in American colleges and universities. *Community Review, 12*(1/2), 27–32.

Shane, L. (2013, January 7). How many student veterans graduate? No one knows. *Stars and Stripes*. Retrieved from http://www.studentclearinghouse.org/about/media_center/articles/files/StarsAndStripes_010713

Shattuck, A. (2011). Exercise: Generative interviewing conflict with civility. Retrieved from https://sites.google.com/a/pdx.edu/leadership-fellows-at-portland-state/home

Shotton, H. J., Oosahwe, E. S. L., & Cintrón, R. (2007). Stories of success: Experiences of American Indian students in a peer-mentoring retention program. *The Review of Higher Education, 31*(1), 81–107.

Single P. B. (2004, June). *Expanding our use of mentoring: Reflection and reaction.* Paper presented at the annual meeting of the American Educational Research Association, San Diego, CA.

Single, P. B., & Muller, C. B. (1999a). *Electronic mentoring: Issues to advance research and practice.* Retrieved from ERIC database. (ED439683).

Single, P. B., & Muller, C. B. (1999b). *Encouraging women students to persist in engineering and science through industrial mentoring using electronic communications.* Retrieved from http://fie-conference.org/fie99/wsdindex.html

Single, P. B., & Muller, C. B. (2001). *When email and mentoring unite: The implementation of a nationwide electronic mentoring program—MentorNet, the national electronic industrial mentoring network for women in engineering and science.* Alexandria, VA: American Society for Training and Development.

Single, P. B., & Single, R. M. (2005). E mentoring for social equity: Review of research to inform program development. *Mentoring & Tutoring: Partnership in Learning, 13*(2), 301–320.

Smith, A., Rainie, L., & Zickuhr, K. (2011). *College students and technology.* Retrieved from http://pewinternet.org/Reports/2011/College-students-and-technology.aspx

Smith, B. (2007). Accessing social capital through the academic mentoring process. *Equity & Excellence in Education, 40*(1), 36–46.

Smith, D. E. (1987). *The everyday world as problematic: A feminist sociology.* Toronto, Ontario, Canada: University of Toronto Press.

Smith, D. E. (2005). *Institutional ethnography: A sociology for people.* Walnut Creek, CA: AltaMira Press.

Smith-Jentsch, K., Scielzo, S., Yarbrough, C., & Rosopa, P. (2008). A comparison of face-to-face and electronic peer-mentoring: Interactions with mentor gender. *Journal of Vocational Behavior, 72*(2), 193–206.

Sodowsky, G. R., & Plake, B. S. (1992). A study of acculturation differences among international people and suggestions for sensitivity to within group differences. *Journal of Counseling & Development, 71*(1), 53–55.

State Disinvestment in Higher Education FY1961 to FY2013. (2013). *PostSecondary Opportunity, 248,* 1–20. Retrieved from http://www.postsecondary.org/last12/248_213pg1_20.pdf

Steele, G., Woods, D., Finkel, R., Crispin, M., Stallman, R., and Goodfellow, G. (1983). *The Hacker's Dictionary.*

Steinberg, J. (2004). Peer mentor program integral to the first-year experience. *E-Source for College Transition, 1*(2), 5–7.

Sternberg, R. L. (1985). *Beyond IQ: A triarchic theory of human intelligence.* New York, NY: Cambridge University Press.

Striplin, J. J. (1999). *Facilitating transfer for first-generation community college students*. Retrieved from ERIC database. (ED430627)

Stryker, S., & Serpe, R. T. (1994). Identity salience and psychological centrality: Equivalent, overlapping or complementary concepts? *Social Psychology Quarterly, 57*(1), 16–34.

Student Affairs Leadership Council. (2009). *From military service to student life: Strategies for supporting student veterans on campus*. Washington, DC: The Advisory Board Company.

Student debt and the class of 2012. (2012). Retrieved from http://projecton studentdebt.org/

Student Veterans of America. (2008). *Campus kit for colleges & universities*. Retrieved from http://www.operationpromiseforservicemembers.com/Campus_Kit_for_Student_Veterans.pdf

Summerlot, J., Green, S. M., & Parker, D. (2009). Student veterans organizations. *New Directions for Student Services, 126*, 71–79.

Symonds, W. C., Schwartz, R. B., & Ferguson, R. (2011). *Pathways to prosperity: Meeting the challenge of preparing young Americans for the 21st century*. Cambridge, MA: Pathways to Prosperity Project, Harvard Graduate School of Education.

Tanielian, T., & Jaycox, L. H. (Eds.) (2008). *Invisible wounds of war: Summary and recommendations for addressing psychological and cognitive injuries* (ADA48099). Santa Monica, CA: Rand Corporation.

Tenenbaum, H. R., Crosby, F. J., & Gliner, M. D. (2001). Mentoring relationships in graduate school. *Journal of Vocational Behavior, 59*(3), 326–341.

Terenzini, P. T., & Pascarella, E. T. (1994). Living with myths: Undergraduate education in America. *Change, 26*(1), 28–32.

Terenzini, P. T., & Reason, R. D. (2005, November). *Parsing the first year of college: A conceptual framework for studying college impacts*. Paper presented at the annual meeting of the Association for the Study of Higher Education, Philadelphia, PA.

Terenzini, P. T., Springer, L., Yaeger, P., Pascarella, E., & Nora, A. (1996). First-generation college students: characteristics, experiences, and cognitive development. *Research in Higher Education, 37*(1), 1–22.

Terrion, J., & Leonard, D. (2007). A taxonomy of the characteristics of student peer mentors in higher education: Findings from a literature review. *Mentoring & Tutoring: Partnership in Learning, 15*(2), 149–164.

Terrion, J. L., R. Philion, & D. Leonard. (2007). An evaluation of a university peer-mentoring training program. *International Journal of Evidence Based Coaching and Mentoring, 5*(1), 42–57.

Thayer, P. B. (2000). *Retention of students from first generation and low income backgrounds*. Retrieved from ERIC database. (ED446633)

Thile, E. L., & Matt, G. E. (1995). The ethnic mentor undergraduate program: A brief description and preliminary findings. *Journal of Multicultural Counseling and Development, 23*(2), 116–126.

Thomas, K., & Althen, G. (1989). Counseling foreign students. In P. B. Pedersen, J. G. Draduns, W. J. Lonner, & J. E. Trimble (Eds.), *Counseling across cultures* (3rd ed., pp. 205–241). Honolulu: University of Hawaii Press.

Thomas, S. L. (2000). Ties that bind. *Journal of Higher Education, 71*(5), 591–615.

Tinto, V. (1975). Dropout from higher education: A theoretical synthesis of recent research. *Review of Educational Research, 45*(1), 89–125.

Tinto, V. (1987). *Leaving college: Rethinking the causes and cures of student attrition.* Chicago, IL: University of Chicago Press.

Tinto, V. (1993). *Leaving college: Rethinking the causes and cures of student attrition* (2nd ed.). Chicago, IL: University of Chicago Press.

Tinto, V. (2008). Access without support is not opportunity. *Change, 40*(1), 46–50.

Tomlin, L. (2015). *Lily Tomlin quotes.* Retrieved from http://www.brainyquote.com/quotes/quotes/l/lilytomlin379145.html

Torres Campos, C. M., Phinney, J. S., Perez-Brena, N., Kim, C., Ornelas, B., Nemanim, L., . . . & Ramirez, C. (2009). A mentor-based targeted intervention for high-risk Latino college freshman: A pilot study. *Journal of Hispanic Higher Education, 8*(2), 158–178.

Towbes, L. C., & Cohen, L. H. (1996). Chronic stress in the lives of college students: Scale development and prospective prediction of distress. *Journal of Youth and Adolescence, 25*(2), 199–217.

Training materials for Portland State University Leadership Fellows Program, Student Activities and Leadership Programs. (n.d.) Retrieved from https://sites.google.com/a/pdx.edu/leadership-fellows-at-portland-state/home

Tversky, A., & Kahneman, D. (1974). Judgment under uncertainty: Heuristics and biases. *Science, 185,* 1124–1131.

2010–11 institutional effectiveness reporting to the PCC Board of Directors: Student success report. (2011). http://www.pcc.edu/ir/iereporting/ie_1011/Success2010Report.pdf

Understanding tuition. (2013). Retrieved from University of Michigan website: http://www.vpcomm.umich.edu/pa/key/understandingtuition.html

Unequal family income and unequal higher educational opportunity 1970 to 2012. (2013). *PostSecondary Opportunity, 256,* 1–20. Retrieved from http://www.postsecondary.org/last12/256_1013pg1-20.pdf

University of New Mexico. (2012–2013). *Fact book.* Retrieved from http://oia.unm.edu/documents/factbook_docs/2012fb_updated.pdf

University of Victoria Teaching and Learning Center. (2011). *DVD 7: Teaching assistant issues.* Available from http://ltc.uvic.ca/servicesprograms/criticalincidents/

U.S. Census Bureau. (2011). State and county quickfacts: New Mexico. Retrieved from http://quickfacts.census.gov/qfd/states/35000.html

Vargas, J. H. (2004). *College knowledge: Addressing information barriers to college.* Boston, MA: College Access Services, Education Resources Institute.

Vivona, J. M. (2000). Parental attachment styles of late adolescents: Qualities of attachment relationships and consequences for adjustment. *Journal of Counseling Psychology, 47*(3), 316–329.

Volunteer rates by educational attainment and gender for people 25 years and over, 2008. (2009). Retrieved from http://www.postsecondary.org/archives/Posters/VolunteerRates.pdf

Von Neumann, J., & Morgenstern, O. (1944). *Theory of games and economic behavior.* Princeton, NJ: Princeton University Press.

Voting for presidential candidates in 2012 by educational attainment. (2012). Retrieved from http://www.postsecondary.org/archives/Posters/VotingforPres2012.pdf

Waldron, T. (2012). *Study: Nearly half of America's college students drop out before receiving a degree.* Retrieved from http://thinkprogress.org/education/2012/03/28/453632/half-college-students-drop-out/

Wells, H. G. (2015). *H. G. Wells quotes.* Retrieved from http://www.brainyquote.com/quotes/quotes/h/hgwells119659.html

Westminster College. (2013). *Student stress calendar.* Retrieved from http://www.westminster-mo.edu/studentlife/housing/Documents/STUDENT%20STRESS%20CALENDAR.pdf

Wheatley, M. J. (2006). *Leadership and the new science: Discovering order in a chaotic world.* San Francisco, CA: Berrett-Koehler.

Withers, B. (1972). Lean on me. On *Still Bill* [CD]. Los Angeles, LA: Sussex Records.

Ye, J. (2006). Traditional and online support networks in the cross-cultural adaptation of Chinese international students in the United States. *Journal of Computer-Mediated Communication, 11*(3), 863–876.

Yeh, C. J., & Inose, M. (2003). International students' reported English fluency, social support satisfaction, and social connectedness as predictors of acculturative stress. *Counseling Psychology Quarterly, 16*(1), 15–28.

Yi, J. K., Giseala Lin, J. C., & Kishimoto, Y. (2003). Utilization of counseling services by international students. *Journal of Instructional Psychology, 30,* 333–342.

York-Anderson, D. C., & Bowman, S. L. (1991). Assessing the college knowledge of 1st and 2nd generation college students. *Journal of College Student Development, 32*(2), 116–122.

Zhai, L. (2002). Studying international students: Adjustment issues and social support. Retrieved from ERIC database. (ED474481)

Zhao, C.-M., Kuh, G. D., & Carini, R. M. (2005). A comparison of international student and American student engagement in effective educational practices. *Journal of Higher Education, 76*(2), 209–231.

Zickuhr, K. (2013). *Who's not online and why.* Retrieved from http://www.pewinternet.org/Reports/2013/Non-internet-users.aspx

INDEX

developmental approach of, 91
duration of, 91
evaluation of, 95
for high school transitions to
    college, 91
inclusiveness of, 91
matching methods of, 98
program description of, 92–94
for students of color, 92, 95, 97
training for, 93, 96–97
returning students
    skill erosion of, 54
    transition issues of, 54–55
    women's programs for, 20
review and revision, of program,
    321–22
Rodger, S., 290
role mastery, 70, 74
    of first-generation students, 58,
    59, 60
    returning students' issues with, 55
    in two-path model of student
    performance, 32–33
role models, 8
    for decision making, 77–78
    peer mentors as, 11, 13, 15, 17,
    18–19, 35–38
    scripts for, 71, 72, 81
    of self-authorship, 47–48
    in two-path model of student
    performance, 35–36
    for understanding professor's
    expectations, 71, 75–77, 79, 81,
    82, 84, 87
Rosopa, P., 12, 166
rubric, for peer mentoring programs,
    2, 19–22, 41, 130

Sacramento State University,
    218–23, 231
sample forms. *See* forms
satisfaction surveys, for mentors,
    304–5
scalability
    of e-mentoring, 161

of group face-to-face mentoring,
    159
scheduling, face-to-face mentoring,
    158
schemas, in decision making,
    211–14
Scielzo, S., 12, 166
sciences, technology, engineering, or
    math (STEM), 23, 105, 119
scripts
    for adjustment issues, 213–14
    for decision making, 213–14
    of role models, 71, 72, 81
selecting mentors, 117–18. *See also*
    recruiting mentors
self-authorship theory, 44–46
    role models in, 47–48
self-concept, 45–46, 48, 67n1
self-efficacy, 12
sequencing
    of mentor training, 261–63
    of program content materials,
    214
    of support materials, 132–33
service-learning
    academic performance tied to, 36
    LSAMP program for, 204
    mentor training about, 250, 252
    program content materials about,
    205–7
    resources about, 217
    SMILE program for, 204
SFMP. *See* Students First Mentoring
    Program
short-answer surveys, 295–96, 300
short-term programs, 19, 20–21
    ISMP as, 312
    program design for, 131–32
    Transfer Connections Program as,
    190
    VETS to VETS Program as, 218
Simon, H., 73
Single, P. B., 154
Single, R. M., 154
size. *See* program size

a career in academic advising. The emphasis placed on developing the skills to become a more independent thinker is essential to understanding the needs of college and university students who are in the early stages of understanding the complexities of becoming successful contributors to society as a whole."

—*NACADA Journal (National Academic Advising Association)*

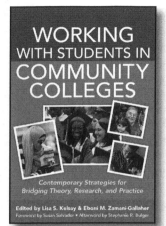

Working With Students in Community Colleges
Contemporary Strategies for Bridging Theory, Research, and Practice
Edited by Lisa S. Kelsay and Eboni M. Zamani-Gallaher
Foreword by Susan Salvador
Afterword by Stephanie R. Bulger

"This is a valuable resource that will help readers to understand community colleges and the needs and characteristics of their students as well as help to gauge how agile and responsive these colleges are to demands and changes.

These chapters provide a timely and valuable resource for the array of professionals working to adapt and evolve their practices in an exciting and challenging time for community colleges. The comprehensive treatment of institutional operations and student progress makes this reading an important resource for practitioners, administrators, and faculty. In addition, this book provides insightful strategies and recommendations for strengthening student services and identifying internal and external barriers for change and partnerships. If you embrace our responsibility to serve the community college student sector effectively, you will turn the pages of this book with the realization that it is a necessary instrument for the community college professional's toolbox."

—*Susan Salvador, Vice President of Student Services, Monroe Community College*

22883 Quicksilver Drive
Sterling, VA 20166-2102   Subscribe to our e-mail alerts: www.Styluspub.com

Als ... *...ble from St...*

Q16

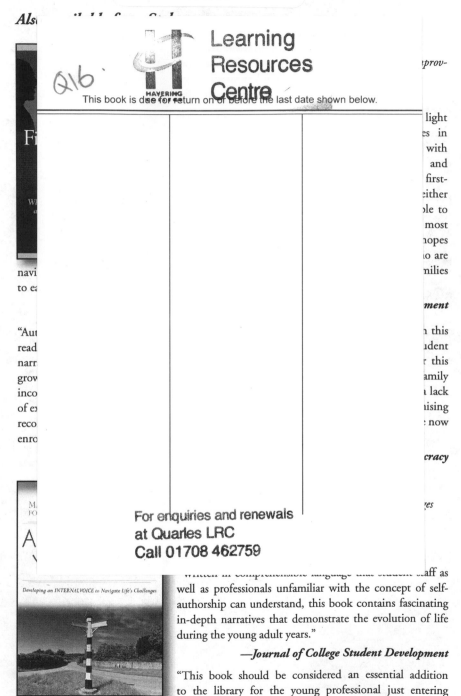

Learning
Resources
Centre

prov-

This book is due for return on or before the last date shown below.

Fi...

W...
a...

light
...es in
with
and
first-
...either
...ble to
most
...opes
...o are
navi...
to ea...
...nilies

...ment

"Aut...
read...
narr...
grow...
inco...
of ex...
reco...
enro...

...n this
...ident
...r this
...amily
...a lack
...ising
...e now

...cracy

M...
FO...

A
...
Developing an INTERNAL VOICE to Navigate Life's Challenges

...es

For enquiries and renewals
at Quarles LRC
Call 01708 462759

...written in comprehensible language that student staff as well as professionals unfamiliar with the concept of self-authorship can understand, this book contains fascinating in-depth narratives that demonstrate the evolution of life during the young adult years."

—*Journal of College Student Development*

"This book should be considered an essential addition to the library for the young professional just entering
(Continues on preceeding page)